UNHOLY BABYLON

UNHOLY BABYLON

The Secret History of Saddam's War

Adel Darwish and
Gregory Alexander

ST. MARTIN'S PRESS
NEW YORK

ISBN 0-312-06530-2 (pbk)
ISBN 0-312-06531-0 (hc)

First published in Great Britain by Victor Gollancz Limited.

First U.S. Edition: March 1991
10 9 8 7 6 5 4 3 2 1

Contents

Maps

Illustrations

Acknowledgements

Planning for this book commenced a month before the invasion of Kuwait on 2nd August 1990, our intention being to publicise the brutal nature of Saddam Hussein and his regime and to draw attention to the assistance that he was receiving from the West for his arms procurement programme. It seemed incredible to us that European companies, with little or no hindrance from their governments, were actively involved in the supply of equipment and technology for the manufacture not only of conventional armaments but also of chemical, biological and nuclear weapons.

The tragic events in Kuwait on 2nd August 1990 interceded, attracting the attention of the world media, and since then there has been much detailed coverage of the Gulf Crisis. This book, however, is concerned with the story of Saddam Hussein and his rise to power, and with the West's role as 'kingmakers': the political assistance afforded him both before, during and after the Gulf War as well as the economic and industrial assistance which enabled him to create the most powerful military machine in the Middle East.

We have received much assistance during the research and writing of this book. We owe special thanks to many brave men and women who provided us with much valuable information from inside Iraq but whose identities we cannot reveal for their sakes. We hope that one day we will be able to thank them personally in a happy Iraq free from tyranny.

Seyyed Abd al-Azziz al-Hakim, Hanni al-Fekaiki, Dr Tahseen Me'alla, Dr Ahmad Chalabi, Dar Majid, Sa'ad Saleh Jabr, Dr Sahib al-Hakim, Dr Bahr al-O'Loum, the Iraqi Communist Party, the Campaign for Human Rights in Iraq, the Islamic Da'wa Party, and the Iraqi Students Society all rendered us invaluable help and to them all we extend our grateful thanks.

Abd al-Majid Farid and Amin al-Ghafari of the Arab Research Centre were extremely kind in granting us interviews and in providing us with much valuable material. We are most grateful to them both.

A number of diplomats and officials from the Middle East, Europe and

America were kind enough to give us interviews and to provide us with first-hand information. For obvious reasons we are unable to identify them but we are most grateful to them for their help and co-operation.

We would also like to express our appreciation to the following for their generous help: Will Fowler, Chris Jenkins and Michael Gething of *Defence* magazine; Henry Dodds of *Jane's Soviet Intelligence Review*; Christopher Foss of *Jane's Defence Weekly*; and Brian Walters, James Shortt, Christopher Bellamy and Anthony Preston, all of whom were extremely generous in providing assistance with technical information on weapon systems.

Dr Eric Groves, Naval Research Director of the Foundation for International Security, was kind enough to provide us with information concerning the 1961 Kuwait Crisis and we are most grateful to him. We also received invaluable assistance from a number of individuals and organisations who have over the years been monitoring the supply of arms and the support given to Saddam Hussein and his regime by Western industry. These include: Herr Norbert Gansel of the Federal German Parliament and Social Democratic Party, who was kind enough to supply us with information concerning the involvement of German companies in the supply of equipment and technology to Iraq; Leonard Spector, of the Carnegie Endowment for International Peace, who provided us with information on Iraq's nuclear development programme; Hugh Dowson of the Clifton Diocesan Justice and Peace Commission, who provided details of chemicals supplied by Western companies to Iraq; the Stockholm International Peace Research Institute; the librarians at the International Institute of Strategic Studies; the Campaign Against the Arms Trade; BUKO-Koordinationsstelle in the Federal German Republic; AMOK in Holland; France's Centre de Documentation et de Recherche; the International Peace Information Service in Belgium; and Sweden's SPASS. To them all we would like to express our sincere thanks.

Justin Arundale, Jon Hall, Ken Gresham, Brita Latham, Stephen McEntee, Jeremy Turner, Barry Perkins, Giovanni Vasco, Gertrud Erbach, Marian Carey, Katharine Jacob and Larry Lawrence of the library at the *Independent* all gave us wonderful support with our research, and no words can express sufficiently our gratitude for the time and effort they devoted to helping us. *Independent* columnist Annika Savill, Deputy Foreign Editor Harvey Morris and Middle East Editor Patrick Cockburn gave us valuable briefings on the Iraqi position during the crisis. Further assistance with research came from Andrew Graham Yool and Philip Spender at Index on Censorship, whilst John Bulloch and Jill Brown both provided us with photographs. Again, to them all, we extend our sincerest thanks.

Much of the information supplied to us came from organisations and individuals in other parts of Europe, and we are most grateful to Mr Jim Beveridge, Sylvia Bahr and Thérèse Chantal Leignel for their help in translating documents for us.

We also wish to express our appreciation to Liz Knights, Editorial Director of our publisher Victor Gollancz, for her great support; to our researcher Caspar Henderson for his tireless work in tracking down material; and to Duncan Snelling, our unpaid sub-editor, for spending so many hours at the keyboard sorting everything out. Last, but by no means least, our gratitude and thanks go to our agent, Dianne Coles, whose idea it was for us to write this book.

Prologue

At 1805 GMT on 1st August 1990, British Airways flight BA149 took off from Heathrow for Kuala Lumpur, via Kuwait and Madras. The plane was carrying 367 passengers, mostly Britons. In Kuwait it was 2105 on a hot August night.

Four hours later, Kuwait City was asleep, the only movement coming from the odd car which could be seen speeding along the wide, well-lit, modern highways. Suddenly, the sound of sirens rent the still night air and shortly afterwards Kuwaiti ministers and officials could be seen running half-dressed for their air-conditioned limousines. Soon the cellphone network was buzzing as they frantically called from their cars, waking up their bank managers or instructing their wives to gather together valuables and documents. Kuwait City was suddenly like a hive of disturbed bees.

Panic and shock rippled throughout the city as the news spread like wildfire that Saddam Hussein, the 'Butcher of Baghdad', had carried out his threat and ordered his tanks to cross the border. Even now, the leading elements of the Iraqi forces were advancing along the Basra–Kuwait Highway on their way to seize control of the tiny emirate.

Two of the diminutive Kuwaiti armed forces' Scorpion light tanks attempted to engage the leading Iraqi armour as it reached the outskirts of Kuwait City at 0200 local time. However, they stood little chance against the 125mm guns of the T-72s – although each T-72 had one shell only; they destroyed the two Kuwaiti tanks within thirty seconds.

Half an hour earlier the Dasman palace, residence of the Emir Sheikh Jaber al-Ahmad al-Sabah and his family, had been alerted by the Saudi Arabians, whose AWACS aircraft had detected the advance of the Iraqi forces. The emir's personal bodyguards bundled him, the crown prince and their families into armoured Mercedes limousines and they sped towards the Saudi borders.

By this time, Captain Richard Brunyate, the pilot of BA149, had already made his first contact with the control tower at Kuwait Airport and had been instructed by the air traffic controller to proceed as normal. From his cockpit, Captain Brunyate could see the city ahead of him, apparently peacefully asleep. At 0113 GMT, or 0413 local time, on 2nd

August, Flight BA149 touched down at Kuwait. Neither the crew nor the passengers were aware that they had landed in a war zone. It was only when a new crew had come aboard and the plane was preparing to take off fifty-two minutes later that the new pilot saw Iraqi tanks near the runway.

Shortly afterwards, the passengers, including eleven children, were disembarked and, with the aircraft's crew, taken by Iraqi troops to a hotel in Kuwait.

When the rest of the world awoke the following morning, it was to the news that Iraq had invaded Kuwait and that there was fighting in and around Kuwait City. As the day wore on, news filtered out of the emirate of the stand made by the emir's brother, Sheikh Fahd al-Ahmad, who was killed whilst leading the royal guards in the defence of the Dasman palace.

As the West recovered from the initial shock, some began to ask very pertinent questions: 'How and why could this happen?' 'Why was there no warning?' 'Why was the pilot of Flight BA149 not warned to divert his plane to another airport?' 'What were our intelligence services doing?' Indeed, there was every reason to ask.

Meanwhile, more Iraqi troops were approaching Kuwait City. With them came members of the Mukhabarat, the dreaded Iraqi intelligence service, equipped with lists of individuals who were to be arrested and taken to Baghdad. Accompanied by detachments of the Iraqi army's special forces, they made their way unerringly to the homes of those unfortunate people whose names were on their lists.

In fact, warning of the Iraqi invasion had been given, but it had been virtually ignored by politicians in the West and the Middle East. America's Central Intelligence Agency and Egypt's Mukhabarat had both presented their governments with over a dozen reports, the last three of which stated that invasion was imminent. The very same leaders who ignored those intelligence reports were now woken by their aides to be told of the invasion. President Hosni Mubarak in the Egyptian city of Alexandria had three days earlier chosen to accept Saddam Hussein's word, confirming that he was not planning to invade Kuwait, against that of his own intelligence service which possessed evidence of the Iraqi dictator's hidden intentions. Mubarak repeated Saddam Hussein's assurances to President George Bush who, on 31st July, ignored the CIA's warning, 'They are ready, they will go.'

During the seven months prior to the invasion, Saddam Hussein had steadily escalated his political confrontation with the West and with his own neighbours; yet Western governments had not acted, despite obvious and increasing concern amongst the Gulf nations. They were merely following a pattern of diplomacy established and adhered to during previous years, despite continual reports and warnings from human rights organisations and the media of Saddam Hussein's relentless brutality towards his own people and his increasing belligerence towards his Gulf neighbours. Even in Britain, those journalists who attempted to focus public attention on the excesses of the Ba'ath regime in Baghdad were subjected to smear campaigns and attempts, some traced to Whitehall, to blacken their names in an effort to deter them from harming Anglo-Iraqi trade and diplomatic relations. It was the same in Washington and Paris.

Nearly 95 per cent of Saddam Hussein's arsenal of weapons of mass destruction was imported – from France, the United States, West Germany, Britain, Egypt, Brazil and Chile, as well as from Eastern Europe and the Soviet Union, his main supplier. Massive financial credit, provided on extremely generous terms, was extended by Western banks with the connivance and support of their respective governments. This enabled Saddam Hussein not only to purchase large numbers of sophisticated aircraft and weapons systems from the West, but also to establish his own arms industry, develop ballistic missiles, construct chemical weapons production plants and further his development of nuclear weapons.

By the time the world had woken up, it was too late for Kuwait. Iraq's seizure of the oil-rich emirate was holding the whole world to ransom – almost every nation in the world seemed to be represented amongst the hostages who were eventually taken to Iraq or amongst those who remained in hiding in Kuwait; there were over a million expatriates working in the emirate and in Iraq at the time of the invasion.

Oil prices rocketed as the world reacted to the fact that Saddam Hussein was not only in possession of Iraqi and Kuwaiti oil fields but also virtually in control of 40 per cent of the world's known oil reserves; Saudi Arabia's oil fields were within range of his missiles and three hours' drive away for his armoured divisions massed on the borders.

President George Bush faced the most serious crisis to confront the world since the Korean War. As troops of the 82nd Airborne Division landed in Saudi Arabia a few days after the invasion, he addressed his nation and the world, declaring that American forces were being deployed to defend Saudi Arabia against an 'imminent' Iraqi attack. The arrival of US forces was the manifestation of the nightmare long feared by conservative pro-Western Arab regimes, resulting in a show of sympathy towards Iraq from elements of the Arab populace throughout the Middle East – sympathy which Saddam Hussein was quick to exploit by linking any solution to the Kuwaiti crisis with one for the Palestinian problem.

Sadly, the people who, at the time this book was written, were taking a moral stand against the Iraqi dictator are themselves far from blameless. It was they who, for one reason or another, allowed him thirteen years of freedom to establish a ruthless and brutal dictatorship supported by a powerful war machine. Worse, in trying to deal with the 1990 crisis, they allied themselves with regimes whose records on human rights were little better than that of the Ba'athists in Baghdad.

Was Saddam Hussein really planning to invade Saudi Arabia? Or was America's military response just an excuse to cover up a major blunder in US foreign policy? The Americans had continually misread Saddam Hussein's hints and signals and had sent him the wrong messages in return. Moreover, why had American analysts failed to see the 'writing on the wall' to such an extent that the Pentagon had no contingency plans to cope with an Iraqi invasion of any of the Gulf States? One valid question asked by a small number of people in the United States after the invasion was 'What happened to $50 billion worth of advanced weapon systems sold to the Saudis for their self-defence over the past few years?'

On the second day after American troops started arriving in Saudi Arabia, the joke being told in a café in Jordan's capital, Amman, where Saddam Hussein enjoyed the most popular support outside Iraq, went as follows:

Saddam Hussein was discussing the plans to outmanoeuvre the Americans who were about to land and he asked his chief of staff, 'How long did it take your men to capture Kuwait?'

The chief of staff replied, 'Six hours, sir.'

The president asked, 'If we were to take Saudi Arabia?'

'Twelve hours, sir.'

'And the United Arab Emirates?'

'Another three hours' drive, sir.'

'What about Bahrain?'

'We can take it by fax, sir.'

THE ROOTS OF CONFLICT

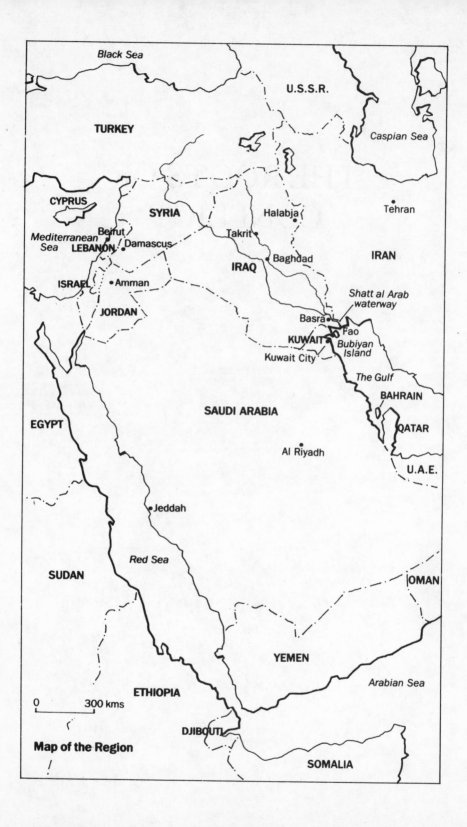

Map of the Region

1 · Lines in the Sand

One Sunday evening in June 1961, twenty-four-year-old Saddam Hussein al-Takriti sat in the Indiana Café in Dukkie, the university quarter of Cairo. He had become a familiar face for the past year after registering at a sixth form college. Now a member of a Ba'ath party 'sleeping cell', Saddam lived nearby in a flat by the Nile. When the evening news bulletin was broadcast on Cairo Radio, Saddam was playing dominoes, drinking sweet black tea and smoking his water-pipe. He suddenly dropped the dominoes, pausing to listen motionlessly to a two-minute item from an Egyptian correspondent in Baghdad. Not bothering to wait for the end of the report, he jumped into a taxi and asked the driver to take him over the Attahrir Bridge, and again over the Qasr al-Nile Bridge, to the late-night post office in Rue Parliament. Quickly drafting a telegram, he sent congratulations and a message supporting the policies and the moves of the man whom he had tried to assassinate eighteen months earlier. It was this botched murder attempt which had forced him into exile, and he was still wanted for a number of crimes in his homeland, Iraq.

The news item that had so excited Saddam was a report on a press conference held by the Iraqi Prime Minister, General Abd al-Karim Qasim, in Baghdad to announce that Kuwait, which had won its independence from Britain only six days earlier, was to become part of Iraq.

Saddam sent his telegram without first discussing the matter with Midhat Juma'h, the man who had recruited him into the cell of Ba'athist exiles in Cairo a year earlier. Juma'h was the most senior member of the cell and had direct links with the Egyptian intelligence service. The Ba'ath party was in fact opposed to General Qasim's move to annex Kuwait for a number of reasons, the most obvious of which was that it needed Cairo's support if it was to make a bid for power.

Britain had recognised Kuwait's independence on 19th June 1961, abrogating an agreement signed in 1899 which had made the emirate a British protectorate – an agreement which Baghdad had always refused to recognise.

During his press conference a few days later, General Qasim said, 'Kuwait is an inseparable part of Iraq; the Iraqi republic has decided not to recognise the 1899 Anglo-Kuwaiti agreement signed by the former Sheikh of Kuwait for 15,000 Indian rupees from the British commissioner in Abadan . . . and the Iraqi republic has decided to protect the people of Kuwait who are the same people of Iraq.' He declared that Kuwait was part of the province of Basra and promised to issue 'a presidential decree appointing the Sheikh of Kuwait an executive administrator to the Muhafadha [county] of Kuwait'. Thus another Middle Eastern crisis was created, but this claim to Kuwait was not the first; it was merely a chapter in a long-running drama.

'It is all the fault of the British,' declared the editorials of the Iraqi papers next morning. 'Kuwait is part of Iraq, we are one nation, separated by the criminal knife of British imperialism.' The story was generations old.

Kuwait emerged as an emirate, as it was known in the Ottoman administration, or sheikhdom as the Arabs knew it, during a period when the entire area was suffering from a political vacuum. Ottoman rule, which had been established in Iraq in 1550, could not control the tribes of the coast whilst at the same time the new European powers had begun to fight over maritime supply lines to secure a route to India. What is now known as Kuwait was part of Lewa'a Al-Basra. In theory, it came under the control of Vali Al-Basra (the Governor of Basra), but his grip on the upper Gulf had weakened by the early eighteenth century.

In about 1710, a new clan led by Sheikh Sabah bin Jaber arrived, with other clans, on the sea coast in the north-eastern corner of the Arabian Peninsula where the coast of the Gulf bends eastwards opposite two small islands. While piracy and conflict were disrupting the lower Gulf, trade agreements with other clans helped the Sabahs to establish an unofficial rule by the mid-1720s. In order to survive, the previously nomadic tribesmen were forced to adopt a new way of life when settling by the coast. They turned to trading, seafaring, fishing, diving for pearls and building small boats. Political organisations began to emerge as the new settlers divided themselves into three groups along family lines: one for administration, another for trade and a third for the economics associated with the sea, under the heading 'pearling'.

Sheikh Sabah, whose family was chosen to administer the affairs of the fledgling settlement, built a mud wall around the town for protection. Failaka and the other islands became part of his administration while trading activities laid the foundations of a basic economy. When Sabah bin Jaber died in 1764, his son Abdallah bin Sabah was elected by other families of the U'tub (migrating tribes) as his successor, thus establishing a precedent that the most suitable member of the Sabah family should be chosen as the new ruler. This tradition was respected by the Ottomans, who in theory ruled Kuwait from Basra but did not intervene in the political process. It was later to be strictly observed by the Kuwaitis, who enshrined it in their post-independence constitution of 1963, although the constitution promised democracy and an elected Parliament to safeguard civil rights.

When the Persians occupied Basra for nearly five years in the mid 1770s, the trade route between India and the West was diverted from Basra to Kuwait, creating an enormous economic boom that was matched only by the discovery of oil some 160 years later. The long-running conflict between the Ottomans and the Persians gave a *de facto* independence to the emirate which had not existed two decades earlier. By the time Abdallah died in 1815, the tribes of U'tubs dominated Bahrain as well as Kuwait, controlling the entire Arab maritime trade and pearling in the Gulf.

Dutch maps dated 1740 make no mention of Kuwait, but they show the island of Failaka, calling it Peleche. It was there that in 322 BC Nearchus, the admiral who led the fleet of Alexander the Great, built a fortress when Alexander ordered him to return from India to the Euphrates via the Gulf, hoping to secure a maritime link between Babylon, the capital of his eastern Empire, and India.

The name Kuwait first appeared, written next to a tower on the coastal area known as Graen, on a navigation map drawn up by the Dutch East India Company and dated 1765. The word is the plural of *kut*, which means a tower or small coastal castle.

The very existence of Kuwait has always hung on a knife's edge, under threat from powerful neighbours who could, if they wished, extinguish it as a sovereign state with a single blow. This taught the Kuwaitis early lessons in political and diplomatic cunning, which they needed if they were to protect their independence.

By the end of the eighteenth century, the entire responsibility for policing the Gulf had become Britain's. India was by then a British possession and the Dutch and the French had been largely evicted from the subcontinent. Britain was happy to restrict its interests in the Gulf to protecting its trade routes and subduing piracy. In 1820, it succeeded in negotiating a General Treaty of Maritime Peace with the sheikhs of the Trucial Coast. (There was no need to make a separate agreement with the Kuwaitis, who took no part in the piracy that plagued the lower Gulf.) Britain required some form of legal framework as a pretext for intervention if needed, as it was worried about the growing presence of Turkish naval power in the waters of the Gulf. The Turks had also been known to encourage Arab piracy against the French and Portuguese.

Britain proceeded to establish posts and naval bases along the trade route to India via the Suez Canal, which was opened in 1866, and also signed exclusive agreements with Arab rulers throughout the Gulf. The first was with Bahrain in 1880, prohibiting the sheikhdom from making any treaties or agreements with any state other than Britain or establishing diplomatic relations with other countries without British consent. With a history of living under threats from hostile neighbours, the Kuwaitis also wanted British protection.

When Sheikh Mubarak became ruler in 1896, he was forced to fight off his two brothers. He managed to defeat and kill them both, this bloody episode marking the start of his reign. Such conflict was unusual among the Sabahs and shocked members of the other ruling families were quick to ally themselves with Mubarak before they shared the same fate. A feud within the Sabah clan was thus prevented. Mubarak subsequently built up a 25,000-strong force of loyal tribesmen and used it to defend the emirate, its caravans and other interests from marauding bedouins.

Mubarak also used the Sabahs' cunning, playing superpowers off against one another. In 1897 the Baghdad Vali – the Ottoman governor of Baghdad – tried to assert control over Kuwait. Mubarak sought British protection in the form of an alliance, but the British refused his request. By 1898 the sheikh had let it be publicly known that he was about to give Britain's arch-rivals, the Russians, a coal-loading station in the emirate. The British were alarmed, because a month earlier the Ottomans had granted Count Kapnist, a Russian entrepreneur, permission to build a railway line to connect the Mediterranean with the Gulf, from the Syrian coast to Kuwait via Baghdad.

Lord Curzon, an expert on the Gulf and a pillar of British imperialism, became India's viceroy. He managed to persuade the British government to sign an agreement with Sheikh Mubarak in 1899, ensuring that no territories would be leased, sold or given to any other power without British consent. At the same time, Britain's growing rival in Europe, imperial Germany, announced that it was to build a railway from Berlin to Baghdad. Mubarak received a letter assuring him of 'the good offices of Her Majesty's Government towards you, your heirs and successors, plus 15,000 rupees'.

His heirs learned this lesson and made good use of it. In 1983 the Kuwaitis forced the US Congress to agree to sell them advanced weapons after buying Soviet arms first. When they hired three Russian tankers in 1987, the Soviet fleet started protecting their shipping in the Gulf; this led to the United States placing the emirate's tankers under the Stars and Stripes.

In July 1913, the storm clouds of war were gathering over Europe and Britain urgently wished to resolve matters in the Gulf. Mubarak, never one to miss an opportunity, wanted to make the best of the options facing him. The British and the Ottomans reached an agreement recognising Kuwait as 'an autonomous district of Ottoman empire'. The agreement defined the frontiers of the emirate, whose population had doubled since 1898, while its pearling and fishing fleet now included more than 800 vessels.

On the eve of the First World War, Britain was conspiring to use the warlike bedouin to protect its interests in the Middle East, either under the leadership of their sheikhs or under British officers – such as T. E. Lawrence – rather than deploying its own soldiers in the desert. To secure the support of Mubarak, Britain agreed to recognise Kuwait as independent of the Ottoman Empire. In exchange, Mubarak was to support Britain against Turkey in the coming war.

Mubarak and his family continued smuggling and trading with all comers and leaving doors open for new deals with many parties. It was war, an ideal situation in which to make money. The Kuwaitis were still poor and ethics could not be permitted to stand in the way of profit.

Turkey joined Germany and her central European allies, while Mubarak took Britain's side but did not fight. He persuaded Abdul Azziz ibn Sa'ud, the Sultan of Najd – later Saudi Arabia – to join the alliance. Sharif Hussein, the Emir of Mecca, whose son Faisal led the Arab tribes with Lawrence against the Turks, also joined.

Mubarak's son Salem, who masterminded smuggling for the Turks, succeeded his father in 1915 and declared his sympathy for Muslim Turkey. He also permitted the Syrians, who were under naval blockade by the Allies, to use Kuwait as a conduit for trade. Seven years later, in 1922, Britain punished the Kuwaitis for their treachery when Sir Percy Cox, the British High Commissioner in Iraq, carved away an oil-rich coastal slice of Kuwaiti land and handed it over to Ibn Sa'ud. However, it continued to honour the 1899 agreement guaranteeing Kuwait's status as a British protectorate.

After the war, Ibn Sa'ud pressed his territorial claims along the border lines agreed by Turkey and Britain. In 1920 he placed an embargo on Kuwaiti trade which caused great damage to the emirate's economy, whilst his Wahhabi warriors carried out many raids across the border. In October 1920, Sheikh Salem marched with his forces to meet those of Ibn Sa'ud at Al-Jahrah, some thirty miles east of Kuwait City. Unlike 2nd

August 1990, the Kuwaitis managed to halt the advance of their well-armed and battle-hardened adversaries. Despite heavy losses, they were able to prevent the invaders from occupying Kuwait City until British warships arrived and landed Royal Marines. The Wahhabis withdrew and Sir Percy Cox proposed to resolve the border dispute a year later.

Cox had arrived in what was to become Iraq in October 1920, replacing as High Commissioner Sir Arnold Wilson, who had wanted to set up a British protectorate. Wilson's plan had been ill-received in the newly founded country, already in turmoil since General Maude had captured Baghdad from the Turks in March 1917 at a cost to the British of two and a half years of bitter fighting and 98,000 casualties. Maude proceeded to put into effect the secret Sykes–Picot agreement, drawn up in 1916 between Britain and France, in which the two powers shared out the spoils of their coming victory over the Ottoman Empire. Mesopotamia, comprising the two former Ottoman velayets (provinces) of Basra and Baghdad, was given to Britain. The northern velayet of Mosul was initially given to France, but was the subject of a dispute which was settled in Britain's favour in 1919.

The Kurds were in constant revolt, demanding an independent home-land, and found the defeat of the Ottomans and the occupation of Mosul a few days after the Armistice a golden opportunity for pressing their claim for a free state. They were further encouraged by the promises of autonomy that American president Woodrow Wilson appeared to offer in his fourteen-point plan. Initially the British had encouraged the appoint-ment of 'suitable' local Kurdish leaders in the administration of Al-Mosul velayet.

However, Britain soon became more committed to establishing a single Arab state under its control than addressing the national needs of the Kurds. When the state of Iraq, comprising Basra and Baghdad, was founded and finally put under British mandate with the approval of the League of Nations in the San Remo agreement of April 1920, the whole nation revolted. The Shia, the majority of the population in the southern and central areas, were demanding an Islamic state, whilst their clergy declared the British rule unlawful as Muslims should not be ruled by non-Muslims. They suffered most as they were the fuel of the revolution.

It was the Sunni minority that gained from the collapse of the Ottoman Empire. A group of Western-educated politicians who wanted an inde-pendent, secular Iraqi state or a British-style constitutional monarch, they included Nuri al-Sa'id and the pro-Western nationalist group Ahd-al'Iraq, who had been encouraged by the Syrian congress in Damascus which had elected Abdallah as King of Transjordan and Faisal King of Syria. They were the sons of Sharif of Mecca who with Lawrence had led the Arabs to fight Britain's war in the desert.

Sir Percy Cox abolished British military rule and implemented an 'Arab solution' by setting a national council of ministers to draft an electoral law and establish a national assembly. Britain insisted, however, on maintaining control of foreign policy. It was the national council which approved Faisal as constitutional monarch when he arrived for the first time on Iraqi soil in June 1921, after the French had dethroned him as King of Syria. With Faisal's help, Cox proceeded to establish a strong hold on the fledgling country.

The borders between Iraq and Kuwait, like the borders with Saudi Arabia, were ill-defined if marked at all. Cox and Faisal had feared that the lawlessness on the country's southern border might be a threat to the stability of the nation. In 1922, in order to put an end to the trouble, Cox summoned Ibn Sa'ud to a conference at Uqair, near the seaport of Al-Hasa on the Gulf coast near Bahrain. Cox wanted to define the northern borders of Najd in an attempt to prevent any further incursions by the king's bedouin followers who cared little for artificial frontiers. Their loyalties were to their own tribal chiefs, not to some distant government or ruler. Raiding the camping grounds of other tribes across the borders was one of the favourite pastimes of the Arabs of the Najd central highlands, and this often resulted in trouble and bloodshed. Sometimes they disrupted trade by attacking caravans heading for the ports of Kuwait and Basra. The Hijaz tribes, who inhabited the western edge of the central highlands, even prompted Ibn Sa'ud to press claims over territories under Kuwait's domain.

The rivalries and tensions between the Saudis and the Iraqis were no better then than they were in 1990. During the Uqair conference, the arguments went on for days. Having suffered heavy casualties at the swords of Ibn Sa'ud's tribesmen, the Kuwaitis let the British political resident represent them. The Arabs guessed that oil, discovered in Iran in 1908, would become the black gold of the future because in 1911, on the advice of Winston Churchill, the Royal Navy had converted its ships from coal to oil power. The border disputes between the Saudis and the Kuwaitis soon concentrated on the areas near the coast where oil was discovered some years later.

To put an end to these disagreements, Cox decided to draw the borders himself. The red pencil line denoting the new borders was arbitrary and unfortunately the map he used was inaccurate, so even the exact geo-

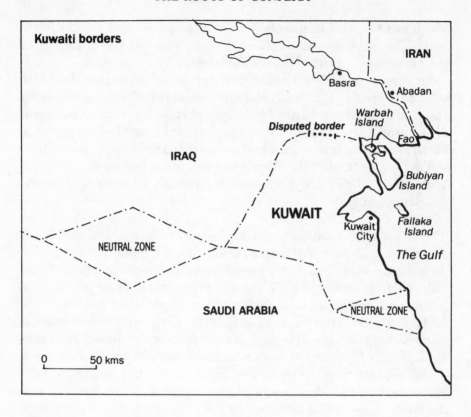

graphical position of the border was far from certain. However, it marked the division between Saudi Arabia and Iraq, as well as two neutral zones, and thus temporarily settled the disputes. The aggressive Ibn Sa'ud accepted Cox's newly marked border at the time, but trouble simmered endlessly thereafter, eventually culminating in the events of 2nd August 1990.

Knowing that many more deals would be made with Faisal in future, Cox gave Iraq a large slice of the Najd territory it claimed. In order to placate Ibn Sa'ud, he had to exact a price from the Kuwaitis for their co-operation with both the Turks and the British during the First World War. He gave the Najd tribes about two thirds of the land that was governed by the Kuwaitis according to a 1913 Anglo-Turkish agreement, now forcibly annulled. Kuwait also lost its right to part of the hinterland south of 1913 agreement lines and this became a neutral zone. Another neutral zone was created between Iraq and Saudi Arabia, and the two zones were the source of endless arguments and feuds for years to come. In compensation, a small slice was carved away from Iraq to be given to

Kuwait, thus reducing Iraqi access to the sea to a mere sixteen miles of useless swamps and marshland.

Cox drew his lines after weighing up claims by the conflicting tribes and assessing their real force on the ground. He later explained to Sheikh Ahmad al-Jaber, Kuwait's ruler, that at the time nothing could be done to prevent Ibn Sa'ud from taking this territory by force if he wished to do so. He added, however, that Britain would not stand in the way if Kuwait was to fight to win it back. Compared to Mubarak, who had ambitiously and vigorously defended Kuwait's interests, Ahmed took fewer risks. He based his policies on the fact that Kuwait needed the help of a powerful friend like Britain while keeping good relations with its neighbours in order to preserve independence. He attempted to balance the interests of regional powers, who preferred to see Kuwait independent rather than annexed, with those of Britain, which was then a world superpower requiring a guaranteed supply of oil. It was a policy his family had followed since they established Kuwait some two hundred years earlier.

After Cox's rearrangement of the borders, which left Iraq virtually landlocked, British officials in the region worked hard to persuade the Arabs to recognise them. When the subject arose again in March 1923, Major Moore, the British political resident (agent) in Kuwait, asked the emir, Sheikh Ahmad Jaber al-Ahmad, to define the borders formally. The latter replied in a letter dated 4th April 1923, referring to Mubarak's letter of 1920 to Cox which stated that 'the borders were the same which Sheikh Salem al-Mubarak defined to the British High Commissioner in Baghdad in a letter dated 17th September 1920 as the green line defined in the Anglo-Ottoman treaty of 1913'. Major Moore reported this to Cox, who replied on 19th April, instructing Moore to inform the emir that Britain recognised his definition of the borders. These borders, which included the islands of Bubiyan and Warbah, remained intact until 1990.

In the summer of 1932, Britain nominated Iraq for membership of the League of Nations, which asked for a copy of the border agreements between Iraq and its neighbours. Iraq's prime minister, Nuri al-Sa'id, wrote on 21st July 1932 to Sir Francis Humphrie, the British High Commissioner in Baghdad, recognising the borders exactly as outlined in Sheikh al-Mubarak's letter of 1920.

Another border crisis followed five years later. In 1935, a retired British officer, one Colonel Ward, was director-general of the port and navigation works in Basra. At that time, developments in artillery had resulted in considerable increases in the maximum ranges of field guns and howitzers. Consequently, Ward was of the opinion that Basra was too near to the Iranian border – a mere thirteen miles away – which put it in danger in any future conflict. He advised the Baghdad government to build a port in Umm Qasr as an outlet to the sea, instead of at Basra which ships could only reach by sailing up the Shatt al-Arab waterway along the Iranian borders. (Thirty years later the Shah of Iran implemented a similar idea by moving oil export facilities from Abadan on the Shatt al-Arab to Kharj Island.) The Baghdad government showed great interest in the project, which was known as Khor Abdallah (the Abdallah Canal).

Over the next two years, the Iraqi foreign ministry developed further the idea of acquiring a proper outlet to the sea. Following the signing, on 4th July 1937, of the Shatt al-Arab agreement between Iran and Iraq, Mahdi Abbas, the Iraqi deputy foreign minister, wrote to the British government on 7th September 1938 saying, 'In the light of Iranian threats to the Shatt al-Arab, we wish to start a project to guarantee an outlet to the sea via Kuwait.' The British replied that Iraq should fear no threat from Iran, since Britain was its ally, and that it was unlikely that the Kuwaitis would agree to a canal being cut through their land. By the end of the month, Tawfeek al-Seweedi, the Iraqi foreign minister, was more explicit in his note to London: 'If Kuwait was to give the island of Warbah to Iraq, then the whole Abdallah waterway would come under Iraq's rule and guarantee a safe port for us.'

Iraq's head of state at the time was young King Ghazi, a playboy with a taste for fast cars who had succeeded his father Faisal in 1933. An inexperienced but sincere Arab nationalist, Ghazi denounced French rule in Syria, Zionist claims in Palestine and the British colonialist presence in the Gulf. Annexing Kuwait was also an important item on his nationalist agenda and he made his first move in this respect in 1938. Using propaganda broadcast through the Iraqi press and his own private broadcasting station in his Baghdad palace of Azzohour, Ghazi exploited political unrest in Kuwait. He preyed on the ambitions of Kuwait's educated younger generation who were demanding a parliament and a written constitution. His actions set an ominous precedent for succeeding Iraqi governments and their attempts to annex the oil-rich emirate.

The 1989–90 pro-democracy movement in Kuwait, started by liberal members of the parliament dissolved in 1986, had its origins in the 1938 pro-democracy movement. The first seeds of a democratic movement inside the emirate were sown amongst the new generation, educated by Ottoman, Egyptian, British and other Western teachers. Some members of families other than the Sabahs presented Sheikh Ahmad al-Jaber with a demand to participate in the government. They called for a parliament modelled on Westminster, a demand that many of their grandchildren copied early in 1990 when they presented Sheikh Jaber, the current Emir of Kuwait, with a petition signed by half the registered electorate. On both occasions the patriarchal tyranny of the bedouin tribal rulers got the better of the emir. However, the rejection of the pro-democracy ideal provided Baghdad with an excuse to force its help upon the dissenting majority of people in Kuwait.

As in 1990, Iraqi newspapers were widely read in Kuwait. In 1938, many articles written by members of the new pro-democracy movement in Kuwait were printed in Iraqi papers, which were read in the emirate or were heard on broadcasts from King Ghazi's palace radio station.

Unlike in 1990, the economic situation in Kuwait in 1938 was dire compared to that of the relatively prosperous Iraq. The 1930s slump in world trade reduced the demand for pearls and the number of vessels arriving at the port of Kuwait City declined, creating mass unemployment and a migration of workers to Basra, Baghdad, Abadan and other places. There was also an acute water shortage and conditions were ripe for a mass revolt inspired by a movement seeking support on the streets for liberalisation.

Clashes between the Kuwaiti authorities and those citizens gathering to discuss democratic demands gave the Iraqis an opportunity to build up a persuasive propaganda campaign in which they extolled the virtues of their constitutional monarchy whilst putting forward persuasive arguments for a Kuwaiti federation with Iraq. The Iraqi media claimed that in this it was supporting popular demands among Arab nationalists in Kuwait.

King Ghazi massed troops near the borders, while the media attacked the 'medieval rule of Sheikh Ahmad al-Jaber al-Sabah, and his denial of civil rights to the people'. At the same time, Ghazi threatened to confiscate Kuwaiti properties and land in the Shatt al-Arab. Editorials in Iraqi newspapers urged Kuwaitis to demonstrate, calling for unity with Iraq. The press columns were full of maps and explanations to their readers of the benefits available to the people of Kuwait, who were short of water and lacking in agriculture. Kuwaitis were promised improvements in education, a stronger economy and better health if they united with their prosperous northern neighbours under the Hashemite flag.

Britain informed the now-independent Iraq that it would militarily intervene if there was any move into Kuwait. However, the Sabah family again had luck on their side. Late at night on 4th April 1939, King Ghazi drove his sports car at high speed into a lamp-post inside the gardens of the Azzohour palace. His instant death drew the curtain on this chapter of Iraqi attempts to annex Kuwait.

*

The events of the Second World War divided the Iraqis into two factions: those led by Abd al-Illah and al-Sa'id, who wanted to support Britain against Italy and Germany, and those who wanted to support the Axis out of sheer hatred for Britain as the colonial power held responsible for the ills of the nation. This phenomenon was visible throughout the Middle East, especially in Egypt, where nationalist groups and officers were sympathising with the Germans. Britain's opponents were led by Rashid Ali al-Gailani and were backed by a powerful faction of officers known as the 'Golden Square', who were influenced by or attracted to ideas of pan-Arab nationalism proposed by scholars mainly from Syria and Palestine.

A number of underground movements continued to flourish. There were the writings of Sati'e al-Husari promoting, without much scientific proof, the racial theory of a 'common Arab heritage'. He also produced reams of emotional prose which expressed support for an 'Arab Nation' made up of Iraq, Syria, Lebanon, Palestine and Transjordan. These nations, he argued, formed an integral part of one another. In the case of Iraq his call was accompanied by the additional claim that the Iraqis were the direct descendants of the Mesopotamians and Babylonians. The claim was made in an effort to promote a common feeling of national loyalty for the country which had not even existed a few years earlier.

This myth was later effectively adopted by the Ba'ath party and Saddam Hussein. During the Gulf War of the 1980s the Baghdad propaganda machine, whilst promoting Iraqi nationalism, glorified the Iraqi leader as the heir of the Babylonian kings and as the leader of Pan-Arabism. This appealed to Arab nationalists – especially those amongst the Palestinians on the West Bank and in Jordan.

Although Iraq as a nation state was, and still is, largely artificial and had no historic roots – unlike Egypt, for example, where the border and the population remained as they were for over seven thousand years – the grouping of the three Ottoman provinces has since the mid-1920s possessed more Arab character than any Arabic-speaking nation. This was due to the commitment of the Sharifian officers and politicians loyal to Faisal I, who came from clans and tribes of northern Arabia; their dream for Arabism was a union of the Fertile Crescent – mainly Iraq, Syria and the Jordan Valley.

Prime Minister Nuri al-Sa'id had attached himself to Britain and was therefore seen by the second generation of Sharifians as an obstacle in the way of Pan-Arabism. However, Pan-Arabism was a flag waved by a large number of otherwise disparate groups. Iraqi and Arab national awareness found its way into other factions such as the reformists of Jma'at al-Ahali, founded by students educated at the Beirut American University who subscribed to the ideas of British Fabianism. Other tendencies were groups faithful to al-Husari's ideas of pan-Arabism and there was also the Iraqi communist party, founded in 1934 from labour groups.

The presence of such political elements were first recognised in huge demonstrations against Britain in 1941 and after 1945, and later still in the bloody events of 1958.

Resentment at the effects of the war and the founding of Israel, which was seen as the theft of Palestine, in 1948 further fuelled anger against the British. Oil workers went on strike and there was widespread anti-British sentiment. Subsequently, martial law was introduced.

In 1949, Nuri al-Sa'id ordered the Iraqi army's withdrawal from forward positions in Palestine. The leaders of the communist party who had been in prison since 1947 were publicly hanged in Baghdad. Between then and the fall of the monarchy in 1958 there were some twenty different cabinets in Iraq. Meanwhile oil revenues were growing rapidly. Despite Britain's awareness of corruption, violation of human rights and the unpopularity of the government, it continued to support the regime as increases in oil income made Britain feel more optimistic. Nuri al-Sa'id was seen as apparently paying more attention to development by establishing the Development Board in 1950. This organisation concentrated on large-scale construction projects, which served to generate more corruption.

The gap between rich and poor was growing wider. Between 1939 and 1957, the cost of living in Iraq increased fivefold. Eighty per cent of the population were illiterate (90 per cent of women), while less than one fifth of all Iraqi children went to school. There was one doctor for every 60,000 head of population and one nurse for every 12,000. There was no form of social security. The percentage of undernourished people rose from thirty-three in 1949 to fifty-six in 1957.

Parties with real programmes for social reforms like the communists were driven underground, as was the Arab nationalist party, the Ba'ath, which had been founded in 1947. The secrecy of underground work and al-Sa'id's oppressive measures led these parties to adopt violence and develop a conspiratorial approach. They realised that the army would be the effective instrument for change and thus sacrificed any remaining shaky belief in parliamentary democracy.

The young king Faisal II, who had succeeded his father, Ghazi, at the age of four, was isolated by his uncle, the Prince Regent Abd al-Illah, and the prime minister. There is no evidence that British diplomats gave Nuri al-Sa'id any advice to change his ways and introduce some form of liberalisation. As Tahseen Me'alla, a founder member of the Ba'ath who split with the party in 1970, later commented on Britain's involvement with Nuri al-Sa'id, 'The British ruling classes wanted democracy and liberty in Britain but not for the peoples they once ruled. They only wanted oil and a slice of the profit given to a ruling oligarchy adopting a British lifestyle and advised by British officials. The oligarchy took all the oil income themselves and, while the local population was being oppressed and deprived of its basic civil rights, Britain looked the other way.'

Faisal II came of age in 1953 but Abd al-Illah was reluctant to loosen his grip on power. Hoping to produce a chamber of deputies that could neutralise his rivals, Abd al-Illah called for parliamentary elections in 1954 while Nuri al-Sa'id was abroad.

The National Front, comprised of the communists, national democrats and Istiqlal (the Independence party), won eleven out of 135 seats. Prudently Abd al-Illah brought in Nuri al-Sa'id as prime minister to form a new security pact, as the 1930 treaty with Britain was about to expire.

The prime minister dissolved the parliament, banned newspapers and arrested activists. Opposition parties such as the Istiqlal or the national democrats boycotted the election and 122 out of the 135 seats were uncontested.

In an editorial in London's *Baghdad Times* on 23rd February 1955, Nuri al-Sa'id was criticised for going too far in banning political parties and withdrawing licences from some sixty newspapers. The writer warned of a possible disaster.

Various events in Iraq and overseas caused nationalist and leftist groups to clamour for change. The nationalisation of oil in Iran inspired popular demand for similar measures in Iraq whilst the communist-led mass demonstrations in Baghdad, known as the Intifada, were joined by other banned parties. The rise to power of Gamal Abd al-Nasser in Egypt and his subsequent defiance of the superpowers also had an effect on the political scene in Iraq, as did the negotiations leading to the signing in 1955 of the Baghdad Pact, which angered Nasser.

The idea of the pact was first encouraged by US Secretary of State John Foster Dulles's 'northern tier' foreign-policy concept of bringing the countries bordering the Soviet Union into a military pact with the West. This appealed to Nuri al-Sa'id, who shared Dulles's obsessive anti-communist sentiments and wanted to place Iraq in the centre of a pro-Western bloc to guard against the spread of communism. The Baghdad Pact was a treaty between Iraq and Turkey in which Muslim countries such as Pakistan and Iran were included. Britain also joined, thus giving it the opportunity of negotiating new leases for its military bases in the region. Nasser, however, refused to join.

By early 1957 the national democratic party, the Iraqi communist party, the Ba'ath party, smaller opposition groups and independent nationalists inspired by Nasser had formed the National Unity Front, which was a loose alliance whose programme was independence, social reforms and land reforms. Their aims were the same as those stated in leaflets distributed among army officers, signed by the 'Free Officers'. Although there were no formal links, many officers belonged to some of the political parties. There had been several plans amongst them for a takeover to force a new government on the king.

At this time it was rumoured that the chief of staff of the Iraqi army had received information on a coup plot prepared by Abd al-Karim Qasim and Abd al-Salam Arif. Qasim, the commander of an armoured brigade from the 3rd Division, had been a favourite of the Prince Regent Abd al-Illah and Nuri al-Sa'id. He was serving with his brigade near the Iranian frontier town of Ba'quba. The commander of the 3rd Division, Major General Daghestani, had no suspicions concerning Qasim's loyalty.

There were also rumours of more than one group of officers preparing for a Nasser-style coup, yet Nuri al-Sa'id was careless of security. In addition to his repeated political and diplomatic errors, which coincided with the rise of anti-British sentiment, Nuri al-Sa'id made another fatal mistake – one which Saddam Hussein is known to have mentioned often to his security men in order to ensure that it is not repeated.

It was a general rule in Iraq that troops from outside the Baghdad garrison were not permitted to move through or around the capital with their ammunition. However, on the night of 13th July 1958 the rule was mysteriously broken. Troops from Baghdad's garrison manning road-blocks and checkpoints did not check to ensure that ammunition had been unloaded from troops and tanks of the 3rd Division as they drove through Baghdad on their way towards the desert road heading west to the border with Jordan on orders from Nuri al-Sa'id.

The king and his uncle were due to travel in the morning to Ankara but as first light was breaking a column of Abd al-Salam Arif's troops moved to the Baghdad radio station, which was captured just before six o'clock. While Abd al-Salam Arif was leading another column of armour towards the palace, Qasim, his partner in the conspiracy, was still with his brigade at Ba'quba.

Outnumbered by the rebels, the king's troops fought bravely but were overwhelmed in a short and bloody battle. The king and his uncle came out into the palace gardens, possibly to listen to the rebels' demands, and were shot on the spot. There was a story later on suggesting that the rebels were planning to spare the life of the king. This seems unlikely, as the rebels would have feared that the king, who was popular, might subsequently lead a liberation movement in exile.

The women in the palace were shot soon afterwards. Whilst the battle at the palace was in progress, the radio announced the success of the revolution and called upon the population to rise in its support. The communists were well prepared, possessing their own organisation among the labour associations and students. They were the first to move on to the streets, pulling down the statues of King Faisal I and Maude, the British general who had captured Baghdad from the Turks during the First World War.

Mobs started to converge on the city. A mood of angry frenzy built up rapidly, exacerbated by the heat which grew more intense as the day wore on, and looting and burning of houses broke out. The bodies of the king and his uncle were hung up by their feet opposite the palace. Nuri al-Sa'id was captured alive trying to flee disguised as a woman. Although only half a leg was left of his body, it was later rumoured that he was still alive when he was subjected to the Sahhl – towing a body by the feet behind a car through the streets of the city. Foreigners who were on the streets and could not reach the protection of troops before they were intercepted by the mob, were torn to pieces – their bodies were later buried in a secret location. Politicians associated with the old regime suffered the same fate as their luckless prime minister. Baghdad was cut off from the outside world in a state of complete lawlessness. As the British ambassador watched helplessly, his embassy on fire, posters bearing the face of Gamal Abd al-Nasser of Egypt were pasted up on the walls of Baghdad.

When Major Abd al-Maguid Farid of the 2nd Signal Regiment of the Egyptian army arrived from Syria twenty-four hours after the killing of Nuri al-Sa'id, he shivered as he saw bodies hanging from lamp-posts. Farid was under orders to deliver a message from Cairo that President Nasser was supporting the revolution and that the United Arab Republic, the name given to the five-month-old Egyptian–Syrian Federation, had put all its resources at its disposal.

To reassure the Iraqis of Cairo's commitment, Farid was also to set up an operations room in the defence ministry, near the offices of Generals Abd al-Karim Qasim and Abd al-Salam Arif. He was allocated a room next to theirs where he set up the radios which he had brought with him and maintained constant contact with Cairo.

On hearing of the Iraqi coup, Nasser's immediate reaction had been to support it. The Egyptian leader was at that moment in Yugoslavia, attending a series of meetings with President Tito. After informing Tito that he would have to cut short his visit, he sent a signal to Alexandria and gave orders that a message of support should be taken to Baghdad and that a communications facility should be installed there. He also sent a signal to Moscow, seeking support from the Soviet Union.

The United States moved its Sixth Fleet into the east Mediterranean after a call for assistance from the pro-Western Lebanese president Chamil Chamoun. On 15th July, Nasser met Soviet premier Nikita Khrushchev in Moscow as the Americans began to flex their muscles on Nasser's northern doorstep by landing marines in Lebanon. Moscow denounced this move, as did the rest of the Eastern bloc, the countries of the non-aligned movement and several other Arab, African and Muslim states. The Lebanon expedition was one of the early American actions which subsequently proved counter-productive in the Middle East, particularly after Chamoun was overthrown and the pro-Nasser Fu'ad Shihab was elected in his place.

Britain also deployed troops to the Middle East. At the request of Jordan's King Hussein, who was related to the Iraqi royal family and had seen the pictures of his uncle and cousin's dismembered bodies in Baghdad, the 16th Independent Parachute Brigade Group was flown to Amman to deter any attempts at a coup against the king.

In Iraq itself, it was too late to salvage the monarchy. As the conspirators were only a handful of men in the 3rd Division, the majority of its troops were still outside Baghdad. The bulk of the Iraqi army hesitated during the first two days and did not lend its full support to the revolution. General Mizra, chief of staff of the Pakistan army (subsequently president of Pakistan), was later reported as stating that if plans for dealing with such an eventuality had existed amongst the armed forces of the Baghdad Pact a joint British–Muslim force could have succeeded in overthrowing the rebel regime in Iraq within the first twenty-four hours, after which it would have been too late. However, there were no such plans and in any case implementing them would have been a very big gamble. Nasser's direct support of the revolution, backed by the Soviet Union, would have made any pro-British government in Baghdad a target for another coup.

Egypt sent two squadrons of MiG-15s and MiG-17s to fly to Syrian air bases in 'a state of readiness to protect the revolution in Iraq'. Twenty-four hours later, Nasser's personal aircraft landed in Aleppo, where he delivered a fiery speech in the main square, denouncing American and British imperialists and stating that the fate of the imperialist servants in Baghdad should act as a warning to others. He was cheered by hundreds of thousands as he was joined by Abd al-Salam Arif, one of the two principal conspirators and architects of the coup. Nasser's Aleppo speech removed any doubt amongst the armed forces, which now united in support of the revolution and swore allegiance to the new regime.

The events of July 1958 in Baghdad set a precedent for the use of violence, terror and conspiracy as a normal instrument of strategy by successive governments which came to power through a series of military coups. During the first five months after the revolution, Qasim survived two assassination attempts organised by Abd al-Salam Arif, his pro-Nasser partner. When Qasim tried to exile Arif by appointing him as ambassador to Germany, the latter stayed in Switzerland. He was recalled and was subsequently arrested, later being tried *in camera*.

Rashid Ali al-Gailani, who had staged a coup in 1941, was called back from exile. However, old habits die hard. He ignored his friends' advice and attempted a coup, which was easily suppressed by Qasim, and he was arrested and sentenced to death. A feud subsequently developed between the communist-supported Qasim and Nasser. Cairo Radio propaganda accused Britain of plotting with the communists against the United Arab Republic and the Muslim world. In fact, the British cabinet was still debating whether to support Qasim against Nasser or to oppose him.

London decided to replace Sir Michael Wright, who as ambassador in Baghdad was still associated with the old regime, and to send Sir Humphrey Trevelyan instead. Meanwhile, the media had become a powerful weapon in the battle. Cairo's accusation of Britain's plotting with communists against Egypt was echoed in the European press. An article which appeared in the German magazine *Der Spiegel* under the headline 'Der Feind steht am Nil' (The Enemy is on the Nile) disclosed more details of British anti-Nasser efforts. This was translated into Arabic and broadcast on Cairo Radio.

Devious tactics were adopted by both sides. Major Farid, the Egyptian signals officer who had subsequently become the assistant military attaché in the United Arab Republic embassy in Baghdad, claimed that the British embassy was reproducing thousands of anti-Nasser leaflets previously published by communists who no longer had the means to produce them.

The communists themselves tried to discredit Nasser. In an attempt to avenge arrests of their comrades in Egypt, Iraqi communists leaked information to a Cairo Radio correspondent that a popular local heroine named Hassinah Mallas Hadid had been arrested after she had shouted Nasser's name while leading nationalists in a street battle against Qasim's troops. When Cairo Radio broadcast the details, after exaggerating the deeds of Hassinah, it caused hilarity in Baghdad coffee houses since the lady in question was running a famous brothel in the Iraqi capital.

Qasim's principal opponents were the new nationalists, mainly the Ba'athists. He thus had to rely increasingly on communist support. They had already drawn up programmes for land reforms, labour laws and plans for health and education. Most importantly, they planned to end the long-running war in Kurdistan.

Qasim appointed one of his cousins, a Colonel Mehdawi, as president of the People's Court. Well known for his somewhat bloodthirsty tendencies, Mehdawi made little or no pretence of administering justice. Every evening the televised court hearings were the main entertainment in the cafés on the streets of the capital. Customers would laugh and cheer as Mehdawi cursed the accused in the dock while delivering speeches attacking Britain, America and later Nasser. On 31st December 1958, at a New Year's Eve party in Baghdad's Railway Club, Mehdawi announced that his New Year present was twelve further executions. At the same time Nasser's police were rounding up and incarcerating over 3,000 members of seven communist parties in Egypt. During this period, reports of attempts on Qasim's life were rife. A number of these attempts were attributed to America's Central Intelligence Agency (CIA) which, in one of the more fanciful accounts, was reported to have sent the Iraqi dictator a poisoned handkerchief as a present. Earlier in 1958, the CIA was also accused by Cairo Radio of plotting to assassinate Nasser. The plan was exposed by Abd al-Hamid al-Sarraj, the head of the Deuxième Bureau in Syria during the Federation, who had been given a large sum of money by King Sa'ud bin Abd al-Azziz of Saudi Arabia to assassinate the Egyptian president.

Qasim's National Front cabinet included a Ba'athist minister, Fua'd al-Rikkabi, who had been the leader of Iraq's Ba'athist elements since 1952. (He was murdered in prison in 1971 on Saddam Hussein's orders.) In February 1959, the National Front collapsed when the Ba'athists and nationalists resigned from the government. The Egyptians backed a nationalist movement in Mosul which took over the city's radio station and declared a new government. Qasim ordered the Iraqi air force to attack the rebels' headquarters and the army to move on Mosul, which it entered after five days. Mention of Nasser's name was forbidden and his pictures were torn down from wherever they had been displayed.

Seven Egyptian and Syrian diplomats were deported from Baghdad, whilst on 22nd February communist students attacked the United Arab Republic embassy during a party attended by a number of Ba'athists.

In January Qasim had asked the British for arms. Selwyn Lloyd, the Foreign Secretary, subscribed to the view that the communists, 'with whom we know how to deal', were a better proposition than Nasser. There were, however, some reservations in London due to Qasim's decision to pull Iraq out of the Baghdad Pact and to request the withdrawal of the Royal Air Force from the air base at Habbaniya. (Britain was planning to leave in any case because of cuts in the defence budget.) Nevertheless, after a year of negotiations, the British cabinet recommended that Qasim's request should be granted and that arms should be supplied. Meanwhile, the Russians had approached Qasim, offering arms at lower prices and with better repayment terms.

It was at this point that the Ba'athists decided to assassinate Qasim. Some selected party members, especially those with medical training and qualifications, were warned to expect casualties. Preparations for a battle with Qasim's supporters were put in hand. The United Arab Republic intelligence service knew that the Ba'athists were planning to assassinate the Iraqi leader, but made no effort to prevent them from doing so.

The Ba'ath leadership gave the orders for Qasim's assassination after two leading party members were executed by Mehdawi's court. On 7th October 1959, a six-man assassination squad was waiting in Al Rashid Street in central Baghdad. The night before, one member of the squad had fallen ill. A new recruit was quickly drafted in: a twenty-two-year-old sympathiser who was not a full party member. An aggressive young man, he had just been released from prison for lack of evidence concerning his involvement, together with his uncle, in the murder of a civil servant. Renowned for his prowess with firearms, he had carried out his first murder at the age of fifteen and a second at the age of twenty – his full name was Saddam Hussein al-Takriti.

The assassination plan called for a car driven by one of the squad members, Salim al-Ze'baq, to obstruct Qasim's car whilst the other five members opened fire on the prime minister himself.

Two months earlier, a Ba'ath member had contacted Mohammed Kabboul, a Syrian national who was a third secretary at the United Arab Republic embassy and had rented his flat opposite the defence ministry in which Qasim's office was located. Kabboul had handed the key to his contact in the Ba'ath, who set up an observation post from which Qasim's movements to and from the defence ministry could be observed. When the prime minister's car left the building on 7th October, a telephone call from the flat reached one of the members of the assassination squad, Taha Yassen al-Alie, who was in a dental clinic at the other end of the street. He rushed out to alert the squad's driver to start the operation but the latter found that he could not move his car as his way was blocked by a delivery van. At that moment the squad saw Qasim's car speeding past them. They decided to try again another day.

As the six men walked through the streets a few minutes later, however, they spied Qasim's car caught in a traffic jam. The squad's leader ordered an immediate attack, but two of his men found that they could not fire: one found his pistol jammed, the second had forgotten to insert the magazine. A third discovered that he could not extract his hand grenade from his pocket. Saddam Hussein, whose job it was to stand on the pavement to cover the escape of his fellow assassins, moved forward and opened fire, killing Qasim's driver and seriously wounding his bodyguard. By this time Qasim, who had been hit in the shoulder and arm, was crouching on the floor of his car.

The assassination attempt degenerated into near farce. The squad's leader was killed, another squad member was hit in the chest and Saddam Hussein was hit in the leg – all in the crossfire from the assassins' own weapons. At this point the squad fled, leaving a scene of total pandemonium behind it. Qasim appeared later on television in his hospital room, declaring that Allah had protected him.

A leading member of the Ba'ath party contacted a doctor, Tahseen Me'alla, who was driven to the district of Alawyiah to treat the two wounded assassins. He operated on Samir al-Najm to take the bullet out of his chest and then attended to Saddam Hussein's leg wound. Later, Saddam Hussein and Samir al-Najm fled to Takrit before making their way to Syria and subsequently flying to Cairo.

As the communists grew stronger in Baghdad, Cairo and Damascus, the propaganda battle against Iraq continued. The Ba'ath party in Iraq had gone underground after the attempt on Qasim's life. Lacking popular support, the Ba'athists decided to plan a military coup as the shortest route to power. They began to forge an alliance with Arab nationalists, Nasserites, the Istiqlal party and others. They were in touch with the Egyptians and a delegation went to Cairo to discuss ways of overthrowing Qasim.

Meanwhile, in Iraq, after a short-lived quarrel with the communists when one of them tried to stage a coup, Qasim appointed four communist ministers whom he needed to maintain popular support. It was at this time that the use of the personality cult entered the world of Iraqi politics. Qasim unashamedly used the media to promote his image, the press referring to him as 'Almunqidh' (the Saviour) and 'Habib al-Mallayien' (the Darling of the Millions). However, plots against his life continued to abound.

In September 1961, Nasser's influence and prestige received a body blow when a group of Syrian Ba'athist officers overthrew the Egyptian administration and ended the federation with Egypt. The Ba'ath party was thus in power in Damascus, but it was to be another two years before it gained control in Baghdad, where its attempt on Qasim's life had damaged its reputation.

A Ba'ath party leader, Ali Saleh al-Sa'adi, returned secretly to Iraq from Syria in April 1960 and became the secretary-general of the regional command, meaning the leadership of the party in Iraq; the national command, based in Syria, controls all elements of the party throughout the Arab world. By late 1962, Sa'adi had succeeded in building up an effective clandestine Ba'ath organisation, whose membership numbered some 850, linked to a number of political groups opposed to Qasim. Most important among these were the military elements, including a group of officers from the northern town of Takrit who were closely bound together by tribal loyalty; they were the core of the Ba'ath party in the army.

Although Qasim had retained his personal popularity among the lower classes after implementing a land reform programme and giving workers their rights, he had created a power vacuum by isolating himself from political parties. Amongst those who were opposed to him were the landowner class and some Western oil companies who plotted with certain members of the military to overthrow him. By late 1962, Qasim had purged a number of army officers because of their membership of the communist party after he had fallen out with his former allies. Thus, by the beginning of 1963, he had effectively deprived himself of the support of those who would have defended him when an alliance of Ba'athist and Pan-Arab nationalist officers stormed the defence ministry where Qasim made his last desperate stand in his office on 8th February 1963.

The February 1963 coup was a classic operation in its planning and execution. Vital installations were seized and the head of state was rapidly removed. The communists had warned Qasim of the coup a week earlier, but he had virtually disregarded them. His only response was to arrest Sa'adi and a leading Ba'athist officer, Mahdi Saleh A'mash.

On the morning of Friday, 8th February, during the fasting month of Ramadan, Ba'athist and other nationalist officers captured and executed the commander of the Iraqi air force. They then seized Baghdad Radio. As news of the coup spread through Baghdad, thousands of people flocked on to the streets from the poorer districts of the city in an attempt to stop the advancing tanks. Qasim arrived at his office at ten o'clock and refused a request by the communists to arm the people, barricading himself inside the defence ministry with 1500 loyal troops.

There was bloody street fighting in Baghdad and Basra as the Ba'athist-led troops and armed gangs gunned down any communists they could find. Ba'athist officers overpowered Qasim and his supporters and slaughtered them. When news of Qasim's death was broadcast, the people on the streets refused to believe it. The Ba'athists responded by transmitting pictures of his bullet-riddled body on television. Shortly afterwards, Abdel Salam Arif, Qasim's fellow conspirator in the 1958 coup, was installed as president.

From their first day in power, the Ba'athists and Arab nationalists showed new dimensions in brutality. At eight o'clock in the evening of the day of the coup, Baghdad Radio broadcast a decree calling for the massacre of all communists after accusing them of plotting to save 'God's enemy, Qasim'. Years later it transpired that the CIA had supplied the Ba'athists with the names and addresses of communist leaders. Five thousand communists and pro-Qasim sympathisers were killed in the first three days of the coup as Ba'athist gangs carried out house-to-house searches and on-the-spot executions.

Despite their extreme methods, the Iraqi communists who supported Qasim had at least planned a political, economic and social programme. However, the Ba'athist-led forces which participated in the coup of 8th February 1963 had no agreed policies; they were united only by their hatred of communism, a feeling which found sympathy in the West.

After the overthrow of Qasim, relations between the Ba'ath and the armed forces began to deteriorate. Some army officers had joined the Ba'ath movement because of its claim to nationalism and its adoption of Nasserite policies as well as its declared opposition to communism. However, the same officers soon became disenchanted with the growing rift between Nasser and the leadership of the Ba'ath, and the growing influence of Al-Haras al-Qawmi (the National Guard), a notorious militia organisation controlled by the Ba'ath and other nationalist groups. By August 1963, the National Guard had increased to 34,000 in number and wielded more power than the army and many government departments.

The Ba'ath party was moving determinedly to assert its hegemony, although it already controlled sixteen out of the eighteen seats on the National Council of Revolutionary Command (NCRC). Soon after the coup, it manoeuvred to oust the Nasserites and other nationalist elements. On 25th May 1963, it turned against its nationalist allies after issuing statements accusing them of conspiring against the regime.

Immediately after the coup, Saddam Hussein returned to Iraq, where he was appointed as the head of Al-Jihaz al-Khas, known popularly as

Jihaz Haneen (the Yearning Apparatus), the clandestine intelligence organisation of the Ba'ath party. Saddam proceeded to turn it into an instrument of terror. It was later reported that the CIA had supplied Jihaz Haneen with lists of names of Iraqi communist activists who were subsequently rounded up and killed in mass executions at Qasr al-Nehayat (the Palace of the End), the interrogation and liquidation centre presided over by Saddam Hussein.

Many older and respected members left the party over elementary issues such as democracy, pluralism and human rights. The Ba'ath was overthrown in November, after only ten months' rule, when the military men in the party sided with fellow officers, taking advantage of a split in the party and ousting the thugs of the Ba'ath National Guard. The party's general secretary, Ali Salih al-Sa'di, who was also deputy prime minister, was dismissed after being held responsible for all the atrocities committed during the past few months. Saddam Hussein's offer to liquidate him, and subsequently make him a scapegoat for the party's bad image, was turned down by the leadership. The sixth Pan-Arab Congress of the Ba'ath party in 1964 presented an account of the infighting that took place. It admitted that the 1963 coup 'did not differ from military *coup d'états* and did not achieve any gains. Rather, there were reactionary deeds.' It also admitted to some excess by the National Guard. Ba'ath party literature of the period began to recognise the split into left-wing and right-wing elements in the party.

On 1st November 1963, the commander of the National Guard was dismissed but refused to step down. On 11th November, while Sa'adi and the members of the Ba'ath ruling clique were holding a meeting to expel right-wing officers from the Regional Command Council of the party, they were arrested by army officers and put on a plane to Spain with passports valid for one day only to stop them returning. The National Guard took to the streets in protest and rampaged through the city for five days. However, on 18th November, the army seized power in a swift military coup led by General Abd al-Salam Arif. As tanks rumbled along the streets of Baghdad, the headquarters of the National Guard was attacked by the Iraqi air force. The new leadership of the Ba'ath party, which had been appointed a week earlier in an attempt to accommodate the military element in the party, was arrested. However, some of its members immediately collaborated with the new regime, whilst others were sent abroad into exile without offering any resistance.

Following the downfall of the Ba'ath, the first few months of the new military government saw a loose coalition of military, pan-Arab nationalists, Nasserites and some Ba'athists. However, these last were soon dismissed from office on discovery of the atrocities and crimes committed by the Ba'ath during 1963. The former Ba'athist prime minister, Ahmad Hassan al-Bakr, who was also vice-president, was made an ambassador at the Ministry of Foreign Affairs. The office of vice-president was abolished.

Abd al-Salam Arif's regime had no basis for legitimacy other than the support of the armed forces. After November 1963 the Republican Guard was created as an élite force to safeguard the regime, its nucleus mainly drawn from the 20th Infantry Brigade. It became part of Iraqi politics as the president's personal instrument of force. Later, during the second Ba'ath regime, Saddam Hussein would expand it into two full divisions.

In the West, fears grew as Arif gave increasing power to pro-Nasser elements who were given a free hand to contact Cairo and discuss possible federation with Egypt. There was no mention at any time of a possible pluralist system to come or of free elections.

In Cairo, following the memories of the federation with Syria, and the noted dislike of Arabs among ordinary Egyptians, Nasser was more cautious. He restricted himself to agreeing, in May 1964, to a joint presidential council to further co-operation between the two nations. The agreement also envisaged close ties in the future between the Socialist Union, the single political party founded in Egypt by Nasser, and a similar state-run organisation to be established in Baghdad. This organisation was formed on 14th July 1964 and included various nationalist groupings, amongst whom were some former Ba'ath members who were sympathetic to Nasser's views.

On the same day, the Iraqi government announced the nationalisation of all banks, insurance companies and thirty-two privately owned trading and manufacturing companies. This was carried out in order to appear in line with the state-controlled system being furthered by Nasser in Egypt. The Iraqi middle classes, who had increased their grip on economic power after the 1958 revolution, saw this move as a direct challenge. The state appointed retired army officers to the top managerial posts in the newly nationalised firms. As a result of their obvious lack of commercial experience and expertise, companies were mismanaged and capital found its way rapidly to foreign banks outside Iraq. Consequently, the Iraqi population saw little improvement in the economic situation whilst unemployment soared. The regime responded by attempting to ease the grip of terror and dissolving the National Guard.

However, thousands of political prisoners were still languishing in jail. One detention centre, the Nuqrat al-Salman desert prison, alone received

2368 prisoners and 1671 detainees between February 1963 and October 1965. Many were subjected to torture at the hands of the Public Directorate for Security under state-of-emergency regulations which remained in effect despite the announcement of a provisional constitution, on 29th April 1964, specifying a three-year transition period. Although the powers of the military governor-general were transferred to the prime minister, effectively nothing changed, since the latter was always a military man and was invested with powers to suspend all civil laws.

Meanwhile, the military courts were renamed state security courts and the war in Kurdistan continued for another three months before agreement was reached on a truce. Negotiations for a peace settlement began on 11th April 1964. The truce lasted until March 1965, when government forces launched a new offensive in the hope of dealing a crushing blow to the Kurdish movement before the end of the summer. This move failed and the regime's crisis deepened.

In an attempt to defuse the growing opposition to military rule, the government appointed a civilian, a lawyer and former diplomat, Abd al-Rahman al-Bazzaz, as prime minister on 21 September 1965. He was denounced by the opposition for being 'too reactionary and a monarchist'.

Bazzaz tried to lessen the impact of the ill-advised nationalisation programme by instituting a policy of his own named 'prudent socialism'. He lifted restrictions on private investment, encouraged joint ventures with foreign capitalists to exploit raw materials and sought to limit the involvement in commerce of the public sector. However, he was no democrat and, like the Ba'athists and the military elements who had preceded him, he sought to ban the public activities of the communist party.

On 13th April 1966 the president, Abd al-Salam Arif, died in mysterious circumstances in a helicopter crash. Nasser immediately pressed the Iraqis to choose Arif's brother, Abd al-Rahman Arif, to replace him.

The following two years saw a period of instability, coup attempts and growing economic difficulties for the government. By the time Abd al-Rahman Arif was sworn in as president, the cost of the military campaign against the Kurds in the north of the country had cost Iraq $270 million, and the economy was deteriorating. The government invited the Kurds for negotiations after declaring a ceasefire on 29th June 1966. A former prime minister, Brigadier Abd al-Rahman Razzaq, attempted to mount a coup within days but it was foiled. There were deep divisions and serious disagreement amongst the top echelons of the ruling clique. Eventually, Bazzaz's administration was dismissed in August 1966 and was succeeded by a series of governments headed by senior military officers who were either nominated or financed by Western multi-national oil companies.

In 1967 the government suffered two serious blows. A dispute had broken out in December 1966 between Syria and the Iraqi Petroleum Company over fees charged on oil pumped through the Trans-Syria pipeline to the Mediterranean. This hit the economy hard and made the Iraqis even more aware of the need for better access to the sea. The second blow was the Six Day War in June, which exposed as hollow the rhetoric of pan-Arab nationalists, since the Iraqis made no effort to go to the aid of Egypt or Syria. Only after public demonstrations throughout the country and mounting political pressure did the president despatch a token force which in the event took no part in any fighting.

Amid deepening crisis within the military regime and a rising tide of resistance, the Ba'ath party returned to power on 17th July 1968 in a military coup carried out by mainly non-Ba'athist army officers. There was no attempt to popularise the movement or to carry out any true democratic changes. Mindful of the events of the February 1963 coup, the party's right wing, headed by Michel A'flaq, Ahmad Hassan al-Bakr and Saddam Hussein al-Takriti, was determined to assert its own authority. Less than two weeks later, they staged yet another coup. On 30th July, against the familiar background of bodies hanging in public places, the Ba'ath party's reign of terror began. The terror which Iraq had experienced during the previous ten years, beginning with the 1958 revolution, was to pale into insignificance in comparison to what the country would experience during the next twenty-two years.

When the pro-British Iraqi monarchy was overthrown in an orgy of blood in July 1958, there were few tears shed in Kuwait, although the older generation were concerned that the new republic might renew claims on the emirate. The emir, Sheikh Abdallah al-Salem al-Sabah, a farsighted and wise man, moved cautiously whilst forging a new alliance with Nasser. He took steps to ensure that Kuwait remained under British protection whilst Iraq cast covetous eyes on it.

Ten weeks after Iraq's 1958 coup, Sheikh Abdallah chose Cairo to announce that Kuwait was to join the Arab States League and would subscribe to the Arab League Development Bank. He also followed Nasser's line by taking strict measures to ensure that oil companies would not allow Kuwaiti oil to be sold to Israel. Kuwait began to take a high profile in co-ordinated diplomacy among Arab nations when it hosted the third Arab Boycott of Israel conference the following month.

In January 1959 the Cairo-based Arab League invited Kuwait to participate in the meetings of the league's high economic council. As the league's charter only permits fully independent states to become members, Cairo plotted to facilitate Kuwait's wider participation in the activities of the economic council by giving the organisation a separate and independent status.

Conservative members of the Arab League, members of the Saudi Arabian royal family and Jordan, were not comfortable with Nasser's 'positive neutrality', which in practical terms meant closer co-operation with the Soviet bloc. Much to Nasser's approval and advantage, the Kuwaitis took a neutral line in Arab League meetings. Their pressure on London for independence brought them even closer to Nasser's side.

Britain reacted initially by suggesting an amendment to the 1899 agreement, but by 1960 the Kuwaitis were pressing for a complete abrogation of the treaty and full independence. Having digested the costly lesson of Anthony Eden's ill-fated Suez campaign, the British government, led by Harold Macmillan, decided not to stand in the way of Kuwait's full independence and its membership of the Arab League.

Macmillan wisely followed advice given by British diplomats and officials in the Gulf which indicated that London's interests, which were mainly concerned with oil, would be safer with a friendly but independent Kuwait. Early in 1961, the emirate's currency changed from the Indian rupee to the Kuwaiti dinar and the emir announced the abrogation of the 1899 treaty on 19th June. Three days later, Kuwait applied for membership of the Arab League and enlisted Nasser's support for its independence.

Iraq's reaction to Kuwait's declaration of independence, which Saddam Hussein heard on the radio in Cairo, promptly sparked yet another Middle East crisis. Although the world was generally caught by surprise, the reaction, especially from Britain, was swift, decisive and productive, wisely taking account of the politics of the Middle East.

Four factors foiled Prime Minister Qasim's intended annexation of Kuwait, factors which were noticeably absent from Western strategy when Saddam Hussein invaded Kuwait twenty-nine years later.

First, British intervention did not undermine Kuwait's sovereignty since it was in accordance with the new treaty signed by the two parties before Kuwaiti independence.

The second factor was Britain's recognition of Egypt's regional leadership role and the former's quick decision to abandon, almost overnight, its policy of frustrating Nasser.

The third factor was Britain's ability, with the consent of other regional powers, to deploy forces in sufficient numbers before Qasim could send his troops into Kuwait.

The fourth was its determination to maintain a dialogue with the Iraqis, and the ability of the Foreign Office, via the embassy in Baghdad, to give a sound assessment, based on good intelligence, that Qasim had taken the decision to annex Kuwait on his own initiative – his announcement had surprised even his own Ministry of Foreign Affairs. The British embassy also provided detailed reports on Iraqi tank and troop movements near the border, thus forewarning Whitehall.

Within twenty hours of Qasim's announcement, the Foreign Office possessed sufficient information to compile a report for Downing Street. Britain subsequently acted in accordance with Foreign Office policy, rather than ignoring it. It is ironic that in 1961, when Britain had no satellites or advanced spy technology, the Foreign Office's intelligence and assessment was more accurate and its measured reaction far more effective than was the case in 1990. In 1961, Kuwait's army was no more than 1500 strong with sixteen tanks and one battery of field artillery. It had no hope of stopping a military attack by Iraq.

The initial view held in Whitehall was that it was unlikely that Iraq would invade. However, this soon changed after the embassy in Baghdad warned that Qasim was taking decisions without consulting his cabinet. Confirmation of this was obtained from a senior Iraqi railways official who advised that railway flat-cars had been transporting tanks to Basra for a subsequent move south as part of a force which would cross the border.

Unlike the American diplomatic personnel in Baghdad in 1990, who failed to warn Saddam Hussein that an invasion of Kuwait would provoke a swift reaction, the British embassy in Baghdad in 1961 played its role extremely effectively. It provided London with accurate military and political intelligence as well as recommending courses to be followed, whilst also warning the Iraqis that Britain would react decisively to any threat against Kuwait.

In Baghdad, Sir Humphrey Trevelyan went to the Iraqi Foreign Ministry whilst the British military attaché visited the Defence Ministry. They both made it plain to the Iraqis that Britain would carry out its obligations to Kuwait under the terms of the agreement. After his meeting Trevelyan sent a signal to London, emphasising that Qasim must not be allowed to enter before British troops were ready. He advised that the Commando carrier HMS *Bulwark*, which was due to arrive in Kuwait on 4th July, should be sent to Kuwait immediately. He also asked for the Swiss to be approached with a view to taking charge of British interests in Baghdad in the event of diplomatic relations being broken off. However,

Trevelyan himself was anxious about Britain taking any military initiative and thus allowing Qasim, who was still getting his task force ready, the opportunity to claim British imperialist occupation of an Arab state.

London's reply pointed out that Iraqi tanks could reach Kuwait City in a night's drive, and Whitehall feared that if the Iraqis arrived first British troops would face great difficulties and high casualties fighting their way into the city.

So Britain took the decision to send troops. Sheikh Abdallah, on advice from London and after consultation with Cairo, formally requested British military aid under the terms of the new Treaty of Friendship. Although his decision was internally opposed by some members of the al-Sabah family, history proved that he had acted wisely. Among those who opposed Sheikh Abdallah's decision was a thirty-five-year-old pro-Nasser nationalist named Sheikh Jaber al-Ahmad who had also objected to the defence agreement with Britain. Twenty-nine years later, sadder but wiser, Sheikh Jaber had to call upon the Americans for military assistance when his 'Iraqi brothers' made him flee from the Dasman palace in the early hours of 2nd August.

Amongst the first British troops to be deployed were the 1st Battalion The Parachute Regiment who arrived in Kuwait on 1st July. Twenty-four hours earlier, the British ambassador in Iraq had instructed the embassy staff to burn their papers, but his orders were premature as there was no breach in diplomatic relations.

A large portion of the British cabinet, backed by the press, were pleased that Kuwait had sought help from Britain, whose armed forces proved capable of quickly deploying 8000 troops without any problems. Royal Marine Commandos were airlifted from HMS *Bulwark* and were soon followed by tanks from Bahrain, with more troops arriving by air and sea from bases in Britain, Cyprus, Aden and Kenya. The British press, who had a large presence in Kuwait, were generally supportive, while the Egyptian media supported British policy in the Middle East for the first time in two years. Some Cairo editorials went so far as to call for Egyptian troops to be sent in to reduce dependency on the British for the policing of the Kuwaiti border. Ordinary Kuwaitis, undoubtedly influenced by broadcasts from Cairo Radio, were cautiously satisfied with the British response but would have preferred an Arab League force.

The Iraqis sent a note to all foreign embassies in Baghdad denouncing Britain's action, denying the validity of the Anglo-Kuwaiti agreement and claiming that they had no intention of invading Kuwait.

It was found out years later that Qasim had drawn up plans – most of which were implemented by Saddam Hussein in 1990 – to annex Kuwait by a coup, the date for which had been set for 14th July, the third anniversary of his own seizing of power. He had planned to create a massive task force under cover of troop rehearsals for the Iraqi national day parade, intending to declare his intentions as soon as the force was in position, towards the end of June. He had already despatched intelligence agents, disguised as Iraqi labourers, into Kuwait, where they were to instigate riots whilst Iraqi journalists fabricated reports of atrocities committed against Iraqi nationals by Britons, Zionists and CIA spies; this was to have been his excuse to despatch his troops into Kuwait. Iraqi armoured columns would have driven the fifty miles from the border to Kuwait City in two hours, subsequently deploying to positions from which they would occupy the emirate.

Qasim made the grave error of miscalculating the British reaction to such a threat. He reasoned that Macmillan, with the bitter lesson of Suez still fresh in his mind, would not use military force. In this he was mistaken. Britain took an extremely tough stance. A principal element of the naval task force despatched to the Gulf by Britain was the fleet aircraft-carrier HMS *Victorious*, which arrived in the Gulf on 9th July carrying a squadron of Scimitars. These were high-altitude interceptors which also had a nuclear strike role. In 1959 the Royal Navy had modified a number of its Scimitars to carry the 'Red Beard' tactical nuclear free-fall bomb. It was British policy up to the early 1960s to deploy tactical nuclear weapons with any task force. Qasim would therefore have been well aware that invading Kuwait would put him at war with Britain and thus open to a possible nuclear strike.

The announcement of Kuwaiti independence on 19th June took Qasim by surprise. As he could not match Nasser's prestige, he had no chance of thwarting Cairo's plan to persuade members of the Arab States League to recognise Kuwait, thus undermining the political basis for any action that Qasim might take.

Despite his quarrel with conservative Arabs, Nasser managed to drum up sufficient Arab support against Qasim. One of his methods was to send to the Saudi ruler, King Saud bin Abdul Aziz, via the Egyptian intelligence service, tape recordings of Qasim's conversations with the Yugoslavian ambassador at the end of June. During these, the Iraqi prime minister stated clearly that he did not recognise the Saudi Arabian borders which had been drawn up by the British in 1922. Qasim was heard to claim that Iraq's borders should include territories which had once belonged to Kuwait but which had been given to Saudi Arabia by the British. After King Saud had heard these tapes, Saudi Arabian support for Nasser's plan was assured. An Egyptian-led Arab League force of two thousand troops, drawn from Egypt, Saudi Arabia, Sudan and Syria, was assembled and despatched to Kuwait to relieve the British forces. King Hussein of Jordan, who twenty-nine years later would support Iraq after its invasion of Kuwait, at that time supported the view that Kuwait was a sovereign state and thus sent his troops to join the Arab League force.

During 1962, the Arab peacekeeping force was reduced and the last troops departed from Kuwait in February 1963 after the coup in which Qasim was overthrown. In October 1963 the new Iraqi government, led by Abd al-Salam Arif, who was pro-Nasser, took control and with him came members of the Ba'ath party.

Socialist and radical in rhetoric, the Ba'ath leaders of 1963 were an opportunistic breed. Whilst repressive internally, their foreign policy appeared moderate and pragmatic. They recognised Kuwait's independence, particularly after the emir paid Iraq a substantial sum of money to supply Kuwait with 120 million gallons of water per day from the Shatt al-Arab. In November 1963, the two countries abolished Customs duties on trade, but a Kuwaiti demand to form a borders commission to iron out any problems was never met.

This was not the end of the matter. Two years later, after the Ba'athists had fallen from power, the Iraqis once again raised the question of the islands in the mouth of the Shatt al-Arab. Baghdad claimed the two islands of Warbah and Bubiyan and other Kuwaiti territory close to the Iraqi border in order to be able to construct the port at Umm Qasr and the railway line attached to it. It insisted that it must be given the islands before there could be a settlement of any outstanding border disputes. The Kuwaitis replied that they would only consider leasing Warbah (the closer of the two islands to Iraq's vital Khor Abdallah Canal) to Iraq for a period of ninety-nine years. The question was not resolved, as Iraq now faced a series of military coups.

Although the claim to Kuwait had been relinquished by the Ba'athists in 1963, it was renewed ten years later, this time with military force as well as with diplomatic belligerence. On 20th March 1973, without any warning, two Iraqi armoured units occupied the Samitha border post inside Kuwait. The Kuwaitis reacted swiftly, mobilising their own small army as well as Arab and international opinion. Saudi forces moved into Kuwait in a show of support, whilst Iran warned Iraq of the grave consequences if it did not withdraw. Faced with such concerted and determined opposition, the Iraqis quietly retreated.

In August 1973, Sheikh Jaber al-Ahmad al-Sabah, then the Kuwaiti prime minister and crown prince, visited Baghdad for talks with Saddam Hussein, the Iraqi vice-president. During their discussions Saddam suggested that Bubiyan Island should be divided in two, with the eastern part going to Iraq and the western half remaining as Kuwaiti territory. No agreement was reached, but in subsequent talks Baghdad seemed to accept Kuwaiti sovereignty over the areas it coveted. In 1978 Izzat Ibrahim, who later became Saddam Hussein's deputy, visited Kuwait and suggested that Kuwait should hand over half of Bubiyan to Iraq. Iraq was committed to the idea that the border should be defined in such a way that it 'guarantees a naval position for Iraq, securing the defence necessary for its national interests and the Arab nation's interests in the Arabian Gulf.' Again, nothing was settled, and two years later the Iraqis became too embroiled in the conflict with Iran to harass their vulnerable southern neighbour further.

2 · The Curse of Black Gold

As the first troops from the 82nd Airborne Division were disembarking from their aircraft on to the hot tarmac of Mishab Airport, a young Saudi Arabian soldier turned to a British journalist and remarked, 'Ironic, isn't it? I suppose it is somehow reassuring that the West is sending troops here, but would they have bothered to "protect" us if we had no oil?' The young Saudi knew the answer, of course. Despite the protestations of Western politicians to the contrary, the international dimension of the 1990 crisis, like all Middle Eastern crises since the First World War, is really about oil – a crisis that has let 'infidels' step on the Muslims' holy sands in order to defend oil fields vital to Western interests. Historians in a hundred years' time might perhaps be tempted to draw parallels between Western action in 1990 and the 'gunboat diplomacy' practised in the nineteenth century – only this time the 'natives' are armed with weapons rather more potent than spears.

King Fahd of Saudi Arabia, who calls himself Khademul H'aramine or 'the Custodian of the Two Shrines' to give his rule true Muslim authority, has always kept the Americans at arm's length, despite his country's heavy reliance on the United States for everything from air-conditioning machines to fighter aircraft. This time he had to bite the bullet and ask the Americans to protect his kingdom, the greatest gamble of his reign. The reason for their alacrity in doing so can be summed up in one magic word – oil.

Fahd was no different from his Arab brothers and from the West, all of whom had appeased Saddam Hussein and looked the other way while he was committing his appalling crimes. As long as the 'Butcher of Baghdad' was keeping the tide of Islamic fundamentalism from their doorsteps, they were happy to contribute arms and finance for his war effort. Even when the conflict with Iran was over, and Saddam Hussein had returned to brutally repressing the Kurdish element of his population whilst building his formidable war machine, the oil-rich states of the Middle East turned a blind eye. Yet, when there was a threat to oil, the knives were unsheathed and the details of his grisly record were put on display, thanks to Saudi Arabian petrodollar influence on Arab journalists.

The discovery of oil on the Iranian side of the Gulf imposed on the Middle East a strategic importance even greater than that which it had formerly possessed when it had provided a series of military bases on the maritime route to India.

Just as the East India Company and the spices trade led to a revolution in maritime politics and the expansion of empires – interrupted by the inevitable wars – so the new oil trade made it difficult to discern the dividing line between the policies of privately owned companies and those of successive governments. It provided a licence to run states within states, conduct policies, mount *coups d'état* and change governments.

Oil was first mentioned in association with the region by the Greek writer Eratosthenes of Cyrene (276–194 BC): 'Asphaltus is found in great abundance in Babylonia. The liquid asphaltus, which is called naphtha ... is of singular nature. When it is brought near the fire, it burns with flames ...'

Oil had been found in Masjid al-Sulaiman, Persia (now Iran), in 1908. In 1903 the Anglo-Persian Oil Company (APOC), later renamed the Anglo-Iranian Oil Company and subsequently British Petroleum, was founded, but it did not commence trading until 1909 when it secured a concession from the Shah. The first oil refinery at Abadan began production in 1912 and by 1914 had exported quarter of a million tons of oil.

Winston Churchill, on becoming First Lord of the Admiralty in the Liberal government in 1911, had been urging the conversion of the ships of the Royal Navy from coal to oil power. A vast three-year programme of conversion headed by Admiral John Fisher – nicknamed 'the Oil Maniac' by Royal Navy officers – was implemented in haste, just in time for the First World War. After the war Lord Curzon remarked, 'The allies floated to victory on a sea of oil.'

When oil was discovered in Persia, Britain was dependent on oil from the United States and from the American-controlled Gulf of Mexico. London wanted to explore the new oil fields in the Middle East to reduce the reliance on America, which was monopolising the supply and emerging as a new superpower with growing overseas interests.

A few days before the outbreak of the First World War in August 1914, the British government bought fifty-one per cent of the shares of the Anglo-Persian Oil Company; Britain later gained a large interest in the Turkish Petroleum Company – which controlled concessions to exploit oil in what would later become Iraq – after Churchill had managed to push the agreement through the House of Commons.

Churchill later stated that the original investment of £2.2 million 'brought the prize from Fairyland far beyond our brightest hopes'. It paid for the cost of the entire naval conversion programme and made southern Persia economically and strategically part of the British Empire in the Middle East.

The Ottomans suspected oil must be present under the sands of territories neighbouring Persia, especially the three of its provinces that now constitute Iraq and Kuwait. A few years earlier, a number of rival international groups had been making bids for oil concessions in the Ottoman Empire's *velayets* – provinces – near the Gulf. The 1903 Baghdad Railway Convention gave the Ottoman Railway Company of Anatolia (controlled by the Deutsche Bank) the rights to build the Berlin to Baghdad Railway, including the licence to excavate and exploit minerals on land seventy-five miles on either side of the tracks.

The oil companies were seeking more concessions from other Ottoman provinces. In 1911, Mr Greenway, the director of APOC, wished to acquire a concession from Sheikh Mubarak of Kuwait to drill for oil but the British resident dissuaded him from writing to the emir. The company tried again in 1913, but Britain told them to wait until after the war.

As Kuwait, with the help of Britain, had just been granted recognition of independence within defined borders from Turkey, the emir had to accede to the British resident's request to agree in writing that 'no Kuwait oil concession would be given except to a person nominated and recommended by the British government'.

The Ottoman Empire had outlived its time. Britain, meanwhile, was establishing itself as the superpower in the region and trying to defend its interests against both American influence and its European rivals and allies. However, Britain knew that deals had to be made with Turkey since it was still the power that the Muslim peoples of the region recognised as their mother state. As deals were negotiated, Turkey concentrated its interest on oil in the provinces that were to form Iraq a decade later. Britain was helping its companies to secure a share, while other European interests were favoured by the Ottomans.

In 1912 the Anglo-Dutch oil company Shell, the British National Bank of Turkey, the German Deutsche Bank and C. S. Gulbenkian, an Ottoman businessman, had formed the Turkish Petroleum Company (TPC, later the Iraqi Petroleum Company). Two years later TPC was granted concessions by the Ottoman authorities to explore oil in the two *velayets* of Mosul and Baghdad. A few months later, it merged with the Anglo-Persian Oil Company (APOC).

In 1913, a British Royal Commission agreed with Winston Churchill that 'we must become the owners or at any rate the controllers at the source of at least a proportion of the oil which we require'.

In 1914, the Turkish Grand Vizir promised TPC the right to exploit oil deposits in areas in the three provinces Mosul, which included Kurdistan, Baghdad, and Basra. Britain, through its oil companies, now had the largest interests and knew it would have to increase its military presence in the area to defend them in the event of war.

War did come to the region when Turkey formally concluded an alliance with Germany on 3rd November 1914 and declared war on France and Britain two days later. However, the Turks chose the wrong side and were subsequently decisively defeated.

When in 1919 the French surrendered their claim to the province of Mosul, in return for the Deutsche Bank's twenty-five per cent share of the Turkish Petroleum Company, Britain decided to include it in Iraq. Despite a number of disagreements between the Iraqi and British governments, there was no dispute about this – thanks to the presence of known oil reserves in Mosul. The arrangement was formally ratified by the Iraqi government in 1925. The British needed to exploit Mosul's oil fields and thus required political control of the area. Such control would, as a result of the agreement, be exercised through the Iraqi government in Baghdad.

There was also a bonus. The regime of King Faisal had little chance of survival in an Iraq dominated by Shia Muslims. With the inclusion of the majority Sunni population of Mosul, life was made a great deal easier for the king.

Iraq also needed Britain's protection against Turkish demands and for help in silencing Kurdish voices demanding independence. However, there was a price that Iraq had to pay: Iraqi government agreement to concession terms that oil companies had demanded.

Lord Curzon, the British Foreign Secretary, was quoted at the Lausanne conference in 1923 as telling the Italian representative, 'When we have definitely settled the question of Mosul [which we have no intention of relinquishing] we would give them [the Iraqis] a share of the oil.'

The Kuwaitis, through their cunning and their negotiating skills, managed to extract better deals than their Iraqi brothers in exchange for granting rights to the exploitation of their oil. In early 1923 Sheikh Ahmad al-Jaber al-Sabah of Kuwait rejected an Anglo-Persian Oil Company offer – made via the British resident – and asked for a minimum twenty-five per cent royalty on net crude oil. The sheikh had a few cards up his sleeve as he drew on his family's famous policy of playing outside forces against one another, thus bringing a new threat to Britain's monopoly over the oil of the region. He had received a cable from a New Zealander, Major Frank Holmes, who was chairman of Eastern and General Syndicates, a small company that had no particular significance at the time. In his cable, Holmes asked the sheikh not to accept any offers until he had an opportunity to discuss matters. Holmes had just won a concession from Sultan ibn Sa'ud to explore for oil in the coastal province of Al-Hasa, just south of the neutral zone.

The Anglo-Persian Oil Company and Britain were convinced by evidence from geologists that there was no oil in the area. Meanwhile, however, Holmes was improving on the offer made previously by APOC. He also became a good friend of Sheikh Ahmad and other Arab sheikhs who liked his company and found him humorous and amusing, according to the Arab writer Amin al-Rihani. When Holmes arrived to negotiate with Ibn Sa'ud, he was carrying an enormous green-lined white parasol and wearing a French-style pith helmet on his head.

Sheikh Ahmad proceeded to outwit the British political agent when the latter reminded him of Kuwait's obligation not to negotiate oil concessions except with persons nominated by the British government. Ahmad replied that he saw no problem, as Holmes was a British subject who had served in the Royal Navy during the war. He was offering better terms than APOC and, furthermore, was on his way to London to present the offers to the British government. The sheikh managed to prolong the negotiations for some ten years, outmanoeuvring the Colonial Office, which wanted to give APOC priority in line with the policy of Churchill, who was now the Colonial Secretary, and Lord Curzon.

In May 1924 the Sabah family managed to obtain their revenge on Britain for Sir Percy Cox's red pencil slicing away the neutral zone two years earlier. Jointly with Ibn Sa'ud, Sheikh Ahmad signed a concession for Holmes to search for oil in the neutral zone, which was outside the area covered by the agreement giving Britain the power to dictate as to who would be given concessions in Kuwait. Holmes went on to secure another concession in Bahrain. His company by itself was not a major danger, as it lacked the essential backing of finance and expertise to turn the concessions into 'mines of black gold'. The Anglo-Persian Oil Company offered him a meagre £50,000 for his rights in the area, as they feared Sheikh Ahmad had opened the door to a major threat to British interests.

In 1927, while Britain was fast losing substantial shares of its oil concessions to non-British interests in northern Iraq, Holmes made a new offer. He had secured the backing of the giant Gulf Oil Corporation of Pennsylvania, which bought options to acquire his concessions. Holmes disclosed to Gulf Oil details of an oil find which he had kept secret for about a year. In 1926 he had found traces of oil while he was drilling for water (another valuable commodity in the deserts) whilst under a contract with Sheikh Ahmad.

Holmes could not understand why the sheikh had turned his offer down despite their friendship and even though he now had the backing of a giant American oil corporation. Ahmad, for his part, wanted to continue the bargaining for as long as possible as he knew that Britain wanted to exclude the Americans.

At the end of the First World War, the United States was the world's largest oil producer. Peace brought a boom in oil-based industries and economic growth dependent upon the consumption of cheap oil. American oil companies sought support from their government because they were being totally excluded from the Middle East by British and European companies while America's own oil resources were being rapidly depleted. Washington declared its 'open door' policy, meaning that the wartime allies should not discriminate against each other in oil supplies. However, American companies still did not enjoy much success when it came to the practicalities of drilling for oil in the deserts of the Middle East.

Meanwhile Britain was having difficulties with the Americans over Iraq. There was intense rivalry and objections by the Americans to the concessions granted by the Ottomans to the Turkish Petroleum Company. The Americans in fact challenged the validity of the concessions. They were in the same situation as the French: both thought their interests would have been served better had the control of the Mosul region remained in Turkish hands. The US State Department stepped up the pressure and in 1923 finally acquired just under twenty-four per cent of the Turkish Petroleum Company's share capital. Meanwhile, TPC refused to allow any share equity participation by the Iraqi government.

The Lausanne conference did not manage to resolve the Mosul boundary problem and it was transferred to the League of Nations. Throughout 1924 Turkey increased its pressure on Mosul, and the Royal Air Force bombed the Kurdish city of Sulaimaniya in November of that year.

In July 1925, the League of Nations Boundary Commission recommended that Mosul should form part of Iraq. There was a condition that Britain's mandatory powers were to be extended for twenty-five years, until Iraq's entry into the League of Nations.

In January 1926 the Anglo-Iraqi Treaty was signed, accepting the conditions laid down by the League of Nations. The official attitude of the Iraqi government at the time was that 'the treaty is not only essential for the retention of the Mosul velayet, but is also essential for the actual existence and the independence of Iraq and its monarchy.'

Six months later the Turkish–Iraqi Treaty was signed, recognising that Iraq would embrace the Mosul velayet and giving Turkey ten per cent of Iraq's oil royalties for twenty-five years.

Enormous amounts of oil were found near Kirkuk, in Mosul, in October 1927, soon after exploration began. During the same year, Iraq's first commercial production of crude oil was recorded at 45,000 tons.

Oil geologists had been maintaining that oil did not exist on the western side of the Gulf, but findings in Iraq increased the suspicion that there might also be large quantities of oil in Kuwait. Britain informed Sheikh Ahmad in November 1928 that a 'British nationality clause' had to be inserted in any concession agreement, excluding non-British companies. The British also tried to impose the same clause on Bahrain.

As recession hit the world following the great crash of 1929, oil companies cut back on expenditure and there was no improvement in Kuwait's bargaining position. American pressure on Britain led to a revision of the 'British nationality clause' which subsequently allowed Standard Oil of California, through its subsidiary, Bahrain Petroleum Company (BAPCO), to prospect for oil. By 1932, BAPCO had discovered large quantities of oil in Bahrain. Other American oil companies then succeeded in gaining access to Kuwait, after the British government had given its permission in April 1932 as a result of efforts by Andrew Mellon, the American ambassador in London, who had large interests in BAPCO. This is one of many clear early examples of diplomacy being interwoven with the interests and politics of oil companies.

The result was fierce competition between British companies and the Americans, via Frank Holmes, to win a concession from Kuwait. The Americans were closing in from the West as Ibn Sa'ud, who had now become the king of Saudi Arabia, granted a concession to Standard Oil.

As the Anglo-Persian Oil Company and Gulf Oil combined forces, without the knowledge of Sheikh Ahmad, to form a jointly owned Kuwaiti Oil Company which they hoped would be able to dictate terms to the ruler, they were astonished to find that he still had other cards to play. Early in 1932, a number of British politicians and businessmen, headed by Lord Lloyd, had formed a company named Traders Ltd with the specific aim of keeping the Gulf exclusively British. They had received advance information concerning the government's decision to favour an 'open door' policy on Kuwait which was to be announced on 6th April. Those companies which had been granted concessions prior to that date would continue to enjoy monopoly interests, but thereafter concessions would have to be sought on a free competition basis. Lloyd and his group, having held negotiations with Sheikh Ahmad and feeling confident that they would be granted concessions, thus announced the formation of Traders Ltd one day earlier, on 5th April.

Ahmad, however, had no intention of granting any concessions to Traders Ltd. Instead, he had deliberately leaked details of the negotiations to the Kuwaiti Oil Company and had let it be known that he was studying an offer. Needless to say, the Kuwaiti Oil Company found itself out-manoeuvred.

The Kuwaiti ruler enjoyed the services of a clever Iraqi lawyer, one J. Gabriel, whilst he himself was a skilled negotiator. By 1934 the two men had managed to obtain the best terms possible from the Kuwaiti Oil Company and had even succeeded in thwarting a British plan to insert clauses giving London greater political controls over the company itself.

Meanwhile, the Iraqis were receiving less than they considered to be their just rewards from British-controlled companies who had fought hard to obtain concession rights for what they knew to be extremely valuable long-term oil assets. This inevitably sowed the seeds of political discontent and resentment against oil companies, which was handed down from one generation of Iraqis to another and culminated during the 1960s and 1970s in policies of confrontation with the West over oil.

Other Arab states achieved better results at much less cost by skilful negotiation. At the time of Iraq's independence in 1932, nearly all Iraqi politicians from a variety of political parties accused the British-controlled companies of deliberately slowing down oil production. However, world demand at that time was low. Moreover, the deposits in northern Iraq were far from the sea and without easy access to an export outlet.

By 1928 the Turkish Petroleum Company had become part of a consortium consisting of the Anglo-Iranian Oil Company, Shell, Mobil and Standard Oil of New Jersey. The company was renamed the Iraq Petroleum Company (IPC). While production from the Persian side was increasing, production from the new oilfields in Iraq was proceeding very slowly. In 1930, Iraq's main exports were still grain and dates, but the same year witnessed a sharp fall in the world price of grain. To compensate for the lost revenue, the Iraqi government sought an advance on royalties from the Iraq Petroleum Company. IPC granted the advance in return for an expansion of its concession area from 192 to 35,000 square miles. This massive increase eventually led to the company's monopoly of

Iraq's entire oil output just prior to the outbreak of the Second World War.

The final concession agreement was signed with the Iraqi government in 1931, one year before the formal ending of the British mandate. In 1933 the total output was only 123,000 tons.

The 1931 agreement on oil concessions secured for the Iraq Petroleum Company the whole of the provinces of Baghdad and Mosul east of the Tigris and was intended to last until the year 2000. The Mosul Petroleum Company had all the areas west of the Tigris and north of latitude 33° N, up to the year 2007, while the Basra Petroleum Company's concession, intended to continue until the year 2013, simply referred to all the Iraqi territory not covered by the two concessions to the Iraq Petroleum Company and the Mosul Petroleum Company.

At first, the Iraqi government share consisted of a royalty paid by the companies on a per-ton-produced basis. Inevitably, the Iraqis persisted in demanding an increase in oil production in order to increase revenue.

In 1932 Britain finally conceded to Iraq's demands for independence in order to give a free hand to Faisal and his officials in restoring tranquillity after the widespread strikes and public demonstrations that had been recurring since 1920 and had reached a peak in 1931.

By 1935 the first oil pipeline from Kirkuk to the Mediterranean had been completed, thus enabling the output to increase to four million tons. Iraqi oil production remained limited to this level until 1950.

Following a sharp increase in world demand for oil after the end of the Second World War, oil companies were eager to expand their activities and increase production. Another pipeline was opened from the northern oilfields to the Mediterranean via Syria. In the south, production began in 1951.

As a result of earlier American and European pressure for ownership of shareholdings in the Iraq Petroleum Company, Iraqi oil production was by the mid-1950s controlled by British, French, Dutch and American groups. IPC's concessions permitted it to extract oil from an area covering the whole of Iraq with the exception of about 680 square miles close to the borders with Iran.

By 1956, Iraq was producing thirty million tons of crude oil per annum, giving the government a revenue of sixty-nine million dinars, which was equal to half the profits declared by the companies for their operations in the same year. This revenue also formed twenty-one per cent of Iraq's national income. Within the country several groups, including many politicians, were voicing their objection to the state of the economy. Dissatisfaction with the size of the country's income from its massive oil wealth was also growing. The government quarrelled with the oil companies over their policies concerning the employment of Iraqis – although the total number of Iraqis employed in the oil industry in 1952 was 10,430, they were carrying out menial work and few of them received the opportunity of being trained to the high technical or administrative standards of Western employees.

Political parties in opposition to the government of Nuri al-Sa'id denounced the concession agreements. As discontent increased, the first calls for the nationalisation of the oil industry were heard on the streets of Baghdad in 1951.

The companies abandoned the royalty system in 1952 as a result of the interruption of Iran's oil exports during the Mossadeq crisis. In March 1951 the Iranian parliament had accepted the advice of Mossadeq, its speaker, and nationalised the Anglo-Iranian Oil Company. Britain had responded by imposing an international boycott of Iranian oil. Mossadeq was subsequently appointed prime minister but was dismissed by the Shah after a disagreement. Shortly afterwards he was reappointed as a result of popular pressure. In the face of growing opposition, the Shah fled from Iran into exile.

Meanwhile the Iraqi government, well aware that the oil companies needed Iraqi oil to compensate for the lost production from Iranian fields, insisted on copying the fifty–fifty profit-sharing system which had been introduced by the Arabian American Oil Company (ARAMCO) in Saudi Arabia. This was one of the early lessons learned by Iraqi politicians – that the West's dependence on Iran and Iraq for oil and for strategic reasons could be manipulated to their advantage.

During the years that followed, those who had hoped for better treatment from the oil companies were disappointed. The companies' activities were limited to the production and marketing of crude oil, enabling them to keep the profits from their Iraqi operations to a minimum since they remained free to sell the crude oil to outlets abroad at very low prices.

Following the 1952 agreement, the companies stepped up oil production. Production increased from 8.4 million tons in 1951 to 29.5 million tons in 1954. The Iraqis' share of the profits rose from 13.7 million dinars in 1951 to 68.4 million dinars in 1954.

Although the Kuwaitis had negotiated better terms in their deals with oil companies, the latter still managed to pay them less than they paid for Iraqi and Iranian oil. When oil production in Kuwait began, the initial sums of money invested by the oil companies were ridiculously low. Since oil was nearer to the surface than in other areas in the Middle East, production costs were low and enormous profits could be made. In return for exemption from all Kuwaiti taxes, the concessionaires paid a bonus of 475,000 rupees (£35,625) and an annual rental of 95,000 rupees (£7125). The royalties were calculated at the rate of three rupees per ton, and were paid in Indian rupees, not in gold as was the case in Iran, Iraq and Saudi Arabia.

When oil first spurted from the wells in 1938, total public revenues in Kuwait – Customs duties, tax on trade and exporting building materials to the Iranian oil-production complex at Abadan – totalled approximately £20,000. The rental charge paid by the Kuwaiti Oil Company added £7125. After payment of government expenses, £1700 was left in the treasury. The Kuwaiti Oil Company had made no provision for the export of oil in the event of war and thus the outbreak of the Second World War delayed the first sales of Kuwaiti oil until 1946 when, on 30th June, Sheikh Ahmad himself ceremonially turned on the tap of the new pipeline which transported the oil to the terminal. Until 1949, the Kuwaiti government was receiving thirteen cents a barrel, ten cents less than the amount paid to Iraq and Saudi Arabia.

However, the real wealth came after the death of Sheikh Ahmad from a heart attack in February 1950. He was succeeded by Sheikh Abdallah al-Salem. In the same year King Ibn Sa'ud began to put pressure on ARAMCO, which was paying him twenty-one cents a barrel, while making a net profit of $1.10 a barrel. The old and ailing king was informed that Venezuela had passed a law in 1948 enforcing a fifty per cent share of income from American oil companies. Meanwhile Iran's Prime Minister Mossadeq was demanding a much improved deal from the Anglo-Iranian Oil Company.

Alarmed by the possibility of Iran setting a precedent for other states in the region, Washington and London had plotted to overthrow Mossadeq on the pretext that he was too close to the communists. Washington's decision was based on a study in January 1953 by the National Security Council. A paper was jointly issued by the State Department, the Department of Defense and the Department of the Interior. It concluded that the political and economic existence of Middle Eastern countries depended upon the rate and terms on which oil is produced, since oil was the principal source of wealth amongst those countries. The paper recognised the operations of oil companies and the level of their production as well as the price they paid as 'instruments of our foreign policy toward those countries'. The paper went on to explain that the way oil companies carried out their operations 'determined the strength of our ties with the Middle Eastern countries and our ability to resist Soviet expansion and influence in the area'. As the paper did not make any distinction between the interests of oil companies and those of the United States, it concluded that 'no settlement with Iran of the Anglo-Iranian dispute was possible'.

Britain's Secret Intelligence Service (SIS), together with the CIA, which provided all the finance, set up an operational bureau in Cyprus during 'Operation Ajax', the operation to topple Mossadeq. Radio broadcasts and newspaper articles were carefully arranged to stir public opinion in Iran and the Middle East against Mossadeq. In August 1953 the CIA organised street mobs in major Iranian cities, setting off a coup that ousted Mossadeq and restored the Shah to the throne whilst the bodies of nationalists and communists were hanging from lamp-posts.

A year later a new Iranian oil consortium agreement was achieved. The Anglo-Iranian company was the largest holder with forty per cent. The five major American companies – Gulf Oil, Socony, Socal, Texas and Standard Oil – each held seven per cent; fourteen per cent was held by Royal Dutch Shell whilst the French Compagnie Française des Pétroles owned six per cent. Another group of independent oil companies controlled the remaining five per cent.

While Britain had dominated Middle East oil resources prior to the Second World War, it was the Americans who exercised post-war control through two avenues which evolved into the 'twin pillar' policy on either side of the Gulf two decades later: firstly, US government assistance in spreading the influence of American companies amongst the Arab sheikhdoms and, secondly, forty per cent control of Iranian oil.

However, the events in 1953 which saw the return of the Shah also sowed the seeds of hatred for the 'Great Satan' – America – which was to boil over a quarter of a century later in a bloody revolution that threw the Gulf into the eye of the storm and led the West – in its rush to contain the Islamic revolution – to condone the behaviour of Saddam Hussein.

The foundation of Israel on land 'stolen' from the Palestinians was in the view of many Arab and Muslim countries a crime of which Britain was largely guilty. In the eyes of the Arabs, therefore, the United States became an accomplice by its continued support for a Jewish state. The subject of Israel proved to be a major complication and frequently a source of conflict between Arab oil-producing countries and Western powers. Inevitably, oil companies became caught in the political crossfire.

However, those Arab oil producers did not possess any real political leverage until 1961, twelve years after Palestine had been 'lost' to the Jews, when they founded the Organisation of the Petroleum Exporting Countries (OPEC) and imposed oil embargoes on Israel. Those twelve years were a bonanza for Western oil companies who made gross profits of $22.2 billion from the Middle East. The oil-producing countries received $9.4 billion, whilst the oil companies netted $12.8 billion.

The co-ordinated policy of OPEC gave members the benefits of collective bargaining and gradually increased their share of the wealth drilled from beneath their sands. However, through the presence of radical members like Libya, Iraq and smaller African countries, OPEC, to the dismay of the West, became an increasingly political organisation. During the early 1970s, there were frequent debates on the issues of the ownership of oil and the control of oil wealth.

In 1973 the Yom Kippur War broke out. Saudi Arabia, Kuwait and Iraq, which between them possess forty per cent of the world's known oil reserves, led the Arab oil producers to place an oil embargo on the United States and the Netherlands for their backing of Israel. As soon as the war broke out, on 6th October, the United States began supplying Israel with advanced weapons and tanks through a massive airlift operation that clearly violated international law. US Air Force transport aircraft landed at airfields in the Egyptian Sinai which had been under Israeli occupation since 1967, despite UN Security Council Resolution 242 which called for Israel to withdraw from the Sinai Peninsula. This violation was proved in Moscow when US Secretary of State Henry Kissinger was shown evidence in the form of an M48 tank captured by the Egyptians in Sinai. The tank's mileometer clearly showed that it had only travelled 48 miles before its capture, proving that it had not crossed the border from Israel which was 120 miles away to the east. American support of Israel was seen by Egypt's Arab allies as an act of aggression.

The Arab oil ministers who co-ordinated the embargo exempted countries like France and Britain, who took a neutral position in the conflict and appeared to contribute positively through diplomatic efforts in the UN Security Council. Meanwhile the Arabs saw the only American function in the council as vetoing any resolution that might have condemned Israeli actions.

Britain and France were tempted to maximise imports of oil from Arab countries at America's expense. Both governments put pressure on oil companies to exploit the status granted by oil producers to the two countries as friends, by diverting the American quota of oil to Britain and France. The British Conservative government under Edward Heath wanted to stockpile oil because of the threat of strikes by the National Union of Mineworkers. Arab diplomats also tried to put more pressure on oil companies by indicating to London, Paris and Washington that they would continue the oil embargo on America and the Netherlands until Western governments pressurised Israel into complying with UN Security Council Resolution 242.

The Yom Kippur War and the subsequent oil crisis had caused oil prices to rise drastically. Iraq's oil revenue, for example, rose by 320 per cent as a result of these prices. The rise in oil prices across the board was almost 400 per cent.

The 1970s also saw Saudi Arabia emerge as an important power in Middle Eastern politics. The country was able to dictate the price of oil simply by threatening to flood the market from its massive reserves. Other OPEC members just had to toe the line.

The Arab sheikhs made massive profits as a result of the conflict, and anger at this led to a flood of Marxist and left-wing calls demanding a fair share for the Egyptians and Syrians whose soldiers had fought and died in the Yom Kippur War. The call by the Marxists was later seized upon by the Palestinians demanding their share to carry on the fight to liberate Palestine, while Arab nationalists developed the idea into shifting the oil wealth into poorer Arab countries for investment there.

President Sadat of Egypt had agreed with the oil-rich Arab states to enter a partnership in which the Gulf States were to contribute $560 million, their capital share in an Egyptian military–industrial enterprise called the Arabic Board for Industry – the organisation which, a decade later, would manufacture the missiles that Saddam Hussein used against Iran, as well as producing air and coastal defence systems for the Gulf States. That these states never paid their share was a contributing factor to Sadat's subsequent decision to negotiate a separate peace with Israel.

A major result of the 1973 embargo was that it made oil companies not only more political but also more independent of Western governments. They were no longer willing to be used as direct instruments of foreign policy. Nor did they concur with the idea of pressurising Israel to implement UN Resolution 242 – a prelude to their independent attitudes during the Gulf War a decade later. Nevertheless the companies' newfound policies of independence were of benefit to the United States: supply of oil was ensured when the companies managed to circumvent the embargo on exporting oil to America and the Netherlands by changing the destination of crude oil on the high seas. This resulted in a drop in oil supplies to Europe since diversions to the US were made from the European quota.

The US State Department could perhaps have averted the Yom

Kippur War, with its human casualties, its material cost and the huge increases in oil prices, had it paid attention to messages sent from King Faisal bin Abd al-Azziz of Saudi Arabia via ARAMCO. As President Sadat was discussing with Faisal the use of oil in the forthcoming battle with Israel, the latter used ARAMCO to convey a sense of urgency about the need for a change of US policy away from a pro-Israeli bias and towards an implementation of a diplomatic compromise solution. ARAMCO's officials' warnings were largely ignored. It was only after the weapon of the oil embargo had been used against America that Washington began to listen.

When the war was over, the United States made it clear that it wished to rebuild its links with some Arab states, including Egypt and Saudi Arabia, and began to use the trade in sophisticated arms in place of oil as a tool of its initiative. Washington also wanted to reassure the Arabs that such weapons would not be an Israeli monopoly. However, the Arabs were required to pay hefty commissions to 'agents' in addition to the cost of the weapons, while Israel either received very favourable terms or was supplied with arms free of charge. This created yet more resentment and contributed to the anti-Americanism which was to become a factor in Middle East politics.

Two successive American administrations, under Presidents Ford and Carter, did make concerted efforts to solve some Middle Eastern political problems. These culminated in President Carter's 1979 peace treaty between Israel and Egypt. However, the core of the problem, the Palestinian–Israeli conflict, remained unsettled.

Early American efforts, by President Nixon and by Henry Kissinger, were not designed to implement a final, comprehensive solution but were intended to reduce the tension in the Middle East in order to assure a steady flow of oil to America, its Western allies and Japan. Part of this policy was also intended to secure the stability of 'friendly' regimes as part of the Nixon Doctrine of promoting the shared hegemony of the two large conservative powers on either side of the Gulf. This was the so-called 'twin pillars' policy which was supposed to ensure the protection of the Saudi royal family and the Shah of Iran.

Not only were arms sales to the two regimes increased but a directive was issued by Henry Kissinger in 1972 which stated that Iran was to be allowed to purchase without restriction the most sophisticated American weapons systems. There were endless machinations by the State Department and the Nixon administration to manoeuvre Congress into authorising the sale of advanced weapons to the Saudis. In order to quieten pro-Israeli voices on Capitol Hill, the Nixon administration and those that followed gave more sophisticated arms to Israel. This served to escalate the arms race in the Middle East as Syria, Libya and Iraq turned to the Soviet Union in an effort to achieve military parity with Israel.

Unfortunately, the United States did not examine the effect of this strategy in the long term, or consider whether Saudi Arabia and Iran would pursue their own interests or balance their interests with those of the West. One of the most disastrous results was to weaken Egypt's position as a major power. A nation state since 2000 BC, its stability had in the past managed to check the extremists among Arab states, the majority of which emerged from the gathering of tribes inside newly drawn borders. They traditionally looked to Cairo for leadership and guidance.

The 'two pillars' strategy also meant projecting American double standards in dealing with the Middle East and in backing medieval ruling oligarchies with appalling records on human rights. The clearest examples of this were the two 'twin pillars' themselves. In the case of Iran, its huge oil revenues were not used to elevate the standard of living of the deprived masses, and Washington only belatedly realised the failure of its policy when it witnessed the ignominious fall of the Shah.

American support for the Pahlavi regime had resulted in the Iranians' violent rejection of Western democracy and discredited the modernist and progressive forces which had previously called for its emulation. The result was a hasty transfer of American support to the other 'pillar', a backward-looking medieval monarchy, again with a shocking record on human rights. The Saudis, unlike the Shah, had channelled their oil revenues into impressive building programmes, prestige projects with no real economic purpose, and imported hundreds of thousands of 'guest workers' who are virtually enslaved without any civil rights. Saudi oil revenues were used to import not only consumer goods but also huge amounts of arms.

The policy of importing Western manufactured goods and arms resulted in the West condoning the policies of the Saudi royal family against deprived sections of its own population – policies which were repeatedly criticised by human rights organisations and in reports by Amnesty International. Because the Saudis were unable to defend their kingdom from potential invaders, they used their money to create an army comprised largely of mercenaries.

Further destabilisation by the Saudis in the region has taken the form of keeping border disputes alive, as is the case with Oman, the United Arab Emirates and Yemen, or financing reactionary forces inside neighbouring countries, as is again the case with Yemen. Pressure has also been applied against those states, such as Kuwait, which wished to liberalise their way of life.

Saudi money also financed a propaganda war against liberal thought amongst Muslims worldwide as well as Islamic groups in Egypt who put pressure on the government to conform to the Islamic code. This has further weakened Egypt economically and politically, leaving a regional leadership vacuum which the Saudis, with a small population and lacking historical stability, were unable to fill themselves. Here was an opportunity for Saddam Hussein to claim the mantle of Arab leadership.

Saudi support of Iraq, which was encouraged by the United States, ultimately backfired. In footing a large proportion of the bill for Western arms supplies for Saddam Hussein, for use in his war against the revolutionary Islamic regime in Iran, the Americans helped to create a monster.

After incorrectly interpreting signals from Washington during 1990, Saddam Hussein approached his oil-wealthy neighbours for grants of money to help pay off the massive debts incurred by eight long years of war. Had he not saved America's allies from the flames of the Islamic revolution?

'But you know you are not the ones who protected your friends during the war with Iran,' he lectured US ambassador April Glaspie on 25th July 1990. 'As a country, we have the right to prosper. We lost so many opportunities and the others should value the Iraqi role in their protection,' said Saddam as he pointed at the interpreter. 'Even this Iraqi feels bitter like all other Iraqis.'

Saddam Hussein was right when he told the ambassador that there was great resentment in Iraq and in many parts of the Arab world that Kuwaitis and Gulf state Arabs were living in luxury, using their money to gamble in Europe's casinos while the children of those who had given their blood to defend Kuwait went hungry. 'Is this Iraq's reward for its role in securing the stability of the region and for protecting it from an unknown flood?' he asked Mrs Glaspie, only eight days before he sent his tanks to the heart of Kuwait City.

The invasion of Kuwait itself posed no immediate threat to any American vital interests as Saddam Hussein himself explained to the American chargé d'affaires on 6th August. He said he was prepared to safeguard such interests once they had been spelled out by the Americans. 'What are legitimate US interests and how can we safeguard them?' said Saddam Hussein to Joseph Wilson, four days after the invasion of Kuwait.

The control of Kuwait's oil reserves will not by itself give Iraq a decisive vote over the oil-price market – Europe only imports six per cent of its oil from Iraq and Kuwait, whilst the United States imports eleven per cent. Even Saddam Hussein would not withhold oil from the market – he desperately needs money. As was demonstrated in 1973, when Western consumers decreased their reliance on Middle Eastern oil, and when Britain and non-OPEC producers started to extract oil from the North Sea, oil prices worldwide fell and led to a glut and further price falls.

The battle inside OPEC was between those led by the Saudi royal family, whose very existence depended on consumers and who thus urged price moderation, and those like Iran and Iraq who were desperate for higher revenues and thus wanted to limit production in order to secure higher prices. Ironically, the invasion of Kuwait pushed oil prices up but Iraq was not to benefit because of United Nations sanctions.

Still there was no major threat to US interests. OPEC cannot control oil prices by itself. Production from non-OPEC countries like Mexico, Angola and the North Sea has increased and this obliges OPEC to be more flexible and to respond to market forces. Even if Iraq were to control combined Kuwaiti and Iraqi oil production – there was no sign of it at the time of writing this book – it would not significantly alter the balance of power between OPEC and non-OPEC producers.

However, what has worried Washington since the invasion is the possible change in the political and economic balance of power in the Gulf region. Saudi Arabia was the dominant power in the lower Gulf, while Iran and Iraq were usually in balance in the north. Between them, these three countries could produce nearly twenty million barrels of oil per day if they were to pump at full capacity – something which Saudi Arabia did in the wake of the takeover of Kuwait to try to stabilise the price of oil.

It is still the Western world which is mainly dependent on Gulf oil supplies: America has cut the amount it imports but still takes five per cent from the Gulf; Europe takes thirty-five per cent. In 1989, France and Italy each imported thirty-five per cent of their oil from the Gulf while the figure for Japan was sixty-four per cent. However, it is not the present which the oil consumers worry about; it is the uncertain future if a dictator like Saddam Hussein is left to dominate the Gulf oil reservoir, the largest in the world, with its reserves increasing as new exploration goes on.

US Secretary of State James Baker told the US House of Representatives on 4th September 1990 that what was at stake was the world's reliance on access to the energy resources of the Gulf. 'It is not about Kuwait and the flow of oil from its wells but about a dictator who, acting alone, could strangle the global economic order, determining whether we all enter into recession or the darkness of a depression.'

There was, however, no credible source or report to suggest that Saddam wanted, intended or even contemplated taking over Saudi Arabia. Bush administration officials admitted that neither the CIA nor the Defense Intelligence Agency thought it was probable that Iraq would invade its vast neighbour.

It is worth remembering that prior to the invasion of Iran in 1980, and Kuwait in 1990, Iraq launched a noisy propaganda campaign spelling out historical claims on the Shatt al-Arab waterway or on the Rumailah oil field on the border with Kuwait. In fact, Iraq signed a non-aggression pact with Saudi Arabia in 1989. 'Had the Kuwaitis signed a non-aggression pact with us, it wouldn't have come to this,' President Saddam told Joseph Wilson as he accused Britain of advising the Kuwaitis against signing such a pact.

However, American officials have argued that, even if Iraq did not invade Saudi Arabia, threatening to do so could enable it to dictate Saudi oil policy. The same also applies to the smaller Gulf states such as the United Arab Emirates, Bahrain, and Qatar, which alone has liquid gas reserves adequate for the next three hundred years at current rates of production. Such a situation would place Iraq effectively in control of production of half the world's oil supplies, and thus give it a leading role in setting oil prices. This alone, in addition to the rule of international law – a point which American officials have not spent much time discussing – presented President Bush with the need to deploy American troops in the Gulf.

3 · Iraq and the West

The fall of the Shah of Iran in 1979 was one of the most devastating blows sustained by US foreign policy since the Vietnam War. Not only had the demise of America's principal ally destroyed the balance of power in the region, but it had also left Washington's Gulf allies vulnerable to the radical forces of Islam.

Saddam Hussein, who that year had become president of Iraq, sought to fill the vacuum left by the fall of the Shah and to assume leadership of the region. At this point it seemed to Western powers that his ambitions were in line with their own interests: halting the advance of the Islamic revolution, securing the flow of oil and preventing Iran from threatening the pro-Western Gulf states. This was not the first time that the priorities of the West had coincided with those of a local regional power but the pursuit of mutual interests had always been a matter of coincidence, never of planned policy. Western policy-makers rarely recognise the existence of legitimate national interests in the Middle East outside the parameters of their own policy aims. When the conditions which have created the coincidence change, there is an inevitable clash of interests.

This pattern has been repeated many times, leading governments with strong nationalist views to distrust Western nations, especially the former colonial powers. Saddam Hussein's regime is no exception. The Ba'ath party started as a secret organisation without popular support; and because of its long years of clandestine activities, including terrorism, the government of the party is by nature secretive and conspiratorial. Its values often clash with those of more open Western societies and this is particularly evident in its paranoia about the Western press. Whenever he meets politicians from the West, Saddam Hussein complains of the 'campaigns in the Western media' being waged against him.

The conspiracy theory that has developed amongst Arab nationalist regimes is a major factor in the conduct of Middle Eastern politics. For Western powers to conduct their policies on the basis of blind pursuit of their own interests, promoting the ambitions of whoever is the most powerful pro-Western leader of the moment, both reinforces existing distrust and creates the conditions for instability and conflict.

Arab nationalists, including Iraqi Ba'athists, are not entirely wrong when they declare that 'Western misunderstanding of Iraqi and other Arab politics is entrenched in the archaeology of a colonialist mentality compounded by America's bias towards Israel'. This kind of statement is printed in many Arab newspapers and publications every time America vetoes a United Nations Security Council resolution condemning an Israeli air raid in Lebanon or some similar outrage. Even at the height of the Gulf crisis, when President Bush was discussing military options to implement UN Resolution 660 (demanding the unconditional withdrawal of Iraq from Kuwait), he failed to make Israel comply with a Security Council resolution demanding that a UN team investigate the Israeli police shooting of twenty-two Palestinians on Temple Mount, territory illegally occupied by Israel. An editorial in *Al Quds*, a Palestinian newspaper, cynically stated that if it had not been for the presence of US troops in Saudi Arabia, America would probably have vetoed altogether the resolution condemning Israel for killing Palestinian civilians.

From the West's point of view, the events of 1958 which ended the pro-British monarchy marked a point after which Iraq could no longer be considered as being in the same camp. Almost all the regimes which succeeded the monarchy were, in one way or another, unpalatable to the West. Although Britain initially welcomed the accession to power of the Ba'ath party in 1963, it was soon disappointed by the lack of improvement in relations with the new regime.

In June 1967, President Nasser received assurances from the United States, via the Soviet ambassador in Cairo, that Israel would not attack Egypt. He in turn gave an undertaking that Egypt would not initiate hostilities. However, on the following morning, Israel, without any warning, launched a series of air strikes on Egyptian air bases, destroying the major part of the Egyptian air force and leaving Nasser's ground forces without air cover in the desert. This led to heavy Egyptian losses and the Israeli occupation of Sinai. Washington subsequently failed to take any action against Israel and continued its support against a background of what was seen by the Arabs as a superpower conspiracy to defeat Nasser and to enable Israel to expand in accordance with the well-known Zionist dream of 'Israel from the Nile to the Euphrates'.

Moscow was quick to exonerate itself. It forced the whole of the Eastern bloc to sever relations with Israel, halted the emigration of Soviet Jews and replaced Egyptian military hardware lost during the conflict. In France, President Charles de Gaulle ordered a ban on selling arms to Israel because it had been responsible for starting the war.

The 1967 defeat of Egypt by Israel, seen by Arab nationalists as an extension of 'Western imperialism', was a major factor in helping the Ba'ath party to seize power in Iraq in 1968. Despite twenty-two years of uninterrupted Ba'athist rule, the West still thinks of Iraq as a 'coup-prone country' – a term sometimes used by British journalists.

In November 1967, seven months before it gained power in Iraq, the Ba'ath party rejected the UN Security Council Resolution 242, an action which was in line with its hard attitude regarding the question of Israel. Drafted by Britain, the resolution called upon Israel to withdraw from territories occupied in June 1967 and upon Arab neighbours to recognise Israel. The United States did little to encourage Israel to implement the resolution.

In 1970 Iraq denounced Egypt's acceptance of a three-month ceasefire plan put forward by US Secretary of State William Rogers. It was later revealed that President Nasser had agreed to it because he needed time to improve Egypt's defences. During the period of the ceasefire, the Russians built an impressive air defence system with SA-2, SA-3 and SA-6 surface-to-air missiles. Prior to this, the Israelis had been carrying out regular air raids on Egypt on an almost daily basis but the installation of the missiles removed their air superiority and the raids ceased thereafter.

It was the Iraqis who persuaded the Palestine Liberation Organisation to attack Nasser's acceptance of the Rogers plan. This resulted in a rift between the Egyptians and the PLO, particularly after the former closed down the Voice of Palestine service on Cairo Radio. These events prompted King Hussein of Jordan, who mistakenly assumed that Nasser had turned on the Palestinians, to order his Arab Legion to move against the Palestinian guerrillas living in refugee camps in Jordan. A massacre ensued in which thousands of Palestinians died. The fighting lasted for two weeks and the episode became known as 'Black September'.

By the early 1970s a close relationship had developed between Iraq and the Soviet bloc, the Iraqi communist party being incorporated into the Progressive National Front in 1973. This appeared to the West to threaten its interests. The stance adopted by the Ba'ath party towards the Israeli–Palestinian question and the Arab–Israeli conflict was of special concern to the United States, where the Jewish lobby is one of the most decisive factors in shaping the administration's Middle Eastern policy. Although opponents of the Ba'ath regime, as well as former Ba'ath party members, argued that in reality the Ba'ath never posed a threat to Israel and never took an active part in the Arab–Israeli wars, a combination of Ba'athist rhetoric and Jewish lobbying convinced Washington that a

Ba'ath-ruled Iraq was incompatible with a lasting peace between Israel and its Arab neighbours.

Between 1977 and 1979, the Iraqis launched a campaign of propaganda against Egypt and its peace accord with Israel, whilst encouraging radical Arab nationalists to take an anti-Egyptian line. Baghdad also hosted terrorist groups like the notorious Abu Nidal and his Fateh Revolutionary Council, which carried out terrorist acts such as the siege of the Egyptian embassy in Turkey in 1978 and the assassination of the PLO representative in his London office in the same year. Iraq's open support for such organisations led the US State Department to put Iraq on the list of states sponsoring terrorism.

The Arab Gulf states attitude to the Ba'ath government in Baghdad was similar to that of the West, except that the physical threat was genuine and more dangerous to Arabs. The Iraqi giant cast its shadow over the Gulf states in many ways. In addition to the threat of direct military action, as in the case of Kuwait, countries in the middle and lower Gulf were subjected to Iraqi threats in the form of internal subversion, Iraqi-backed opposition groups and Iraqi-sponsored terrorism. The main objective of the Iraqi intelligence service, the Mukhabarat, was to create internal instability in targeted countries and to push their regimes into increasing conflict with opposition groups. Meanwhile the national leadership of the Ba'ath party – which in their terminology covered all Arabic-speaking countries – worked on establishing a number of Ba'ath party cells which were financed and supported from Baghdad in places like Bahrain, Qatar and the United Arab Emirates.

The smaller Gulf states had to put up with interference from Iraq, whose leadership was desperate to simulate a Nasser-type role in unifying regional Arab countries into one political bloc. This interference was increased after the isolation of Egypt during 1977–8, following President Anwar Sadat's visit to Jerusalem and his bid for peace with Israel.

Iraq's ambition to play a leading role had been thwarted in the early 1970s by the US 'twin pillars' strategy, which allowed the Shah of Iran to become the 'gendarme of the Gulf', supported to a certain extent by Saudi Arabia. That status quo gave the smaller Gulf states some comfort, since the growing strength of Iran under the Shah helped to counterbalance the unwelcome interference by their domineering 'Arab brothers' in Iraq. The other six Gulf states – Saudi Arabia, Kuwait, UAE, Bahrain, Qatar, Oman – did not dare to establish the Gulf Co-operation Council until 1981 when Iraq was embroiled in its war with Iran.

Such was the geopolitical structure of the area up to 1979 when the fall of the Shah changed all bases of calculation. The stronger of the 'twin pillars' had collapsed. Once the revolution had succeeded in Iran, and an Islamic republic had been declared in February 1979, the Ba'ath regime in Baghdad prepared itself to exploit the opportunity of replacing Iran as the main power in the Gulf. By then, the new calls of Islamic fundamentalism from Tehran were sending shivers down the spines of the Western-supported rulers of the Gulf states.

The overthrow of the Shah provided Saddam Hussein with the chance of a fruitful partnership with the West, and he grasped it: Iraq assumed the role of regional policeman, with the West supplying arms and high technology. Saddam began to divest himself of his communist partners in the government of the Progressive National Front, executing twenty-one members of the Iraqi communist party in July 1979 and imprisoning hundreds of others. Three thousand Iraqi communists were forced into exile in Western Europe, Kuwait, Syria and Egypt.

Washington had been seriously embarrassed by the CIA's failure to detect Islam as the main ideology of the Iranian revolution, which replaced the reliable, predictable, pro-Western monarchy in Iran with a volatile, unpredictable and radical revolutionary regime. There was confusion and near panic within the Carter administration, and the lack of firm response from the United States definitely contributed towards the eventual sacking of its embassy in Tehran and the taking hostage of all the embassy staff. Indeed, any chance of an effective American response was swiftly removed by the loss of virtually all CIA 'assets' in Iran at that time. SAVAM, the revolutionary regime's equally ruthless replacement for the Shah's much-feared intelligence service, SAVAK, moved swiftly and scores of suspected American agents were arrested.

Lack of a co-ordinated and decisive response led to the drawing up of unsophisticated and irrational plans. The ill-fated attempted rescue of the hostages in Tehran ended in fiasco and the deaths of some of the rescue force without so much as a shot being fired. The Carter administration was seen as increasingly impotent and America's stock in the Middle East sank even lower.

Meanwhile, the Ba'ath party was still undermining American foreign policy in the Middle East by rapidly spreading its influence among Arab radicals of the 'rejectionist front' that opposed the Egypt–Israel peace treaty. However, Washington ignored the threat of an Iraqi-led Arab nationalist movement towards peace and stability in the Middle East, whilst CIA reports exaggerated the danger posed by the Islamic revolution. Under President Carter, the main objective of the US Gulf policy, hastily redrafted after the fall of the Shah, was to contain the Islamic revolution and prevent it spreading to the Gulf states.

One serious after-effect of the upheaval in Iran was the occupation in November 1979 of the Grand Mosque in Mecca by a group of radical Muslims inspired by the Islamic revolution. The matter was resolved with the assistance of members of France's Groupe Intervention de la Gendarmerie Nationale (GIGN), who were flown in at the request of the Saudi Arabian government, and former members of Britain's 22nd Special Air Service Regiment who were at that time working for a British company on contract to the Saudi Arabian National Guard. The GIGN troops and the former SAS soldiers assisted in the planning and organisation of the operation to clear the mosque. This was carried out by the National Guard anti-terrorist unit, trained by Grenzschutsgruppe-9 (GSG-9), the anti-terrorist unit of the West German Bundesgrenzschutz (Federal Border Guard). The troops from GIGN used explosives to clear an entrance for the assault teams.

The 1979 peace treaty between Israel and Egypt had led to the latter's isolation from the Arab economic market in which millions of Egyptians were working, remitting in excess of $30 billion per annum, a sum which formed an important part of their country's national income. Under pressure from Iraq, Arab states cancelled Egyptian workers' contracts or changed them so as to prevent them sending remittances, normally consisting of between twenty-five and fifty per cent of their net pay, to Egypt each month. This inevitably had a debilitating effect on the Egyptian economy. In addition, several states welshed on previous agreements to pay their share in joint Arab economic ventures spearheaded by Egypt, including military, industrial, petrochemical and construction programmes. This served to weaken Egypt's economic position still further.

Meanwhile Israel, under the right-wing government led by Menachem Begin, carried out air raids on refugee camps in Lebanon, annexed East Jerusalem and the Syrian Golan Heights, and failed to honour its obligations under the 1979 peace treaty to grant autonomy to the West Bank and Gaza Palestinians. This only increased Egypt's embarrassment and weakened its political influence throughout the Middle East, fuelling Saddam Hussein's idea of making Iraq the dominant force in the region.

Instead of assisting Egypt to overcome its financial difficulties – ultimately only doing so in 1990 as a result of the Gulf crisis – or checking Israel's aggression, especially in Lebanon, the United States looked the other way, its attention focused on containing revolutionary Islam. On 4th November 1979, radical Islamic students, including a number of left-wing elements, occupied the American embassy in Tehran. There had been no early warning of any threat to the embassy and consequently the ambassador and his staff were hard pressed to carry out the destruction of secret documents, many of which were shredded rather than incinerated. As a result, Iranian students spent lengthy periods reassembling documents, the contents of which provided the revolutionary government with valuable intelligence. The information they gained apparently only served to increase the fears of the Iranians and their paranoia about the 'Great Satan'.

At the same time, the Cold War was intensified by the Soviet Union's intervention in Afghanistan. When the American embassy was seized, Moscow did not support the US calling for the upholding of international law or for the enforcement of the Vienna Convention on diplomatic missions. On the contrary, it appeared to lend moral support to the Iranians, limiting its criticism to a gentle rebuke in *Pravda*, in December 1979, which noted in very mild terms that the action seemed to be in violation of international law. In the same article, however, *Pravda* accused the United States of violating international law by conducting naval manoeuvres in the Arabian Sea. Although Moscow supported a United Nations Security Council call for the release of the American hostages, it abstained on a further resolution threatening Iran with economic sanctions if they were not released.

These developments understandably increased the fear both of the US State Department and of the CIA that the Islamic revolution was a real threat to Western interests.

On 22nd September 1980, suddenly and with no warning, Iraq invaded Iran. The Western permanent members of the United Nations Security Council delayed the convening of a meeting and discouraged a resolution that was unequivocal in its condemnation of Iraqi aggression. It is impossible to judge whether a strong Security Council resolution, urging Iraq to withdraw from Iran, would have shortened the Gulf War and spared the Middle East and the West the spill-over effects of terrorism, the kidnapping of Western hostages by Iranian-supported fundamentalist groups and the spread of radical Islamic ideology. These resulted in increasingly strong anti-Iranian feelings in the West which saw Islamic fundamentalism as a potentially destabilising factor, not only in the Middle East but also in Muslim nations elsewhere. Western sympathy and support therefore swung in Iraq's favour, with Saddam Hussein being seen as a bulwark against the regime of Ayatollah Ruhollah Khomeini. Such support ultimately enabled the Iraqi dictator to build his giant war machine and to invade Kuwait a decade later.

Sir Anthony Parsons, Britain's ambassador to the United Nations, and a former ambassador to Iran, has always been critical of the failure of the five permanent members of the Security Council to convene quickly and condemn Iraq. Their motive for not doing so was that they expected Saddam Hussein's sudden *blitzkrieg* against Iran to succeed, but this did not happen. When the United Nations Security Council eventually adopted Resolution 479 on the Gulf War in September 1980, it only called for a ceasefire and did not demand a withdrawal of Iraqi forces from Iranian territory or condemn Iraq for its aggression. Iran was thus left with the impression that it had been abandoned to its fate.

It must have seemed to those in power in Tehran that the world had plotted to give Saddam Hussein the time he needed to destroy the Islamic revolution. They concluded that Iran was facing the combined enmity of the outside world in a conspiracy orchestrated by America.

Saddam Hussein read the implicit message of the United Nations resolution as giving him a green light to continue with his campaign against Iran. Ten years later, on the understanding that Resolution 479 and the way it was adopted had been 'an anti-Iranian plot masterminded by the West', Saddam interpreted the 1990 Security Council's swift adoption of Resolution 660, condemning his occupation of Kuwait, as 'another Western plot', but this time against Iraq. His propaganda machine adopted the Iranian tactics of 1980, saying that the Security Council had turned into an 'instrument in the hands of the Zionists and Imperialists'.

It was almost like the reversal of roles in the same scenario. Iran's 1980 cry against the 'injustice' of the 'imperialist-controlled United Nations' found a sympathetic echo among the down-trodden Shias who drove their car bombs in suicide missions against American interests. In 1990, Iraq's railing against the 'biased and anti-Arab' resolutions of the 'Zionist- and Imperialist-controlled' UN also found a sympathetic ear among Palestinians and other deprived Arabs. These groups saw great injustice in the lack of any attempt to address their needs by wealthy Gulf states or indeed their American friends in the West who denied economic aid to the poor and did little to force Israel to implement one single – amongst scores of – UN resolution.

Saddam also doubtless realised that he could use the West's phobia about Islamic fundamentalism to his own advantage. In his meeting with Ambassador Glaspie, he threatened to make peace with Iran and form a common alliance to confront the United States. Mrs Glaspie seems not to have understood this message. But in 1982 he had exploited America's fears and managed to involve the US in direct maritime confrontation with Iran.

At that time, when Iran appeared to be gaining the upper hand, America and its allies became concerned and it was decided in Washington that Iraq should be offered support in the form of money and arms. There was, however, a major problem in that American legislation prohibits giving credits or loans or forging extensive links with countries on the list of those known to be involved with terrorism. In March 1982 the State Department, without any consultation with Congress, moved swiftly to strike Iraq off the list. American officials first struck a deal with the Iraqis which led to the Abu Nidal terrorist group moving out of Baghdad, ostensibly having been evicted by the Iraqi government. However, a small group remained behind, together with a bank account containing $13 million which was frozen by the Iraqis.

The memory of the seizure of the American embassy in Iran in 1979 also helped to provide political support for Iraq. According to Geoffrey Kemp, the head of the Middle East section in the National Security Council during the Reagan administration, that disaster was still fresh in American minds and 'the Ayatollah was calling us the Great Satan and trying to undermine governments throughout the Gulf States'. He confessed that the plan was to stop Iran. 'It wasn't that we wanted Iraq to win the war, we didn't want Iraq to lose. We really weren't that naïve. We knew he [Saddam] was an SOB, but he was our SOB.'

Then came the bizarre operation which became known as 'Irangate'. It was revealed that arms had been sold secretly to Iran in an attempt to secure the release of Western hostages held in Lebanon by the pro-Iranian Shi'ite group Hezbollah (the Party of God). It was planned that the money from the sale should be used to finance the Contra guerrillas fighting the Sandinista government of Nicaragua, despite a decision by Congress to the contrary.

The taking of Western hostages in Lebanon formed part of a vicious circle of revenge. To start with, a Lebanese Muslim fanatic drove a car bomb into the American embassy in Beirut in April 1983, killing sixty-three people, amongst whom were the CIA station chief, his deputy and the agency's chief Middle East analyst Robert Ames.

America retaliated by ordering the US Sixth Fleet to bombard Shia villages in the mountains. US navy aircraft carried out bombing raids whilst the battleship USS *New Jersey* used her massive sixteen-inch guns. Hezbollah then responded by sending a second car bomb into the headquarters of the US Marines in Beirut, killing 241 men.

Shia villages were bombarded again by the US navy. Subsequently, in December, the Shia Islamic Dawa (the Call) party – whose leaders had been persecuted in Iraq – drove car bombs into French and US embassies in Kuwait. The Kuwaitis, acting on information received from the Iraqi Mukhabarat, rounded up hundreds of Shia suspects. Seventeen of them, all members of the Dawa party, were subsequently convicted. Ironically, the seventeen escaped on 2nd August 1990 under the nose of the invading Iraqi troops, who facilitated their escape to Iran as part of the effort to improve relations with the foe of yesteryear. In another irony, the main armed resistance against the Iraqis in Kuwait was carried out by members of the Dawa party, who had previously been treated by the Sabahs, the ruling family in Kuwait, as second-class citizens.

Two of the convicted men were related to Imad Mughniyeh, an influential Lebanese leader of Hezbollah. To secure their release, Hezbollah began a campaign of kidnapping. On 16th March 1984, they kidnapped William Buckley, who had recently arrived in Lebanon as the new CIA station chief. The kidnappers later sent the CIA a videotape of Buckley being interrogated under torture and divulging information to his interrogators. The CIA were prepared to make virtually any deal to recover him but their rivals, the National Security Council, insisted on pressing ahead with 'Irangate'.

The CIA retaliated on 8th March 1985 by planting a car bomb with the intention of assassinating Hezbollah's spiritual leader, Sheikh Mohammed Hussein Fadlallah, a disciple of Ayatollah Khomeini. Fadlallah escaped unhurt but eighty-one people were killed in the explosion. This led to more kidnapping of Westerners and the hijacking a month later of a TWA airliner.

Shia fanaticism in Lebanon, reinforced by successes against the Americans, made Washington even more determined to expedite the defeat of the Islamic republic on the Iraqi front. Reports by human rights organisations and opposition groups, including the Kurds, about the dangers of befriending the Ba'ath regime and of entrusting it to look after Western interests were dismissed in Washington and other major Western capitals.

In fact, according to the *Washington Post*, the Baghdad regime actively continued to sponsor terrorism. The *Post* quoted Noel Koch, the Defense Department's Director for Counter-Terrorism, who stated that there were no doubts about Iraq's continued involvement with terrorist organisations but that the real reason for removing Iraq from the list was to help them in the war against Iran.

The Iraqis went so far as to employ terrorists directly and to use them when it came to manipulating events to further their aims, regardless of the possible consequences. Although it had departed from Iraq three months previously, the Abu Nidal group was still in the employ of Saddam Hussein. On the night of 3rd June 1982 Shlomo Argov, the Israeli ambassador in Britain, was shot on the steps of the Dorchester Hotel in Park Lane, London. Like the assassination of the Archduke Franz Ferdinand in Sarajevo in June 1914, which changed the course of history, this attempted murder sparked off a devastating chain reaction in the Middle East and resulted in the deaths of thousands of innocent civilians, over three hundred Israeli troops and approximately fifteen hundred Palestinian and Lebanese guerrillas.

The assassination attempt provided the Israelis with the excuse they had been seeking to invade Lebanon and attempt to destroy the PLO as part of their 'final solution' to the Palestinian problem. In revenge for the wounding of Argov they bombed PLO offices and refugee camps in Lebanon, breaking a year-long American-sponsored ceasefire. The PLO retaliated by attacking Israel's northern posts, which the Israelis used as a pretext to start 'Operation Peace for Galilee' – the invasion of Lebanon – on 6th June 1982.

In fact, the attempt on Argov's life was nothing to do with the PLO. It was carried out by an Abu Nidal cell led by Marwan al-Banna, the nephew of the head of the organisation, Abu Nidal, whose real name is Sabri al-Banna. The London-based cell had been set up in 1980 by the Iraqis for use in operations in Europe as dictated by Baghdad. It had 'slept' until activated a week before the assassination attempt by Nawaf Rosan, a member of Abu Nidal and also an officer in the Iraqi Mukhabarat.

On 10th June, the Israelis started their three-month-long siege of Beirut, subjecting it to a heavy bombardment which killed thousands of Lebanese civilians. On the same day, the Iraqi ruling Revolutionary Command Council presented Iran with a proposal for a unilateral ceasefire, saying that they were ready to withdraw all forces from Iranian soil in two weeks because of 'the urgent necessity of directing all efforts towards confronting the ferocious Zionist aggression against the Arab world, the Palestinian people and Lebanon'.

All this took place only three months after the State Department had struck Iraq off the list of countries sponsoring terrorism, enabling Baghdad to obtain $300 million in credits from the US Department of Agriculture's Commodity Credit Corporation (CCC) – ostensibly for the sale of grain to Baghdad, which was in dire need of hard currency to pay for imported consumer goods. The CCC arrangement meant that if Iraq defaulted on payments, the United States government would be liable instead.

With the re-election of President Reagan in 1984, Washington recognised the positive role played by Iraq by restoring diplomatic relations between Baghdad and Washington. The Iraqis co-operated by providing the CIA with information about Soviet weapons in its arsenal and about Baghdad-trained terrorists. The information proved worthless, according to a CIA source. Nevertheless, in 1986 the CIA, in exchange for this information, gave Iraq satellite pictures of Iranian troops and their positions, which proved invaluable to Baghdad.

Financial support, however, was not sufficient for Saddam Hussein. Somehow, because Iraq no longer had the resources or capability to defeat Iran on its own, he had to manipulate events so that the United States became directly involved in the war. For the previous three years, Iraqi pilots had been carrying out attacks on oil tankers passing through the Gulf, taking Iranian oil from Kharg Island to overseas destinations. The Iranians had threatened to attack tankers carrying oil from the Arab side of the Gulf unless these Iraqi attacks ceased. The Western response was to send warships to the Straits of Hormuz to deter the Iranians, who had deployed Silkworm coastal-defence missiles on the Iranian side of the straits, from carrying out their threat. With British, French and American warships patrolling the straits, the scene was set for a confrontation.

It was already dark on 17th May 1987 when a lone Iraqi Mirage F-1 fighter bomber, observed by an American-crewed Saudi AWACS surveillance aircraft, flew low along the coast of Saudi Arabia. As the Mirage approached Bahrain it suddenly veered back northwards, climbing to an altitude of 5000 feet over the Gulf. Its movement was followed by the radar operator aboard the 3585-ton USS *Stark*, an Oliver Hazard Perry class frigate on routine patrol in the shipping lanes south of the Iranian coast. The radar crew notified officers on the bridge that the Mirage's weapons system was locked on to the frigate. However, the bridge continued to regard the jet as 'friendly' – after all, Iraq was fighting America's enemy, Iran. That was why the ship did not engage the Iraqi jet, as its commander, Captain Glenn Brindel, admitted in Bahrain a day later.

The television pictures of the young British servicemen badly burned from the explosion of an Argentinian Exocet, which had hit the British logistics ship RFA *Sir Galahad* during the Falklands War five years earlier, flashed through Captain Brindel's mind as the approaching Exocet, only a few feet above the waves, could be seen with the naked eye. It was too late. In accordance with the rules imposed on all American warships in the Gulf at the time, the frigate's computerised, radar-controlled 'Phalanx' Close-In Weapon System (a multi-barrelled air defence weapon), which was designed to engage attacking aircraft or incoming missiles, had been switched from automatic to manual mode in order to prevent an inadvertent attack on friendly aircraft.

The USS *Stark*'s commander later stated that the Phalanx had not been switched back to automatic mode because the Iraqi pilot had received two warnings from the frigate. When a Pentagon investigation team visited Baghdad a few months later, it was told that the Iraqi pilot was not listening on the frequency used by the *Stark* and did not hear the warning. The Iraqis also claimed that tape-recordings of radio communications to and from the Iraqi aircraft were not available. Defense Secretary Caspar Weinberger therefore demanded to interview the pilot who had fired the fatal missile. This request cut no ice with the Iraqis, who insisted that the *Stark* was inside Iranian waters and the pilot had thought it was an Iranian frigate – a story later repeated by Radio Damascus, quoting an Iranian army spokesman. The Americans disputed this allegation, firmly maintaining that the frigate was in international waters. Although President Reagan stated three days after the attack that no country had the right to deny use of international waters, the two sides agreed to disagree on the location of the *Stark* for the sake of 'friendship between the two nations'.

In fact, when the Iraqi pilot launched his two Exocets, with an interval of ninety seconds between them, the *Stark*'s radar for some reason did not register the separation of the missiles from the Mirage. It was 10.45 p.m. when the first Exocet smashed into the *Stark*'s port side, boring its way through to the crew's quarters below the bridge and detonating in a massive explosion.

As Petty Officer O'Keefe fought his way through the now-darkened interior of the ship, pulling his comrades from their bunks and handing breathing apparatus to the wounded while sea water gushed in on top of him, the second Exocet hit the frigate. None of the vessel's three radar systems, or the American-manned Saudi AWACS, had picked up the second missile's signature. Mercifully, it failed to explode.

By 10.48, the decks were buckled with the intense heat which melted the ship's computers on one side of a bulkhead. On the other side, Petty Officer Mark Samples was in a darkened ammunition store spraying water on three dozen missiles to prevent them from exploding. He continued to do so for thirteen hours.

The upshot of this incident was that the Iraqis apologised and later paid compensation to the injured and the families of the dead sailors. The United States government accepted the Iraqi explanation – by 1.30 the following morning, Washington was referring to the attack as 'a mistake'. They accepted that the Iraqis had not meant to fire at an American ship. It was 'inadvertent' and there had been no 'hostile intent'. 'We've never considered the Iraqis hostile at all,' President Reagan said two weeks later. 'They've never been in any way hostile . . . And the villain of the piece is Iran.'

The pilot whom the Iraqis had refused to allow the American investigation team to question was later executed, according to an Iraqi air force pilot who defected in August 1988. An Egyptian-based Iraqi dissident claimed in early 1989 that it had been revealed that, in the spring of 1987, the Iraqi air force was encouraged to try and instigate incidents which would result in direct confrontations between the Americans and the Iranians. However, no evidence was ever produced to support this claim and Egyptian officials who debriefed the defecting pilot would not deny or confirm it.

As a result of the USS *Stark* incident, the rules of engagement were changed and commanders of American warships in the region were empowered to take action in their own defence without reference to Washington. Thus the United States became directly involved in the Gulf War, sinking or disabling two thirds of Iran's navy during confrontations over the following nine months.

By 1987, a *de facto* alliance had developed between Baghdad and Washington. Since the Kuwaitis had placed their oil tankers under the protection of the American flag in summer 1987, American warships were physically stopping the Iranians from disrupting Iraqi and other Arab oil exports, while the Iraqi air force was using its French-supplied Exocet missiles to attack tankers carrying Iranian oil and thus causing mayhem with the Iranian economy. The decision to re-flag eleven Kuwaiti tankers under the Stars and Stripes was not a carefully studied one. It was rather a hasty response to Kuwait shipping oil in Soviet-flagged tankers protected by Russian warships.

As a result of Tehran's reluctance to accept the United Nations Resolution 598, which demanded a ceasefire, there was an embargo on the supply of arms to Iran. Western technology, aerial photographs supplied by American spy satellites and surveillance data supplied by American-manned Saudi AWACS aircraft all gave Saddam Hussein the upper hand. Egyptian pilots provided Iraqi bombers with mid-air refuelling during raids on targets deep inside Iran. Egyptian technicians, aided by others from North Korea and China, modified Iraqi missiles to increase their maximum range greatly so that Iraq could strike at cities further inside Iran.

In April 1988, the US navy engaged Iranian warships near the Straits of Hormuz, its F14 Tomcat fighters sinking three boats and disabling the two Iranian frigates *Sahanad* and *Sabalan*. The radar systems on these two vessels were Iran's only working surveillance in the southern part of the Gulf. (The three French-made P3 Orion reconnaissance planes had been grounded in Mashhad since late 1987 for lack of spare parts.)

The last decisive battles in 1988 ended with the Iraqi liberation of the Fao Peninsula, occupied by Iran since early 1986 after a massive land attack which nearly isolated Basra. This had sent tremors through the Gulf States, which had nightmarish visions of Iranian forces breaking through and moving south to Kuwait and Saudi Arabia instead of towards Iraq. In fact, Khomeini never entertained any such intentions. His military establishment had never prepared any plans for the taking of Kuwait or of oilfields. His aim was basic and simple – the defeat of the forces of evil which were embodied in the aggressor Saddam Hussein.

When the Fao was recaptured, the Iraqi festivities, which coincided with Saddam Hussein's birthday, continued for a month with Arab delegations arriving in Baghdad to congratulate him. The Kuwaitis presented Saddam with a miniature mosque fashioned in solid gold.

During the mass festivities, Baghdad invited journalists and television crews from all over the world to visit the Fao. However, the Iraqis, who thrive on publicity and put great priority on propaganda, failed to produce a single soldier who could provide an account of how the Iranian fortifications had been stormed. The reason for this was quite simple – such a soldier did not exist.

After the Iranians captured the Fao Peninsula in 1986, numerous Iraqi counter-attacks had foundered against the Iranians' iron will to resist. The Iranians had deployed the Chinese-supplied Silkworm missiles, which subsequently reminded the Kuwaitis of their vulnerability to retribution for having supplied financial and material aid to Iraq. In addition, Kuwait allowed Iraq the use of its port, which became a conduit for the supply of arms and much-needed material, and had allowed Iraqi pilots to use Kuwaiti air space for attacks on tankers carrying Iranian oil through the Gulf.

In December 1987, there was a dinner party in Kuwait at which the main guest was Egypt's defence minister, Field Marshal Abd al-Halim Abu Ghazalla; he was visiting the Egyptian air defence experts installing Amoon air defence systems for the Kuwaiti armed forces. At the table there was a discussion as to how to guard against Iranian Silkworm missiles launched from the Fao Peninsula to attack Kuwaiti port facilities. The Egyptian field marshal indicated that the most practical solution would be for the Iraqis to recapture the peninsula. 'Our Iraqi brothers', said his host, Defence Minister Sheikh Salem Sabah al-Salem, as he looked at the Iraqi military attaché in the usual wily Kuwaiti manner and in the tradition of playing outside powers against one another, 'have tried a number of times but the Iranian defences were too strong.' As he spoke, he glanced at the field marshal, who replied dismissively, 'My boys can capture it in six hours.'

Five months later his 'boys' enabled him to win a bet with Saddam Hussein. Saddam had enlisted Egyptian assistance in the recapture of the Fao – Defence Minister Adnan Khairallah, the president's brother-in-law, had made a bet with his Egyptian counterpart, who took up the challenge and stated that he would present the Fao to Saddam Hussein as a birthday present.

On the night of 16th April 1988, disguised as Kuwaiti fishermen, Egyptian combat swimmers landed on Kuwait's Bubiyan Island, surprising the Iranians in a swift attack using silenced automatic weapons. Meanwhile Egyptian sappers were building bridges over the marshlands and waterways. Egyptian special forces were the first to storm the Iranian fortifications in the Fao, whilst the T72 and T54 tanks of the Iraqi Republican Guards formed the second wave which drove into the Fao at dawn on 17th April. They were followed by Iraqi mechanised infantry in armoured personnel-carriers who flushed out the last pockets of resistance. The Iraqi flag was flying over the Fao five hours and thirty-five minutes after the first assault craft carrying Egyptian frogmen left Bubiyan Island. Meanwhile, helicopters were carrying the Egyptian special forces back to the Iraqi air base at Shui'ebah, near Basra, where two C-130 transport aircraft were waiting to fly them home to the Egyptian air base at Al-Madha.

This action coincided with the US navy attacking Iranian targets while Iranian radar was jammed. The Iranians carried out a desperate attack in the Fish Lake area north of Basra and managed to break through. However, the Iraqis deployed one of their Republican Guards divisions, the only formations in the Iraqi army which possessed radios, and managed to repulse the Iranians, who suffered considerable losses. A combination of all these factors, for none of which Saddam Hussein could claim credit, forced Ayatollah Khomeini to declare a ceasefire – which he compared to drinking a poison chalice – in July 1988. Saddam Hussein, however, deceived himself into believing that he himself was responsible for the victory.

The world, happy at the prospect of Khomeini surrendering, did little to destroy the illusion of the victorious Iraqi leader. By this stage, Saddam Hussein believed that he could achieve any objective as long as he gave clear signals to the West, mainly the United States and Britain, that their interests would be best served, or at least not harmed, if he was to be allowed to carry on with his plans.

On 5th September 1990, in a comment on the Western response to Iraq's invasion of Kuwait, Moroccan writer Abdellatif Laabi wrote in the magazine *Jeune Afrique*, 'Everything which the Arab reality offers that is generous, open and creative is crushed by regimes whose only anxiety is to perpetuate their own power and self-serving interests. And what is often worse is to see that the West remains insensitive to the daily tragedy while at the same time accommodating, not to say supporting, the ruling classes who strangle the free will and aspirations of their people.'

The ending of the Iran–Iraq conflict in theory removed Iran's threat to the Gulf, though this was not reflected in any change in Western policy towards the Middle East. Saddam Hussein was able to expand his influence as well as rebuild his military might after the heavy losses sustained during the war. Moreover, now that the war was over, he had every intention of settling old scores, some of which were of long standing. He decided to combine furthering his ambitions with seeking revenge on those whose support had not been totally wholehearted during the war; invading Kuwait and holding the world oil market to ransom was but one milestone along the road to establishing his dominance of the Arab world.

It is naïve to place all the blame for the 1990 Gulf Crisis on Saddam Hussein. Others, including Middle Eastern and Western powers, should also share the responsibility. 'Who enabled Saddam to survive the war that he started, and armed him to start another one, but the West?' asked Doctor Bahr al-O'loum, a respected Iraqi-born Islamic scholar at the Ahlul Bayit Centre in London.

Historically, politicians and leaders of the Western world have always applied double standards in their definitions of terms like 'legitimate interests' or 'regional stability'. While they argued and discussed the best policies needed to protect British, French or American interests in areas like the Middle East, they ignored legitimate claims of other nations or groupings of nations outside the Western domain. It was not until 1987 and thereafter that 'think-tanks' in the West began to accept the idea that the Soviet Union and the Eastern bloc might also possess 'legitimate interests' in the Gulf. However, the same strategy thinkers and planners have always been reluctant to admit that Third World states also have interests which are to them of equal importance and legitimacy as those of the West.

Intellectuals in the Middle East, whether Arab or Jewish nationalists,

Marxists, Islamic or Jewish fundamentalists, argue that ignoring the legitimate interests of countries in the region has led to a situation in which world stability, as seen by the West, clashes with basic universal concepts like national sovereignty, human rights, freedom of expression or the rights of ethnic minorities.

Almost any region in the Middle East could provide a clear example of how failure to strike a balance between regional and Western interests can lead to disaster. Western policy-makers believe most problems can be resolved by 'maintaining stability' in a region. 'Stability' is the word they use to mean 'preserving the status quo even if it is against the interests of the majority of the people in one country or group of countries'. This falsified argument, believed by the West to the extent that it has supported regimes with appalling records on human rights, has resulted in considerable losses of Western interests in the long term.

The case of the Shah of Iran is one example. Not only did the United States ignore human rights issues in Iran, it also indirectly aided the Shah's regime in suppressing opposition and sowing the seeds for future conflict by supporting him at the expense of his neighbours.

Britain, under the Labour government of Harold Wilson, decided to withdraw from east of Suez. It had neither the ability nor the will to maintain troops in the Gulf. Before they began to implement their plans of withdrawing from the Gulf by December 1971, however, the British expressed the hope that the United States would fill the vacuum. But with the flame in Vietnam burning high Washington was unwilling to commit itself to direct involvement in the Gulf.

President Richard Nixon and Henry Kissinger – the 'modern Machiavelli', as left-wing Arab intellectuals call him – generated the idea of control by proxy; the Shah of Iran would be the new guarantor of the security of the Gulf region and thus ensure stability, secure oil supplies to the West and provide a bulwark against revolutionary changes in the area. He contributed forces, heavily equipped with American arms, as part of the effort to help quell the Dhofar revolution in the sultanate of Oman in the mid-1970s.

As Britain was preparing to evacuate the Gulf, the Shah decided to take over three islands of strategic importance: the Lesser and Greater Tunb, historically part of Ras al-Khaima principality, which later joined the federation of the United Arab Emirates, and Abu Musa, which was the property of the principality of Sharjah, now also part of the UAE. The Shah wanted to add these to another three islands already in his possession: Qeshm, Larak and Hormuz. Together, the six islands form a crescent which covers the entrance to the Straits of Hormuz, the only maritime route for the shipping of oil from the Gulf to the West and Japan. (Iran later found the islands of great strategic value during the Gulf War, deploying Silkworm missiles on them to threaten shipping, and using them as bases from which Revolutionary Guard units attacked tankers and mined the Gulf. Most importantly, however, Iran used the islands, which were beyond the range of Iraqi aircraft, to moor floating barges containing its strategic oil reserves – eighteen days' supply for export.)

On 30th November 1971, the day before the termination of the British treaty with Ras al-Khaima, Iran occupied the uninhabited Lesser Tunb Island and captured Greater Tunb after some fighting. Britain assisted the Shah in securing part-possession of Abu Musa Island in exchange for a promise by Tehran of an annual payment to Sharjah's ruler. Ironically, when Saddam Hussein started the war against Iran in 1980, he wanted to Arabise his crusade. So he added the return of the two Tunb and Abu Musa Islands to 'Arab sovereignty' to his list of demands, at the top of which was sovereignty over the Shatt al-Arab.

The Shah's British-backed move to seize the islands had a snowball effect. It fanned the flames already lit by the Arab nationalist movement on the western side of the Gulf, as it was considered a threat to the national interests of Gulf Arab countries. In April 1972 Baghdad signed a fifteen-year friendship and co-operation treaty with the Soviet Union which included a defence co-operation clause.

Throughout 1970 and 1971, the Iraqi Ba'athists increased their suppression of the Shia religious leaders – whose nationality papers indicated that they were of Iranian origin – and as the propaganda war escalated with Tehran thousands of them were expelled. In order to curry favour with Moscow, the Ba'athists invited the Iraqi communist party to share power in the Progressive National Front government.

The treaty with Moscow was seen by Washington as the means of the Soviet Union securing an advanced post in the region and thus a threat to the status quo in the Gulf. This view was the result of a greater misunderstanding on the part of the United States of the internal and regional situation in almost all the countries of the Gulf. Instead of seeking new channels to explain American policy to Baghdad, President Richard Nixon announced in May 1972 that the Shah could buy any American arms that he required – with the exception of nuclear weapons.

The CIA decided to conduct covert operations against the Ba'ath regime in Baghdad by offering support to the Kurds, who had refused to join the Progressive National Front government coalition, although a Kurdish member of the communist party became a cabinet minister. The

Kurds had renewed their demands for autonomy. With a history of oppression dating back over half a century at the hands of the Iraqis, the Iranians and the Turks, aided by the superpower controlling the region – Britain – the Kurds welcomed the aid from the CIA, who had also made a secret deal with the Shah to aid the rebellion. As a result, the Kurds started a new campaign in the north.

CIA reports on the dangers facing the Shah's regime had meanwhile identified the Soviet-backed communist organisations in Iran as the main threat to the country's stability. It was obviously in the West's interests to ensure that any such threats were continually monitored.

For decades, the West tolerated large-scale suppression by certain regimes of their own ethnic minorities, such as the measures taken by the government of Saudi Arabia against the Shia population in the eastern provinces and the laws passed by the Turkish government against the Kurds, prohibiting any activities which displayed any aspects of Kurdish national culture and forbidding the use of the Kurdish language in public. On numerous occasions the West looked the other way when large ethnic populations suffered aggression and genocide of the kind perpetrated by the Iraqi regime against the Kurds. During the Gulf War, Iraqi forces used chemical weapons against Kurdish guerrillas with the full knowledge of Western diplomats who reported to their foreign ministries.

In fact, the first proven use by Iraq of chemical weapons was reported as early as 1982, when they were used against Iranian troops on the Majnoon Islands in the southern marshes. But it was not until March 1988 that some politicians in the West decided to condemn the use of such weapons, and even then this was due to coincidence rather than to planned policy. On 16th March 1988, only hours before Saddam Hussein gave his approval for the use of hydrogen cyanide and mustard gas against its seven thousand inhabitants, the Kurdish mountain village of Halabja fell into Iranian hands. It was thus subsequently possible for the Iranians to fly Western television camera crews to the village and for the world to see the horrific effects of Iraqi genocide which had resulted in the deaths of over five thousand Kurds, mainly women and children.

When Western interests were at stake, such behaviour was met with only muted condemnation or was simply ignored. Maintenance of the status quo, as long as it was compatible with Western interests, was the main concern. This was the case with Iraq during the Gulf War, Israel in the occupied territories of Palestine and in Lebanon in 1978, 1981 and 1982, and Syria in Lebanon in 1976, 1988 and 1990.

It was against this background of Western double standards that the Iraqis began to implement policies and plans which they believed would secure what they saw as their national interests. This included a massive programme of rearmament, including the acquisition of technology from the West to permit Iraq to develop its own arms industry. In addition, priority was once again given to the development of ballistic missiles as well as chemical and nuclear weapons – all of which were seen as potent factors in any swaying of the balance of power in the Gulf.

A study by the London-based Royal Institute for International Affairs, published in London just a few weeks before the beginning of the Gulf crisis in 1990, classified the interests of the Iraqis as: external and foreign policy; internal security and the survival of the Ba'ath regime; the economy, mainly based on oil; and Saddam Hussein's regional and Arab world aims in relation to his ambition to play a major leading role within the sphere of the Arabic-speaking nations.

However, the writer acknowledged that the nature of the Ba'athist regime and the ambitious designs by its leader had begun, especially since the Gulf War, to project Iraqi interests beyond the limits of legitimacy under international law. This had led to a clash of interests with other nations in the Gulf, posing a threat to its stability and ultimately, because of the region's global importance, to the world as a whole. Ironically, many quarters in the West held the view – perhaps through wishful thinking more than as a result of real observation – that Saddam Hussein, in preserving and securing the national interests of Iraq, would digest the lessons of the Gulf War and concentrate on developing co-operative relations with his neighbours. However, Saddam's unswerving ambition to be the dominant force in the Gulf prevented him from accommodating such hopes.

The barbaric methods used by the Ba'athists against their opponents at home and against Iran during the Gulf War – including genocide – have remained part of their measures to maintain their grip on power. The Baghdad regime has also exploited the hypocrisy of the West, which had previously tolerated such methods, sparing Iraq from condemnation in the United Nations Security Council or at international conferences. In 1989, during a conference in Paris on chemical weapons, many Third World delegates were more interested in purchasing chemical agents from Iraq than they were in condemning the Ba'athist regime for the use of them.

Baghdad's foreign policy concentrated on two avenues, the first leading to security for Iraq against external or externally inspired internal threats. The second involved building bridges with the West in order to establish further trade links, thereby muting any criticism of the regime's oppressive internal measures, while at the same time obtaining much-needed equipment and technology.

Saddam Hussein's decision to turn to the West was made early, even before he started the Gulf War. He intended the ending of the coalition with the communists to be a clear signal to Washington. Halfway through the war, it was obvious that Iraq was securing its place in the Western camp, by purchasing large quantities of weapons, enlisting political support and implementing policies designed to contain the spread of Islamic fundamentalism into friendly nations, namely the Gulf States. Iraq also began to supply arms to the Christian and Arab nationalist militias in Lebanon who were fighting the Iranian- and Syrian-backed Shia groups.

Linking itself to the West and its interests became part of the Baghdad regime's thinking, despite the socialist and Arab nationalist ideologies which it had espoused in the past. The active co-operation between Washington and Baghdad was rendered easier by the effect of the eight years of war on other aspects of Ba'ath party politics which had in the past been anathema to the West, resulting in a decrease in radicalism. By the end of the war, Baghdad had taken a more moderate position on the Palestinian issue. In autumn 1988, the Iraqis were among the first Arab nations to accept PLO chairman Yasser Arafat's newly declared moderate position and his denouncing of terrorism, which helped establish a dialogue with the United States.

It was also recognised that there was an urgent need to effect a reconciliation with Cairo, since it was evident that Iraq would need to obtain military and strategic assistance from Egypt. Up until spring 1990, strong rhetoric was directed only at Syria, the bitter enemy of the Iraqi Ba'athists, while Saddam continued to concentrate on building bridges with Egypt, the West and the moderate Arab countries.

Saddam's domestic policies began to move away from the rigid social-ism previously entrenched in the Ba'athist creed. From early 1987, the year Washington made the commitment to defeat Iran, there was a steady move away from centralised state economic planning. Some American senators and congressmen started to lobby on behalf of Iraq in mid-1987, arguing for the creation of further links with Baghdad and for increases in trade and investment in order to keep Iraq within the Western camp and thus prevent Saddam Hussein from establishing warmer relations with the Soviet Union after the end of the Gulf War.

By November 1987, the Iraqi government was openly praising the American role in escorting convoys of tankers sailing under the Iraqi flag as well as attacking Iranian targets in the Gulf. In a briefing to four British journalists, including one of the authors, Iraq's foreign minister, Tariq Aziz, praised America for its 'positive efforts to keep the military balance in the Gulf'. At the same time, he expressed his disappointment with the Soviet Union's policy, saying, 'If they convince me that they are willing to make Tehran accept the United Nations Security Council Resolution 598, I will take them more seriously.'

Internally, Iraq began to give more opportunities to the private sector as the leadership sought to open the economy to the West. Older members of the Socialist Arab Ba'ath party, who resisted the attempts, were eased out of the party and moved to well-paid posts without real power. In February 1987, new regulations came into effect to encourage the private sector in poultry and meat production. Shareholdings in some sections of the public transport system were sold to the private sector. At the same time, new lists were published to allow the import of more spare parts for vehicles and a project was launched to build some fifteen factories for the production of automotive components. All these changes sent welcome signals to a new pro-Iraqi lobby of American congressmen who sought more political and economic support for Baghdad.

Yet the regime was unwilling, perhaps through its inability to imagine an alternative system of rule, to end the state of fear to which it subjected its populace. By 1990 it had done little to reassure foreign investors that it was on its way to changing its repressive nature. It used chemical weapons on a large scale against Kurdish civilians after the war with Iran had ended, despite arguments that some internal relaxation was essential to improve the image of the regime in the eyes of the outside world.

Active external support for the regime's internal opponents had been one of the main reasons for the eruption of the Gulf War. Both Iraq and Iran used a classic Middle Eastern phrase when accusing the other of 'intervention in domestic affairs'. At the beginning of the conflict, both sides tried to 'liberate' areas on each other's territory. The Ba'ath regime produced slogans to the effect that the war was to liberate the Arab-populated Arabistan areas of south Iran, as well as the two Tunb Islands and the island of Abu Musa. Tehran also called for the liberation of Najjaf, Karbala and the Shia-dominated southern areas of Iraq.

Bearing this in mind, the Ba'athists continued to keep a tight grip on security, both internal and external. In their view any opposition group, regardless of its political persuasion or aims, was an instrument of a foreign enemy.

The war had exposed Iraq's vulnerability as a state composed of different ethnic groups of whom two, the Shia in the south and the Kurds in the north, had at some time or other enjoyed Iran's support or had been allied with it. To maintain internal security and thus ensure its survival, the Ba'ath regime became even less tolerant of these two groups. Defeating the Kurds, who are still seeking their own autonomous state, remained an important item on the Ba'ath list of priorities.

During the Gulf War, a massive security operation of unprecedented size, led by Saddam Hussein's cousin Ali Hassan al-Majid, had been implemented against the Kurds. This included regular sweeps by Iraqi troops, massive bombardments of Kurdish-held areas, the use of chemical weapons, destruction of crops and mass deportations to create free-fire zones as a buffer between the Kurds and the Iranian borders. In the process, Iraq was deprived of orchards that provided more than forty per cent of its fruit, but the policy continued nevertheless – when Ali Hassan al-Majid, Saddam's cousin and Minister of Local Government, was placed in charge of Kuwait soon after the invasion in 1990, his brief was to 'Iraqise' the emirate by repeating the Kurdistan experiment.

Despite the harsh measures of the early and mid-1980s, Kurdish guerrillas continued their resistance. They tied down at least four infantry and armoured divisions of the Iraqi army, numbering some 33,000 troops.

Iran announced its acceptance of United Nations Resolution 598 (demanding a ceasefire and a negotiated settlement) on 18th July 1988. At first light on 19th July, and for the next six weeks, aircraft of the Iraqi air force carried out missions against Kurdish villages and strongholds. Meanwhile, Iraqi troops were engaged in operations against the guerrillas in which over one thousand people were killed. Many guerrillas stood on the tops of hills, helpless as they watched their women and children dying by the dozen in the villages below as Iraqi air force fighter bombers and army helicopters dropped hydrogen cyanide and mustard gas. Over three thousand Kurdish civilians were killed in these attacks. Hundreds of cases of severely burned children were reported by Red Cross doctors visiting refugee camps in Turkey, where over 100,000 Kurds had fled across the borders from Iraqi Kurdistan. Some 20,000 others had taken refuge in Iran.

The 'Arabisation' programme for Kurdistan was subsequently accelerated. Thousands of Kurds were deported from their villages to areas of desert near the borders with Saudi Arabia while their villages were razed to the ground. Meanwhile, new settlements were built in Kurdistan for Arabs coming from other parts of Iraq.

News of the deployment of nerve agents and mustard gas against the Kurds reached Western television screens as United Nations Secretary-General Perez de Cuellar was putting his skills to the test at the commencement of the Iran–Iraq peace talks in Geneva. No one in the

West wanted to see the talks collapse, so nothing was allowed to jeopardise them. The West feared that Iraq, now confident of its military strength, might resume hostilities if it were provoked; once again Saddam Hussein literally 'got away with murder' as the world turned a blind eye. Western interests were perceived as being more important than 'the lives of a few Kurds'.

Only the Western media paid much attention to the story of Iraq's brutality. Arab newspapers either ignored the issue altogether or printed anti-Kurdish articles written by Iraqi officials who praised the 'heroic action' of the armed forces and accused the Kurds of working for Israel. The Kuwaiti press was amongst the most enthusiastic of the Arab media in supporting Baghdad's crusade against the Kurds.

Western diplomats in the region showed little enthusiasm for the evidence obtained by journalists. The same diplomats, who were normally eager to be briefed by journalists coming from the border zone, spoke of the 'need for medical evidence and scientific proof', but did nothing to obtain such proof, despite continuing reports in the Western media. There was one exception: American embassy staff in Ankara interviewed and photographed Kurdish refugees. The CIA presented the US State Department with a report and evidence that Iraq had used chemical weapons.

Only after the most careful weighing up of the situation did Secretary of State George Shulz finally go on record as saying that the United States had the evidence that Iraq had used chemical weapons against Kurdish villages. Again, this intervention was for political rather than ethical or humanitarian reasons and was in line with American interests in the region. The decision was taken that the US had swung too far towards Iraq during 1987 and 1988 and a pretext was needed to redress the balance, if the United States were to continue to play an influential role in the Gulf. But the criticism remained verbal. Attempts by American congressmen to denounce Iraq and apply sanctions against it were bitterly opposed by the Reagan administration.

In September 1988, the Senate Foreign Relations Committee sent two of its members, Peter Galbraith and Christopher Van Hollen, to Turkey. They compiled a report on Saddam Hussein's 'final offensive' against his own Kurdish population. After finding 'overwhelming evidence of extensive use of chemical weapons against civilians', the report concluded that international acquiescence towards previous Iraqi use of chemical weapons had undoubtedly been a major factor in Baghdad's belief that it could use them against the Kurds with impunity.

Senate Foreign Relations Committee Chairman Claiborne Pell intro-

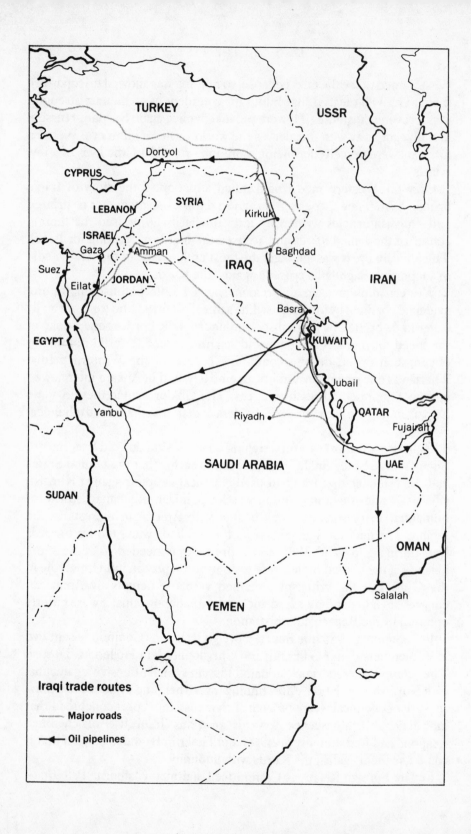

Iraqi trade routes

— Major roads

◄— Oil pipelines

duced the Prevention of Genocide Act 1988. It was passed unanimously. Senator Pell told the Senate: 'While people are gassed, the world is largely silent. There are reasons for this: Iraq's great oil wealth, its military strength, a desire not to upset the delicate negotiations seeking an end to the Iran–Iraq War. Silence, however, is complicity. Half a century ago, the world was silent as Hitler began a campaign that culminated in the near extermination of Europe's Jews. We cannot be silent to genocide again.'

The White House argued that sanctions would be counterproductive. A sanction bill gained the approval of the House of Representatives, but the legislation was dropped in the rush to wind up business in Congress before the 1988 presidential election. Meanwhile, Washington continued to preserve improved relations with Iraq.

To understand the strategic importance of Iraq's claim over Kuwait, in terms of money and an outlet to the sea, one has to examine the development of events that affected Iraqi imports and exports during the Gulf War. One of Iraq's prime strategic objectives in peace or at war is, and always will be, to maintain the production and export of its oil. Its prosperity and strength, regardless of the political persuasion of the ruling regime in Baghdad, depends on its ability to produce large quantities of oil and to export them at the highest price possible.

A few months prior to the start of the Gulf War in 1980, the value of Iraqi crude oil exports had risen fast to over $26 billion per annum. During the early part of the conflict, however, Iraq's ability to export its oil was greatly reduced. Iraqi oil installations at the head of the Gulf were destroyed. Matters were made even worse for Baghdad when, as a result of the intensification of the ideological 'war' with Syria, which had sided with Iran, Damascus closed down the only pipeline to the Mediterranean. Attempts to transport some crude and refined products by tanker truck through Jordan and Turkey proved to be costly and limited the volume of exported oil. Consequently, Iraq's oil exports dropped to 725,000 barrels a day in 1983 compared to 2.5 million barrels a day during the period before the war broke out. This represented a massive fall in earnings of some $16 billion per annum.

Before the war, the main supply route for the vast majority of Iraq's imports and oil exports was through the long and narrow waters of the Gulf. The only port facilities were at Umm Qasar, on the Gulf coastline, and Basra, at the top of the narrow Shatt al-Arab. This route proved to be precarious and insecure, and was closed in the early days of the war.

As its offensive ground to a halt by the end of the first year of the war, and its losses grew, Iraq needed to increase military procurement to avoid a near disastrous defeat. Initially, it drew on its considerable financial reserves. However, it soon had to resort to borrowing and by 1988 Iraq owed the West an estimated $30 billion. Saudi Arabia and Kuwait between them extended loans of over $25 billion, as well as selling the oil extracted from the neutral zone and passing the income to Iraq. Another estimated $15 billion was owed to other Arab countries. Undisclosed sums, believed to be in the region of $10–15 billion, were given by Arab states in the Gulf, not out of good will but because they needed Iraq to continue engaging Iran in war.

In 1988, Iraq's position was strategically boosted when the construction of a second oil pipeline across Turkey was completed, providing a combined pumping capacity of one and a half million barrels per day. A few months earlier, a pipeline laid across Saudi Arabia to Yanbu had also come into operation, with a pumping capacity of half a million barrels per day. By the time the war ended, the diversity of Iraq's supply routes meant that international trade was much more secure.

In mid 1990, Iraqi oil exports were flowing across Turkey and Saudi Arabia, via the new pipelines constructed during the war, and through its oil jetties in the Shatt al-Arab. Imports of heavy machinery and food were coming through four different routes: through Aqaba port in Jordan and overland by trucks; by road transport from Europe via Turkey; via Ahmedy port in Kuwait and overland; and through Saudi ports and overland. The maintenance of these routes meant remaining friendly with Egypt because of the Suez Canal, and establishing some form of 'understanding' with Israel, because of Aqaba, as well as with Kuwait, Turkey, Saudi Arabia and Yemen.

Saddam Hussein's aim should therefore have been to maintain good relations with his neighbours, to make them more appreciative of Iraq's legitimate interests, and to ensure that the pursuit of such interests would not be misinterpreted. However, foreign policy decisions taken in Iraq often rest on aims different from those pursued by other countries. Personal political survival and the pan-Arabist regional ambitions inherent in Ba'athist ideology are frequently the governing factors. Thus, to outsiders, certain decisions taken by the Iraqi dictator have seemed totally illogical.

Up until August 1990, a respectable body of policy-making in the West believed that the diversification of supply routes should, by itself, have made Iraq less interventionist in its regional policy. They were wrong.

THE MAKING OF A
WAR MACHINE

4 · Guarded Secrets

I

'For me it is quite unthinkable that individuals from within the Federal Republic should for motives of profit participate in plans which endanger peace in parts of the world.'

Chancellor Helmut Kohl, 1989

In November 1986, 'X', a former Dutch naval radar specialist who had retired a year previously, was approached by the Dutch navy. They asked if he knew of anyone who would be interested in working on a 'special project' overseas. After volunteering his own services, he was sent to Frankfurt, where he was briefed on his new employment before flying to Iraq. His ultimate destination was the northern city of Mosul. Here he was employed by MBB Transtechnica, a subsidiary of the West German aerospace and armaments giant Messerschmitt-Bolkow-Blohm, in the construction of what he believed to be either a missile base or a facility at which short-range missiles would be assembled.

'X' was employed on a two-year contract during which he worked alongside Germans, Yugoslavs and Americans. He received 200,000 Dutch guilders in payment, returning to Holland every three months for three weeks' leave. On each trip, he flew via Iraqi Airlines and was accompanied by bodyguards who remained with him throughout his time in Holland.

In fact, the installation at which 'X' worked for two years was a missile design and development complex, the construction of which was a highly guarded secret. Called Saad 16, or the Research and Development Centre, it was completed in 1989 and equipped with extensive facilities for the development not only of missiles but also of chemical weapons.

The history of the Iraqi missile development programme had begun two years before 'X' was recruited, in 1984 when Iraq joined forces with Egypt and Argentina to work on the development of a missile. During the late 1970s, the Argentinians had for some time been engaged in the development of a rocket, designated Condor-1 and intended for weather research purposes. They had been assisted in this work by Messerschmitt-Bolkow-Blohm. However, the Argentinians had eventually reached a stage where they discovered that further technical assistance and additional funds were needed. They turned to Egypt for the technology. The Egyptians in turn approached the Iraqis, who were willing not only to participate in the project but also to arrange the required finance, estimated to be in excess of $5 billion. The new joint project, designated Condor-2, would concentrate on the development of a two-stage solid-fuel-powered vehicle possessing a payload capacity of 500kg and a range of approximately 1000km.

Equipment and components were required for the Condor-2 programme and for these the three project partners turned to the West. The list of required items included solid-fuel propellants, inertial guidance and navigation systems, and carbon composite materials for missile nose-cones. Egypt was working on a variety of missiles. Iraq was not only coming in with the cash; it was also providing a test ground in war conditions to try out the missiles. Iranian cities were to be targeted a year later. In addition Egypt acted as a conduit between Baghdad and Buenos Aires through which money, equipment and technology passed.

In 1987, the Iraqis proceeded to set up a procurement network, based upon European companies willing to obtain technology and equipment on their behalf, whilst at the same time assuming a more dominant role in the project and allocating greater financial resources to it. The Iraqi ministry responsible for this was the Technical Corps for Special Projects (Techcorp), a state-owned organisation forming part of the Ministry of Industry and Military Industrialisation. Part of this network consisted of a group headed by the Swiss concern Consen of Zug, which included: Consen SAM and Consen Investment SAM of Monaco; Condor Projekt AG, Consen SA, Ifat Corporation Ltd and Desintec AG of Zug, Switzerland; Delta Consult Gmbh and Delta System Gmbh of Salzburg, Austria; GPA of Munich, West Germany; Transtechno Ltd of Jersey and Transtechno UK Ltd of Britain; Aerotec and Conseltec SA of Buenos Aires, Argentina; and Intesa SA of Córdoba, Argentina. One of the Swiss companies, Ifat Corporation Ltd, had previously been involved in the initial stages of the Condor-1 project in Argentina.

Other companies involved were Messerschmitt-Bolkow-Blohm, which was apparently to supply guidance systems and missile technology; Snia-BPD of Italy, a supplier of rocket motors and fuel; the West German company MAN, which was to manufacture the mobile transporter-erector-launcher for the missile; Sagem of France, which would supply inertial navigation systems; Wegmann, a West German manufacturer of multiple launch rocket systems; and Bofors, the Swedish armaments manufacturer whose role is unknown.

Whilst work on Condor-2 continued in Argentina, carried out by German and Italian technicians at an Argentinian air force establishment near the city of Córdoba, research and development was also carried on in Egypt at a top secret facility outside Cairo known as Factory 17. In 1987, however, Argentina was forced to withdraw from the project because of lack of money and it was left to the Egyptians and Iraqis to continue development of the missile.

The Iraqis decided to improve the capability of the SS-1 Scud-B missiles supplied to them by the Soviet Union. With the assistance of technicians from Egypt, Iraqi engineers were able to modify the missiles by reducing the size of the warheads from 1000kg to 500kg and by increasing the size of the missiles' fuel tanks in such a way that their range was increased from 300km to 600km, sufficient to enable them to reach the Iranian capital, Tehran. The modified Scud-B, designated 'Al Hussein', was subsequently used with devastating effect against Iranian cities in the final stages of the conflict. It was estimated that Iraq used a total of approximately 360 missiles during the Gulf War, launching some two hundred on Iran over a period of forty days between February and April 1988. It was known as the war of the cities. The Iraqi missiles had a devastating effect, mainly psychological, and played a major role in bringing forward the Iranian decision to accept a ceasefire in July 1988.

Iraq also purchased over 120 Badr-2000 missiles from Egypt, subsequently using them, too, to blitz Tehran.. These were also modified Scud-Bs, each with a reduced payload of 275kg and a range of 600km. The Iraqis' use of these missiles enabled the Egyptians to evaluate the efficiency and ultimate effect of the weapons whilst at the same time earning hard currency from their sale. Egypt, then emerging as the second-largest exporter of arms in the Middle East, had foreseen that the missile was the weapon to sway the balance of power in the region. It was this particular weapon that worried most of Iraq's neighbours after Saddam Hussein invaded Kuwait in 1990; they feared that he might use missiles to hit Saudi towns and oil installations. It also presented the allied forces with a dilemma as Saddam threatened to unleash his missiles with chemical warheads against Israel if he was attacked.

The spread of missiles in the Middle East is another major sign of failure of Western, mainly American, foreign policy in the region. Not only was control of missile technology inadequate; so too was the Western resolve to settle the long-standing Arab–Israeli dispute. Inevitably this is seen by Arab states – not without justification – as American bias towards

Israel. Throughout five wars involving the Jewish state – three initiated by Israel in addition to two invasions of Lebanon – the United States ensured that Israel had a more than adequate supply of arms in order to tip the balance in its favour.

It was essentially American technology that enabled Israel to create an advanced air force which could reach all the territories of the member countries of the Arab States League. An air raid on the Palestine Liberation Organisation headquarters in Tunis on 1st October 1985 resulted in the deaths of twenty Tunisian civilians. Meanwhile, the United States Congress continued to block any sale of advanced weapons to even moderate Arab states.

During the early stages of the Gulf War, the Israeli air force destroyed the Iraqi nuclear reactor at Al-Tuwaitha. Soon after this, not only Iraq but also other Arab countries gave missile development programmes the highest priority in order to create a deterrent to balance Israeli superiority in the air. In effect, the Israeli destruction of the Iraqi nuclear facilities and its air raids on other parts of the Arab world started the missile race in the Middle East.

In 1987, following further modifications which had increased its range to 800km, the Egyptians shipped three missile kits, including a prototype Condor-2, to Iraq for trial use against the Iranians. Whilst this enabled the Egyptians to evaluate its performance, it also furnished the Israeli intelligence service, Mossad, with the proof which it had been seeking for four years – that the Egyptians had been collaborating with the Argentinians to produce a missile with a range of 1000km. The Israelis knew that this would be of particular concern to the British as the weapon would be able to reach the Falkland Islands if launched from the Argentinian mainland.

Israel passed photographs and information to the CIA on the Egyptian shipment of three missile kits of which one was a Condor-2 to be assembled and tried in Iraq. However, the Americans did not pass the information on to Britain until three months later. When Washington finally did so, there was resentment in London that it had not been given it earlier. Subsequently, Britain raised the matter with the Egyptians, who denied that they were assisting the Argentinians to develop missiles.

As a result, Britain pushed forward with an agreement which it had drafted, called the Missile Technology Control Regime (MTCR). It was signed by Britain, the United States, France, West Germany, Italy, Canada and Japan in an attempt to curb the spread of missile technology to the Third World. The agreement obliged signatories to exercise control in their own country of exports of equipment and technology which could be used in the manufacture of ballistic missiles. Despite this, there was little response from countries, including Egypt, which had already benefited from technology acquired from the West. It was known, for example, that propellants and guidance systems supplied by Messerschmitt-Bolkow-Blohm were being modified by the Egyptians and exported to Iraq and Argentina.

During the first half of 1988, the Egyptians supplied the Iraqis with approximately sixteen prototype Condor-2s for test launches against Iranian targets. These were reported to have reached ranges of between 675 and 1000km, carrying payloads of 500kg.

In 1987, 'a friendly' intelligence source informed the Mukhabarat that Israel had plans to knock out strategic military production sites and carry out major sabotage against the Iraqi missile programme. The source of this information was the Saudi Arabian intelligence service which is known to employ former members of Britain's Secret Intelligence Service. However, unbeknownst to the Iraqis, the Saudis themselves were also entering the missile race.

During the second half of 1987, the Saudis purchased from China over one hundred CSS-2 long-range ballistic missiles with a maximum range of over 1500 miles. However, their method of doing so caused a row between London, Washington and Riyadh. The Americans were informed by the Saudis that they were acquiring a short-range version of the HY-2 Silkworm coastal-defence missile from China for supply to the Iraqis. Washington sanctioned the deal because it was in line with its policy of aiding the Baghdad regime in its war against Iran. The individual responsible for organising the deal with China was Prince Bandar bin Sultan, the Saudi Arabian ambassador in Washington, who is considered by the White House to be a close friend of the United States.

Arrangements were made for the 'Silkworms' to be transported by sea from China to Yanbu in Saudi Arabia, from where they would be transported by road to Iraq. An American spy satellite observed the passage of the missiles, which were being delivered in a number of consignments, and registered nothing unusual. During the day, under the watchful eye of the American satellites, the missile transporters moved slowly north. As soon as darkness had fallen, however, the convoys carried out a swift U-turn and headed at high speed to Al-Rab'e al-Khali, in the desert not far from the borders with the Sultanate of Oman, where the missiles were assembled and installed in silos already prepared for them.

It was by pure chance that the United States discovered the existence of the silos after careful examination of satellite photographs. The Americans were assured by Prince Bandar bin Sultan that the silos were in fact parts of an ordinary ammunition depot. It was not until a year later, in early 1988, that they finally discovered the full facts. Meanwhile the British, whose GCHQ listening posts in Oman had monitored the Saudis' activities, had known about the missiles but had not informed the Americans. There was subsequent speculation that this was in mild retaliation for the latter not having informed London sooner of Argentina's Condor-2 missile programme.

Eventually, the Americans accepted King Fahd's word that he would not place 'weapons of mass destruction' in the warheads of his missiles. This was perhaps the only time that the 'Jewish lobby' in the United States did not have its way, but there was little it could do. In any case, Israel was later given all the necessary assistance to develop its Arrow anti-ballistic shield system.

During 1988, the Iraqis announced that they had developed and tested a second modified version of the Scud-B missile. Designated 'Al Abbas', it had a smaller warhead of 300kg and a further increased range of 900km. This caused considerable concern in London where it was rapidly assumed that the source of technology for this weapon was Egypt.

During a visit to Britain in September 1988 by President Mubarak, the subject of Egypt's missile programme, and in particular the Condor-2, was raised by Prime Minister Margaret Thatcher. She was reported to have made her feelings very clear on the matter. The Egyptians at that time were seeking Britain's support in two areas: firstly, to back Egypt in its difficulties with the International Monetary Fund over rescheduling of some of its massive debts; secondly, to accept an Egyptian plan to persuade PLO chairman Yasser Arafat to denounce terrorism, to declare an independent Palestinian state in exile and to recognise Israel's right to exist.

It was reported at the time that Mubarak promised Mrs Thatcher that Egypt would withdraw from the joint missile project. The Gulf War had already ended and Iraq was seriously behind with repayment of considerable sums of money owed to Cairo.

In June 1989, when President Mubarak visited Britain again, Margaret Thatcher once more expressed concern about Egypt's continued involvement in the Condor-2. However, Egyptian officials assured their British counterparts that Egypt had severed its connections with the project.

The world paid little attention to Saddam Hussein's missile programme until September 1989, when the *Independent* revealed details of the huge explosion which destroyed the missile solid-fuel plant at Al-Hillah, south of Baghdad, when some seven hundred people were killed, including many Egyptian technicians. It took the Iraqis months to recover

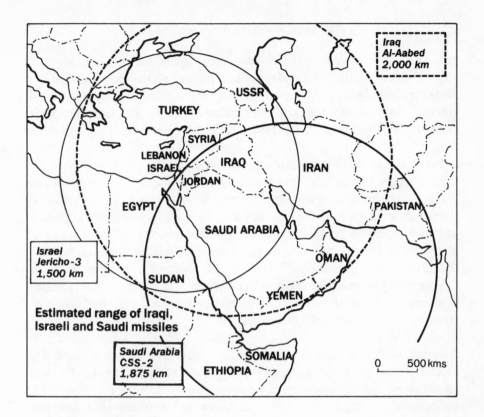

Estimated range of Iraqi,
Israeli and Saudi missiles

Iraq
Al-Aabed
2,000 km

Israel
Jericho-3
1,500 km

Saudi Arabia
CSS-2
1,875 km

0   500 kms

from the explosion. Despite heavy press coverage of the incident, no alarm was raised and Western governments did nothing to bring pressure to bear on Baghdad.

On 5th December 1989, the Iraqis launched a three-stage rocket designed to carry a satellite. Designated Tammuz-1, it was launched from the space centre at Al-Anbar. According to subsequent reports, only the first stage of the rocket was tested, the second and third stages being dummies. It was also reported that it was liquid-fuelled, with the first stage consisting of five Scud-B boosters fastened together. Later in the same month, the Iraqis claimed that they had also tested an intermediate-range ballistic missile, referred to as 'Al Aabed', which had a range of 2000km. It is believed that this missile is similar to Tammuz-1 and is a development of the 'Al Abbas', being a three-stage type carrying a 750kg payload and powered by five Scud-B boosters.

A further development took place in November 1990 when the Iraqis announced that they had successfully tested yet another missile. Designated 'Al Hijara', it was reported as having been launched over a distance of 1200km at the Iraqis' test range in Mauritania. The Iraqis' claim that its maximum range was 2000km put Western intelligence experts on their guard, because such a capability would have made the missile a threat to allied warships in the Gulf and to ground forces in Saudi Arabia. The US Defense Intelligence Agency took the announcement seriously and voiced its opinion that the Iraqis were more advanced than had previously been thought and that the 'Al Hijara' might have been put into production.

Iraq has invested heavily in missile research and development. With the help of technology, equipment and components acquired from the West, it has also been able to develop other weapons, such as the 'Al Ababil' short-range surface-to-surface missile. This weapon carries a cluster munition warhead containing two hundred bomblets and has a range of thirty-five miles. It is reported to have been used during the final stages of the Gulf War. The Iraqis have been conducting a number of such development programmes requiring extensive and sophisticated facilities in which the necessary research and development can be carried out. The construction of such facilities has been another area of heavy investment.

The main Iraqi missile research and development centre is Saad 16, located outside Mosul in the north of the country. The centre was constructed in strict secrecy by a consortium of European companies. Completed in 1989, its highly extensive and sophisticated facilities include two 12-metre supersonic wind tunnels capable of simulating speeds up to three times the speed of sound. These were designed by the Austrian company AVL and constructed by Aviatest of West Germany, a subsidiary of the armaments manufacturer Rheinmetall. Other facilities include a 120-metre underground firing range, laboratories for electronic and chemical developments, missile test bays, test monitoring laboratories, control rooms and climatic test chambers. The entire complex is very heavily guarded, being surrounded by a perimeter fence equipped with electronic sensors and closed circuit television. Watchtowers are positioned at intervals along the fence and Daimler Benz Unimog trucks, equipped with surveillance equipment, patrol the entire area.

Overall responsibility for the design and construction of Saad 16 lay with an Austrian firm of consultant engineers, Consultco of Vienna. In turn, Consultco sub-contracted the actual building of the base to several Austrian companies, including Hutter & Schrantz, Grazer Construction and installation engineers Swatek & Cerny. Overall management of equipping the base was in the hands of the West German company Gildemeister Projecta of Bielefeld, but the main contractor for supply of equipment and technology was MBB-Transtechnica, the subsidiary of Messerschmitt-Bolkow-Blohm.

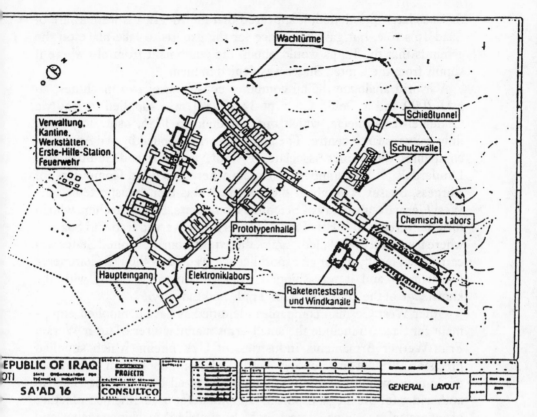

Layout of the Saad 16 missile and chemical weapon research and development centre

The equipment for Saad 16 was supplied from sources in the West. In 1986, a shipment consisting of $1 million worth of analogue computers and electronic test and measurement equipment was supplied by Hewlett Packard to Iraq under a US government-supplied export licence. These are known to have been installed in the Saad 16 missile development complex. Hewlett Packard subsequently claimed that it had been unaware that the computers were intended for military use.

Tektronix, a major US manufacturer of electronic test equipment, supplied more than $50,000 worth of electronic test equipment to Gildemeister Projecta, whilst in 1986 another American manufacturer of test equipment, Wiltron, supplied a scalar network analyser for testing microwave communications. In both cases, export of the equipment was carried out legally under export licences issued by the US government after clearance had been granted by the National Security Council. When this was later questioned, it appeared that the Americans were aware of Saad 16's role, but gave clearance for the exports to take place on the grounds that the Iraqis would obtain the equipment from elsewhere if supply from the United States was denied to them.

A hybrid analogue digital computer consisting of two machines, an EAI 2000 and a Gould Concept 32/2705/1, was supplied to Iraq via Gildemeister Projecta, which ordered them in 1986, ostensibly for a university research centre. The computer was supplied by two American companies, Electronics Associates (EAI) of New Jersey and Gould of Fort Lauderdale. It was shipped to Britain where Scientific Computers, of Burgess, Sussex, assembled the system. It was then transported to the West German subsidiary of Scientific Computers, EAI of Aachen, who in turn delivered it to MBB-Transtechnica for delivery to Iraq and Saad 16 where it was finally installed. Again, the export from the United States was carried out legally under an export licence granted by the US Commerce Department and it was shipped from Britain to Germany with the knowledge of the Department of Trade and Industry.

Other West German companies identified as having supplied equipment for Saad 16 include the small-arms manufacturer Mauser Werke; Fritz Werner Armaments-Industries, of Geisenheim, which supplied precision drilling machinery; Karl Kolb, a supplier of laboratory equipment, which is currently being prosecuted by the West German authorities for the illegal export of equipment for use in the manufacture of chemical weapons; Voest, which supplied machine tools; and Messerschmitt-Bolkow-Blohm, which supplied a complete meteorological station including balloons, parachutes, wind and temperature measuring instruments and a radio station complete with a computer and the relevant software. Other companies included Carl Zeiss of Baden-Württemberg, which supplied equipment, and Degussa of Stuttgart, which was involved in the general management of Saad 16.

A web of West German, Swiss and Austrian companies formed a link between Saad 16 and the Condor-2 project. This was confirmed by evidence obtained by the West German magazine *Profil*, consisting of copies of telexes sent between Gildemeister Projecta and a company named Induplan Chemicals of Salzburg, Austria. These telexes were reported as referring to training courses in 'explosives analysis', which Gildemeister Projecta wished the Austrian company to conduct. Induplan Chemicals, subsequently renamed Bowas Induplan, was a company specialising in the construction of chemical plants. It was owned by the Von Bohlen and Halbach families, who also owned two other companies,

Bohlen Industrie of Essen and Bohlen International SA of Luxemburg, former parent companies of Consen, which headed the group involved in Project 395, the Iraqi missile development programme.

During the Condor-2 project, Induplan Chemicals supplied plans for the construction of a fuel plant. Until 1984, its managing director was a sixty-two-year-old Bavarian named Helmut Raiser who subsequently became head of the Consen organisation. In 1984, Raiser left Induplan Chemicals together with two other employees, Werner Schoffel and Ludwig Anmayr. The latter became managing director of Delta Consult Gmbh, formed in Salzburg in 1984 and part of the Consen group, whilst Schoffel became the company's attorney. The majority shareholder in Delta Consult was another company in the Consen group, Ifat Corporation Ltd, in which Helmut Raiser appeared again as a major figure.

Connections with another company, Tencom Ltd, were also established when it was discovered that its joint managing director and attorney were Ludwig Anmayr and Werner Schoffel respectively. The other joint managing director was identified as Frau Francine Painthiauz-Schmidt, wife of a senior Messerschmitt-Bolkow-Blohm technical expert, Hermann Schmidt. A link with another company named PBG Project Consultancy Ltd, based in Freising, Bavaria, was also shown. Apart from the fact that Werner Schoffel was also this company's attorney, a minority shareholder proved to be Delta Consult.

Another company with a similar name, Delta Systems, featured Ludwig Anmayr as its attorney whilst its joint managing directors were Adolf Hammer and Ekkehard Schrotz, both former senior engineers with Messerschmitt-Bolkow-Blohm and both formerly involved in the Condor project. In May 1988, Schrotz's car was blown up in Monte Carlo. A group claiming to be Iranian and calling itself the 'Guardians of Islam' admitted responsibility. It gave the reason for the attack as the fact that Schrotz was involved in sales of missiles to Iraq. Schrotz disappeared for a while after this incident but then re-emerged as joint managing director of Delta Systems.

Britain first became aware of the Saad 16 project when a senior consultant employed by a leading British aviation company made two visits to Iraq in December 1989 and one in February 1990 to advise on advanced aerodynamics. According to testimony given to the authors, he saw evidence in the offices, the laboratories and the missile booster testing tunnels which left him in no doubt as to the role of the complex.

Between his visits to Iraq, the consultant discussed problems which had occurred with the Saad 16 wind tunnels with Aircraft Research Association in Bedford, which is frequently used by the Ministry of Defence's

Royal Aircraft Establishment for testing their models. He also raised the matter with another firm, APECS, a consultancy service set up in 1983 by Leo Townend, a former employee of the Royal Aircraft Establishment, and his partner, who is also expert in ultrasonic dynamics. Although ARA informed the Ministry of Defence about the Iraqi requests, no action was taken. As he received no advice from the Ministry of Defence or the Foreign Office, the consultant said it was not for him to pass judgement on what the Iraqis were doing with their equipment. Subsequently, he returned to Baghdad in February 1990.

Circumstantial evidence suggests that British officials had little or no information about Iraq's missile programme or whether British firms and technical experts were involved with it. When British firms sought export licences or volunteered information, as in the case of ARA, no action was taken by the appropriate government departments. After the return of two British consultants from Baghdad, including the one mentioned above, one of the authors published a detailed account, in the *Independent* of 3rd March 1990, of the trouble facing the Iraqis with their missiles and their inability to test the boosters. The reasons for their difficulties were quoted as being 'cracks in the testing blocks' built by the Germans, as well as the fact that Baghdad had sought assistance from two British aerodynamics experts to correct the supersonic airflow in their wind tunnels. Two weeks later, an officer of the Secret Intelligence Service was lunching with old friends, including a journalist from the *Independent on Sunday*. 'By the way,' said the SIS officer to the journalist, 'I don't suppose Darwish would tell you the names of the two consultants who went to Iraq, would he?'

One major problem which faced the Iraqis was the lack of space in which long-range trials of missiles could be carried out. In May 1990, however, it appeared that they had found the solution to this problem: it was revealed that Iraqi engineers had commenced constructing missile test facilities in Mauritania. This information emanated from the United States whose satellites had detected early stages of construction work in a remote part of the country.

Close relations between Iraq and Mauritania were established in 1989 when Saddam Hussein supported the Mauritanian ruler, Colonel Muawiya Ould Sidi Ahmed Taya, in his dispute with Senegal over the border between the two countries. It was no doubt as a token of his appreciation that Muawiya permitted the Iraqis to establish a missile test range in one of his country's vast areas of desert. Needless to say, this development in the Iraqi missile test programme sounded further alarm bells in Washington, London and Tel Aviv.

With so much effort and investment being put into missile research and development, the question then arises as to where the weapons would be put into production. The answer is to be found in 'Project DOT'.

In 1986, an Ifat Corporation representative approached the Vienna-based company Consultco about a project in Iraq codenamed DOT. Another firm of consultants already co-operating with Ifat Corporation was the Austrian firm Feneberg, based in Graz, which had also been involved in the Condor-1 project in Argentina and a similar programme in Egypt. The latter, codenamed RS-120, was a project to develop a short-range missile with a range of 120km. Consultco, which was already working for the Iraqis in the role of project management of the construction of Saad 16, was told that DOT was similar to two other projects already in existence in Argentina and Egypt. The Iraqi government agency responsible for DOT was the State Organisation for Technical Industries (SOTI).

The DOT project involved the construction in Iraq of three complexes, codenamed DO1, DO2 and DO3 respectively. DO1 was to be a missile fuel research and production centre located near the town of Al-Hilla, 50km south of Baghdad, whilst DO2 would be established as an engineering production facility near the town of Fallujah. DO3 would consist of a missile test range situated some 95km south of Baghdad near the city of Karbala.

Consultco, in co-operation with two other Austrian companies, submitted a quotation, but the price was too high. The Iraqis then commenced construction of the three complexes with local labour under the supervision of Feneberg, the Graz-based firm of engineering consultants. However, some installation work was carried out by European companies such as BBC Brown Boveri of Mannheim, West Germany, which was responsible for electrical installations. Other companies supplied equipment, although certain items were provided by the Egyptians, who had at that time almost completed a similar project of their own, codenamed DOS. These included a computerised control system for DO1 which had originally been supplied to Egypt by the West German company Siemens.

In November 1988, whilst attending a summit meeting in the United States, Chancellor Helmut Kohl was confronted with secret information and satellite photographs which provided irrefutable evidence of participation by West German companies in the Iraqi missile programme. This material had in fact been given initially to his Foreign Minister Hans Dietrich Genscher by US Secretary of State George Shulz.

During the previous five years, the West German government had received over one thousand reports from Washington of the involvement of West German companies in armaments projects in several parts of the world, including the Middle East, South America, Asia, and the Far East. These projects were in the main concerned with the development and production of long-range missiles and chemical weapons.

In 1989, American satellites photographed the Libyan chemical weapons factory at Rabta. Close inspection of the photographs revealed an additional complex, which American experts are almost certain is a missile production facility. A report from the US Arms Control and Disarmament Agency states that the Libyan missile has a range of 500km and that it is of 'West German design'. This evidence is supported by reports in the British media which stated that one hundred West German technicians were working on the Libyan missile project. These reports were investigated by a West German public prosecutor and at least one company was summoned before the courts for illegal export to Libya of valve control mechanisms for use in missile production.

Until 1989, West German companies had few obstacles to becoming involved in such projects. It was not until October of that year that a law was passed requiring West German technicians to obtain an official licence to work abroad. Efforts by the Social Democratic party in the Bundestag to persuade the government to tighten the law further so as to forbid the participation of German nationals in projects involving the production of chemical weapons and missiles met with the following comment from Count Lambsdorff, the former head of the Federal Economic Ministry, which is responsible for the control of exports and technology and equipment: 'If your conception of legality got a look-in, then in all probability my late brother-in-law, who helped the Americans get on to the moon, would have been punished and put in prison . . . It is well known that missiles can be used for peaceful purposes: for example, satellites can be sent up. Evil things, as you call them, can also be carried by them.'

This statement is disturbing when one bears in mind the office which Lambsdorff had previously held. During the period of his tenure at the Federal Economic Ministry, missiles were being developed in Brazil, Argentina, Egypt, Iraq, Pakistan, Libya and South Africa – all with the assistance of West German companies.

As has already been mentioned, it was only as a result of pressure from the Americans that the German government in 1985 brought pressure to bear on Messerschmitt-Bolkow-Blohm to withdraw from the Argentinian Condor-1 project. In the following year, further complaints from the

Americans about continuing West German involvement prompted the company's board to 'discover' that Argentina was still developing the missile with the assistance of West German technicians, many of whom were allegedly 'former employees'. In 1989, as the result of a parliamentary question by the Social Democratic party, the government made a statement admitting that, in 1985, a West German company had been involved, together with the government's own Research Institute for Air and Space Travel, in carrying out wind tunnel tests on a model of an Argentinian two-stage rocket codenamed 'Vector'. This project was subsequently renamed 'Condor'.

In 1985, when Egypt and Iraq joined the Condor project, equipment for so-called 'research purposes' was exported by a subsidiary of Messerschmitt-Bolkow-Blohm. The company encountered no difficulty, the export licence application having stated that the equipment was required for a satellite project. Two years previously, the company had sold the Egyptians a multi-sensor platform for testing rocket trajectories. In 1985, it sold another to the South Africans, supposedly for use in meteorological research – at the same time that Pretoria was purchasing West German plans for the construction of submarines which were to be equipped as missile carrying vessels.

In 1988, one of Messerschmitt-Bolkow-Blohm's subsidiaries, MBB-Transtechnica, supplied the Egyptians with three consignments of laboratory equipment. Messerschmitt-Bolkow-Blohm itself had been approached previously by Ifat Corporation concerning the Egyptian RS-120 project, but had agreed to carry out only some of the required work because of concern about West German export restrictions. As a result, the rest had been undertaken by the Italian company SNIA, a subsidiary of Fiat. The West German government's foreign trade ministry had initially approved the deal with SNIA, but in December 1987 the West German security services had recommended that Messerschmitt-Bolkow-Blohm should sever its connections with the project. In addition, the company had been made aware that it might become subject to American blacklisting unless it withdrew.

Accordingly, in early 1988, Messerschmitt-Bolkow-Blohm stopped co-operating with the Egyptians on its missile projects, using the excuse that it had only just discovered that the Egyptians were involved in research and development for military purposes. However, as has already been stated, the Consen Group, which took over the role of masterminding the procurement of technology and equipment for the Condor-2 project, included many former senior employees of Messerschmitt-Bolkow-Blohm amongst the management of its companies, as well as a large number of technicians signed up after the latter's withdrawal.

In November 1990, it was reported that the Consen Group was being liquidated. As a result of exposure by the media, the Zug-based parent company, Consen, had been liquidated earlier in 1990, whilst Ifat Corporation, which played a central role in recruiting companies for the Saad 16 project, was liquidated at the end of the year. Other subsidiaries, including Delta Consult, Delta Systems and the French-based company Tema, also went into liquidation.

It appears that the West German government turned a blind eye to the matter of German participation in overseas armaments projects until 1987, when Iraq began using missiles against Iran. It was apparent to experts with detailed knowledge of the Iraqi missile armoury that the ranges at which the missiles were being used were far in excess of the capability of the Scud-B known to have been supplied to Baghdad. Extensive modifications had obviously been carried out and these would only have been possible with expert technical assistance. The German government thus took the step of refusing export licence applications for any further exports of technology and equipment related to missile production. However, this measure did not deter West German companies from continuing their involvement in the Iraqi missile programme. Elsewhere, West German firms continue to be involved in similar projects in India, Pakistan, South Africa and Brazil. This is despite the fact that the first three have been reported as being on the threshold of possessing nuclear weapons. West German export regulations are such that there are gaps and grey areas which have been used to advantage by certain companies seeking to bypass export controls.

There were two aspects of the federal government's past behaviour which puzzled, and in some cases alarmed, those who had been keeping a close watch on West German commercial participation in overseas armaments programmes. Firstly, when the Missile Technology Control Regime (MTCR) was signed in 1987, the agreement was never publicised by the German federal government – although the other signatories proclaimed it as a major event. The information was apparently limited to elements in the West German aerospace industry and major research establishments within the republic. Under the terms of the MTCR, the export of equipment and technology was not banned and could be permitted under West German law. For some reason, the federal Customs authorities were provided with the minimum amount of information, as were the Bundestag parliamentary committees concerned with such matters, and thus it was impossible to increase the effectiveness of export controls.

Secondly, until June 1984, West Germany was forbidden by a West European Union agreement to manufacture missiles which possessed a range of more than 70km. This restraint was lifted after the government had complained that it was 'discriminating'. At the time, Foreign Minister Hans Dietrich Genscher made a statement to the Western European Union, justifying the removal of the restriction: 'The lifting of these legal requirements is really more than a case of the obvious. It is necessary to assure our co-operation. Whether we are allowed to do something or whether we do it are two different things. But we want to be allowed to do it. Whether we do it is quite another question. It will in no way influence the arms export policy of the Federal Republic of Germany.'

The Social Democratic party immediately demanded a total ban on commercial trade and exports of equipment and technology related to the production of missiles. The federal government dragged its feet, relegating the matter to parliamentary committees for study and discussion. This situation continued for two years until June 1986, when the government refused to implement such a measure. As observers noted at the time, it was during this two-year period that the West German armaments industry was particularly active in missile development programmes overseas.

The West German government has always refused to publish statistics and details concerning arms exports. However, assessments made in 1989 by the US Arms Control and Disarmament Agency state that West Germany had moved up from seventh to fourth place in the world league of arms suppliers. After the many warnings from the United States and from the West German Federal Intelligence Service, it is inconceivable that the government was not fully aware, from the very beginning, of the involvement of West German companies in missile development programmes in countries which have highly dubious motives for acquiring such a capability.

II

It was early in the morning on 25th August 1988 that eight-year-old A'agiza saw Iraqi aircraft approaching the Kurdish village of Aikmala where she lived in north-eastern Iraq. As she watched, she saw bombs dropping from them. Instead of the normal loud explosions, however, yellow clouds of smoke were formed. A few seconds later, the villagers of Aikmala started to fall to the ground dying as they unsuspectingly inhaled the foul-smelling smoke which drifted through the village. A'agiza watched, mystified, as her parents and brother died before her eyes – blood coming from their mouths as their skins slowly blackened. Elsewhere in the village, others crouched in their homes and died as the mustard gas and hydrogen cyanide nerve agent filtered in and asphyxiated them.

A'agiza was one of the few survivors of the attack on Aikmala. With the remaining members of the village, she later made her way painfully over the mountains into south-eastern Turkey. As she did so, her small body was racked by severe coughing, vomiting, internal bleeding and diarrhoea whilst her skin was covered in painful blisters.

During that last week in August 1988, another seventy Kurdish villages were attacked from the air with chemical weapons. In the Bassay Valley alone, two hundred families were reported as having been wiped out. During the following three weeks, four hundred and fifty more villages were destroyed. It has been estimated that three thousand out of a total of four thousand villages were razed to the ground by the Iraqis.

The story of Iraq's development of 'Aslihatul Dammar Ashammel' – translated literally as 'weapons of mass destruction' – starts in 1974 with the formation of a three-man committee headed by Saddam Hussein, who was then vice-president of Iraq. The other two members of the committee were Vice-Premier Adnan Hamdani and Chief of Staff General Adnan Khairallah, who was Saddam's cousin and brother-in-law. The decision to pursue the development of chemical weapons came as a result of their wish for military parity with Israel, which has on a number of occasions refused to join the Non-Proliferation Treaty that exists to prevent the spread of nuclear weapons. At that time, the Iraqis, who had yet to start their own nuclear weapon development programme, felt that chemical weapons could offer a viable deterrent against Israeli attack.

To assist it in this task, the committee engaged the services of a Beirut-based consultancy called Arab Projects and Developments (APD). This was a Palestinian non-profit-making organisation sponsored by construction magnates Kamel Abdel Rahman and Hasib Sabbagh. APD was formed to help Arab countries with their development plans and policies, thus enabling the Palestinian people to repay their Arab brothers for supporting them in their unending struggle against Israel.

Rahman and Sabbagh were both close friends of the Palestine Liberation Organisation chairman Yasser Arafat and were heavily committed to the idea that Palestinian abilities and talents could do much for the Arab Nation. It was with their solid support that APD eventually expanded to become a four hundred-strong organisation staffed by highly talented

Palestinians. It was involved in a number of projects in Arab countries, including reclamation of land, construction of railways, development of plans to allow Arab states to become self-sufficient in sugar and development in areas of high technology, including the Arab Satellite Project.

In 1975, after studying the Iraqi requirements, although it had no previous experience in the field of armaments, APD recommended to the committee that the initial requirement for the creation of a development programme, aimed at producing weapons capable of giving Iraq military parity with Israel, was the recruitment of the necessary technical expertise. Because Iraq did not already possess this, APD recommended that a major effort should be made to recruit suitably qualified Arab scientists, technicians and engineers from wherever they were working in countries throughout the world.

Saddam Hussein and his committee accepted APD's recommendations. Between 1974 and 1977, despite misgivings on the part of some individuals within APD, over four thousand Arab nuclear scientists, chemists, chemical engineers and other technically qualified personnel were recruited. They included Iraqis, Egyptians, Moroccans, Palestinians, Algerians, Syrians and Arabs of other nationalities. They arrived in Iraq from America, Canada, Britain, Brazil and a host of other countries, bringing with them their knowledge and expertise in the fields of nuclear physics, chemistry, biological research and other related sciences.

APD had used a twofold method of recruitment when approaching a prospective candidate. They appealed to his pocket by offering twice as much money as he was being paid in his current employment, reinforcing this with added incentives such as a car and free housing; and to his patriotic sentiments towards the Arab Nation by extolling the honour of taking part in such an all-Arab programme which was ultimately aimed against Israel.

There is reason to believe that the governments of the United States, Britain, France and Israel were well aware of what was happening. The movement of a large number of Arabs, very highly qualified in such sophisticated areas of science, must have triggered alarm bells amongst the intelligence services in the West and the Middle East, inevitably leading to a 'comparing of notes' amongst some of them and conclusions being drawn accordingly. The reason behind the West's lack of action to disrupt or halt the Iraqi recruitment programme has never been clarified but there were two factors which possibly contributed to it. During that period, the Cold War still divided East and West, and Iraq was the Soviet Union's principal protégé in the Middle East. Any protest from the West would almost inevitably have fallen on deaf ears. The second, more sinister, factor is that the West was at that time actively attempting to loosen the ties between the Soviet Union and Iraq, lessening the latter's dependence on Moscow through arms sales. In other words, the West was taking risks in the long term for the sake of political expediency.

Once the recruitment programme was complete, APD made further recommendations – including one that Iraq should concentrate initially on the development of chemical and biological weapons, because the technology was simpler to acquire and master than that required for nuclear devices. Saddam Hussein, who had by then executed Adnan Hamdani, one of his two fellow committee members who had grown too popular for comfort, accepted this recommendation, but insisted that development in the nuclear field should still continue in parallel with the simpler chemical and biological efforts. APD personnel were subsequently sent to America, France, Canada and Britain to obtain the required equipment and technology.

Blueprints for the construction of the first Iraqi chemical warfare plant were provided by Pfaulder Corporation of Rochester, New York. Despite the fact that the drawings were described as 'flow charts for a pesticide plant', even a novice would have recognised that the chemicals it was supposed to produce – Amition, Demeton, Paraoxon and Parathion – could be used to manufacture nerve agents. Early in 1978, the US government refused to grant Pfaulder a licence to export the machinery for building the plant, but the Iraqis managed to acquire the single most important component – the drawings and technical specifications. Subsequently, the Iraqis turned to European companies to build the plant and attempted to obtain co-operation by amending their usual trading practices – they announced that the construction contract would be negotiated rather than being open to tender.

Companies contacted by APD and its intermediaries included ICI and Babcock & Wilcox of Britain, Montedison of Italy and Ferrostahl of West Germany. ICI was sufficiently perturbed by the Iraqi requirement to inform the Foreign Office, but the other companies were apparently interested in participating in the project. Although the British government took no known action, the Iraqis somehow learned of ICI's warning to the Foreign Office. As a result, they changed their approach to constructing their own chemical weapon production facilities. They decided to construct the plant themselves and thus resorted to purchasing equipment and components from several companies under the pretext of constructing a pesticide production factory.

Several European companies, deceived by this ploy, assisted in the project. Thus, Iraq's first and somewhat crude chemical warfare plant, with a production capacity of two thousand tons per year, was built in early 1979 near the town of Akashat in the north-western part of Iraq which borders with Syria and Jordan. The facility itself cost $50 million, with safety and protective equipment costing an additional $10 million – the protective clothing used by workers in the plant was obtained from Britain under an export licence granted by the Department of Trade and Industry. How this particular purchase was effected, one of the last before production of the chemicals commenced, is not totally clear, but the first British companies approached to supply protective suits were the textiles giant Courtaulds and a Midlands-based company named SOS.

In 1979, APD was closed down when it lost its Beirut base. However, the scientists whom it had recruited for Iraq were still attached to the defence ministry and they continued to form the nucleus of Iraq's determined effort to develop chemical and biological weapons. By that time, the Ibn Al Haitham Institute, a highly secret establishment engaged in 'strategic scientific projects', had been founded and it is believed that many of the specialists recruited by APD were also employed there.

Of the three members of the committee, only Saddam Hussein himself is still alive. In 1989, Adnan Khairallah was killed in a helicopter crash in which Saddam Hussein's hand was suspected as having played a part.

Having begun construction of the first of several chemical production plants, and recruited a large number of technical personnel, Iraq also needed a supply of considerable quantities of chemicals. Once again, it turned to Western industry. In July 1983, five hundred tons of thiodiglycol, a component of mustard gas, were purchased at a cost of approximately £500,000 by KBS Holland BV from a Belgian subsidiary of Phillips Petroleum USA on behalf of the Iraqi State Enterprise for the Production of Pesticides (SEPP). A second, much larger order for 500 tons of thiodiglycol, 200 tons of trimethyl phosphite, 250 tons of phosphorus oxychloride and 200 tons of potassium fluoride was placed with KBS at the end of 1983, after Iraq had used chemical weapons for the first time during the Gulf War. However, the contract for this order was cancelled, reportedly after pressure from the Dutch government. In February 1984, a consignment of seventy-four drums of potassium fluoride was discovered by US Customs at New York's Kennedy Airport, addressed to SEPP and awaiting despatch to Baghdad. Whilst thiodiglycol is used in the manufacture of mustard gas, the other chemicals are ingredients for nerve agents.

Another company which supplied chemicals to Iraq was Melchemie BV, located at Arnhem in the Netherlands. In February 1985 the Dutch authorities obtained evidence that between November 1984 and January

1985 the company had legally exported over 1200 tons of chloroethyl, dimethylamine, thiodiglycol, and 20,000 kilograms of phosphorous trichloride, all of which are components for the manufacture of mustard gas. In 1986, after export controls had been introduced by the Dutch government, Melchemie was found guilty of attempting to export to Iraq phosphorous oxychloride, a component of the nerve agent tabun.

One source of chemicals for Baghdad was uncovered by the US Customs Service whilst it was engaged in an operation to prevent the export of chemicals to Iran during the Gulf War. The story began in 1984 when a Dutchman, Frans van Anraat, who operated a Singapore-based company which traded in chemicals, met a Japanese named Charles Tanaka. Van Anraat was looking for a source of thiodiglycol, which has several industrial applications as well as being an ingredient of mustard gas. Tanaka was able to find a quantity of the chemical in Japan. After the consignment had been shipped to Europe, van Anraat despatched it to Iraq.

By the latter part of the Gulf War, international export controls on thiodiglycol had made the supply of the chemical scarcer and Tanaka could no longer satisfy van Anraat's requirements from his sources in Japan. He therefore turned to possible sources in America, despite the fact that export of the chemical to countries other than certain European states had been banned. Tanaka approached a contact who eventually tracked down Alcolac International, which was a supplier of thiodiglycol but normally only in small amounts – for use in the manufacture of ballpoint pens. Not surprisingly, when approached to supply several hundred tons of the chemical, the company leaped at the opportunity. Consignments were shipped to Europe under the description of 'textile additive'. That the company was aware of the illegality of its actions is demonstrated by the fact that it initially planned to ship the consignments to Liberia or to a non-existent company in the Belgian port of Antwerp.

When US Customs investigators initially discovered the shipments to Iran, they substituted water for the thiodiglycol before the consignments were allowed to leave the United States. Unbeknownst to them, however, another large consignment of three hundred barrels, containing almost 520 tons of the chemical, had also been exported to Iraq. Details of this consignment were only discovered when the investigators raided the offices of Alcolac International and studied the company's files.

Charles Tanaka's intermediaries and Alcolac International were subsequently prosecuted for violation of export regulations. Tanaka himself was arrested and charged after being duped into returning to the United States. Van Anraat, however, was never apprehended.

It was in early 1984 that the West first learned that European and American companies had been supplying chemicals and equipment which had subsequently been used by Iraq for the development and manufacture of chemical weapons. There was a great deal of concern amongst Western intelligence agencies as they submitted reports to their respective governments. The United States was the first to react, and in March of that year banned the export to Iraq or Iran of five different chemicals which could be used to produce nerve agents and mustard gas. In 1986, the list of chemicals subject to export controls was increased and Syria was added to the ban. In the following year, growing concern about chemical weapon proliferation led to eight further chemicals being included and the list of prohibited countries was considerably extended to cover all but eighteen Western nations.

Meanwhile, efforts had also been made elsewhere to control the export of chemicals. In early 1984, West Germany had instituted export controls on certain chemicals, as had a number of other countries including Britain, the Netherlands, Denmark, Eire, Canada, Australia and Japan. The West Germans were particularly concerned, as there had been reports that a pesticide plant constructed by a West German company was being used for the production of nerve gases.

However, a major problem facing those trying to control the proliferation of chemical weapons was that individual countries listed different chemicals as being subject to export controls. In 1985, Australia took the initiative in putting forward proposals to co-ordinate international efforts and formed a body named the Australian Group which by 1987 included twenty member countries and the European Commission.

During the Gulf War, the United States, Britain and France tempered their strictures against Iraq and its production and use of chemical weapons because they were already preoccupied with confronting a more immediate threat – Ayatollah Khomeini and his fiery brand of Shia fundamentalism which was threatening to spread throughout the Islamic world.

However, on 16th March 1988, Iraq used chemical weapons against the Kurdish town of Halabja. The entire world was shocked by this barbaric act. Nevertheless, despite all the exclamations of horror and outrage, no really effective action was taken against the Baghdad regime. Once again the West considered that it had other, more pressing priorities.

On the cessation of hostilities between Iraq and Iran, despite the continuing international effort to control the proliferation of chemical weapons worldwide, several European governments, including Britain,

France and Germany, were still anxious to retain Iraq as a major trading customer and thus turned a blind eye to the chemical weapon development programme, which continued unabated. They continued to encourage their respective commercial companies to forge even further links with Baghdad.

At this point, it would perhaps be useful to explain in outline the usual types of agent encountered in chemical weapons and their characteristics.

Chemical agents are categorised as lethal, damaging or incapacitating. They are further specified as being either non-persistent, lasting a few minutes or hours, or persistent, when their effect lasts for periods of up to a few days, depending upon climatic conditions. Persistent agents are produced in liquid form and are normally delivered by aircraft in the form of a spray or vapour which manifests itself on targets in the form of droplets. When detected, their presence would be sufficient for an area to be declared uninhabitable and, depending on the type of agent, possibly denied even to troops equipped with protective clothing and equipment. Non-persistent agents can be delivered by aircraft, artillery or missiles and can consist of liquids or gases.

Within these categories, there are different types of agent designed to carry out different functions. Lethal nerve agents such as sarin, tabun, soman and VX are designed to attack the central nervous system after inhalation or on contact with the skin, causing difficulty in breathing and loss of muscular co-ordination with eventual convulsions and death. Sarin and tabun were developed from insecticides by the Germans during the Second World War, sarin being ten times more lethal than tabun. Lethal blood agents such as hydrogen cyanide cause almost instant death after inhalation by preventing the absorption of oxygen into the body's bloodstream. Non-persistent lethal choking agents such as phosgene and chlorine cause asphyxiation, whilst non-persistent damaging blister agents, such as mustard gas, cause severe inflammation and blisters. In addition, there are toxins which are manufactured from the poisonous by-products of micro-organisms; these can be either lethal or incapacitating, depending on the purpose required of them. It was reported in October 1990 that Iraq was in possession of two such toxins, mykotoxins HT-2 and T-2, one hundred milligrams of each having been supplied by the West German company Josef Kuhn in co-operation with another firm named Plato. The effects of exposure to such toxins are irritation of the skin, blisters, dizziness, nausea and diarrhoea – if not treated, they can lead to death.

The Iraqi government department responsible for overseeing Iraq's chemical weapon development programme is the State Enterprise for Pesticide Production (SEPP). Production facilities consist of four complexes at Salman Pak (at which biological weapons are also developed), Samarra, Akashat and Al Fallujah. The largest of these is at Samarra, 60km north-west of Baghdad. This 25-square-km plant, which is surrounded by a 160-square-km exclusion zone, produces sulphur and nitrogen mustard gases as well as tabun and sarin.

The mustard gas produced at Samarra has been reported as being a highly refined type of distilled agent which is delayed in effect, attacking the mucous membranes and resulting in violent inflammation of the lungs and eyes as well as severe blisters on the skin which, when punctured, form again. If the gas is inhaled, it causes internal blistering of the throat and lungs, leading to possible death from pulmonary oedema – the lungs become filled with fluid and death is caused by what is known as 'dry land drowning'. Iraqi production capabilities are believed to extend to the production of binary weapons – devices which contain two substances which are harmless until mixed after launching, at which point they become toxic – and to the thickening of liquid and aerosol chemicals which delays evaporation in high temperatures.

It is known that Iraq has devoted considerable effort to developing other types of chemical agent. It has been reported that trials of prototype agents have been carried out on political prisoners in the notorious Abu Gharib prison near Baghdad. Some of those produced at Akashat were tested on Kurds captured by Iraqi forces in 1983, many of whom died as a result. It has also been reported that the Iraqis may possibly have developed a new type of chemical agent known as perfluoroisobutene (PFIB) which is a completely colourless and odourless but extremely toxic agent. Produced by subjecting teflon to extreme heat under highly controlled conditions, PFIB causes pulmonary oedema. Current types of chemical warfare protective equipment are apparently ineffective against PFIB, which penetrates the activated charcoal used in gas respirators and NBC suits.

It was reported in 1989 that Iraq was manufacturing a highly concentrated chemical agent called 'blue acid', which is also said to be capable of penetrating current types of gas respirator and protective clothing. The agent is apparently manufactured at three plants constructed by West German companies and codenamed Ieas, Meda and Ghasi, the locations of which are unconfirmed.

Monthly production figures, quoted in 1989, for the manufacture of certain chemical agents at Samarra are quoted as being sixty tonnes of mustard gas and four tonnes of sarin and tabun respectively. Both these nerve agents are colourless and odourless and a quantity equivalent to the size of a cube of sugar would be sufficient to kill 2500 people.

The construction and equipping of Samarra and the other Iraqi chemical plants was carried out by a number of West German companies, including the two construction firms Walter Thosti Boswau and Heberger Bau. Equipment was furnished by companies such as Messerschmitt-Bolkow-Blohm and Karl Kolb, which supplied laboratory equipment and the pilot plant for the production of poison gas, and Sigma Chemie, which supplied chemicals. Mobile toxological laboratories were supplied by Anton Irle, whilst containers, pipes and centrifuges, manufactured from a special highly corrosion-resistant metal, were provided by Quast.

Other suppliers included Preussag, which sold SEPP chlorine as well as containers to hold the chemical, and Rhema, which supplied a gas chamber. Water Engineering Trading (WET) of Hamburg delivered raw materials for the production of sarin and tabun, which were brought in via Turkey for delivery to Fallujah. In 1985, WET supplied chemicals, including phosphorous oxychloride, for use at Samarra, as well as supplying SEPP with incubation equipment for the production of biological agents. The cultures themselves were acquired from Oxoid GmbH, which has since been renamed Unipath GmbH.

There is little hard intelligence available concerning Iraq's biological warfare capability, but it is known that from 1979 onwards increased effort was channelled into construction of biological warfare plants at Salman Pak and in the north of the country, as well as into research and development of biological agents which have been reported to include different strains of cholera, pulmonary anthrax and typhoid. It is believed, but has not been confirmed, that the Iraqis are also in possession of cultures of tularaemia, otherwise called 'rabbit fever', and it is therefore possible that they may also have attempted to develop this as a biological agent.

Export controls on possible components for biological weapons were not, it seems, applied to the same extent as was the case with chemicals. Indeed, it would have been extremely difficult for such measures to have been introduced, bearing in mind the lack of evidence to support any suspicion of the Iraqis' intentions. Baghdad acquired the necessary items in the same way as it had procured equipment for its chemical programme, component by seemingly innocent component, and often under the pretext of perfectly legitimate medical research. In 1985 the Centre for Disease Control (CDC) in Atlanta, Georgia, sent three shipments of 'West Nile fever' virus to Iraq for research purposes at the request of an Iraqi doctor who was apparently known to CDC. No check was carried out as to whether the virus, which causes fever and nausea, was used for its intended purpose. In any case, there was ultimately no way in which CDC could have discovered whether or not it had been used in biological warfare research.

In terms of large scale conflict, chemical weapons can be delivered by three methods: by aircraft, either by spraying or by free-fall bomb; by artillery shell or rocket; and by ballistic missile. The Iraqis possess the capability to deliver them by all three means, their armed forces having been trained in the use of chemical weapons by instructors from East Germany. Specialists of the now disbanded Volksarmee installed a large chemical warfare training centre in Iraq during the mid-1980s. The Iraqi army is reported to include chemical warfare battalions in its order of battle.

Iraqi forces are issued with protective clothing, some of it of Soviet pattern. It is known that Iraq does produce its own locally manufactured suits and respirators, as they have been seen on display at defence exhibitions in Baghdad and elsewhere. They are reported to be similar in design to those produced in the West, but there are no confirmed details about their performance. Units equipped with Western and Soviet-supplied tanks and armoured personnel-carriers would be protected by the nuclear, biological and chemical (NBC) protection systems incorporated in those vehicles equipped with them.

The war with Iran provided the opportunity for Iraqi forces to gain experience in the use of chemical agents, as has already been well documented. However, the Iraqis soon discovered that chemicals can be a two-edged weapon when they first used them in February and March 1984 during operations in the Majnoon Marshes. The weather conditions were adverse and mustard gas was blown back amongst the Iraqi forces, causing casualties. Adverse weather conditions also affected the use of chemicals during the offensive in the Fao Peninsula in February 1986, when rain and humidity diluted the effects of mustard gas.

The Iraqis also found that chemical weapons were effective against large numbers of men in relatively confined areas. However, the major effect was the psychological one on Iranian forces who in any case found it virtually impossible to operate in temperatures as high as 104° Fahrenheit when wearing gas respirators. Protective clothing, other than respirators, was scarce because of the international embargo on supplies of arms to combatants on both sides. Iran was forced to spend large sums of money acquiring it, although it was never able to do so in sufficient quantities.

During the Gulf War, a large proportion of the delivery of chemical agents was carried out by the use of bombs dropped from aircraft. In 1988, attacks against Kurdish tribesmen were reported as having been carried out by Swiss-supplied FFA AS-202 Bravo trainer aircraft.

The Iraqi air force currently has several types of aircraft in its squadrons which are capable of carrying chemical weapons. Amongst these are the Su-20/22 'Fitter', the Su-24 'Fencer' and the Su-25 'Frogfoot' which possess weapon payload capacities of 4250kg, 300kg and 4400kg respectively over ranges of between 1050 and 1400km. In addition, the MiG-21 and certain versions of the MiG-23 and Mirage, with which the Iraqis are equipped, can also carry bombs or chemical weapons. Typically, aircraft would be used to strike at targets in rear areas, such as airfields, communications centres and lines of supply, headquarters locations and civilian installations such as oilfields.

Iraq also made frequent use of its artillery's capability to use chemical agents during the Gulf War. In April 1988, massive artillery barrages at the start of the offensive on the Fao Peninsula consisted of high-explosive and chemical shells, the latter containing cyanide gas and nerve agents. Towards the end of the following month, the Iraqis employed chemical weapons in artillery and rocket barrages to drive Iranians from the Shalamche bridgehead, again using cyanide gas and nerve agents together with high explosive shells and rockets. In June, they employed both aircraft and artillery to deliver chemicals simultaneously, firing cyanide gas and nerve agent-filled artillery shells and nerve agents at Iranian front lines whilst dropping mustard gas bombs from the air on rear formations. This tactic proved highly successful.

The Iraqi army possesses in its arsenal several types of artillery which are capable of firing chemical ammunition. In addition to Soviet-supplied weapons, these include G-5, GHN-45 and FH-70 155mm howitzers which possess maximum ranges of approximately 40,000, 30,000 and 24,000 metres respectively and which fire a shell containing a chemical payload of 5–10kg. Some artillery units are equipped with the Astros II multiple-launch rocket system, which fires the SS-60 rocket; it can also be fitted with a chemical warhead weighing 100–300kg. The SS-60, along with the smaller-calibre SS-30 and SS-40, is manufactured by the Iraqis under licence from Avibras of Brazil and it is almost certain that attempts will have been made to fit them with chemical warheads.

In late October 1983, the Iraqis used their missiles in anger for the first time, launching Scud-Bs at six Iranian cities. In December, they launched Scuds at five Iranian towns, killing twenty-one people and injuring 222. During the entire period of the conflict, Iraq launched a total of over three hundred missiles.

The main advantage offered by ballistic missiles is speed of delivery – a missile can cover 2000km in approximately ten minutes. Moreover, a number can be launched simultaneously in the form of a saturation bombardment. However, ballistic missiles are not particularly accurate weapons, their accuracy being measured in terms of Circular Error Probable (CEP) at two-thirds of their maximum ranges. The CEP of a missile system is the area in which 50 per cent of the number of missiles launched at a specific target will fall. In the case of short- and intermediate-range ballistic missiles, with maximum ranges of between 1000km and 5000km respectively, the CEP is between 200 and 1000 metres. When one considers the 10–50 metre CEP of a cruise missile, it can be seen that ballistic missiles are not weapons to use against pinpoint targets. They would therefore be used against area targets such as major troop concentrations, towns or cities for which a large chemical warhead would be required in order to be effective, as well as to allow for the inherent inaccuracy of the weapon.

Iraq is known definitely to be in possession of five different types of missile which are capable of carrying chemical warheads. The Scud-B, which was used by both Iraq and Iran during the Gulf War, in its standard unmodified configuration, can carry a 555kg chemical warhead of viscous VX liquid nerve agent. With a maximum range of 280km, it has a CEP of 930 metres at 180km which reduces to 450 metres at maximum range. The Al Hussein, in essence a modified Scud-B, has a greater maximum range of 650km but has a much smaller chemical warhead payload capacity of 136kg. Likewise the Al Abbas, also a modified Scud, has an even greater range, 900km, but its payload capacity is reduced further to 300kg. The Al Aabed is a totally different proposition with its range of 2000km and a warhead payload capacity of 750kg.

The FROG-7 is another Soviet-supplied missile which the Iraqis used during the Gulf War to bombard Iranian cities immediately behind the battle zone. It has a maximum range of 70km and the FROG-7b variant carries a 390kg chemical warhead. It has a CEP of 450–700 metres. This missile, with its short range, would in all probability be used against troop concentrations in forward positions and concentration areas, as well as against other targets such as forward headquarters locations, bridging sites or communications centres.

There have been reports that the Iraqis also possess SS-21 Scarab missiles, although the Soviet Union has denied supplying these weapons, and it is believed that they are organised as a brigade of eighteen launchers. This missile can carry a chemical warhead and has a maximum range of 120km and a CEP of 50–100 metres.

The deployment of a chemical agent from a missile warhead would be

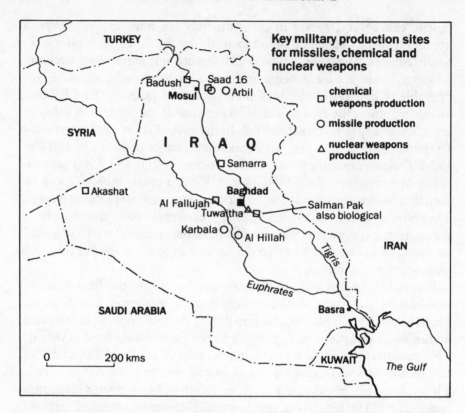

Key military production sites for missiles, chemical and nuclear weapons

□ chemical weapons production

○ missile production

△ nuclear weapons production

TURKEY

Badush Saad 16
Mosul ○ Arbil

SYRIA

I R A Q

□ Samarra

□ Akashat

Al Fallujah □ **Baghdad**
Tuwaitha △ □ — Salman Pak also biological
Karbala ○ ○ Al Hillah

IRAN

Tigris

Euphrates

SAUDI ARABIA

Basra

0   200 kms

KUWAIT   The Gulf

in the form of an airburst, probably at a height of some four thousand feet in order to gain maximum effect through drift. The area affected would depend much on wind conditions but coverage from a Scud warhead bursting at that height would measure approximately four kilometres in length by half a kilometre in width at the point nearest to the chemical's deployment. A 136kg payload of VX nerve gas deployed from an Al Hussein warhead would, depending on wind conditions, affect an area covering approximately one third of a square mile.

During the last sixteen years, Western intelligence agencies repeatedly warned their respective governments of Iraq's active pursuit of further advancement in chemical weapons, to little avail judging by the support given by Western industry to Baghdad's chemical warfare development programme. At the same time, those same intelligence agencies were also becoming increasingly concerned at another greater threat which had far greater ramifications with regard to the balance of power in the Middle East and for world peace in general.

III

Iraq's nuclear effort commenced in 1959 when Baghdad established the Iraqi Nuclear Energy Committee and in the same year joined the International Atomic Energy Agency. Ten years later, on 29th October 1969, it signed the Nuclear Non-Proliferation Treaty and three years later, in March 1972, ratified it.

In 1960, Iraq signed an agreement with the Soviet Union for the supply of a IRT 2000 two megawatt thermal-powered research reactor. Construction was begun at Al Tuwaitha in 1963 and completed in 1968. The Soviets also supplied the Iraqis with extensive facilities which enabled them to construct a complete nuclear research complex, including a laboratory for the production of radio isotopes. At the same time, Iraqis were sent to the Soviet Union to be trained in nuclear physics.

However, the Iraqis were not satisfied with the Soviet-supplied system and were well aware that the regular close inspections by teams of Soviet technicians precluded any chance of obtaining sufficient military grade material for the production of a nuclear weapon. This was despite the fact that in 1978 the Soviets upgraded the fuel in the reactor from 10 per cent enriched U-235 to 80 per cent enriched uranium in order to increase the reactor's power to five megawatts.

The Iraqis realised that they would have to turn elsewhere to obtain assistance in acquiring the facilities and military-grade material to produce nuclear weapons. They rapidly realised that their best prospects lay in Europe, where there was greater readiness to supply Iraq with technology which was in any case more advanced than that of the Soviet Union.

In April 1975, a conference took place in Baghdad which was attended by European, American and Arab scientists. It was there that links were established between the Iraqis and the head of the fuel department of the Italian Nuclear Energy Committee (CNEN). Later in the year, in September, Saddam Hussein, who was then vice-president, visited France and two months later a nuclear co-operation agreement was signed between the two countries. The Iraqis almost immediately afterwards approached the French about the supply of a five hundred megawatt electrically powered gas graphite reactor but this request was refused.

The French did, however, offer as an alternative an Osiris research reactor operating on enriched uranium. This was of a type known as a Material Test Reactor (MTR), normally used in the development of reactors intended to produce power. It produced a far higher degree of thermal power than the standard types of research reactor and it did possess one attribute which made it attractive to the Iraqis – it could produce weapon-grade plutonium.

At the beginning of 1976, Iraq signed an agreement with Italy for the supply of equipment and nuclear technology, including recycling nuclear fuel and reprocessing radiated fuel. During the following year, the French built two reactors under what was initially called the Osirak Project but was subsequently designated Project Tammuz 17. One was the Osiris-type seventy-megawatt reactor named Tammuz I and the other a much smaller, one-megawatt research model called Tammuz II. Both were powered by 93 per cent enriched uranium which is itself weapon-grade material. Moreover, Tammuz I was capable of producing approximately 10kg of weapon-grade plutonium per year – the amount required for one nuclear weapon was about 6kg.

The entire Tammuz 17 project was constructed by a consortium of French companies which operated under the title of CERBAG – Centre d'Etudes et Recherche Baghdad. This consisted of five companies: Technicatome, which was responsible for the design of the complex housing for both reactors as well as for the supervision of construction, the training of Iraqi personnel and part of the operation of CERBAG; Bouygues, which provided all civil engineering and construction expertise and also assisted in the operation of CERBAG; Société Générale Techniques Nouvelles (SGTN), which handled all planning, erection and running-up of all equipment installed in the complex; COHSIP, which installed all control and electrical systems; and Constructions Navales et Industrielles de la Méditerranée (CNIM), which constructed the reactor cores and the metal coatings for the reactor pools.

Whilst work was progressing on the Tammuz 17 complex, the Iraqis signed another agreement in early February 1978 with the Italian CNEN and two Italian companies, SNIA Techint and AMN, for the supply of another complex housing extensive research and test facilities. This project was named 30 July and provided what is described as a 'technological hall for chemical engineering research' – a 'cold' facility for training personnel in the recycling of spent fuel – and a 'technological hall for testing materials', which provided facilities for research into nuclear structure, including a thermo-hydraulic research centre. The 30 July complex also included a laboratory and twenty-six 'hot cells' for radio isotope production.

Meanwhile, up to 200 Iraqi technicians and scientists were sent to France for training, whilst another 150 went to Italy. At the same time, Iraq was still looking elsewhere to obtain further assistance and in particular to Brazil, which was known to be receiving uranium-enrichment technology from West Germany. Brazil proved receptive to Iraqi approaches and in 1980 an agreement was signed under which it would supply Iraq with uranium ore and low-grade enriched uranium. In June of that year, Brazilian scientists travelled to Baghdad to explore the prospects of mining uranium in Iraq itself.

Iraq was also making every effort to acquire uranium from sources worldwide. A hundred and twenty tons were acquired from Portugal in 1980 and a further 200 tons from Niger. Attempts to purchase uranium elsewhere were unsuccessful. In several instances, they were made through the use of dealers in the international arms trade.

By July 1980, the French had shipped an initial 12kg of 93 per cent enriched uranium to Iraq, the total amount to be supplied being 80kg. Tammuz I required three loads of 12kg of U-235 per annum; the smaller Tammuz II required only one load, of 12kg, which would operate it for several years. At that stage, Saddam Hussein was being briefed by his scientists as to how they planned to produce sufficient plutonium for the manufacture of nuclear weapons. However, he himself had already fully appreciated that, before this could be done, there would have to be sufficient fully trained Iraqi personnel capable of running the project – he was under no illusions that either France or Italy would permit him to produce nuclear weapons. All foreign scientists and technicians would therefore have to be removed from Iraq before that would become possible.

Whilst the Iraqis were making apparently steady progress towards their goal, there was increasing unease about Tammuz 17 elsewhere. In France there had been dissension over the nuclear co-operation agreement ever since its signing in 1975. However, Jacques Chirac, prime minister at the time, saw Iraq as the future leading power in the Middle East and as France's principal supplier of oil. Fully realising Saddam Hussein's nuclear ambitions, he decided to turn a blind eye to them and decreed that the deal to supply the reactors should be completed. When André Giraud, the head of the French nuclear energy committee, protested strongly, Chirac threatened to sack him if the deal was not completed according to the signed agreement. Indeed, the matter was considered to be of such importance that President Giscard d'Estaing took personal control of the affair in order to ensure its smooth passage.

The Americans were also well aware of Iraq's nuclear activities and of French support of them. Accordingly, Washington placed an embargo on any American-supplied uranium being transferred to Baghdad. Inevitably, however, the French circumvented this obstacle by supplying uranium from their own stocks.

However, there was one country which had been monitoring the progress of Project Tammuz 17 closest of all – Israel. From the very beginnings of Franco-Iraqi nuclear co-operation, the Israelis had protested against the assistance being given to Baghdad. In 1978, the Israeli intelligence service, Mossad, began an operation codenamed Operation Sphinx, to penetrate the Iraqi nuclear effort and obtain accurate information on the progress of Tammuz 17. A number of Iraqi scientists were working in France, some at the Sarcelles nuclear plant north of Paris. From a list of them, obtained by a Jewish contact who was employed in the plant's personnel department, Mossad was able to target one particular Iraqi – a forty-two-year-old scientist named Butrus Eben Halim.

Over a period of a few months, Mossad carried out an operation which commenced with a supposedly chance encounter between Halim and an Israeli agent masquerading as an Englishman named Donovan. This had in fact been cleverly engineered by the Israelis, who had carefully studied the profile they had built up on the Iraqi – for example, the fact that he and his wife were childless indicated that his marriage was possibly not a happy one. This was confirmed when a female Mossad agent, posing as a door-to-door perfume saleswoman, was successful in striking up a brief friendship with Halim's wife who turned out to be an unhappy and rather bitter woman.

Halim's wife subsequently returned to Iraq for a few weeks and the Israelis took advantage of her absence. 'Donovan' proceeded to befriend the Iraqi, entertaining him and introducing him to a young prostitute called Marie-Claude Magal, who was in the pay of Mossad. Halim proved easy prey and shortly afterwards 'Donovan' took him to Amsterdam to meet two 'business acquaintances', who were in fact a Mossad agent and an Israeli nuclear physicist. The two men explained that they were working on a scheme to sell nuclear reactors to Third World countries but needed details of a suitable type which they could market to prospective clients. Halim believed this story and agreed to provide details of the Tammuz 17 project. Over the next few weeks, he photocopied detailed technical information and passed the information to the two Israelis, who continually pressed him to provide further material.

Inevitably, however, the Iraqi grew increasingly concerned about the risk of being caught but the Israelis calmed his fears with generous payments, entertainment and prostitutes. Eventually, however, Halim was in such a state of anxiety that it was decided that 'Donovan', with whom he still had a good relationship and whom he still believed to be an Englishman, should tell him that it was the Americans with whom he had been dealing and that the two 'business acquaintances' had turned out to be CIA agents.

Not surprisingly, Halim was devastated by this revelation and terrified that the Iraqis would discover his treachery and return him to Iraq for trial and execution. 'Donovan' once again calmed his nerves and informed him that the 'Americans' required only one further item of information – Iraq's likely reaction to a French suggestion that 'caramel', an alternative fuel from which nuclear energy (but not weapon-grade material) can be produced, should be provided by France for the Tammuz 17 project instead of enriched uranium. Halim was able to reply that Iraq would want the enriched uranium, but he added that a nuclear physicist, an Egyptian named Yahia El Meshad, would shortly be travelling to France from Al Tuwaitha to check progress on the project and to decide on such matters.

A few days later, Yahia El Meshad arrived in Paris. Shortly afterwards Halim engineered a meeting between himself, Yahia and 'Donovan' in a restaurant. Yahia, however, was reserved and unforthcoming, being evidently unwilling to talk in front of a stranger.

Not long afterwards, Halim's wife returned from Iraq. His new-found wealth, resulting from the generous payments received from Mossad, initially improved their relationship. However, he was unwise enough to tell her about his dealings with 'Donovan' and the two 'CIA agents'. His wife was suspicious and angered by her husband's stupidity and gullibility. She immediately saw the hand of Mossad in the affair.

It was by then early April 1979. All had gone well with both the Tammuz 17 and 30 July projects and CNIM, the French manufacturer of the cores for the two reactors, had completed its task and prepared the cores for shipment to Iraq. However, events took a dramatic turn when, at three o'clock in the morning of 7th April, there was an explosion in a huge hangar in the port of La Seyne-sur-Mer near Toulon.

The French authorities rapidly deduced that a small group of saboteurs had entered the hangar belonging to CNIM and had planted explosive charges on the two cores, which had been completely destroyed. Other equipment in the hangar had been left untouched. On the following day, a group calling itself 'the French Ecological Group' claimed responsibility for the attack, stating that its motive was to 'neutralise dangerous weapons for the sake of the future of the human race'. The French security service, the Direction de la Surveillance du Territoire (DST), was not convinced. The raid had the hallmarks of highly trained professionals and to the French that in itself pointed the finger of suspicion at one particular organisation – Mossad.

The French were correct in deducing that the Israelis were responsible. Early on the morning of 5th April a team of five Mossad operatives, accompanied by an Israeli nuclear physicist, had infiltrated the guarded high-security area in the port. With the assistance of one of the guards, another Mossad operative, the team gained entry to the CNIM hangar where the cores were being stored prior to shipment. Under the guidance of the nuclear physicist, who showed them the best locations for the explosives, the Israelis placed their charges on the cores. As they stealthily withdrew, a diversion was started by more Mossad agents in the street outside the secure area's perimeter – a young woman had apparently suffered a glancing blow from a car and the ensuing shouting match between her and the driver served to distract the attention of the guards at the main gate. As the charges exploded, the team of saboteurs rapidly disappeared – as did the 'injured pedestrian' and the offending driver, together with his car.

The news of the destruction of the cores had a devastating effect on Halim; he was terrified that the Iraqis would launch a witch hunt amongst those Iraqis working on the Tammuz 17 project in France. Once again, his wife was convinced that the Israelis were responsible. Despite the best efforts of 'Donovan' to reassure him, Halim decided that he would return to Iraq to avoid any further contact with those whom he considered to have embroiled him in the whole affair. Shortly afterwards, he and his wife did so.

Just over a year later, on 6th June 1980, Yahia El Meshad returned to France on the latest of a number of visits during the previous months. On this occasion he would be checking equipment which had been manufactured in France and was ready for delivery to Baghdad. Amongst the items he was to inspect was the first consignment of 12kg of 93-per-cent-enriched uranium. Meshad visited the French Nuclear Centre at Fontenay-aux-Rares as well as equipment suppliers at Saclay, Cadarache and Pierrelatte. On 13th June, he returned to Paris where he was staying at the Hôtel Méridien.

On the following day, a chambermaid went to room 9041. Despite the 'Do Not Disturb' notice hung on the door handle, she entered the room and found a scene of carnage – Yahia El Meshad was lying on the floor between the two beds in the room with his throat cut.

The French authorities were certain that Meshad's murder was directly linked to Tammuz – he was known to them as one of the most prominent and highly trained scientists working on the project. They were certain that robbery had not been a motive because his wallet, containing 1400 francs, was found untouched in his pocket. They did, however, discover that Meshad had been approached by an attractive young prostitute. On further investigation, they were able to identify her as Marie-Claude Magal – unbeknownst to them, the same young woman introduced to Butrus Eben Halim by her Mossad paymasters.

The involvement of the young prostitute on the fringe of this affair might not have seemed untoward to the French investigators except for the fact that when the DST, who had interviewed her on 1st July, decided to recall her for further questioning they discovered that she had been killed in a hit-and-run accident. The DST were convinced that she had been involved in some way with Meshad's death and that she had been murdered to ensure her silence. This led them to question whether she had been hired to seduce Meshad in an attempt to keep him away from his room whilst it was being searched. In the event, this ploy had failed and the killer had decided that he had no option other than to murder the Egyptian. The French also considered another alternative – that Meshad had been murdered as a warning to others working on Tammuz 17.

Initially, the finger of suspicion was once again pointed at Mossad, but the Israelis themselves denied any involvement in the affair. Subsequently, however, Egyptian intelligence sources reported that they believed that Meshad had been murdered by Syrian agents working on behalf of the KGB, the Soviet intelligence service. Their version of events stated that the Soviets had been anxious to discover the state of progress of Tammuz 17 and had commissioned the Syrians to copy documents being carried by Meshad. Unfortunately for him, he had discovered the Syrians in his hotel room and had been murdered.

In fact, the French had been correct in guessing the identity of those responsible. Mossad had decided that an attempt should be made to recruit Meshad – if this proved impossible, he would have to be eliminated. Interception of telexes between Baghdad and the nuclear plant at Sarcelles had revealed details of his travel arrangements for his impending visit to France. On his arrival in Paris, Meshad had contacted Marie-Claude Magal, whom he used regularly for 'entertainment' during his visits to Paris. Mossad, on researching Meshad's background, had discovered that he possessed a penchant for sexual perversions and had ensured that the girl they supplied was willing to accommodate these. Marie-Claude herself was completely unaware of her employers' true identities but does not appear to have been concerned, as long as they continued to reward her generously.

Marie-Claude was due to arrive at Meshad's hotel room at 7.30 p.m. Shortly beforehand, a Mossad agent knocked on the scientist's door and attempted to make an offer to him – would he exchange information for considerable amounts of money? Meshad's reaction was swift and to the point. He slammed the door shut after threatening to call the police. Shortly afterwards, Marie-Claude arrived and stayed for approximately two hours. Later in the night, two Mossad agents entered Meshad's room and cut his throat as he slept.

On hearing of the murder, Marie-Claude Magal contacted the police and gave them an account of her visit to Meshad. She mentioned that he had been angered by an approach prior to her arrival by someone who had offered him money for information.

Approximately a month later, on the night of 12th July, Marie-Claude was plying for trade in the Boulevard St-Germain when a car drew up beside her as she walked down the pavement. Thinking that the driver was a prospective customer, she walked around to the offside of the vehicle to talk to him. As she bent down by the car window and engaged the driver in conversation, another vehicle approached. Just before it drew level, she was pushed backwards into its path. The young Frenchwoman was killed outright and, as she lay in the street, the two cars disappeared.

France was not the only battleground on which attempts to halt Tammuz 17 took place. On the night of 7th August 1980, on the Via della Lungearetta in Rome, a bomb exploded outside the front door of a flat belonging to the general manager of SNIA Techint, the company manufacturing the laboratories for the 30 July project. Almost simultaneously, two other bombs exploded in the Via A. Bargoni outside the company's offices.

A group styling itself 'the Committee to Safeguard the Islamic Revolution' claimed responsibility for the attacks. This organisation was unknown to the SISMI, the Italian security service, or to anyone else, and no further information was forthcoming as to the real identity of the perpetrators. However, of one thing the Italians were certain – the attacks were intended as warnings not only to the Iraqis, but also to those who were assisting them in their nuclear development programme. Indeed, a message demanding that SNIA Techint end its participation in the project, and warning that further action would be taken against Fiorelli and his family if it did not do so, was left near Fiorelli's flat.

'The Committee to Safeguard the Islamic Revolution' proceeded to send letters to scientists in France, Italy and Iraq making the same threat. Initially it was suggested that the Iranians were responsible but, after investigation by the French and Italian security services, Mossad once again became the principal suspect. These threats had the initial effect of frightening some scientists, but this wore off after the French, Italian and Iraqi authorities reassured them that they and their families would be well protected.

On 22nd September 1980, the war between Iraq and Iran broke out. A week later, on 30th September, the Iranians carried out a surprise air attack on the Tammuz 17 complex at Al Tuwaitha. Two Iranian F-4 Phantoms attacked with rockets and cannon and swiftly disappeared. The Iraqis were taken completely by surprise, to the extent that none of the anti-aircraft defences opened fire on the two Phantoms.

The damage caused to the complex was only slight. Neither reactor had been hit and the laboratory complex suffered only minimal damage: the water-cooling system for the reactors had been damaged, as had the storage facility for radioactive waste material. The main effect on the project was the delay caused by the absence of French scientists and technicians who had left Iraq on the outbreak of war. The bombing served to aggravate this problem as the remaining foreign personnel working on the project also left Al Tuwaitha immediately afterwards.

The Iraqis, however, took the opportunity of turning the situation to their advantage. In the absence of foreign technicians, they removed from Tammuz II the major part of the 12kg of enriched uranium, only a small amount of which had been used to operate the reactor. This was stored in a secure location. Thereafter, Iraq denied French or International Atomic Energy Agency inspection access on the grounds that wartime security regulations did not permit it.

The Iranian air attack had served to alert the Iraqis to the fact that Al Tuwaitha was poorly defended and they turned their attention to remedying the situation as quickly as possible. In October 1980, they signed an $800 million contract with Thomson-CSF of France for the supply of Crotale surface-to-air missile systems, Magic R-550 air-to-air missiles and Exocet missiles. A further $900 million contract was also signed for the establishment of an electronics manufacturing facility at Samarra, to produce military radio communications and radar equipment. In January of the following year, a third contract was signed with Thomson-CSF for the supply of surface-to-surface missiles and radar systems. In February 1981, the foreign scientists and technicians returned to Al Tuwaitha, having been confidently reassured of their safety by the Iraqis. In April, full-scale work on Tammuz 17 was resumed.

In fact, the Iraqis' confidence was misplaced. At that very moment Israel was completing its plans for the destruction of Tammuz 17.

In making their plans to destroy the reactors, the Israelis had considered several options. They had discounted the idea of sabotage, because of the very tight security within the complex – all personnel, Iraqi and foreign, were thoroughly searched when entering restricted areas. Armed guards within these areas kept a close watch and the entire complex was under closed-circuit television surveillance. The reactors themselves were surrounded by a high concrete wall and by a fence fitted with electronic sensors which would give the alarm if touched or breached. The entire complex perimeter was patrolled by heavily armed mobile patrols.

A second option was the mounting of an attack by special forces and airborne troops. The main obstacle militating against such an operation was the distance of over five hundred miles over which a force of at least two hundred troops would have to be transported. This would involve the use of large transport aircraft to carry not only the troops but also the helicopters which would be required to fly the troops into the target area. In addition to the requirement for landing strips, which would have had to be secured covertly beforehand, the aircraft would have to be refuelled en route, adding a further complication to the operation. There was also the possibility of unforeseen problems, such as aircraft malfunction. Added to these factors was the risk that the aircraft would be detected on the way to the target, although this would have been minimised by sophisticated deception measures. Such an operation would also very probably result in unacceptably heavy casualties being sustained.

For these and other reasons, the idea of an attack mounted by airborne troops was discarded. Other options were considered, including an approach overland by troops disguised as Iraqis, but in the end it was decided that the task of destroying Tammuz 17 should be given to the Israeli air force.

The Israelis had amassed a large amount of information on Tammuz 17 but they now increased their intelligence effort to acquire even more data on the complex. As well as high altitude reconnaissance flights reportedly carried out by Phantom RF-4E aircraft, the Israelis obtained aerial photographs from SAVAM, the Iranian intelligence service. Despite the fact that diplomatic relations between Israel and Iran had been cut off when Ayatollah Khomeini came to power, unofficial contact had been maintained – to the extent that Israel supplied Iran with spare parts for the latter's American-manufactured aircraft and weapons as well as occasionally swapping intelligence. Politics notwithstanding, both countries had a common cause in frustrating Saddam Hussein's ambitions.

According to a story leaked by the Israelis, a formation of eight F-15 fighters and eight F-16 fighter-bombers took off from an air base at Beersheba on 7th June, just after 4 p.m. The F-15s, whose task it would be to provide escort cover for the F-16s and to jam the radar of the Iraqi air defence systems, were equipped with electronic counter-measures equipment and a combination of Sidewinder AIM-9, Sparrow AIM-7 and Shafrir Mk 3 Python air-to-air missiles. The F-16s, which would carry out the attack on the reactors, each carried two Mk 84 2000lb iron bombs capable of piercing eleven feet of concrete and up to fifteen metres of steel.

In addition to the main formation, another, smaller one took off at the same time. This consisted of an IAF tanker aircraft which had been repainted in the colours of Aer Lingus, the Irish airline which frequently leased its aircraft to Middle East airlines. It was accompanied by an escort of eight F-15 fighters.

The aircraft flew very low at heights of between thirty and sixty feet, radio silence being maintained throughout the two and a half hour flight from Israel to Al Tuwaitha. In addition to the use of the advanced navigation systems fitted in the aircraft, the formation was also guided towards the target during the latter stages of the flight by signals from an electronic beacon which had been planted in the area of the Tammuz 17 complex by an Israeli agent.

Approximately halfway through the flight, after entering Iraqi air space, the main formation of F-15s and F-16s refuelled from the tanker aircraft. Once this operation was complete, the tanker swung away and headed for Cyprus, where it landed as if carrying out a normal commercial flight. Its escort, which had remained with it until it had left Iraq, returned to Beersheba.

At 5.33 p.m. precisely, the pilot of the leading F-15 sighted the Tammuz 17 complex. The F-15s climbed to a height of one thousand feet from which they would cover the F-16s during the attack. The F-16s meanwhile climbed to a few hundred feet, deploying so as to approach the target from different directions and angles.

The speed and suddenness of the attack caught the Iraqis totally unawares. The radar-controlled, quadruple-barrelled ZSU-23 anti-aircraft guns opened fire as the eight aircraft attacked but were unable to hit the small, fast-flying F-16s. The bombing was precise and all sixteen 2000lb bombs found their mark, hitting the target within thirty feet of its centre. Within two minutes it was all over and the Israeli aircraft were heading for home.

Although the bombing was of unerring accuracy, the destruction of Tammuz I was in fact almost guaranteed by another factor hitherto never admitted by the Israelis. In his book *By Way of Deception*, the Mossad defector Victor Ostrovsky reveals that a Jewish-French technician named Damien Chassepied, who had been recruited by Mossad, had taken a briefcase, supposedly containing an electronic beacon, into the Tammuz I reactor. He was apparently under specific orders from Mossad to place the briefcase inside the reactor at a given time on a given day, although he would not have known why. In fact, Chassepied was inside the reactor when the F-16s carried out their bombing runs and was killed, the only casualty among the technicians working in the reactor at the time. It is inconceivable that he would have remained there during an attack and there has been speculation that his briefcase, unbeknownst to him, might also have contained a radio triggering device which, when it was switched on, initiated explosives pre-positioned in the reactor core.

In his book *The Invisible Bomb*, the British scientist and arms control specialist Frank Barnaby quotes reports that the reactor core was destroyed by charges previously placed inside it. He states that the charges were reportedly initiated by a radio signal from Israel and that such a signal was detected by monitoring stations in Jordan at the time of the attack.

However, remote initiation by this means would have been almost impossible to achieve because, due to the long range over which such a signal would have had to be transmitted, the antenna on the receiver attached to the explosive would have had to have been sited on top of the reactor in order to pick up the signal – this would have been impossible. Moreover, because of the distance involved, any such signal would have had to be transmitted on short wave, as opposed to high frequency, and would have been prone to problems caused by atmospherics.

The siting of an antenna inside the reactor would have been useless because it would have been totally shielded and unable to pick up any incoming signal from outside the building. Initiation of any explosive charges inside the reactor core would have had to be carried out from within the building itself. It is possible, therefore, that Damien Chassepied's briefcase did indeed contain a small ultra-high frequency radio transmitter which could have been activated as he switched on his 'beacon'. This would have sent a signal, coded so as not to be corrupted by any electronic emissions from within the reactor, to small receivers attached to the charges. Whatever the direct cause of his death, Chassepied's silence was ensured.

However, more than one Western intelligence service attempted to cast doubt on the Israeli story. CIA experts described it as 'frankly incredible', adding that in their opinion there was little doubt that the raid was mounted from Iranian territory. The CIA report at the time stated that it would have been impossible for the Israeli aircraft to fly such a distance undetected, especially with American-manned AWACS aircraft which scan the entire area of northern Saudi Arabia airspace and which can observe all the way to the Mediterranean.

Whatever the route taken by the Israeli aircraft, the raid had the desired effect. The Iraqis were stunned by the attack and for a few days afterwards there was no reaction from Baghdad. In fact, they had no idea who had carried out the raid. It was subsequently admitted by the Iraqi ambassador in Italy, Taha Ahmed el Dahud, that, until the Israeli government made an official statement about the attack, Baghdad had no knowledge who was responsible. The Iraqis were powerless to retaliate against Israel and had to content themselves with broadcasting propaganda. Saddam Hussein himself remained silent whilst he doubtless pondered long and hard over longer-term measures.

The rest of the world was also taken completely by surprise by the raid. The United States, Israel's closest ally, expressed surprise, dismay and disapproval. However, Israel stuck to its guns, maintaining that it had previously warned the Americans on a number of occasions about the Iraqi nuclear effort and had continually requested that Washington bring pressure to bear on the French and Italians to cease supplying equipment and technology to Iraq. The Israelis' pleas had fallen on deaf ears and so they had decided to take matters into their own hands.

In May 1981, a month before the raid, François Mitterrand had been elected president of France. Prior to this, he had on several occasions promised the Israelis that France's involvement with the Iraqi nuclear effort would be terminated and he had repeated this as part of his election manifesto in an attempt to win votes amongst France's large Jewish population. However, after successfully winning the election, Mitterrand and his administration performed a volte-face by announcing that the agreements previously undertaken by Giscard d'Estaing's government would be honoured and fulfilled. This reneging on the undertakings previously given by Mitterrand was one of the major factors which influenced Menachem Begin and his government to destroy Tammuz 17.

On the day following the raid Pierre Mauroy, the French prime minister, condemned the raid and ten days later President Mitterrand also expressed his disapproval. This response was no doubt due to the fact that, whilst the raid had provided them with an excuse to wriggle out of their involvement in the Iraqi nuclear programme, the French also wanted to ensure that relations with Iraq were not damaged: it was important that the high levels of sales of French arms to Baghdad remained unaffected and that the supply of Iraqi oil to France continued to flow.

With the destruction of Tammuz 17, the Iraqi nuclear development programme was halted for the time being. Iraq was by then fully committed to its war against Iran and the European scientists and technicians had again left Al Tuwaitha and returned to their own countries. It was at this point that Baghdad made the decision to change course from trying to use its reactors to produce weapon-grade material. Its main reason for doing so was that, although the two smaller research reactors had survived the raid and some 14kg of enriched uranium had been recovered, all surviving elements of the Tammuz 17 complex were still subject to regular inspection by teams from the IAEA. From then on, the Iraqis set out to procure equipment, material and technology by covert means for the purpose of setting up separate and highly secret uranium-enrichment facilities.

One of the first occasions when evidence of this came to light was in 1984 during the trial in Italy of members of an arms-smuggling organisation. It transpired that two years earlier, in 1982, the smugglers had offered to sell the Iraqis 33.9kg of plutonium. One of the defendants in the trial stated that he had attended meetings with Iraqi officials in Baghdad and subsequently in Rome. However, the proposed sale turned out to be a 'scam' on the part of the smugglers who did not possess any of the material but were using the scheme as a method of persuading the Iraqis to purchase conventional weapons.

The revelations from the trial revealed that the Iraqis were still actively interested in acquiring material for their nuclear development programme. In the following year, the Iraqis again declared their interests when they established a joint nuclear co-operation programme with Egypt and Pakistan. This was to involve the building of an experimental reactor in Egypt at Al Wadi Al-Gadid and the formation of a tripartite nuclear safety commission which would have its headquarters in Cairo and representatives based in both the other two countries. Although apparently intended to carry out nuclear research for purely non-military purposes, such an organisation would undoubtedly have facilitated the transfer of technology and material for military use. The relationship between Iraq and Pakistan, which has been reported as also having engaged in covert and illegal acquisition of technology and equipment for its own 'Project 706' nuclear weapon development programme, has since been of great interest to Western intelligence agencies; for some time they have monitored the exchange of scientists and technicians between the two countries.

In 1987, Saddam Hussein directed that the Iraqi effort to produce nuclear weapons should be stepped up and given the highest priority. By late in the following year, after the end of the war with Iran, the Iraqis were once again making every effort to acquire the technology, equipment and material which they required to construct their own nuclear production facilities. To assist them in doing so, they enlisted the aid of procurement agents and commercial companies in Europe and the United States.

At that time, Britain's Secret Intelligence Service had received reports of Saddam Hussein's directives ordering a major effort in nuclear weapon development. SIS produced an assessment which stated that if the Iraqis were successful in producing a nuclear weapon they would probably use it against Iran in order to bring the war to a swift conclusion. As a result of this report, SIS was ordered to co-operate fully with the CIA and Mossad in order to try and prevent Saddam Hussein from achieving his nuclear ambitions.

Meanwhile, the Iraqis also took measures to ensure that their nuclear development facilities were properly protected against any attack. A one-hundred-foot-high earthen rampart was constructed around Al Tuwaitha and batteries of radar-controlled ZSU-23 anti-aircraft guns, as well as surface-to-air missiles, have since been positioned around the complex. The missile and chemical weapon research centre at Saad 16 and the three Project DOT sites are all similarly protected whilst all key laboratories have been relocated underground.

In early 1989 press reports of a US Commerce Department ban on the export of a shipment of vacuum pumps to Iraq, on the grounds that they could be used in the production of nuclear fuel, indicated American concern. Indeed, in February of that year, the Director of US Naval Intelligence, Rear Admiral Thomas A. Brooks, had declared before a congressional committee that the Iraqis were once again actively involved in a nuclear weapons development programme.

In December 1989 the West German magazine *Der Spiegel* revealed that the Federal Criminal Police Bureau (BKA) and the Federal Intelligence Service (BND), together with the West German Customs, were investigating reports that the engineering company H & H Metalform Gmbh of Drensteinfurt had been involved in the supply to Iraq of equipment for the manufacture of gas ultra-centrifuges which would enable the enrichment of uranium to a level of 90 per cent.

It transpired that the alleged mastermind behind the affair was a seventy-seven-year-old man named Walter Busse who had formerly been a departmental manager in the Munich-based firm of MAN Technology Gmbh. Busse was alleged to have formed, without the knowledge of his employers, close relationships with nuclear scientists and technicians in Iraq and Brazil, as well as with West German suppliers of equipment and components.

Busse was said to have first made contact with the Iraqis through

Avibras, the Brazilian armaments manufacturer whom H & H Metalform had reportedly supplied with rocket engine components and casings. According to the *Der Spiegel* report, H & H Metalform had also previously supplied Iraq with rocket components. The Iraqis were actively seeking contacts through whom they could obtain nuclear technology and the Brazilians had apparently introduced them to Busse.

The West German investigators were reported to have discovered that Busse had visited Iraq four times during 1988 and 1989 and that in the course of these visits he had established contact with two senior Iraqi officials – Anees Mansour Wadi and Safaa al-Habobi – whose names would subsequently feature elsewhere during investigations into Iraqi procurement operations. Busse was accompanied by another West German, Bruno Stemmler, who was still employed by MAN Technology and was an expert in rotary technology. His employers were totally unaware of his journeys to Iraq with Busse.

MAN Technology is a company specialising in centrifuge technology and the Iraqis were in urgent need of Stemmler's expertise in producing centrifuges for use in uranium enrichment. Busse apparently arranged and supervised the installation of the special rolling machines and lathes supplied by H & H Metalform, he and Stemmler subsequently overseeing the start-up of the plant.

The ingredient that forms the basis for a nuclear weapon is raw uranium, which is mined from deposits in the ground. Previously, Iraq had imported large quantities from countries such as Brazil, Portugal, Italy and Niger. However, in August 1990, it was reported that Iraq was carrying out the mining of uranium from a mine not far from its northern border with Turkey. According to sources amongst Kurdish guerrillas, the mine is located near the village of Sarsenk, which is itself between the towns of Amadiyah and Dahok.

There are two methods by which weapon-grade material can be produced, depending on whether a nuclear weapon is to be based on enriched uranium or on plutonium. In the case of the former, the raw ore is converted by a chemical process into uranium hexafluoride gas at a conversion plant – it is known that the Iraqi phosphate plant located at Al Qaim also houses a hydrogen fluoride production facility, hydrogen fluoride being a component in the production of uranium hexafluoride as well as being used in the production of nerve agents.

Enriched uranium is then produced by a process which consists of the uranium hexafluoride being spun in a device known as a high speed centrifuge – in the case of weapon-grade uranium, a special version of this device is required to separate the radioactive U-235 from the inert U-238 of which it composes approximately 0.7 per cent. This process enriches the U-235 content to some 90 per cent, at which point it is weapon-grade uranium and can be used to manufacture a nuclear device.

In the initial stage of production of plutonium, uranium ore is processed through a purification plant, which converts it into uranium oxide. It then undergoes further processing in a fuel fabrication plant before being used as fuel in a reactor. Depending on the type of reactor, enriched uranium can also be used as fuel. The spent fuel is then reprocessed, plutonium being produced from it by irradiation.

Once sufficient enriched uranium or plutonium has been produced, it is formed into a hollow sphere comprising two halves. This is then wrapped in high explosive which is formed into a series of segments or 'lenses'. The design and construction of these 'lenses' is a critical process, as they must explode simultaneously with equal force on initiation. The timing of triggering of the explosives is therefore also critical and thus a series of ultra-high-speed high-voltage switches, known as 'krytrons', which operate at a speed of less than one tenth of a millionth of a second, are used to ensure that the detonators are initiated precisely at the same moment.

On initiation, the high explosive causes the enriched uranium or plutonium sphere to implode and compress to the size of an orange. At this point, an electronic gun inside the weapon discharges a stream of neutrons into the sphere, causing it to react in the form of a massive explosion.

It is known that, up until the invasion of Kuwait, Iraq's nuclear shopping list included components for centrifuges, amongst them special magnets manufactured from samarium cobalt which hold the centrifuges in place without contact whilst they are spinning. The Iraqis made several attempts during 1989 to acquire these magnets but it was later reported that China had agreed to assist Baghdad in the manufacture of them. Iraq was also seeking components for the construction of a plant to manufacture high-melting-point and rapid-detonation explosives. Other items included test equipment and krytrons.

In July 1990, the American authorities blocked the export of three furnaces, manufactured by Consarc Corporation of Rancocas, New Jersey, which could have been used for the melting and casting of titanium. According to reports, these furnaces, which could heat metals to temperatures of over 1800° Celsius, had been ordered by the Iraqi Ministry of Industry and Minerals. However, the American authorities stated that there was no such agency and that the furnaces were actually intended for installation at an Iraqi military research site at Karbala, south of Baghdad. The British government, at the request of the American authorities, placed a ban on the export to Iraq of two similar furnaces being manufactured by Consarc Corporation's British subsidiary, Consarc Engineering of Glasgow.

Despite the fact that the supply of equipment and components from the West and elsewhere was cut off after the invasion of Kuwait by the United Nations embargo, there were reports in September 1990 that Iraq was obtaining material from China, notably seven tons of the chemical lithium hydride which is used in the production of nuclear weapons and missile fuel. The deal, which was apparently worth $15 million, was reported to have been struck with China Wanbao Engineering Company, an engineering and construction subsidiary of the Chinese state-owned arms-manufacturing giant, Norinco. In documentation apparently circulated to a number of arms dealers, ten tons of the chemical had been included in a list of items being offered by the Chinese. Within a matter of days, Iraq had agreed to buy seven tons. A small quantity of 10kg was said to have been delivered, followed by a consignment of two tons.

China has been producing lithium since the 1950s and has legally exported lithium-based products, excluding lithium hydride, to countries such as Japan. Trading in the chemical has been handled in the past by another subsidiary of Norinco, China National Non-Ferrous Metals Import Export Corporation, which is not involved in the defence sector. China Wanbao Engineering Company, on the other hand, has previously been involved in defence-related projects – its own sales literature states that the company specialises in the 'construction of military and civil engineering products', including factories for the production of 'various solid propellants of rocket and missile'. It is believed that the company may have carried out factory construction projects in Iraq.

Needless to say, the Chinese were quick to deny the allegations and it was considered by sources in Britain and the United States that the Chinese government may not have been aware of the deal until news of it was broken in the media. Indeed, it is likely that Peking was extremely embarrassed – it had voted in favour of the United Nations embargo, no doubt as part of its attempt to rebuild diplomatic bridges with the West after the rift caused by the massacre in Tiananmen Square.

There have been varying estimates as to when Saddam Hussein will possess nuclear weapons. Evidence certainly suggests that the Iraqis have been concentrating on the construction of a centrifuge enrichment facility which would enable them to produce weapon-grade uranium. Given the fact that they have a large number of highly qualified scientists working on their nuclear development programme, and that they already possess a well-equipped arms manufacturing and engineering capability, it is unlikely that the Iraqis would find such a task beyond their capabilities.

With the absence of a suitable reactor and with the 14kg of enriched uranium salvaged from Tammuz 1 being regularly checked by the IAEA, it is unlikely that the Iraqis will attempt to produce plutonium-based weapons. The more feasible option would be devices based upon weapon-grade uranium produced in a gas-centrifuge enrichment facility. Having produced them, however, the Iraqis will be faced with the problem of producing some form of delivery system – either in bomb configuration to be delivered by aircraft or, rather more likely, a missile warhead. The engineering of nuclear warheads is not a simple process and would require extensive production facilities which would be un-avoidably large and vulnerable to air attack.

There is little hard evidence of the current state of the Iraqi nuclear effort, but expert estimates initially stated they might produce a nuclear weapon system within five years. In some cases, as more evidence has come to light concerning Baghdad's procurement of equipment and technology, this has been revised to between two and three years.

However, in November 1990, *The Sunday Times* carried a report claiming that America's Defense Intelligence Agency (DIA) had issued a report to the Department of Defense which stated that Iraq was far more advanced in the development of a nuclear weapon than had previously been estimated and that it was possible that such a weapon could be produced within two months. The information on which the report was based had apparently been supplied by two agents inside Iraq. When this was analysed together with data concerning Iraqi procurement of nuclear-related technology, the DIA had come to the conclusion that the production of an Iraqi nuclear weapon could be imminent.

Reactions to the DIA report were mixed. It was inevitably seen in some quarters as being an attempt to stem the waning of political support within America for military action to resolve the Gulf crisis. In response, the DIA quoted further evidence which had given it reason to believe that Iraqi nuclear weapon production was further advanced than had previously been thought – in July 1990, Swiss police raided a factory in Berne where they discovered details of transactions involving the supply to Iraq of special scoops used in gas centrifuges. It was this information which gave rise to the suspicion that the centrifuges themselves had been constructed and were in position.

In order to obtain the technology, equipment and material to permit it to develop its own nuclear capability, Iraq has been forced to acquire it covertly and sometimes illegally from countries in the West, Asia and the East. It would not have been able to achieve its degree of progress so far without the co-operation of certain individuals, commercial organisations and even governments for whom the prospect of considerable financial and political gains assumed greater importance than the ethics of dealing with a brutal, repressive regime which would be able to threaten the stability of the entire Middle East, and consequently world peace, once it possessed the ultimate weapon.

5 · Merchants of Death

I

A small number of British journalists have for the past three years been publishing reports calling attention to the Baghdad regime's appalling record on human rights, its use of chemical weapons, its support for terrorist groups and its efforts to destabilise certain parts of the Middle East. The *Independent*, in particular, had attempted to alert its readers to the continuous supply of arms to Iraq by Western countries. Shortly before *Observer* journalist Farzad Bazoft's trial in March 1990, it had published an account of how the Department of Trade and Industry gave its support to the granting of a £450 million line of credit to Iraq, which already owed huge sums of money to British companies. The agreement for the credit was signed despite the fact that Bazoft had earlier been arrested and accused of spying, together with the British nurse Daphne Parish, and that another Briton, Ian Richter, had for some time been languishing in an Iraqi prison on trumped-up corruption charges. At the time that this huge amount of credit was arranged, none of the British government departments involved in sanctioning and arranging the deal raised the question of the three captives.

However, the British were not alone in their ambivalence towards dealings with Iraq. The French and Italians were even more so, whilst the Bonn government seems for some years to have steadfastly turned a blind eye to the activities of West German companies supplying Iraq with technology and equipment for its conventional, chemical and nuclear weapon development programmes.

In its issue of 24 September 1990, the West German magazine *Der Spiegel* alleged that Messerschmitt-Bolkow-Blohm had supplied Iraq with a 'fuel air explosive' weapon which created a blast equivalent in power to a 'small atomic explosion'. The article stated that the company had carried out trials on the weapon at its test site at Schrobhausen before supplying blueprints of the weapon and test equipment to Egypt, at the time one of Iraq's main arms suppliers and an ally in the Western plan to stop the spread of the Islamic revolution from Iran. The blueprints were apparently passed on to the Iraqis, who immediately commenced production. The article also reported that the Iraqis were in possession of technology purchased from West Germany which would enable them to manufacture highly concentrated 'blue acid', the chemical reported as capable of destroying the filters in the gas respirators worn by the troops of the allied nations.

This report highlighted once again the West's past willingness to sell Saddam Hussein sufficient arms and technology to enable him to build a war machine capable of providing powerful opposition to the combined forces arrayed against him in Saudi Arabia since the invasion of Kuwait. This was in spite of embargoes placed by Britain, the US, the European Commission and other individual Western nations on the supply of arms to either side in the Gulf War.

As has already become patently obvious, both East and West must share equal blame for helping to create Saddam Hussein's war machine. In the mid-1980s, Iraq was the world's leading importer of arms, its expenditure reported as reaching $33.3 billion at the height of the Gulf War in 1984. In 1989, with the Gulf War over, it was still spending heavily on arms – to the tune of $15 billion. Estimates by the Stockholm International Peace Research Institute (SIPRI) indicate that Iraq may have spent a staggering $80 billion during the period 1980–90. Another study, carried out by Iraqi officials who defected from Baghdad, put the figure for the first eight years of the war at $105 billion. When compared with Britain's expenditure of $69.5 billion and France's $68.6 billion during the same period, the scale of Baghdad's arms procurement rapidly becomes apparent.

At the end of the Gulf War, Iraq was in possession of the most powerful war machine in the Middle East. During the eight years of hostilities with Iran, Baghdad imported from the Soviet Union alone $10 billion worth of arms which included Mi-24 Hind and Mi-8 Hip helicopters, MiG and Sukhoi fighter aircraft, Tupolev bombers, Ilyushin 67 transport aircraft, Frog-7 and Scud-B missiles, T-62 and T-72 main battle tanks, BM-21 rocket launchers, artillery and vast quantities of small arms and ammunition. However, payment for much of this weaponry still remains outstanding. As at August 1990, the Soviet Union was owed 3.7 billion roubles.

During the 1980s, Iraq was one of a small number of nations which accounted for a large proportion of the Soviet Union's thirty-seven per cent share of all weapons sales to the Third World. However, by the beginning of the decade, it had already increasingly found that much Soviet equipment, which was in any case mainly of low technology category, was second-rate. Saddam started to turn elsewhere for more sophisticated hardware.

Another major factor which caused Iraq to seek arms from sources other than the Soviet Union was that Moscow wanted to earn more hard currency from overseas arms sales and was increasingly reluctant to extend further credit to a customer who had already proved to be unreliable over repayment. It was apparently because of payment problems that Iraq was refused MiG-27 aircraft during the Iranian offensive of spring 1987.

Iraq's decision was made on the advice of Egyptian military experts. Former defence minister Abd el-Halim Abu Ghazalla and General Abdel Ghanni al-Gamsi recalled how, in 1971, the Egyptians had been forced to delay a large-scale attack on the Israeli positions in Sinai for two years because they had to retrain their troops, who had used solely Soviet weapons for the previous fifteen years, on equipment purchased from Britain, France and West Germany. It was thus not until 1973 that the Egyptians were able to initiate the 'Operation Ramadan' which started the Yom Kippur War.

Early in the Gulf War, the Iraqis stepped up their arms procurement from the West in an attempt to pressurise a reluctant Soviet Union into abiding by the terms of a friendship and co-operation treaty signed by the two countries in April 1972. The Iraqis were aware that the treaty ended in April 1987 and that Moscow, anxious to improve ties with its southern neighbour, Iran, was unlikely to carry on providing Iraq with weapons on the same scale as before. In view of the fact that Iraq was the blatant aggressor in its conflict with Iran, the Soviets were reluctant to sell it weapons of an offensive nature, preferring to restrict supply to those intended for purely defensive roles.

It was thus for both strategic and political reasons, as well as to seek high technology, that Baghdad decided to obtain arms from the West. The Ba'ath government was well aware that reliance on any one supplier made it vulnerable to political blackmail at a possibly crucial moment. It also decided to rely wherever possible on direct dealings with arms manufacturers, knowing full well that in several countries commercial expediency and the pursuit of profit, rather than ethics, were the governing factors in sales of arms. To assist in establishing contact with manufacturers and suppliers, Baghdad enlisted the aid of Iraqi businessmen resident abroad, as well as that of arms dealers in Egypt, Jordan and Saudi Arabia.

Whilst they improved their procurement network in the West, the Iraqis were also establishing sources in communist countries in the East, such as China and North Korea, whose products were in the main copies of Soviet weapons and equipment already in service with Iraqi forces.

From the late 1970s onwards, China established a place for itself amongst the suppliers of arms in the international market and played a particularly prominent role during the Gulf War, supplying arms to both sides. It has one arms sales organisation, the government-owned company Norinco, which owns a large number of subsidiaries. Norinco markets a very wide range of Chinese-manufactured products which extends from small arms and artillery to fighter aircraft and Hai Ying-2 Silkworm missiles of the type purchased and used by Iran and Iraq during the Gulf War.

Chinese arms sales to Iraq during the 1980s were considerable. During the period 1981 to 1984, Peking supplied 700 T-59 and 600 T-69 tanks, 650 Type YW-531 armoured personnel carriers and 720 Type 59/1 130mm artillery pieces. Between 1981 and 1987, F-6, F-7 and F-8 fighter aircraft were also supplied, the F-6s and F-7s having been assembled in Egypt. During the last two years of the war, four B-6 bombers, which were Chinese copies of the Soviet 'Badger', and seventy-two Hai Ying-2 Silkworm coastal-defence missiles were also supplied. The Chinese were, however, assiduously supplying arms to Iran at the same time.

However, once Iraq found it could gain access to superior Western equipment, mainly because of extremely generous loans and credit terms from European banks who were in most cases tacitly encouraged by their respective governments, it increasingly turned away from Moscow and Peking towards the West. Whilst it still relied predominantly on Soviet-type weaponry, it obtained most of its advanced equipment from the French.

France had begun supplying Iraq with arms in 1967 and continued until early 1990, by which time it had overtaken China as Baghdad's second-largest supplier after the Soviet Union. The inventory of items supplied during thirteen years is lengthy. In addition to Mystère and Mirage fighters, it includes Alouette, Gazelle, Puma and Super Frelon helicopters supplied by Aerospatiale; HOT and Milan anti-tank missiles and Exocet AM-39 and MM-40 anti-ship missiles from Euromissile; as well as AMX-10P mechanised combat vehicles and AMX-30 main battle tanks supplied by GIAT. Other French companies who have supplied weapons and equipment to Baghdad include Panhard, Thompson-Brandt, Matra, Thomson CSF, Luchaire, COFRAS, Raclet, Matra Manurhin Défense and Lacroix.

In 1980, shortly after declaring war on Iran, the Iraqis had turned to France in desperation after Baghdad itself was subjected to air raids. Saddam Hussein had been advised, by former generals of the deposed Shah's imperial army, that the Iranians were desperately short of trained pilots and that those who had previously served the Shah would, if permitted to fly, take off and not return to Iran. In fact, this was totally incorrect and it was a grave miscalculation on Saddam Hussein's part to allow himself to be convinced by such ill-founded beliefs. Not only did the Iraqis fail to knock out the Iranian air force but the Iranian pilots, putting duty before ideology, also carried the war into the Iraqi heartlands. Baghdad, which is only four minutes' flying time from the border with Iran, was subjected to a series of well-planned air attacks which exposed the inadequacy of the Iraqi air defences. The Iraqis immediately placed orders with the French for considerable amounts of air defence systems and eighty Mirage fighters.

The French arms industry has always enjoyed a full measure of support from its government, the latter's attitude apparently being that arms exports are in the interest of national security and that they enable France to afford to manufacture its own arsenal.

There is no doubt that France considered Iraq an important client deserving preferential treatment. There is evidence that the French intelligence services tolerated several 'irregularities' by the Iraqi Mukhabarat on their own soil in order to keep the path smooth for lucrative arms deals. In 1979 Barzan Takriti, Saddam Hussein's half-brother and the head of the Mukhabarat, commissioned his deputy, Sabaawi Ibrahim, to oversee the creation of a new network in Europe. This consisted in part of companies owned by Iraqi residents in France which acted as fronts for both covert procurement tasks and intelligence operations. Sabaawi Ibrahim in turn sent Saad Saleh Al-Jabouri, a Mukhabarat officer, to Paris as the chief of a new bureau housed at the Iraqi Airways office in the French capital. Part of his brief was to mastermind the hunting down and elimination of opponents of Saddam Hussein's regime as well as carrying out operations against Syrian targets.

Al-Jabouri was subsequently joined by two other Iraqis – Kadhem Al-Rabie and Nizar Hamdoun, the former an Iraqi businessman who subsequently used his connections to set up a 'front' company and was successful in striking a number of important arms deals in France. Nizar Hamdoun, currently Saddam Hussein's deputy foreign minister, played the part of Ba'ath party representative on the National Union of Iraqi Students (NUIS), but in reality was a Mukhabarat officer, senior in rank to both his Paris-based colleagues. Hamdoun masterminded the kidnapping of two Iraqi students, Muhammed Hassan Khair al-Din and Fawzy Muhammed. They were drugged and smuggled comatose out of France back to Iraq.

Several years later, in 1988, al-Jabouri and al-Rabie were instructed to return to Iraq. The former departed from France first and was arrested and executed soon after his arrival in Baghdad. News of his death reached al-Rabie, who went into hiding and obtained protection from the French. He is still sought by the Mukhabarat but remains in France under guard.

According to a defector from the Mukhabarat, the French intelligence services were aware of the activities of the bureau, but there was a tacit understanding that these would not harm French interests and there would be no breaking of French law. As far as the French were concerned, the bureau's role was to work with agents of the Christian forces in Lebanon who were supported by the Iraqis – the same forces who in 1982, led by the Israelis into the Sabra and Chattilla refugee camps, massacred over eight hundred Palestinian women and children. The bureau was also to liaise with Lebanese-born French arms dealers and drug traffickers, mainly Christian Maronites, in organising anti-Syrian operations in Syria, Lebanon, Europe and Cyprus. In fact the Iraqis only carried out one murder in Paris during this period, in the Champs Elysées, in 1986; the victim was a Syrian named Hassan al-Haidari.

Despite French efforts to ensure that the Iraqis adhered to the agreement and confined their activities to anti-Syrian targets, Sabaawi Ibrahim supplied the Paris cell with fresh instructions to start another operation to be led by Nizar Hamdoun, who would report directly to Sabaawi Ibrahim himself. By the end of 1980, a second bureau had grown out of the first one and was run as an import and export company by Fadel Jawad Kadhem and Safaa al-Habobi, two post-graduate students living in France. These two would feature later in a procurement operation set up by Iraq in Britain.

The company was a front for the purchase of heavy metal presses and precision milling machines for use in one of the plants being constructed by the Nassr State Enterprise for Mechanical Industries (NSEMI) at Salman Pak on the Kut–Baghdad highway. After finishing his studies in France, Safaa al-Habobi subsequently became the chairman of NSEMI.

In 1967, France's stock in the Arab world had gone up following General de Gaulle's decision to stop supplying arms to Israel after it started the Six Day War against Egypt and Syria. However, in 1968, following the military coup that brought a Ba'ath party to power in Iraq, the French had suffered a major setback when the new regime cancelled an order for Mystère fighters. Former Ba'ath party members later accused the pro-British element in the party – led by Saddam Hussein and Hassan al-Bakr – of cancelling the deal for the benefit of Britain.

Thus the French learned an important lesson. During the Gulf War they co-ordinated their arms trade policies so that they tied in with regional as well as global political developments. At the same time, Paris kept an eye on the Baghdad regime and assisted it with some of its ambitious plans, including co-operation in the fields of intelligence and security.

During the first half of the 1980s, French assistance to Iraq also extended to the loan of aircraft and personnel for use in the conflict against Iran. On 26th May 1983 a secret agreement was signed by President François Mitterrand, covering the supply on lease of five Super Etendard aircraft. In February of that year there had been reports in the French media that the government was planning to sell the aircraft, complete with Exocet missiles, to Iraq, but the Defence Minister at that time, Charles Hernu, denied the report. However, at the beginning of June, Hernu signed an agreement with the manufacturers of the aircraft, Dassault and Snecma. Subsequently, Iraqi pilots and technicians underwent fourteen weeks of intensive training at an airbase at Cuers.

On the morning of 7 October 1983 five Super Etendards left the Brittany base of Landivisiau, staging at Corsica before eventually making a rendezvous with the aircraft carrier *Clemenceau* in the Mediterranean. During the following week, the aircraft were repainted in Iraqi colours whilst checks were carried out to ensure that the pilots removed all identifying insignia from their personal equipment and that they were not carrying any incriminating documentation. The aircraft were then flown to Iraq.

A detachment of thirty French military personnel, including seven pilots and several technicians from Dassault, Snecma, Aerospatiale and Matra, were based in Iraq to provide training and logistical support. It was subsequently reported but not confirmed that the pilots also participated in missions. The five aircraft were returned to France in September 1985.

During their two years in Iraqi service, the Super Etendards and their Exocet missiles proved a decisive factor in the outcome of the Gulf War. The five aircraft enabled Iraq to intensify what was known as the 'tanker war', which achieved wider political objectives for the Iraqis. As mentioned in a previous chapter, it was a French-supplied Exocet which in 1987 crippled the American frigate USS *Stark*, causing the US navy's rules of engagement to be changed and ultimately resulting in America's direct involvement in the Gulf War.

In May 1989, it was revealed that France was negotiating with Iraq for the supply of fifty Dassault Mirage 2000 and fifty Alpha Jet trainer/ ground attack aircraft. It was, however, France and not Iraq which had sought the deal. In efforts intensified during 1989, Defence Minister Jean-Pierre Chevènement's visit to the four Gulf states also included Iraq. The Iraqis were impressed by the performance of the Mirage 2000 at the Dubai Air Show on 29th January 1989, when two aircraft flew all the way from France, stopping once in Egypt and refuelling in mid-air several times en route.

Dassault, one of the jewels in the French arms industry's crown, had supplied the Iraqis with aircraft since 1976, when it sold them thirty-two Mirage F1EQ and four F1BQ. A second order for twenty-eight F1EQ-4 and three F1BQ was placed in the same year and all these aircraft were delivered between 1980 and 1982. A third order for twenty Mirage F1EQ-5, equipped to carry Exocet missiles, was placed in 1981 and these were delivered between 1983 and 1985. At the same time, a further eighteen F1EQ-6 and six F1BQ were ordered, delivery being planned to take place at intervals between 1987 and 1989.

However, by 1987 Dassault had a virtually empty order book and had sold only one aircraft the previous year. Previously, the company had been heavily dependent upon Iraqi orders. By 1988 the situation looked extremely grim and thus Dassault, as well as the French government, was desperate to obtain the contract for the supply of Mirage 2000s and Alpha Jets to Baghdad. During a defence exhibition which took place in Iraq in May 1989, the chairman and chief executive of the company, Serge Dassault, was in attendance, together with the French chief of staff, General Maurice Schmitt.

Other companies were competing for the contract to supply Iraq with advanced jet trainers, including British Aerospace with its Hawk 100, Spain's CASA with the C-101 and Italy's Aermacchi which was offering its MB-339. Dassault also faced tough competition as far as its Mirage 2000 was concerned, in the shape of the Panavia Tornado and the Russian MiG-29 Fulcrum.

However, there was one far greater problem which threatened to jeopardise Dassault's chances of winning these two vital contracts, worth a total of FFr22 billion. Iraq already owed France more than FFr25 billion, of which approximately half had been spent on purchases of arms, credits for which had been guaranteed by the Compagnie Française d'Assurance pour le Commerce Extérieur (COFACE), the state export insurance agency. To make matters worse, Iraq had already refused to pay instalments due. For the period 1988–9 alone, the amount owed was FFr8 billion but the Iraqis intended to pay only FFr1 billion. The French retaliated by impounding the eighteen Mirage F1EQ-6 which had been completed and were awaiting delivery to Baghdad.

Both Dassault and the French government were in a dilemma. The government was naturally reluctant to increase its exposure to any further default on Iraqi debt, but Dassault was keen to deliver the eighteen aircraft and to secure further orders.

In September 1989, however, it was announced that the French had reached an agreement with Baghdad over the rescheduling of the debt. Under the new arrangement Iraq would pay FFr1.8 billion immediately, the remaining FFr7 billion for the period 1988–9 being repaid over six years.

In the face of strong competition from Britain and the Soviet Union, Dassault was also ready to compromise. As a result, four of the F1EQ-6 aircraft were delivered in November 1989. During the following month a further ten were delivered.

A few days after the aircraft landed in Iraq, Jean-Pierre Chevènement, who was in the Gulf as a guest of the United Arab Emirates to attend their national day celebrations, made a rapid visit to Baghdad on which he was accompanied by George Marcel Dassault, Jr. An argument ensued between the French and the Iraqis over the amount of money owed by Baghdad to France for previous deliveries of arms. The Iraqis claimed that it was FFr25 billion, while the French maintained that the figure was over FFr44 billion when taking into account the cost of modifications to weapon systems, such as adding extra missile pylons to enable the Mirages to carry Exocet and other, non-French missiles, as well as the fitting of in-flight refuelling equipment and additional avionics.

In December 1989, a high-level delegation headed by Jacques Mitterrand, the president's brother, visited Baghdad to discuss closer co-operation on aerospace and other projects. It included in its ranks representatives of several French companies. During their stay, which included a visit to the Saad-16 missile development complex near Mosul, meetings took place with the Iraqi Deputy Prime Minister, Sadoun Hammadi, Minister of Industry and Military Industrialisation General Hussein Kamal Al-Majid, Transport and Communications Minister Mohammad Hamza Al-Zubiadi, and Oil Minister Issam Abdul Rahim al-Chalabi.

In February 1990, Jean-Pierre Chevénement paid a further visit to Baghdad, where he met Saddam Hussein. Prior to the visit, Iraq had placed a FFr900 million order with Thomson-CSF for advanced electronic equipment and had paid for it in cash. This unusual gesture was later reported to have been made in order to persuade the French to sell

Iraq the Mirage 2000. It proved to be a successful ploy – Chevènement agreed in principle not only to sell the Mirage 2000 but also to permit the aircraft to be manufactured in Iraq. In September of the previous year, the Iraqis had already started constructing the Mirage assembly facilities in the Al-Iskandria military industrial complex near Al-Hillah, south of Baghdad. The entire area was rebuilt after the massive explosion, in a missile-booster solid-fuel manufacturing facility, on 18th August 1989, which killed seven hundred people.

The rescheduling of Iraq's debt repayments having already apparently overcome any objections from the French Ministry of Finance, an agreement was drawn up and was due to be signed on 2nd August 1990 – the day that Saddam Hussein invaded Kuwait.

Despite fears over possible Iraqi defaults on debt repayments, the flow of French equipment and technology to Baghdad was never halted. Sales of the latter included assistance in the development of an Iraqi AWACS aircraft, designated Adnan-1 and based on an Ilyushin-76 equipped with a Thomson-CSF 'Tiger' radar, as well as the provision of expertise in maintaining and operating it. The Iraqis never made any attempt to conceal the existence of this aircraft and thus Baghdad's version of AWACS was seen by several Western journalists during visits to Iraq.

French technicians also helped the Iraqis to upgrade some of their Scud-B missiles for which the Iraqis badly needed an effective guidance system. When Egyptian technicians had reduced the payload and lengthened the boosters, the missiles had become notoriously inaccurate and had fallen some ten miles away from targets when launched against Tehran in 1987 and early 1988. As Saddam Hussein's forces came under pressure from Iranian counter-attacks, so he wanted to blitz more Iranian cities and power stations as well as to destroy Kharg and Larak Islands in order to prevent Iran exporting oil. He could not wait for Egyptian and Korean scientists to finish tests on guidance systems under development and so he called upon the French.

By mid-April 1988 the missiles, now renamed Al-Hussein and Al-Abbas, were fitted with a sophisticated inertial guidance system alleged to have been manufactured and supplied by Sagem, despite the fact that France is a signatory with six other industrialised nations – the US, Britain, West Germany, Italy, Canada and Japan – to the Missile Technology Control Regime which forbids the export of such equipment and obliges signatories to stop companies under their jurisdiction from supplying components for missiles possessing ranges of over three hundred miles and capable of carrying 500kg warheads. The maximum

1 King Faisal II of Iraq (centre) with the Prince Regent Abd al-Illah (left) in 1952.

2 President Nasser of Egypt, who opposed Iraq's attempt to annexe Kuwait in 1961.

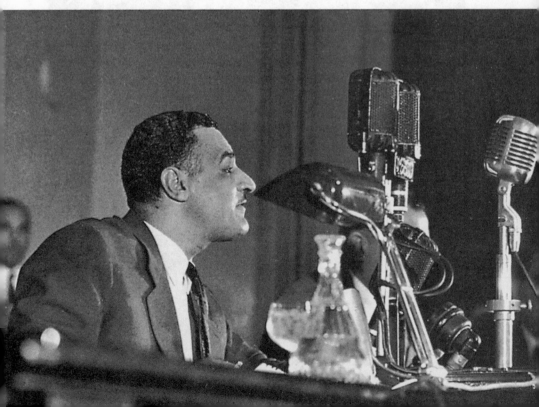

3 General Qasim of Iraq, cheered by crowds after his move against Kuwait.

4 Saddam Hussein and President Brezhnev: the signing of the Iraqi–Soviet friendship treaty in 1972 encouraged the US to support the Shah of Iran.

5 The late Ayatollah Khomeini. The Islamic revolution he led in 1979
   encouraged the West to support Saddam Hussein.

6 The *USS Stark*, crippled by an Iraqi Exocet missile in 1987.

7 Kurdish victims of the Iraqi poison gas attack on Halabja in 1988.

8 Saddam Hussein orders his troops into the Fao Peninsula, a decisive point in the Gulf War.

9 Iraq recaptures the Fao Peninsula, the first Iraqi advance in eight years.

10 Former French Prime Minister Chirac with Saddam Hussein in 1974.
France moved early into the Iraqi arms market.

11 (below left) The Adnan-1, an early warning aircraft, was produced by Iraq
with French assistance.

12 (bottom left) A German MBB Bo105 helicopter fitted with HOT anti-tank
missiles. A large number of these were supplied to Iraq via Casa of Spain.

13 (below right) An Al-Abbas surface-to-surface missile – the majority of
Iraq's missiles are based upon modified Soviet Scud-Bs.

14 (above left) The Paragon, one of the three guns constructed for Dr Gerald
    Bull's project HARP during the 1960s.

15 (above right) Gerald Bull (left) with one of the project HARP guns in 1965.
    He is accompanied by Jean Lesage, then premier of Quebec.

16 Components for a large rail-mounted gun, codenamed Project 839,
    impounded by Greek customs officials in 1990, en route to Iraq.

17 Massive posters portray Saddam's war as a rebirth of glorious Arab history.
This one depicts Sa'd bin Abi Waqqass who imposed Arab Islamic
hegemony in Mesopotamia.

ranges of Al-Abbas and Al-Hussein were increased from two hundred to three hundred and five hundred miles respectively.

Despite stringent laws governing the export of arms, West Germany has also figured prominently amongst those Western countries from which military equipment and sophisticated technology have found their way to Baghdad. Over a period of eight years commencing in 1982, a total of sixty-eight West German companies supplied equipment and assisted in setting up arms production facilities in Iraq as part of Baghdad's efforts to become self-sufficient.

In July 1990, West German authorities began investigating a contract placed in Iraq with Ferrostaal of Essen for the supply of a forging plant located at the town of Taji, north of Baghdad. This formed part of a complete steel-manufacturing complex consisting of a casting foundry, a forging line and a rolling mill. A consortium of German companies under Klockner INA of Duisburg constructed the foundry whilst the forging plant was built by Ferrostaal in co-operation with SMS Hasenclever of Düsseldorf, the latter being responsible for the supply of a 2500-ton hydraulic open die forging press. The construction of the rolling mill was being carried out by Danielli, an Italian company. The supply of engineering services, machining equipment and moulding lines was provided by a Swiss company, Georg Fischer.

Other German contractors involved in the project included Zublin of Stuttgart, ABB of Mannheim, which supplied an electricity substation, and MDH of Duisburg, which provided furnaces and horizontal casting equipment. Cranes for the complex were supplied by Mannesmann Demag of Duisburg and MAN of Nuremburg, whilst Thyssen Rheinstaal provided cranes and transportation equipment for the plant's melting shop. The supply of two heat treatment furnaces and civil engineering was the responsibility of two Italian companies, Marano Ticini of Siti and Icomsa of Padova. The entire production complex was due to be commissioned in 1991 and would have had an annual output of 350,000 tons.

Some of these companies also helped Iraq to construct a similar complex near Salman Pak, part of which is a plant used for the manufacturing of chemical and biological weapons. The reasons for locating such a plant in the middle of a heavy industrial complex are twofold: firstly, to conceal the production of chemical and biological weapons, which is the responsibility of the Nassr State Enterprise for Mechanical Industries (NSEMI); secondly, all Iraqi establishments of military and strategic importance are protected by sophisticated air defence systems and are surrounded by massive ramparts of sand, the lesson having been learned from the Israeli attack on Al Tuwaitha in 1981.

When the existence of the complex was publicised in the *Guardian* newspaper in July 1990, all the German companies involved in its construction maintained that it was intended for the production of industrial components and pipelines. However, the *Guardian* obtained documents which proved that the plant was intended to produce 1000 barrels per annum for artillery pieces ranging in calibre from 105mm to 203mm.

It was also a West German company which in 1981 constructed three large bomb- and gas-proof shelter complexes in the Al-Yarmouk, Al-Badr and Al-Saad areas of Baghdad for use as emergency seats of government. A further similar complex is reported to have been constructed underneath Saddam Hussein's presidential palace. All four complexes are apparently fitted with sophisticated ventilation and air filtration systems which were reported as having been designed and fitted by a British company.

Other West German companies which supplied Iraq with equipment include Daimler Benz which, from 1976 to 1986, sold Baghdad 6737 of its highly versatile Unimog 4×4 trucks and other vehicles. Daimler Benz also featured as the supplier of engines for a large quantity of Brazilian-manufactured armoured vehicles purchased by Iraq, whilst Magirus-Deutz supplied cross-country vehicles.

Revelations about the activities of one particular German company shed light on South African connections with the Baghdad regime. The giant arms manufacturer Rheinmetall was discovered to have supplied Paraguay with a complete plant for the filling and priming of 155mm artillery shells. Subsequent investigations by the West German authorities revealed that the plant had in fact been transhipped to South Africa, where it had been assembled and installed by Armscor, the state-owned arms manufacturing conglomerate. It transpired that Armscor was providing Iraq with 155mm ammunition for use in a number of FH-70 howitzers supplied by Saudi Arabia. These weapons are manufactured jointly by Britain, Italy and West Germany and it was subsequently discovered that a total of seventy-two were sold to Saudi Arabia during the period 1982–3 by International Military Services Ltd, the commercial arm of the British Ministry of Defence.

In addition to its involvement in the Iraqi missile development programme and allegedly in the provision of 'fuel air explosive' technology, Messerschmitt-Bolkow-Blohm has also been reported as being involved in the supply of aircraft, through contracts fulfilled through companies in other countries, which ended up in Baghdad. Between 1983 and 1985, the company sold twenty-three of its BO-105 helicopters as part of a 'package' assembled by the Spanish company CASA, in which Messerschmitt-Bolkow-Blohm held an 11 per cent shareholding at the time. The package included HOT anti-tank missiles supplied by Euromissile, of which Messerschmitt-Bolkow-Blohm owns 50 per cent in partnership with Aérospatiale of France.

In 1985, however, the Spanish government blocked the export of sixty more BO-105CBs armed with HOT anti-tank missiles. Three years later, Messerschmitt-Bolkow-Blohm indirectly supplied Iraq with twenty-two BK-117 helicopters. These were sold to a Bavarian company in civilian configuration, but were subsequently converted for military use by the Austrian firm of Densel, which is based in Augsburg, in Germany, before being sent on to Iraq.

Other Spanish companies who have conducted business with the Baghdad regime include Santana, which sold Land Rovers on which were mounted 106mm recoilless rifles. Other exports to Iraq from Spain include mortar ammunition and aircraft bombs. Explosives and mortar ammunition were also supplied to Baghdad from Spain's neighbour Portugal, the exporter being the company SPEL. In 1988 the Portuguese lifted the ban on exports of arms to Iraq which had been in force during the Gulf War.

Italy has also been an important source of arms for Baghdad and at the beginning of the Gulf War played a major part in modernising Iraq's small navy.

In 1981, Iraq placed a large order for naval vessels with the Italian manufacturer Fincantieri. It comprised a supply ship, a floating dock, four Lupo class frigates and six Assad class corvettes, the total value of the contract being $2.86 billion. The supply ship *Agnadeen* and the floating dock were delivered just prior to an embargo being placed on exports to Iraq by the Italian government in late 1986 because of payment problems. In fact, they never reached Iraq. They were sailed to the Egyptian port of Alexandria and are still there today. Two of the corvettes were also handed over to Iraqi crews but were impounded and have since remained moored in the Italian naval base at La Spezia. The crews of these two vessels, who number approximately one hundred personnel, are still living in La Spezia together with their families. The other four frigates and four corvettes remained undelivered and impounded at La Spezia where they are to this day.

However, 1988 saw the start of a two-year dispute when the Iraqis threatened to tear up the contract on the grounds of default by the suppliers and to refuse delivery of the remaining vessels. The Iraqi threats caused considerable consternation within the Italian government because the total penalty to Italian companies would have been some $3.9 billion. Following legal advice, the Italians commenced negotiations with Baghdad in an attempt to resolve the situation. However, the Iraqis were pressing for compensation for the delay in delivery, claiming that they had already paid $441 million. They demanded extra financial arrangements, the transfer of technology from Fincantieri worth $150 million, the supply free of charge of the *Saettia*, a prototype high-speed fast-attack craft developed as a private venture by the company, delivery of ten Agusta B-212 naval helicopters ordered in 1983 and 1986, and supply of $150 million worth of naval command and control technology developed by another state-owned company, Selenia. Negotiations were still continuing when the invasion of Kuwait took place.

Supplies of aircraft, weapons and equipment from Italy were maintained throughout the Gulf War. The helicopter manufacturer Agusta, which produces aircraft under licence from Bell, Sikorsky and McDonnell Douglas in addition to manufacturing its own models, allegedly played a principal role. Between 1980 and 1988, it is reported as having supplied a large number of helicopters which included two of its own A-109, six S61A-4, thirty Model 500C, fifty-four Model 500D, five anti-submarine variants of the AB-212, twelve AB-412 Griffons and six AB-412.

During the same period, Iraq also purchased naval weapon systems from Italy. These included ten Aspide/Albatross SAM launchers, together with 224 Aspide surface-to-air missiles, and ten Otomat-2L launchers with sixty Otomat-2 anti-ship missiles.

Other items supplied by Italy included Valsella anti-tank and anti-personnel mines, 4 × 4 light armoured vehicles manufactured by ASA, and Mirach 100 helicopter-launched reconnaissance drones produced by Meteor. Italian companies also assisted Iraq in assembling its own ammunition production facilities. Until April 1987, Iraqi pilots were undergoing flying training at an Italian air base at Villanova d'Albenga. It was only after a storm of publicity in the Italian media that the arrangement was terminated.

Even countries normally regarded as maintaining a strictly neutral stance appear to have been involved in supplying arms to Saddam Hussein. Norway's Dyno Industrier supplied Iraq with 1200 tons of explosives in 1988 through Nitro Nobel, its Swedish subsidiary. The export licence was granted on the understanding that the explosives would be used in the construction of a dam in northern Iraq as part of a hydro-electricity and irrigation project. However, most of the order was clustered nitro-glycerine – a highly explosive jellified substance made by adding nitric and sulphuric acids to glycerine. The clustered version is in the shape of small balls connected via fine wiring systems which conduct the electric charges setting off a chain of electronically controlled explosions, the number of which depends on the number of clusters in a chain – at precise, split-second intervals as fine as sixteen milliseconds.

Clustered nitroglycerine is used in industry to make tunnels and bore into rocks, but it is also used in the manufacture of missiles. The chains of clusters are used to produce minute explosions to control the precise timing of the ignition of solid fuel in missile boosters and either to accelerate or to reduce the speed of combustion according to pressure, speed and height of the missile in relation to its payload as it leaves the launching pad and heads towards its target. This control is vital in calculating the speed of the rocket to achieve maximum results. It is very likely that the Iraqis have diverted the Norwegian-supplied explosives for such use.

Switzerland is another normally neutral country which has supplied arms to Iraq. It is listed as having supplied fifty Roland armoured personnel carriers during the period 1980–81, in addition to having sold a large number of training aircraft to the Iraqi air force between 1979 and 1988: forty-eight AS-202 Bravos, fifty-two PC-7s and twenty PC-9s. The AS-202 Bravos proved to be ideal aircraft for carrying out operations against the Kurdish villages in the mountains. Kurdish Pashmerga guerrillas have alleged that these aircraft were used to drop chemical agents on them.

As has already been mentioned, the Austrian company Consultco designed the Saad-16 missile and chemical weapon research and development complex at which missile boosters are tested in a supersonic wind tunnel designed by another Austrian firm, AVL. During the Gulf War, the state-owned arms manufacturer Noricum supplied two hundred of its GHN-45 155mm-calibre long-range howitzers to Iraq via Jordan. The ammunition for these guns was supplied by Hirtenberger, another Austrian company which was reported to have sold ammunition in large quantities to both sides during the Gulf War. Other Austrian firms are known to have been involved, with the assistance of British and Polish companies, in the construction of an ammunition factory in Iraq and in the supply of military vehicles. During the subsequent trial of eighteen members of the Noricum management in April 1990, on charges of illegal export of arms to the Gulf, it was revealed that the company had also supplied Iran with $300 million worth of arms and ammunition during the eight year conflict.

Dutch industry has also played its part in supplying conventional weapons and equipment to arm Saddam Hussein. Between 1982 and 1985, ammunition manufacturer Eurometaal delivered 220,000 propellant charges and 30,000 155mm artillery shells. Originally, the contract had been barred by the Dutch government but the company managed to circumvent this by selling the propellant and shells to a firm alleged to have experience in running embargoes, Pouderies Réunies Belges (PRB) of Belgium, which exported the consignments to Iraq via Jordan.

In 1983 the Dutch authorities announced that they were investigating possible evasion of export regulations by the Dutch night vision equipment manufacturer Oldelft, suspected of having supplied image intensifiers to Iraq. It was subsequently revealed that the company had exported 1120 million florins' worth of night vision equipment direct to Baghdad between 1974 and 1980, but thereafter had made deliveries via another company identified as Montagrex and its Portuguese subsidiary Optagrew, based in Lisbon. The export of these consignments was covered by an end-user certificate apparently provided by General José Maria de Costa Alvares who was then in charge of equipment procurement for the Portuguese army. In 1987 Oldelft was prosecuted for illegal export of equipment to Iraq, but was cleared on a legal technicality which enabled the firm to avoid declaring the final destination of the equipment on the export documents. In November 1988, however, the company was prosecuted again on the same charges in the High Court at The Hague and was fined 25,000 florins, a fine so tiny that it might be considered to have been a token penalty.

In August 1990, Oldelft's name featured once again when questions were raised in the Dutch parliament about reports that the company had supplied Iraq with airborne reconnaissance systems and night vision equipment via its Belgian subsidiary Instrubel, which is based in Oudenaarde. These deliveries, whose total value was reported as being 1500 million florins, apparently continued until the beginning of August when they were halted by the United Nations embargo.

The Philips group of companies was also reported as having been involved in the supply of equipment to Iraq. In 1986 a consignment of fifty night vision devices, worth 1500 million florins, was exported to Iraq by the Philips subsidiary in Germany. The consignment was shipped after an application for an export licence had been turned down. Allegations were made that falsified documentation was apparently used, which was reported to have been provided by a corrupt general in the Jordanian army.

Britain is no innocent as far as the creation of Baghdad's war machine is concerned, although the nature of its exports tended to be less obviously lethal than those items supplied by other countries. During the period of the Gulf War, the government's attitude towards the supply of arms appeared at times to be somewhat ambiguous – no doubt reflecting its regard for Iraq as a bulwark against Iranian Shi'ite fundamentalism.

In 1981, contracts were signed by British companies for the supply to Iraq of approximately £312.5 million worth of 'defence-related but non-lethal equipment'. One contract fulfilled by Primary Medical Aid, a company based in Fareham, Hampshire, supplied over ten thousand 'protection kits' at a total cost of over £300,000. These reportedly consisted of nuclear, biological and chemical (NBC) protective clothing apparently designed to give protection to personnel handling chemicals or filling artillery shells. This contract was alleged to have been fulfilled with the support of the Ministry of Defence's Defence Sales Organisation (now the Defence Export Services Organisation).

In 1982 a large quantity of one thousand Land Rovers, constructed to military specification, were supplied together with a further sixty vehicles fitted with radio communications equipment and fifty Range Rovers at a total cost of £28 million. It was reported that this contract was effected through International Military Services Ltd. In addition, the Iraqis also purchased a large amount of Cymbeline mortar-location radar equipment. The manufacturers of Cymbeline, Thorn EMI, were reported as still conducting training courses in Britain for Iraqi military personnel in early 1990.

During the early part of the Gulf War, Britain continued to train military personnel from both Iraq and Iran. Eighty Iraqi air force pilots were trained by a commercial company, Specialist Flying Training, at Carlisle. Meanwhile, ten Iranian officers were being trained in the use of 'Skyguard' air defence weapon systems by the British Manufacture and Research Company at its headquarters on the former RAF base at Faldringworth in Lincolnshire. Britain continued to train Iraqi personnel throughout the war, but the Iranians were denied such facilities from the end of 1982.

Evidence of one apparent attempt to export weapons from Britain to Iraq during the Gulf War relates to an incident which occurred in 1987. On 16th October, the Italian authorities boarded the 10,000-ton cargo vessel *Fathulkair* which had arrived in the port of Savona en route to Dubai. Their suspicions apparently aroused by discrepancies in the shipping documents giving details of the cargo, although it was subsequently rumoured that they had received an intelligence tip-off, the Italians searched the ship and found that it was carrying a consignment of 350 Heckler & Koch 5.56mm-calibre light machine guns. On further investigation, it was discovered that these weapons had been made under licence by Royal Ordnance at its factory in Enfield, Middlesex. Also found were 357 crates of spare parts for heavy weapons.

Prior to sailing to Savona, the *Fathulkair* had called at Liverpool, where the consignment had been loaded. Further investigations revealed that the vessel, owned by the United Arab Shipping Company and registered in Qatar, had called at ports in Belgium, France and West Germany before sailing to Britain. Amongst the crew were four Iraqis and it transpired that the consignment was ultimately due for delivery to Baghdad via Dubai, which was the *Fathulkair*'s final destination. The captain of the vessel was arrested and charged with illegal arms trafficking. He was subsequently sentenced to four years' imprisonment but given parole as long as he remained within the confines of Savona itself.

Three years later, the *Fathulkair* once again collected a cargo from a British port but this time its contents were far more lethal. On 25th February 1990, containers of potassium cyanide were found washed ashore on the Sussex coastline. It was subsequently confirmed by the Department of Transport that sixteen containers of the chemical had been washed overboard from the *Fathulkair* during heavy storms and that the cargo, which also included a quantity of toxic resin and 160 gallons of another unspecified chemical, had been loaded aboard the vessel at Sheerness. As yet, the supplier of the cyanide has remained unidentified; it was claimed at the time that the *Fathulkair*'s destination was Saudi Arabia. However, bearing in mind the ship's previous connection with shipment of arms to the Gulf region, there were suspicions that the cyanide was intended for use in Iraq's chemical weapon development programme.

During the early 1960s, the United States sold Iraq $12,486 million worth of arms and equipment, including 75mm artillery pieces, vehicles and radio communications equipment. In late 1981, when the Iraqis' campaign against Iran ran into unexpected difficulties, there were calls in the United States for restoring relations with Iraq, broken off in 1967 after the Six Day War. During the previous three years, Baghdad had been giving increasing indications of its wish to re-establish links with America, where a pro-Iraqi lobby had been growing for some time. On 26th November 1984, full diplomatic relations were restored between the two countries.

Two years prior to that, however, in 1982, a total of sixty Hughes 300C and 500D helicopters had been sold to Iraq. Delivered in 1983, these aircraft were apparently intended for use by the Iraqi Ministry of Communications and Transport. That sale was followed in 1985 by another, worth $27.4 million and authorised by the United States government, of twenty-six McDonnell Douglas MD-530MF helicopters. In 1986 seventeen Bell 214ST helicopters, part of an order for a total of forty-five aircraft, were delivered to Iraq. Despite the fact that these aircraft were sold in civilian configuration, they would have required little or no modification for military use. Indeed, it was subsequently reported – in September 1988, by American journalists visiting Iraqi forces engaged in operations in Northern Iraq – that they had travelled in some of the Bell 214ST aircraft which were painted in military camouflage. They had seen others at air bases at Kirkuk, Arbil and Mosul.

The sales of these aircraft were negotiated by a Miami-based Lebanese arms dealer named Sarkis Soghanalian who had been appointed by Saddam Hussein to act as an intermediary. He was assisted in this role by a Washington-based company, Global Research International, operated by Colonel John V. Brennan, who had been military adviser to President Richard Nixon during his administration. Brennan's partner was John Mitchell, Nixon's former Attorney-General. Global Research was reported to have been involved in the Hughes and McDonnell Douglas helicopter deals and to have collected a commission from Soghanalian of $548,000 on the 1985 sale, though not without some difficulty.

Global's relationship with the Lebanese middleman finally foundered after Soghanalian's apparent failure to pay the company $8.7 million in commission on a deal involving the supply of $181 million worth of Romanian-manufactured uniforms to Iraq. The deal allegedly involved other well-known figures, including Richard Nixon, who is reported to have corresponded with the late president Nicolae Ceauşescu on the matter, and former Vice-President Spiro Agnew, who is alleged to have acted as an intermediary between Global Research and another company, Pan-East International, which contracted with the Romanian Ministry of Light Industries for the manufacture of the uniforms. In March 1990, the dispute between Global Research and Soghanalian became the subject of legal proceedings when the company filed a lawsuit in Washington in its claim for the $8.7 million commission.

One of Iraq's principal suppliers of arms has been Egypt. It is ironic that Iraq, which led the anti-Egyptian Arab front in 1978 and 1979 after President Sadat signed the Camp David peace treaty with Israel, should have rushed to seek Cairo's help after the tide turned against it, during the early part of the Gulf conflict when the Soviet Union refused to continue supplying Iraq with arms. In addition to providing Iraq with technical assistance for its missile, nuclear and chemical weapon development programmes, Egypt has acted as a major supplier of arms since the beginning of the Gulf War. This was despite the absence of diplomatic relations which had been broken off in 1977 and were not resumed officially until November 1987. In 1981 Iraqi imports of arms from Egypt were estimated at $700 million, rising to $1.5 billion in 1982 but falling to $500 million in 1983. By the end of the conflict, Iraqi expenditure with Egypt totalled an estimated $11 billion, with the Iraqis still owing the Egyptians over $3.5 billion in 1990.

Anwar Sadat, a wily and pragmatic politician, paid scant heed to ethics when he saw in Saddam's predicament a way out of Cairo's isolation and an opportunity to reinstate Egypt in its leading role in Middle East politics. He ordered a massive airlift of Egyptian-manufactured ammunition and spare parts. As other Arab states, namely Saudi Arabia, Kuwait and the United Arab Emirates, already owed Egypt over $560 billion as their share for a joint arms industry project, Sadat saw in the arming of Iraq a chance to extract payment with interest – Iraq was supported by those states in its conflict against Iran and thus they had an interest in ensuring that Baghdad received the arms that it required. In fact, the Egyptians never received payment.

Amongst the arms supplied to Iraq were American weapons assembled or manufactured under licence in Egypt. This was done with the full knowledge of Washington and after obtaining the relevant licences from America. The major part of Iraq's requirements, however, was for Soviet-designed arms and ammunition manufactured under licence in Egypt since the bulk of Iraqi weapons and equipment were Soviet-made. This suited the Egyptians for a number of reasons. Firstly, they were looking for hard currency as well as for markets to which to export their home-produced arms whilst they entered into fierce competition with Israel for arms exports to Africa and other Third World markets. Secondly, the war between Iraq and Iran provided a good testing ground for weapons designed by the Egyptian arms industry; and finally, the massive sales of arms to Iraq resulted in increased employment in Egypt – and in Iraq, where Egyptians filled vacancies caused by an acute shortage in manpower. By the end of the war with Iran, there were 1.3 million Egyptians working in Iraq.

There are considerable quantities of arms supplied by Egypt to Iraq which have not been recorded in Western estimates. However, those arms listed as having been supplied between 1981 and 1989 include 250 T-55 tanks, 300 BM-21 multiple rocket-launchers, 300 122mm SAKR rocket-launchers, 200 D-30 122mm howitzers, ninety-six M-46 artillery pieces, 100 AT-3 Sagger anti-tank guided weapons and an unspecified number of SAKR-Eye surface-to-air missiles. Romanian-manufactured M-77 tanks were also supplied in 1984.

Egyptian aircraft sales to Iraq during the same period included forty F-6 and eighty F-7 fighters, these being Chinese copies of Soviet-designed aircraft which were assembled under licence in Egypt. Eighty EMB-312 trainers, assembled under licence from Embraer of Brazil, were also supplied between 1985 and 1988.

Egypt also provided much technical assistance and expertise. Egyptian instructors served on attachment in the Iraqi armed forces, as did technicians who maintained sophisticated weapons and equipment or serviced aircraft.

Egyptian pilots and radar technicians played a major role in destroying Iran's economic base and internal morale in the decisive period which began in December 1987. In addition to Kuwait, the United Arab Emirates and the eastern coast of Saudi Arabia being secured by Egyptian-manned air defence systems, Egyptian pilots took part in air raids deep into Iran. Egyptian tanker aircraft provided mid-air refuelling for Iraqi bombers raiding power stations and industrial plants in the far east of Iran and on the coast of the Caspian Sea whilst their colleagues on the ground were jamming the Iranian radars. Technical co-operation between the two countries was at a high level, with the Egyptians imparting to the Iraqis much of the knowledge and expertise that they had gained during the construction of their own industries, which had been achieved with American and European assistance. In March 1989, Egypt signed an agreement for the construction of two plants in Iraq for the production of iron and steel.

It was Saudi Arabian money which helped to underwrite Iraq during the eight years of the Gulf War. Like the United States, Britain, France and the Gulf States, Saudi Arabia saw Iraq as being the main bastion against the spread of extreme Shia fundamentalism emanating from Tehran. It was thus in the Saudis' interests to ensure that Iraq was able to sustain its war against Iran and to that end they, together with Kuwait, provided Baghdad with financial support whilst also opening up a route through the country along which arms were transported.

Jordan also acted as a conduit for arms being shipped to Iraq during the Gulf War, the port of Aqaba being the point through which all consignments shipped by sea were unloaded and transported onwards by road. In addition, Jordan also supplied arms which, during the period 1980 to 1986, included thirty M-114 155mm howitzers, 100 M-109 155mm self-propelled howitzers, fifty Khalid main battle tanks and 200 GHN-45 155mm long-range howitzers. Between 1983 and 1984, Jordan also supplied Iraq with twenty F-6 fighters.

South America has also played a major part in the supply of conventional weapon systems to Iraq – Brazil, Chile and Argentina being the principal sources. During the war with Iran and subsequently until early 1990, Iraq was Brazil's largest customer. In 1984 it was reported that the value of deliveries of Brazilian arms to Iraq had reached a level of $100 million per annum. The total value of deliveries over the last fourteen years has since been estimated at $3 billion.

One Brazilian company which has exported large quantities of its products to Iraq is Engesa, well-known in international defence circles for its range of armoured vehicles. Between 1979 and 1985, the company's sales to Baghdad included 500 EE-11 Urutu armoured personnel-carriers, 1026 EE-9 Cascavel armoured cars and 300 EE-3 Jararaca reconnaissance vehicles. The company also provided about fifty technical staff who were based in Iraq to provide after-sales technical support.

In November 1986, an Iraqi delegation went to Brazil to negotiate a $2 billion contract for the supply of 300 Osorio tanks, 300 Cascavel armoured cars and an unspecified quantity of Avibras Astros II multiple rocket-launchers. These last items, manufactured by Avibras Aerospacial, were subsequently used by Iraqi forces in the latter stages of the Gulf War. The launcher is supplied in 127mm, 180mm and 300mm calibre versions which fire thirty-two SS-30, sixteen SS-40 and four SS-60 rockets respectively and which have ranges of thirty, thirty-five and sixty kilometres. The SS-30 carries a high-explosive warhead, whilst the two larger rockets have cluster munition warheads which contain dual-effect anti-personnel and anti-armour bombs. During the period 1980 to 1985 Iraq purchased seventy-eight Astros II SS-30 multiple rocket-launchers together with an unspecified number of SS-30 rockets, thirteen Astros Guidance fire-control radars, twenty Astros II SS-60 multiple rocket-launchers, 960 SS-60 rockets and 100 Cobra 2000 anti-tank guided weapons.

The intermediary reported to have played a central role in negotiating many of these contracts between Iraq and Brazilian suppliers is José Luis Whitaker Ribeiro. A principal character in the Brazilian arms industry, Ribeiro is reputed to have made a vast fortune from sales of arms to Iraq. He is said to have been a regular visitor to Baghdad, flying to and fro between Brazil and Iraq in his own private Boeing 707 airliner.

In late 1988 discussions took place between the Brazilian aircraft manufacturer Empresa Brasiliera de Aeronautica (Embraer) and the Iraqis concerning an agreement for the assembly under licence of the EMB-312 Tucano trainer. The Iraqis were already operating eighty of these aircraft which had been purchased from Egypt, where they had been assembled. In early 1989, Iraq was negotiating a large arms deal covering the supply of Pirhana air-to-air missiles, Astros II rocket-launchers, SS-30 and SS-60 rockets, and armoured personnel carriers.

As a result of having lost the American and Egyptian airborne surveillance support which was provided until the end of the Gulf War, Iraq was keen to replace it with its own capability as soon as possible. The decision was taken to develop a satellite system which would provide Baghdad with surveillance of Israel, Syria and Iran as well as the mountainous region of northern Iraq where Kurdish guerrillas were active. The Iraqis turned to Brazil and in particular to the Brazilian space agency, the Instituto de Pesquisas Espaciais (INPE).

Discussions took place between INPE and Iraq's Scientific Research Centre (SRC). In addition, contact was established with Orbita Space Systems, the Brazilian rocket manufacturer. The proposed satellite system would have been placed in orbit at a height of 700km. Weighing 150kg, it would have been equipped with a French high-resolution infra-red camera. In addition to the satellite itself, Brazil would have supplied the laboratory, which would have enabled Iraq to construct its own satellites, and the necessary training for Iraqi technicians. The total cost to Iraq would have been in the region of $50 million.

There was much speculation as to how the Iraqis planned to launch their satellites into orbit. Various alternatives would have been open to them, including the use of one of their Condor-2 missiles adapted for the task or, alternatively, a Brazilian-supplied rocket. An alternative option, which they decided to develop themselves, was a ground-based satellite-launcher.

Brazil also featured in the Iraqi missile programme. A retired Brazilian air force general named Hugo de Oliveira Piva was contracted by the Iraqis to produce an air-to-air missile called 'Piranha'. In October 1989, he took a team of engineers and technicians to the Saad-16 research and development centre at Mosul where, in addition to their work on the 'Piranha', they carried out upgrading work on Scud-B missiles.

Twelve years ago, nobody had heard of Cardoen Industries or of its owner, Carlos Cardoen, a stocky Chilean entrepreneur, doctor of engineering and producer of mining explosives. Currently, Mr Cardoen, aged forty-nine, is one of the richest men in Chile, living in a mansion in Santiago where the walls are said to be lined with silk. He possesses his own private army, runs one of the biggest privately owned arms companies in Latin America and is reputed to have assets of some $400 million. On the wall of his office a portrait of President Saddam Hussein occupies pride of place. It is an appropriate tribute to the Iraqi leader, because Carlos Cardoen has made his fortune selling arms to Iraq.

In 1988, Cardoen Industries was reported as carrying out ninety-five per cent of its business with Iraq, totalling in excess of $100 million per annum. The company started supplying Baghdad at the beginning of the Gulf War and it has been estimated that, during the period of the conflict, it was profiting to the tune of $80 million per year from sales of cluster bombs to Saddam Hussein's regime. One of the major contracts fulfilled by Cardoen Industries during the war was the sale to Iraq of 100 G-5 155mm howitzers which it manufactures under licence from Armscor of South Africa.

In early 1990, it was reported that Cardoen had been approached by the Iraqis to supply missile guidance systems for mounting on helicopters. At that time, Cardoen was conducting a project which involved the conversion of civilian Bell 206 helicopters to gunship configuration and it had been reported that Iraq was keen to purchase up to fifty of these aircraft.

It was on the trail of these reports that, in March 1990, Jonathan Moyle, a former RAF helicopter pilot and the editor of *Defence Helicopter World*, a British defence industry publication, arrived in Chile as a visitor to FIDAE, the annual Chilean international aerospace exhibition. On 31st March, however, Moyle was found hanging in the wardrobe in his room at the Hotel Carrera in Santiago.

There was much speculation concerning Moyle's death, as it transpired that he had confided in another defence journalist that one of his purposes in going to Chile was to investigate reports that Cardoen was developing a low-cost attack helicopter for sale to Third World countries and that Iraq had ordered fifty of the converted Bell 206s. The only feasible explanation so far suggested for Moyle's death is that he had discovered that these aircraft were to be armed with Helios, an advanced guidance system used in conjunction with the Emerson Electric TOW missile, which is manufactured in Britain, America and Sweden. Helios is on the list of items barred for export to both Chile and Iraq but it is possible that efforts might have been made to obtain it illegally. Sources amongst other defence journalists have stated that the information concerning the Bell 206 conversion was common knowledge but that there had been no mention of Helios.

If Cardoen Industries had planned to obtain Helios for the Iraqis, it would have had to do so illegally and the political consequences of the exposure of such a plan would have been far-reaching. The United States would have undoubtedly prevented any further export of helicopters to Chile and considerable embarrassment would have been caused to the government of President Patricio Aylwin, which has been making every effort to rehabilitate itself with the West since the departure of the Pinochet regime. There were reports during 1990 that the Chilean government had already become increasingly embarrassed by reports of Cardoen's continuing commercial connections with Iraq, not least because it is well known that Carlos Cardoen himself contributed $1 million to Aylwin's election campaign and is reportedly an associate of the president.

Thus, if Jonathan Moyle had discovered the existence of such a plan, he might have posed a serious threat to Cardoen's continuation of its lucrative supply of arms to Baghdad and to its political relationship with the Chilean government. As far as the Iraqis were concerned, he would have been a threat to one of their principal sources of arms.

The conclusion reached by the Chilean police, that Moyle had committed suicide, was little less than extraordinary and raises the question of whether the Chilean authorities initially tried to cover up the affair. The circumstances of his death make suicide highly suspicious to even the most inexperienced investigator – a man five foot eight inches in height does not hang himself from a wardrobe rail five feet from the floor – but other factors also dictated against such a conclusion.

On the day following the night of his death, Moyle was due to depart for La Paz, Bolivia, where he was due to accompany a unit of the Bolivian Air Force on an anti-narcotics operation. He had telephoned his parents an hour before the estimated time of his murder to tell them of the trip to which he was looking forward with much enthusiasm – an unlikely action of a man about to commit suicide. Moreover, Moyle was due to be married three months later and an unfinished letter to his West German fiancée was found in his hotel room. In addition, the hotel chambermaid gave evidence to the local police that she had seen blood on the sheets of Moyle's bed and subsequently noticed that a briefcase and two folders, which she had observed previously, were missing from the room.

The chambermaid also told the police that she had heard Moyle having an argument with someone in his room on the night before his death. The identity of Moyle's visitor has not been revealed, but it was reported that Raul Montecinos, the chief of public relations for Cardoen Industries, visited Moyle that evening in his hotel. Montecinos was reported as having admitted that he had done so but subsequently issued a denial. On the following morning, according to hotel reception staff, a man booked a taxi in the name of Moyle and left the hotel.

The lack of action on the part of the British embassy and its refusal to put pressure on the Chilean authorities to investigate the matter further was inexplicable, as was an attempt to smear Moyle's name by a British official as yet unidentified. An allegation was made, apparently at a reception held at the embassy for the Archbishop of Canterbury, that Moyle had accidentally killed himself whilst engaged in a bizarre sexual act. Incredibly, this same disgraceful allegation was apparently repeated during briefings to journalists by Foreign Office officials in London. It was only retracted after the intervention of Foreign Office minister Tim Sainsbury who telephoned Moyle's father to express his sympathy and to reveal the identity of the official responsible. Moyle's family, who were naturally distressed and infuriated by the slur cast on their son, later received a letter of apology from the individual concerned.

At the subsequent coroner's inquest, the results of the autopsy on Moyle were revealed as showing that he had been subjected to a forcibly administered injection and that traces of a sedative had been discovered in his stomach. In addition, heavy bruising was discovered on his shins, indicating that he had been forcibly restrained on his bed before being sedated and hung in his wardrobe. Moreover, it was also revealed that he had been discovered with a makeshift nappy, fashioned from towels and plastic bags, wrapped round him – the only feasible reason for his killers dressing his body in such a way would be to prevent body fluids escaping and drawing attention by their odour. It was only after learning these facts that the magistrate responsible for the case ordered that there should be a new investigation by OS-7, the specialist criminal investigation department of the Chilean national police.

Some strange occurrences took place in the aftermath of this tragic and as yet unsolved affair. The chambermaid who had found Moyle's body and the hotel telephonist through whom Moyle had placed his last telephone call on the evening he died both disappeared from their employment at the Hotel Carrera. Meanwhile, the naval and air attachés at the British embassy, whom Moyle had met during his visit, returned to London shortly afterwards, whilst the First Secretary at the embassy was apparently posted elsewhere.

Despite the official reactions of the British and Chilean governments to

Moyle's death, it was apparent to most people that Moyle had been murdered. Moyle's notebook, which was in the possession of the Chilean authorities, apparently contained references to the Helios-Helitow system. It is generally believed that Moyle did stumble upon details of the Iraqi deal with Cardoen which is thought to have also included a supply of special oscilloscopes required as test equipment for Baghdad's nuclear development programme.

What has not been revealed until now is that Moyle was warned not to continue his investigations into the suspected deal between Cardoen Industries and Iraq for the acquisition of Helios. A former intelligence officer in the Mukhabarat, now in hiding in Europe, has confirmed that, during a meeting with a representative of Cardoen Industries, Moyle was advised that if he continued his efforts to discover the facts concerning the attack helicopters for Iraq he would suffer the consequences.

Despite its previously notorious treatment of opponents of its ruling regimes, Chile has long enjoyed good relations with the West. Indeed, the British government had particular reason to be grateful for Chilean assistance during the Falklands War in 1982. Consequently, Chile is an acceptable country for the export of technology and is involved in several joint ventures with elements of the international defence industry. These include a joint marketing agreement between FAMAE, another Chilean arms manufacturer, and Britain's Royal Ordnance. The two companies are co-operating in the marketing of the Royal Ordnance RAYO 160mm artillery rocket system currently being promoted as a cheaper alternative to the Multiple Launch Rocket System (MLRS) which is in service with the British and American armed forces.

In October 1990, it was reported that the Libyan leader, Muammar Gaddafi, was acting as a secret intermediary between Iraq and Cardoen Industries in negotiations for the supply of fuel air explosive (FAE) weapons. Libya had previously acted as a supplier to Iraq in 1982 when it sold four hundred Brazilian-manufactured EE-9 Cascavel armoured cars to the Baghdad regime, and when it subsequently supplied bottom-laid acoustic/magnetic mines procured from Armscor of South Africa.

In principle, FAE weapons release on initiation a fuel-gas vapour which permeates everything within the target area, including buildings and armoured vehicles. Almost immediately after its release, the vapour would be ignited by a detonation system within the bomb itself. The result would be a huge fireball and massive shockwave over an area of approximately 150 square yards. FAE weapons would be particularly effective against targets such as airfields, oil installations and concentrated numbers of troops or vehicles.

During the Vietnam War, the Americans developed a similar system for use in clearing mines from landing zones prior to the arrival of heliborne troops. The concussion from the resultant blast was designed to initiate any mines laid on the zones, but it also had the effect of neutralising any enemy troops in close proximity. As yet, however, all attempts to develop FAE weapons have proved unsuccessful. The Americans terminated their development programme five years ago and it is known that Soviet attempts to develop 'sub-nuclear weapons' were also unsuccessful. The technology required to produce them is sophisticated, but once all development problems had been resolved FAE weapons would be cheap to produce and could be dropped by aircraft in the form of bombs or delivered by missiles.

Cardoen Industries is known to have tested FAE weapons in Chile's Atacama Desert, about fifty miles north of Iquique. The weapon under test was apparently developed by a Spanish company, Expal, which designed the system for the Spanish air force. It was manufactured by MS Systems of Madrid, and the company's chief engineer, José Allepuz, was reported to have been present at the tests in Chile. Cardoen's contribution to the weapon was the fuse system. Due to the Spanish embargo on sales of arms to Iraq or Libya, exports of Spanish weapons would have to be channelled through a third party – in this case, Chile.

Cardoen Industries was also reported to be building a $60 million factory for the manufacture of fuses. Situated near Baghdad, the factory is equipped with precision machine tools supplied by the British firm Matrix-Churchill, a subsidiary of Technology Development Group of London. In addition, two other factories have been installed by the company, producing aircraft bombs which include the cluster types CB-130, CB-250K and CB-500.

For some years, the Chilean navy worked closely with Marconi in the development of tube-launched mines. Inevitably, in its capacity as a principal manufacturer, Cardoen Industries had access to some of the technology used in this project and it is believed that the company may have transferred some of this technology to some of its other customers, including Iraq.

In addition to its extensive involvement with Iraq and Egypt in the development of the Condor-2 missile, Argentina also supplied weapons and equipment to Baghdad during the Gulf War in the form of vehicles, mortars, rifles and ammunition. In addition, one hundred 'Tanque Argentina Mediano' tanks of West German design were sold at a total cost of $1.7 million.

*

Other countries that have contributed to Saddam Hussein's arsenal or have provided technical support include Greece, India and North Korea. The Eastern bloc was also active in offering its wares, East Germany supplying fifty T-55 tanks and Poland delivering four hundred of the same type during the first two years of the Gulf War. During 1981–5, Czechoslovakia supplied two hundred OT-64 armoured personnel-carriers, one thousand BMP-1 mechanised infantry combat vehicles and a further four hundred T-55 tanks. In the same period, Romania sold Baghdad 150 T-55 tanks whilst Hungary supplied two hundred Fug-70 scout cars. Yugoslavia sold small arms and 122mm artillery ammunition as well as providing assistance in the design and construction of air bases which included underground hangars for aircraft.

There have been extensive links between South Africa and Iraq since before the Gulf War. During the late 1970s and throughout the 1980s, South Africa bought considerable amounts of oil from Iraq and stockpiled them, because of its uncertainty over the outcome of the American presidential elections in 1980, 1984 and 1988. Pretoria was nervous that a Democratic president would increase sanctions as a result of South African operations in Angola.

From 1984 to 1986, South Africa supplied Iraq with considerable quantities of artillery ammunition. Consignments were shipped in oil tankers which were half loaded with water, their remaining tanks being loaded with ammunition. These were delivered to the Jordanian port of Aqaba where they were unloaded. The vessels then proceeded to the Kuwaiti oil port of Al Hamadi where Kuwaiti or Saudi Arabian oil, donated by the two countries to Iraq for its war effort, was loaded and taken back to South Africa in payment for the ammunition. It was for this reason that the Iranians launched some of their Silkworm missiles against the oil platforms at Al Hamadi in October 1987.

In 1988, a pipeline stretching from Al Zubair in Iraq to Yanbu in Saudi Arabia was completed and put into operation. Oil was thereafter pumped directly to Saudi Arabia, which sold it to South Africa, on behalf of Iraq, for hard currency or arms. In 1990 the pipeline was closed as a result of the imposition of United Nations sanctions against Iraq after the invasion of Kuwait.

South Africa also supplied Iraq with arms via third parties. The 1984 sale of G-5 155mm howitzers via Cardoen Industries of Chile has already been mentioned. South Africa has also used Libya as an intermediary, as was illustrated by the sale of naval acoustic/magnetic mines.

II

Due to the tight controls exercised by most governments on conventional weapons, as well as on many of the components and materials required for both nuclear and chemical weapon research and development, Iraq was forced to resort to mainly covert methods of acquisition. As a result, it set up a worldwide network of procurement 'fronts' by purchasing established companies, some of which were manufacturing concerns, in Britain, Germany, Switzerland, Spain, France and Italy. It was through such 'fronts' that equipment, materials, expertise and even other companies were acquired. The creation of such a network was not illegal and it appears that the Iraqis were in most instances careful to avoid breaking any laws in order not to attract unwelcome attention. In addition, Iraqi trainee technicians were sent to work in companies throughout Europe in order to obtain access to the latest technologies legally.

In 1987 a Baghdad-based company named Al-Arabi Trading formed the British company Technology and Development Group (TDG), located in west London. A number of Iraqis were placed on the company's board of directors, including four named as Fadel Jawad Kadhum, Nassir al-Nainsi, Safaa al-Habobi and Hana Jon – names which had already figured elsewhere in Baghdad's covert procurement network in Europe.

In the same year, TDG purchased a number of British engineering companies. One of these was the Coventry-based precision machine-tool manufacturer TI Machine Tools Ltd, which was bought from the TI Group. The company, subsequently renamed Matrix-Churchill Ltd, was acquired through one of TDG's subsidiaries, TMG Engineering Ltd, with Iraqi funds of which some were channelled via the Dresdner bank in West Germany. Three Iraqis were identified as being on Matrix-Churchill's board of directors: Fadel Jawad Kadhum, Safaa al-Habobi and Adnan al-Amiri. The company already numbered British Aerospace amongst its customers, its milling machines being used to manufacture components for missiles.

After its buy-out by TDG, Matrix-Churchill received a number of orders for precision machine tools from Iraq. The company was later reported as having a £30 million turnover, 20 per cent of which was from sales to Middle Eastern countries, of which Iraq was the largest customer. When questioned later about these contracts, the company insisted that it had obtained export licences from the Department of Trade and Industry for all overseas sales, including those to Iraq.

In September 1989, it was revealed that a $14 million machine tool project was being undertaken by Matrix-Churchill and an American company, XYZ Options of Tuscaloosa, Alabama, on behalf of the Iraqi state-owned Machine Trade Company. The project involved the construction of a plant designed to produce precision tungsten carbide tools which Matrix-Churchill and XYZ Options stated would be used for machining components for commercial use. However, during a visit by officials from the American embassy in Baghdad, concern was expressed when a sophisticated computerised jig grinder was spotted by officials involved in export control. This particular piece of equipment could apparently be retooled easily for machining components for weapons and missiles.

Matrix-Churchill also provided a link for TDG with other companies. The company is a 50 per cent shareholder in Coventry-based Matrix-Churchill Takisawa, in partnership with Takisawa Machine Tool Company of Japan. In the United States, the company has an American arm in the form of Matrix-Churchill Corporation. In addition, it owns Newcast Foundries of Newcastle-under-Lyme and has a 50 per cent shareholding in a London firm of architects and project management specialists, Archiconsult.

TDG itself always denied being an Iraqi procurement organisation, but British intelligence officers had identified one of the company's directors, Fadel Jawad Kadhum, as being a senior official in Saddam Hussein's administration. Suspicions about the company were further strengthened when Matrix-Churchill allegedly became involved in a deal which involved a $3 billion loan by the American branch of an Italian bank, the Banca Nazionale del Lavoro, without the approval of its board of directors. The Iraqis had ordered one hundred computerised machine tools, which could have been used for making a variety of items including artillery shells, and the bank underwrote the entire deal. Some of the machine tools were delivered to Iraq, the remaining consignments being halted by the United Nations trade embargo after the invasion of Kuwait.

TDG again came to the British government's attention in October 1989 when it was involved in the purchase, through a part-owned subsidiary, of an aerospace factory in Northern Ireland which had been owned previously by Lear Fan. It had been used for the production of a turbo-prop executive aircraft manufactured from carbon fibre and advanced composite materials and its equipment included filament-winding machines which could be used in the manufacture of missile components.

The factory was purchased by SRC Composites Ltd, a subsidiary of Canira Technical Corporation Ltd, which was in turn a jointly owned subsidiary of TDG and SRC Engineering, a Geneva-based subsidiary of

Space Research Corporation, the company headed by one Dr Gerald Bull, of whom more will be said in the next chapter. The directors of Canira and SRC Composites included the two Iraqis, Fadel Jawad Kadhum and Nassir al-Nainsi. SRC Composites Ltd applied for a £2 million grant from the Northern Ireland Industrial Development Board. Initially the company's application received a positive response, but it was subsequently turned down after the intervention of the Foreign Office, which apparently feared that the factory might be used to manufacture missile components for the Iraqi missile development programme. The British authorities seemed to have been alarmed at the Iraqi involvement with the company and by the fact that SRC Composites Ltd's technical director was an individual named James Brooks who had previously worked for Short Brothers, the Belfast-based missile manufacturers, where he had been the project manager for the Blowpipe shoulder-fired surface-to-air missile programme.

As well as establishing commercial 'fronts', Iraq also made use of a number of companies which it hired to act as procurement agents on its behalf. One such organisation, which is reported to have had close connections with TDG, was another London-based company, Meed International, which figured largely in Iraqi procurement operations in Europe.

Formed in 1987, Meed International was operated by two directors: a Briton named as Roy Ricks and an Iraqi engineer identified as Anees Mansour Wadi whom he had met in the Middle East when the latter had represented the company for which Ricks had previously worked, Modern Fire Alarms International. On leaving MFA, where he had been managing director, Ricks had contacted Wadi with a view to the possibility of their continuing to do business together. Ricks's approach was a fortunate one for both himself and the Iraqi. A year earlier, Wadi had been approached by an Iraqi government official named Kassim Abbass, who had been tasked by his masters with acquiring Western equipment and technology for Iraq's arms industry. Abbass was at that time looking for someone to work in co-operation with him by setting up a company in Britain. Subsequently, Wadi and Ricks established Meed International, situated in Mayfair.

During 1987 and 1988, Ricks and Wadi maintained frequent and close contact with the commercial attaché at the Iraqi embassy in Bonn, Ali Abd al-Mutalib Ali. Working from a list of requirements provided by him, they established contacts with a number of British engineering firms. During that period, they were successful in arranging contracts for the supply of machine tools to Iraq. In 1987, a series of meetings took place at the embassy in Bonn between representatives of six different European manufacturers, Ali Abd al-Mutalib Ali and Abbas Yass, an engineer from Iraq's Nassr State Enterprise for Mechanical Industries.

All these meetings were apparently arranged by Meed International and resulted in very large contracts being placed for the supply of machine tools for Iraqi ammunition factories. Some of the contracts were perfectly explicit as to the purpose for which the machinery was to be used – one clearly stated that it was required for the production of casings for 60mm, 81mm and 120mm mortar bombs. The machine tool manufacturers involved in these contracts included Biglia of Italy and TI Machine Tools Ltd (renamed Matrix-Churchill after its takeover by TDG later in the same year), BSA Tools Ltd and Whickman Bennett of Britain. All four of these companies received contracts varying in value from £6 million to £19 million each, BSA Tools Ltd being contracted to supply fifty machines and TI Machine Tools Ltd 150 lathes. Other companies awarded contracts were Index of West Germany and Georg Fischer of Switzerland.

During 1987, Meed International also negotiated a contract for Colchester Lathes, a subsidiary of the 600 Group, to supply machine tools to the Qaqa Establishment, an Iraqi munitions manufacturing company. At the same time, it was conducting negotiations with other machine tool manufacturers, including Brown & Sharpe Ltd and Bennett Mahler.

Meed International also approached companies involved in computers and high technology, items high in priority on the Iraqi procurement list. These included International Computer Systems (London) Ltd and Deltacam Systems, whom Meed International contacted on behalf of the Nassr State Enterprise for Mechanical Industries, which was keen to acquire computer design systems for plastic injection moulding processes. Both companies were subsequently awarded contracts, Deltacam supplying 3-D computer modelling software during the following year, by which time Meed International had given way to TDG as the premier Iraqi procurement organisation in Europe. By the time it did so, however, it had arranged contracts with British machine tool manufacturers worth approximately £40 million.

Meed International was also revealed to have held discussions with the ammunition and pyrotechnics manufacturer Astra Holdings. The Iraqis were keen to be self-sufficient in the manufacture of American-type fuses and 155mm artillery ammunition and were thus seeking to obtain the necessary technology. Astra confirmed that it could provide such material, offering a choice of either the data and technology for manufacture or, alternatively, the installation of an entire factory. The Iraqis did not accept the proposals but instead approached Cardoen Industries of Chile, which accepted a £27.5 million contract to construct and equip the factory. Amongst the equipment ordered for installation in the plant was machinery for manufacturing fuses for artillery shells. This was ordered from Matrix-Churchill under a £12 million contract. During the period from early 1989 until early 1990, the company dispatched consignments of ammunition-manufacturing equipment to Iraq. By the middle of 1990, the factory was in full production of 155mm long-range artillery shells.

Another company which acted as a procurement agent for Iraq was Euromac, the Italian company owned by the Iraqi Kassim Abbass. It had been involved in negotiations over contracts awarded for the construction of the steel production complex north of Baghdad and had been investigated by the Italian authorities in 1988 for possible involvement in the supply of cluster-bomb components to Iraq.

Euromac first came to the attention of the American authorities in the autumn of 1988 when the US Customs Service was informed by CSI Technologies, a California-based manufacturer of high-speed electronic capacitators known as 'krytrons', that a British company had contacted its London office and was attempting to obtain such items on behalf of Iraq. Krytrons are used to trigger the detonators which form part of the initiation system in a nuclear explosive device. They can also be used in missile technology, being used to initiate motor ignition or missile stage separation. The US authorities have previously prevented two attempts, by Pakistan and Israel, to smuggle krytrons out of the United States, but it is known that Pakistan has been successful in doing so on at least one other occasion.

Euromac Ltd, a British company closely connected with Euromac of Italy, was based in Thames Ditton, Surrey, and was operated by an Anglo-Iraqi called Ali Ashour Daghir, a Briton named Michael Hand and Jeanine Speckman, a Frenchwoman married to an Englishman. The company had connections with Meed International and Technology Development Group Ltd, both principal components in the international procurement network set up by Baghdad.

A joint operation was mounted in co-operation with the British Customs and Excise to ensnare Euromac Ltd together with another company, Atlas Equipment (UK) Ltd, and the Iraqis. Another krytron manufacturer, EG & G, was requested by the American authorities to manufacture a quantity of forty dummy capacitators.

In September, two representatives of CSI Technologies flew to London for a meeting with Ali Ashour Daghir and Jeanine Speckman in London. Unknown to Daghir and Speckman, one of the two Americans was a US Customs Service undercover agent.

At the meeting, which was also attended by two Iraqi technical experts, the krytrons were discussed in detail. Initially, Daghir and the Iraqis maintained that the capacitators were required for use in laser research but the requirement specification was changed a number of times during the discussion until it became obvious that the devices were required for nuclear initiation purposes.

On 19th March of the following year, the dummy krytrons were flown from Los Angeles to Heathrow Airport in London, where they were stored in a warehouse. A few days later, as the consignment was about to be loaded aboard an Iraqi Airways flight on which it would have been flown to Baghdad, it was seized by British and American Customs officers. At the same time, several suspects were arrested at the airport, including Daghir, Speckman and a Lebanese engineer named as Toufic Fouad Amyuni. They were later charged with attempting to export the krytrons illegally. At the same time Omar Latif, the London-based official of Iraqi Airways, was also arrested and subsequently deported. It transpired that he was the head of the Mukhabarat's intelligence network in Britain but, unlike the others arrested, had not been charged with any offence in order to avoid any further deterioration in relations between Britain and Iraq which had already been strained by the execution of the *Observer* journalist Farzad Bazoft.

Omar Latif's name was also connected with reports of attempts by the Iraqis to smuggle components for underwater mines out of Britain. On 29th March 1990 Customs officers raided the premises of a company specialising in the manufacture of acoustic detonators and other equipment used in mines. This raid took place at the same time as others in Edinburgh and north-west England. During these raids, documents were found which mentioned Latif. One of the companies raided was Global Technical and Management Services International, a Deeside-based company which specialised in the clearance of underwater mines and explosives and which had not long before been involved in the survey and clearance of ordnance from Iraqi waters. In part of a statement issued at the time in which it denied any wrongdoing and claimed that British government approval had been obtained, the company described its activities in Iraq in outline:

'The project involved the supply of equipment and personnel (many of whom were ex-special British forces) to carry out the contract of works and also to train Iraqi navy personnel.

'Prior to the award of the contract, it was discussed in depth with British embassy officials in Baghdad. Copies of the contract document were distributed to the British embassy, all major UK suppliers and third parties involved within the project.'

During investigations in Europe and the United States, links between the Iraqi procurement organisation in Britain and others in Switzerland and Germany were revealed. Investigators soon discovered that the Iraqi Fadel Jawad Kadhum again featured prominently and frequently.

Switzerland has figured for some time in Iraqi procurement operations. In 1987 a Swiss arms dealer, Walter Demuth, was arrested by the Italian authorities under an international warrant issued by the Americans, who were at that time investigating the Iran–Contra affair. When arrested, Demuth was in possession of documents concerning arms deals totalling in excess of $300 billion. It transpired that his company, Helitrade, had been selling to both sides during the Gulf War.

Investigations by the Swiss and the Americans uncovered the existence of an Egyptian scientist, Abdelkadir Helmy, who was working in California for the Aerojet General Corporation in Rancho Cordova. Helmy, a naturalised American, was a senior scientist in the company and was engaged at that time on a project concerned with the development of a new type of shell for a 120mm gun. In March 1988, the US Customs Service was informed that there was a possibility that Helmy might be involved in the joint Iraqi–Egyptian missile project, Condor-2.

Helmy was put under twenty-four-hour surveillance and the Customs investigators had little difficulty in obtaining evidence of his clandestine activities. In fact, he made little effort to conceal them. He talked openly over the telephone, despatched material to the military attaché at the Egyptian embassy in Washington and failed to destroy memos and notes, merely throwing them away with his household rubbish. Regular searches of his dustbins proved very fruitful, revealing documents which included notes on the construction of missile nose cones in carbon-carbon.

Helmy had recruited an assistant, an American named James Huffman who lived in Lexington, Ohio. Monitoring of their telephone conversations revealed much about Helmy's operation and on one occasion led to the interception of a shipment of chemicals used in the production of missile fuel.

Telephone surveillance also revealed that Helmy had formed a company named Science and Technology Applications. Further investigations revealed that this was a 'front' into which more than $1 million had been paid by a subsidiary of the Consen group, Ifat Corporation. The Customs investigators dug further and discovered that Helmy, through

Science and Technology, had purchased carbon composite material and missile nose cones from suppliers in California. It also transpired that Helmy's controller was an Egyptian officer based in Austria, Colonel Hussam Yossef. He provided lists of items which Helmy was to purchase and despatch to Washington. These would then be exported via the Egyptian diplomatic bag.

As the US Customs Service continued to eavesdrop on Helmy's telephone conversations, it learned that the Egyptian defence minister, Field Marshal Abd el-Halim Abu Ghazala, was also involved in the affair. During one particular conversation, it was revealed that Rear Admiral El Gohary, who was based at the Egyptian embassy in Washington, was becoming increasingly anxious about the growing volume of material being sent to him for despatch to Cairo via the diplomatic bag. Helmy, using the defence minister as his authority, became forceful in insisting that his instructions be followed. The admiral eventually caved in and agreed that in future all material would be despatched via the weekly Egyptian air force flight from Washington to Cairo.

On 24th June, the US Customs investigators pounced. They intercepted a consignment of 195kg of carbon fibre, intended for the production of missile nose cones, as it was being loaded aboard an Egyptian air force aircraft at Baltimore-Washington airport. At the same time, Helmy and his American accomplice, together with Helmy's wife, were arrested and charged with illegal export of materials without the required licence.

The Swiss were under the impression that they had halted Iraqi operations in their country, but they were wrong. In August 1990, the West German authorities intercepted a shipment of nuclear components to Iraq. On investigation, it was discovered that both the suppliers were Swiss companies, Schmiedemeccanica SA and Schaublin AG. It was subsequently revealed that an Iraqi commercial organisation, the Iraqi Industrial Company in Baghdad, had placed an order with Schmiedemeccanica for what were described as 'gear forgings' and had supplied the hard steel for manufacturing them. In fact the finished items were components for gas centrifuges. The company predictably denied all knowledge of the true nature of these items. Likewise, Schaublin AG was emphatic that the machine tools which it had supplied, as a result of an order placed in 1988, could be used in the manufacture of a wide range of items.

The Iraqi procurement network in West Germany was perhaps the most extensive and was mainly devoted to the acquisition of equipment for production of conventional and chemical weapons as well as for the Iraqi nuclear development programme. During 1990 the West German authorities carried out investigations into fifty companies suspected of supplying equipment and components for the production of chemical agents and biological weapons. On 17th August seven people were arrested, including an Iraqi named al-Kahdi, a specialist employed by the West German intelligence services. Al-Kahdi, who had fallen foul of the Iraqis and had been saved from the death sentence by the intervention of the West German President, Richard von Weizsacker, was the manager of a company in Hamburg, Water Engineering Trading. The other six arrested were employees of a subsidiary of Preussag, based in Hanover. It was suspected that equipment and components for the production of poison gas had been shipped via Turkey to Iraq, and that al-Kahdi may have been paid $10 million for supplying the components for the con- struction of a chemical weapons production facility.

During the Gulf War it was oil donated by Kuwait via Saudi Arabia, in addition to Saudi money, which underwrote Iraqi expenditure on arms. Since the end of the conflict, however, Saddam Hussein would have been unable to assemble his present military might and to construct his military industrial base without the financial facilities offered to him by the West in the form of extensive credits granted by European banks.

The British government, anxious to ensure that Britain secured a large proportion of trade with Iraq, actively encouraged banks to grant Baghdad huge amounts of trade credit. In 1989 the Midland Bank played a leading role in the setting up of credits for Iraq to the tune of £340 million. This loan was governed by a preferential rate of interest of 9.5 per cent – considerably below commercial rates at that time. By June 1990 most of this credit facility had been drawn upon, but by then exporters were being denied further access to it because of increasing arrears in Iraqi repay- ments. However, in the following year a syndicate of banks led by the Midland established further credit facilities of £250 million, despite the fact that by then the Iraqi deficit on repayments to British suppliers and banks was in excess of £100 million. This deficit was underwritten by the government's Export Credit Guarantee Department which had already covered earlier losses suffered by the Midland with regard to previous credits granted to Iraq.

It is suspected that a multi-million-pound deal set up by the Ministry of Defence with Jordan may have been used to channel further supplies of arms to Iraq. The agreement, which was signed in Amman by Prime Minister Margaret Thatcher in 1985, provided a total credit facility of £275 million for the Jordanians. Finance was provided by a consortium of banks led by Morgan Grenfell and including Midland Montagu and the

Arab Bank Investment Company. However, it was later revealed that only £125 million had been paid out to British suppliers. Assuming that the full amount of the credit facility was drawn upon, this left £150 million unaccounted for. This deal had been arranged by the Defence Export Services Organisation of the Ministry of Defence and was managed by International Military Services (IMS), the Ministry of Defence's own commercial organisation specialising in the export of arms.

From the period 1986 to 1988, British manufacturers in the defence industry could also indirectly turn to the Ministry of Defence for help in financing deals. In 1986, IMS formed its own finance organisation, IMS Export Finance House, to offer a financial service to British companies enabling them to obtain insurance for deals which the government Export Credit Guarantee Department would not cover. This was effected through a system known as 'forfeiting', whereby a supplier would be paid, for example, 85 per cent of a contract price by IMS which would claim the full value from the client and pocket the 15 per cent difference as its fee.

Prior to the 1990 Gulf crisis, the government was unmoved by suggestions that British companies involved in sales of arms to Baghdad might have been drawing on finance provided by British banks. William Waldegrave, Minister of State at the Foreign and Commonwealth Office, said in a statement to the House of Commons on 5th April 1990: 'There is no question of isolating Iraq. The Arab League unanimously supports Iraq on the Bazoft case . . . Therefore I fear that it is being hopeful to have the idea that cutting off British trade credits and trying to prevent British businessmen from going to the market – not that we could legally do it – would isolate Iraq. That could create satisfaction among our industrial competitors and it would lose us jobs and orders in Britain. It would have no other effect.'

It was in the United States and Italy, however, that real evidence emerged as to the scale of the international financing of Iraqi arms procurement. In August 1989, the US Federal Reserve was advised by the Federal Bureau of Investigation that it was investigating possible irregular activities by the Atlanta branch of the Banca Nazionale del Lavoro (BNL), Italy's largest bank. By the following month, FBI agents were able to reveal that they had discovered a secret operation set up to finance Iraqi military procurement to the tune of a staggering $2.2 billion in loans and $830 million in commodity export credits. It had been carried out by some middle management of BNL acting without the bank's official sanction.

Their investigations have suggested that one of the principal characters in this was a thirty-six-year-old naturalised American of French-Algerian descent, Christopher Drogoul, who was the manager of BNL's Atlanta branch. They indicate that Drogoul had allegedly set up a total of three thousand letters of credit, details of which were not recorded on the bank's books but were concealed on his own personal computer at his home. All of these related to shipments of arms which were listed on Iraqi Airways cargo manifests as agricultural machinery and machine parts but which in reality, according to the Italian authorities, were high technology electronic equipment and missile parts produced in several countries throughout the US and Europe. All the consignments had been shipped to Fiumicino Airport in Rome, from where they were despatched on twice-weekly flights to Baghdad. The investigations continue and as yet no legal proceedings have been brought.

At least twenty European companies from Britain, France, West Germany, Spain and Italy featured on the letters of credit, including Lummus Crest, Thiessen, Mannesmann Demag, Mannesmann Handel, Potain, Rotec Industries, Servas, Techno Export, XYZ Options and Dresser. One of the British companies identified as being involved was Ferranti International Signal, whose American subsidiary, ISC Technology, was reported to have been awarded contracts worth a total of £50 million by Iraq for the supply of naval electronic systems during the Gulf War. Another was Matrix-Churchill, the Iraqi-controlled and Coventry-based subsidiary of TDG which was said to have exported £8.5 million worth of machinery to Iraq during 1988–9 alone. In September 1989, the company confirmed that an irrevocable letter of credit for £26.4 million had been established with the Atlanta branch of BNL for the purpose of funding a contract to manufacture forging dies for Iraq, supposedly for use in the production of automotive components.

Interrogation of one of the senior executives of the Atlanta branch of BNL unearthed the fact that there had been a plan to set up a bank whose role would have been to finance the acquisition of technology and arms procurement for Iraq. Paul von Wedel, the branch's deputy manager, was reported as having told investigators that the plan had been discussed with Hussein Kamal, the Iraqi Minister of Industry and Military Production, who is also Saddam Hussein's son-in-law.

As investigators in the United States and Italy dug further, it was revealed that members of the middle-level management in BNL's headquarters in Rome had in fact been aware of the letters of credit and had been involved in processing the unauthorised payments. This resulted in September 1989 in the resignations of BNL's president, Signor Nerio Nesi, and its director-general Signor Giacomo Pedde. Directors and senior management were not aware of the secret operation.

Evidence was also discovered suggesting that BNL had previously been involved in financing the illegal supply of arms to Iran. Signor Felice Casson, an investigating magistrate in Venice who was appointed to prepare cases against Nesi and Pedde, had for the previous three years been amassing a considerable amount of information which had convinced him that BNL was one of a number of banks throughout Europe that were financing the arms trade with Tehran. As a result of his discoveries, warrants were subsequently issued for the arrest of individuals involved in three companies which had supplied fuses and artillery shell components. Warrants were also issued against senior members of BNL's management for suspected complicity. At the time of writing none of these individuals has yet been tried in the courts.

The investigators discovered that tracking down the movement of the disbursed credits was a difficult task. Money had been raised by the Atlanta branch of BNL on the interbank money markets from amongst fifty or so European, American and Japanese banks in amounts averaging between $20 million and $30 million.

The revelations over BNL may well have a bearing upon another aspect of Iraqi arms procurement. In January 1990, the French were intrigued when Iraq offered to pay cash for a large order of FFr900 million worth of advanced electronic equipment from Thomson-CSF as part of a plan to persuade Defence Minister Chevènement to agree to the sale of the Mirage 2000. Knowing Iraq's financial position to be somewhat parlous, there was curiosity amongst the French as to the source of this sudden wealth. In all probability it was money previously obtained from BNL. The Iraqi ploy was successful: not only did the French agree to sell the aircraft but also to permit its manufacture under licence in Iraq. Moreover, they agreed to reschedule Iraqi FFr25 billion debt repayments on which interest had not been paid since 1986.

There is no doubt that one result of the Gulf crisis has been to expose the extent to which Western countries and the Eastern bloc have armed Saddam Hussein, and that considerable embarrassment has been caused as a result. The Soviet Union, China and France are particularly guilty of having supplied Iraq with huge quantities of conventional arms, the French together with other European countries and the United States supporting Iraq as a bulwark against Iranian Shi'ite fundamentalism. Equally, elements of European industry, mainly in Germany but also elsewhere, have apparently had few qualms in recent years about supplying the technology and equipment for Saddam Hussein's chemical and nuclear weapons development programmes, frequently in violation of national and international laws, treaties and trade regulations.

In Britain, this issue came to the fore when, on 2nd December 1990,

The Sunday Times carried a report concerning the alleged involvement of a government minister and senior civil servants in providing assistance to British companies exporting equipment to Iraq for military purposes.

The paper's well-known 'Insight' investigative team had been carrying out a detailed study of the role played by the Department of Trade and Industry into the granting of export licences to companies producing equipment for the manufacture of munitions. They claimed that a principal figure in the matter was Alan Clark who, at the time of writing, is Minister for Defence Procurement but during the period in question was a minister at the Department of Trade and Industry.

In 1984, Britain had embargoed exports of all military equipment to both Iraq and Iran. However, in November 1986, Clark visited Baghdad to promote British business interests in Iraq with whom, despite the arms embargo, trade was flourishing. One of the principal reasons for his visit was a meeting with the Iraqi trade minister, Hassan Ali, at which he would discuss a new agreement to cover credit which would be financed by the DTI's Export Credit and Guarantee Department and would bring the total credit extended to Iraq by Britain to £750 million.

In early 1988, the then Foreign Secretary, Sir Geoffrey Howe, put forward a request to the cabinet that there should be further restrictions on export of equipment to Iraq. This was the result of concern at the Foreign Office about the large contracts for machine tools and other equipment which had been exported to Iraq. Indeed, Foreign Office officials had brought the matter to the attention of the DTI, pointing out that the factories and plants in which the machinery had been installed were operated by Iraq's Ministry of Industry and Military Industrialisation.

The result was increasing disagreement between the Foreign Office and the Department of Trade and Industry, which it advises on the acceptability of individual export-licence applications. Inevitably, because Foreign Office approval was being withheld on certain applications for further exports of equipment to Iraq, the companies concerned were becoming increasingly anxious about being able to fulfil their contracts within the timeframes specified. Several of them communicated their anxieties to the Department of Trade's export-licensing branch but were advised to contact the minister directly responsible, Alan Clark.

On 20th January 1988, a meeting took place at the London headquarters of the Department of Trade and Industry. It was attended by representatives of Matrix-Churchill, BSA Tools Ltd and Colchester Lathes, as well as representatives of the Machine Tool Trades Association. Minutes of the meeting taken by one of those organisations present state that during his address to those assembled, Clark, who was accompanied by senior representatives of his department, not only congratulated those companies present on having secured such lucrative contracts, but also advised them on the manner in which future applications for exports to Iraq should be completed. The impression given to one attender was that he advised them to minimise the military potential of their products in any such applications in order to avoid the possibility of licences being refused.

According to the minutes, Clark made clear that he supported the granting of export licences for machine tools to be sold to Iraq and also advised that applications should be submitted at the earliest opportunity in order to avoid delays caused by 'bureaucratic interference'. He did, however, add the rider that he had given such advice based on the circumstances in existence at that time and that should political conditions undergo change, particularly with regard to any shift in American support of either of the Gulf war combatants, then 'the current order may change'.

Clark ended by giving his assurance that he would support the companies' case 'strenuously up to cabinet committee'. It is not alleged that this is what the minister did in fact say at the meeting but the impression given to some of those present was that they would be allowed to continue exporting their machine tool products to Iraq, even though it was fully appreciated by all concerned that they would be used for the manufacture of mortar and artillery ammunition. This was subsequently reinforced by a document sent to the Department of Trade and Industry by Matrix-Churchill, giving details of the company's business with Iraq and emphasising the company's reliance on defence as one of its major markets.

It was also fully appreciated by all those present that the matter was one of the utmost sensitivity. The minutes of the meeting apparently include a reference to the fact that maximum effort was to be devoted to ensuring that details did not come to the attention of the media.

Trade with Iraq boomed during the rest of 1988. By the end of the year, it had risen from £2.9 million in 1987 to £31.5 million.

In the event of a war in the Gulf, the forces of the allied nations will face an enemy well equipped by the arms industries of Europe, the Eastern bloc and China. It can only be hoped that some form of action will be taken against those who, in pursuit of profit, violated national or international laws in arming the 'Butcher of Baghdad'. Those who permitted them to do so will, no doubt, escape unscathed.

6 · 'Project Babylon'

Late in the evening of 22nd March 1990, the dead body of sixty-two-year-old Dr Gerald Bull, a Canadian artillery expert who gained posthumous notoriety as the scientific genius behind what was to become known as the 'Super Gun', was found lying in a pool of blood outside his flat in the Brussels district of Uccles. He had been shot from behind with a silenced 7.65mm pistol, fired by a killer who had waited for him in the dark as he stepped from the lift of the apartment building where he lived. The $20,000 in cash he had with him was untouched and his killing bore the hallmarks of a professional assassin.

The prime suspect was the Israeli intelligence service, Mossad, which had an interest in preventing Bull from continuing to help the Iraqis to develop long-range weapon systems. Naturally, the Israelis denied any involvement in his death and carefully organised leaks to the media which suggested that he had been killed by the Iraqis after they had discovered that he was a CIA agent working on a 'sting' operation to discover details of their chemical and nuclear weapon development programmes. Another theory, which was also traced back to Israeli sources, proposed that Bull was killed by either the CIA or Britain's Secret Intelligence Service to prevent him from examining the consignment of forty 'krytron' high-speed electronic switches which was due to be smuggled out of the United States to Britain and ultimately to Iraq. This particular theory propounded the idea that if Bull had discovered that the krytrons were dummies the 'sting' operation which had been mounted by the British and the Americans would have been compromised.

Gerald Bull had paid grievously for his ambition to realise a lifelong dream. Ironically, the international recognition he had sought for his commitment to ballistics and long-range artillery systems came less than a month after his murder. His death, however, led to revelations concerning not only his work for the Baghdad regime but also the role played by British government departments.

Born in Ontario in 1928, Gerald Bull was a brilliant mathematician, a respected scientist and businessman whose career in ballistics spanned four decades. His involvement with long-range projectiles and launching systems began in 1951 when he joined the Canadian Armament Research and Development Establishment, where he worked on guided missile and ballistic projects. In 1964, he was appointed to be Director of the Space Research Institute at McGill University in Montreal. An expert in long-range artillery, Bull had long been convinced of the value of a gun launcher for launching projectiles into space, seeing it as a cheaper alternative to rockets. He managed to convince the American and Canadian governments, who set up a research team, with him at its head, and invested millions of dollars in his project. His principal assistant was Charles Murphy of the US Army Research Laboratories.

Known as the High Altitude Research Project (HARP), Bull's launcher system was initially based on 16-inch-calibre smooth-bore naval guns, three of which had been supplied by the US navy. In 1965, however, Bull had received a windfall in the form of some data originally produced by the late Dr Fritz Rausenberger, the designer of the German long-range artillery guns used to shell Paris from ranges of up to a hundred miles during the latter stages of the First World War. This data included plans for the construction of the guns and Bull was able to use this information to reconstruct them on his computers.

Subsequently, three HARP guns were built by joining together the barrels of 16-inch naval guns. The largest one, with a barrel length of 172 feet, was located at a test range at Highwater, on the border between the United States and Canada. A smaller version, equipped with a 120-foot barrel, was at the US army proving range at Yuma in Arizona, whilst the third, also with a 120-foot barrel and named the Paragon, was positioned on a highly secret test range on the Caribbean island of Barbados, where it remains to this day.

During trials in Barbados, a rocket-propelled fin-stabilised 'Martlet' shell was fired into space to a height of approximately 112 miles above the earth's surface, setting a new high-altitude record. Although restrictions prevented them from doing so, the project research team maintained that a projectile weighing up to six hundred pounds and up to sixteen feet in length could be fired to a height of 1150 miles.

Despite the successes achieved by HARP, it was terminated at the end of June 1967 by both governments, on the grounds that rockets remained the better option. Up until then, rockets had relied on liquid fuel mixed with oxygen, which was both costly and dangerous. Then came the development of solid fuel, which was cheaper, safer and more efficient, and enabled scientists to produce rockets half the size with double the range and payload capacity. This new generation of solid-fuelled rockets was cheaper than Bull's HARP guns and projectiles. That was why the

HARP programme was terminated at the end of 1967. At the time, however, it was suspected that there were additional reasons, including suspicions that Bull had made several enemies in American and Canadian government departments through his often arrogant behaviour.

In 1968, Bull proceeded to form his own company, the Space Research Corporation (SRC). He registered it in the state of Delaware, financing it with capital raised from commercial contacts. He also formed a company in Canada, Space Research Corporation (Quebec) Ltd, and continued to develop his concepts for long-range artillery and launching systems, having purchased all the HARP material from the American and Canadian governments for a nominal figure. SRC proceeded to enjoy considerable success, being awarded contracts worth more than $9 million by the US Department of Defense for design and development of long-range munitions, projectiles, fuses and propellants.

At the same time, Bull developed his own long-range 155mm artillery shell and commenced production of it. SRC established a close relationship with Pouderies Réunies Belges (PRB) in Belgium and a Brussels-based subsidiary, Space Research Corporation International (SCRI), was set up as a joint venture in partnership with PRB in order to tender for NATO contracts.

SRC was by then carrying out work of a highly sensitive nature for the Pentagon, including the development of components for 8-inch nuclear artillery ammunition. By 1977, the company had obtained contracts to produce up to 50,000 155mm shells. Despite this, it was in financial trouble and was in arrears on loan payments to its bankers.

It was at this point that salvation appeared in the form of the South Africans, who were introduced to Bull by the Central Intelligence Agency. During the 1970s, they had been attempting to develop long-range artillery to counter the Soviet-made 122mm howitzers being used by Cuban forces fighting against South African troops in Angola, but had had little success. Bull's technology was thus an answer to their prayers.

The US embargo on the sale of arms to South Africa prevented Bull from selling his weapons to Pretoria. However, he circumvented this by using shell companies in Spain and Antigua, in the West Indies, and selling the South Africans the technology to develop a long-range artillery piece and several consignments of his special long-range 155mm ammunition. These were shipped, ostensibly for trials, to Antigua, where Bull had set up a test range; en route they were transhipped to South Africa. As a result, the South Africans were able to develop their G-5 155mm howitzer based on Bull's design. Considered by many defence experts to be the most effective long-range artillery piece worldwide, the

G-5 (and its self-propelled version the G-6) has a maximum range of thirty-two miles and is an extremely accurate weapon. Equally importantly, it can fire conventional, chemical and nuclear ammunition.

However, the South Africans did not limit themselves to buying technology and ammunition. In 1977, nervous about SRC's precarious financial position and anxious to retain access to Bull's technology, the South African government-owned arms manufacturing conglomerate Armscor purchased 20 per cent of SRC's holding company and acquired Bull's patents and licences.

Unfortunately for Bull, however, when the South Africans broadcast the details of their new weapon two years later, in 1979, his involvement in the G-5 programme was revealed. The American authorities discovered the details of SRC's sales to Pretoria, and, after an investigation by the US Justice Department, prosecuted Bull for violation of the arms embargo. After being tried and convicted in 1980, he was sentenced to a term of imprisonment of three months. The short sentence perhaps reflects the embarrassment of the US government – there had been American complicity in the supply of 155mm ammunition to South Africa in that the shells had been manufactured in a US army ordnance factory and the Office of Munitions Control of the US Department of Commerce had waived the requirement for an export licence.

On his release from prison, somewhat embittered by what he considered to be shabby and unfair treatment by the Americans, Bull left the United States and moved to Brussels. SRC's companies in America and Canada had gone bankrupt and so he was forced to rebuild his empire from scratch. At the same time, PRB had dissolved its partnership with SRC and had taken over SRCI, changing the company's name to International Ordnance Sales and Services (IOSS).

On establishing himself in Brussels, Bull once again set up Space Research Corporation and proceeded to develop his contacts with several countries, including Spain, Chile, Austria, Yugoslavia, China and South Africa. He expanded SRC into a truly international concern, establishing subsidiary companies and offices in a number of places, including London, Vienna, Geneva, Madrid and Belgrade. The organisation concentrated on design; production was handled by sub-contractors throughout Europe.

One of the first major contracts for SRC was the design of a long-range artillery weapon for Norinco, the Chinese government-owned arms and munitions manufacturing organisation. This eventually manifested itself in the form of the WA-021 155mm howitzer with which the People's Liberation Army is currently equipped. A similar design project was carried out by SRC for the Austrian company Noricum, which produced it as the GHN-45 155mm howitzer and sold it to both sides during the Iran–Iraq War. A quantity of two hundred of these weapons was sold to Iraq via Jordan in 1982, the ammunition being supplied by another Austrian company, Hirtenberger.

Other projects included a conversion kit for the Soviet-made M-146 130mm artillery pieces of the Yugoslav army, which enabled the weapons to fire long-range ammunition. Somehow, this equipment also found its way from Yugoslavia to Iraq.

SRC also carried out development work for the Israelis, designing special ammunition for use by the Israeli defence forces' M-107 175mm self-propelled guns. During the 1980s, artillery weapons based on Bull's designs were manufactured by a number of companies in other countries, including SITESCA of Spain, CITEFA in Argentina, Cardoen Industries of Chile and Taiwan's Army Arsenals.

Bull's direct personal connections with Iraq and Saddam Hussein began early in 1988, during the latter stages of the Gulf War, when Iraq was under severe pressure from Iranian forces threatening to break through in the area of Basra. The Iraqis were familiar with Bull's technology, the Austrian GHN-45 and South African G-5 howitzers having been in service with them since 1982 and 1984 respectively.

In January, Bull travelled to Baghdad, where he attended a series of meetings during which the Iraqis enlisted his assistance in overhauling and upgrading their entire artillery arsenal. He was able to show them two of his existing designs for a 155mm and a 210mm self-propelled howitzer. As a result, SRC was awarded a contract to develop these guns, as well as special ammunition for use with them, and to provide training in enhanced ballistics for Iraqi technical personnel. These two weapons were subsequently developed as the 155mm Majnoon and 210mm Al Fao. Prototypes were eventually assembled by the Spanish company Forex SA from components manufactured by companies in Germany, France and Spain; these were then flow to Iraq. The Al Fao, mounted on a self-propelled 6 × 6 chassis, is reputed to have the longest range of any artillery piece in the world, being capable of delivering shells to a distance of approximately 36 miles when using the special long-range 'base bleed' ammunition developed by SRC. This particular type of shell is fitted with a burning charge attached to its base, which reduces drag during flight.

During discussions at one meeting, the Iraqis also made plain their requirement for both a satellite launching capability and an ultra-long-range weapon system. At that time, there was one particular threat which was of increasing concern to them – Israel.

With the memory of the destruction of their Tammuz I reactor still uppermost in their minds, the Iraqis feared an Israeli pre-emptive strike, especially as the support which they had enjoyed in the West began to evaporate after they were universally condemned for the use of chemical weapons. They firmly believed that the threat of retaliation against Israel with weapons of mass destruction was the only effective deterrent: high casualty figures have always been a factor unacceptable to the Israelis.

However, the existence of a system such as the Arrow anti-ballistic missile system threatened to make such a concept obsolete. The Iraqis had thus begun to look for a delivery system which would not only provide a surveillance capability but which would also circumvent an anti-ballistic missile shield.

Bull apparently expressed his enthusiasm at the idea of developing such a system as well as an ultra-long-range artillery weapon. Saddam Hussein, who had been kept informed by telephone, asked to see Bull that evening and at 8.30 p.m. the Canadian was driven to the presidential palace.

An account of the meeting states that it was an extremely friendly one. Bull apparently sat cross-legged on a cushion on the floor of a lavish reception room which opened on to a veranda and a garden. He and his host ate dates and between them demolished a bottle of Johnny Walker Black Label, Saddam Hussein's favourite tipple. For three hours, Bull held forth non-stop on his theories and ideas, drawing a series of diagrams on a sketchpad.

At the end of the meeting, by which time it was well past midnight, Saddam Hussein ordered that Brigadier-General Hassan Kamal al-Majed, the Minister of Industry and the man responsible for overseeing Iraq's most advanced armament programmes, should be woken from his sleep and summoned to the presidential palace at once. Thus was 'Project Babylon' conceived – over a bottle of whisky on the cushions of Saddam Hussein's palace.

Through his work for the Iraqis, Bull subsequently became a close friend of Hassan Kamal al-Majed who, besides being the Minister of Industry, is a cousin and son-in-law of Saddam Hussein and thus an influential figure in the Ba'athist regime.

Four months later, SRC had completed the technical plans and specifications for the 'Project Babylon' launcher system. These were drawn up by an Athens-registered subsidiary of SRC, Advanced Technology Institute (ATI), which had been formed specifically for the project.

Design experts and draughtsmen had been recruited by a British company, European Research and Design Ltd, which was based in Wales and Brussels. Its company secretary, a Welshman named Paul Shaw who lived in Brussels, was also an employee of SRC. The ATI design team was reportedly headed by a Briton named John Heath, a highly skilled draughtsman. Those specialists recruited by ATI found themselves working on specifications and designs for projectiles which were to be fired from a giant gun or launcher; one of the experts supervising their work was an aerodynamics specialist named Tony Slack. ATI employees were recruited from throughout Europe and included Britons, Italians, Frenchmen and a South African in their ranks. The director of the company responsible for this stage of the project was an American, Alex Pappas, who was also a director of SRC. He had worked with Gerald Bull for several years and had assisted him with the designs for the South African G-5 155mm howitzer.

Early in 1988, a meeting took place at the offices of a British metal-forging company in Birmingham, Walters Somers Ltd. Those in attendance included an intermediary representing the Iraqi government and representatives of Walter Somers Ltd and another metal-forging company, Forgemasters Engineering Ltd of Sheffield. The Iraqis' intermediary was a director of SRC, Dr Christopher Cowley, who was a metallurgist by profession. During the meeting, Cowley outlined a plan for a petro-chemical plant which was apparently to be constructed in Iraq. He also put forward proposals for tasks to be carried out by the two companies and extended an invitation for them to attend a meeting at SRC's offices in Brussels in June.

A few days prior to the Brussels meeting, three directors of Forgemasters Engineering's parent company, Sheffield Forgemasters, attended a meeting with the company's solicitors to discuss the proposal. They were apparently dubious about SRC and were curious as to why a company specialising in defence was involved in a petro-chemical project. Despite their misgivings and their suspicions that the project might really be of a military nature, however, the directors decided to attend the meeting and to proceed with further discussions with SRC.

The meeting in Brussels was attended by directors of Sheffield Forgemasters and Forgemasters Engineering. Also present were representatives of River Don Castings, another subsidiary of Sheffield Forgemasters, and an Iraqi who was introduced as being the individual who was in control of the entire project. During the meeting, the directors of Sheffield Forgemasters asked if the project was of a military nature; their suspicions had been aroused by the technical specification of the metal from which the tubes were to be manufactured: forging steel with a high content of chrome, molybdenum and vanadium. To anyone well versed in steel production, it would have been obvious that such steel possessed strength far in excess of that required for use in the manufacture of pipelines. However, Cowley allegedly assured them that the tubes were required for petro-chemical applications.

The proposals put forward to Sheffield Forgemasters by Cowley and SRC involved the manufacture of fifty-two steel tubes, each six metres in length and one metre in internal diameter, by Forgemasters Engineering Ltd. Cowley announced that an order had already been placed with Walter Somers Ltd for twelve steel tubes, each ten metres long and 350mm in internal diameter. At the meeting, it was agreed that the Department of Trade and Industry should be consulted in order to ensure that the project was in accordance with regulations. In principle, however, Sheffield Forgemasters accepted the proposals.

Several further meetings took place and by August 1988 contracts with the Iraqi Ministry of Petroleum had been agreed. During the latter part of 1988 and throughout 1989, Forgemasters Engineering manufactured a total of fifty-two tube sections according to plans and specifications provided by ATI.

Personnel from ATI were responsible for exercising quality control on other components for the project being manufactured by companies elsewhere in Europe, including the Societa delle Fucine steelworks in Terni, Italy, and the Von Roll steelworks at Berne in Switzerland.

Development of the propellant for the launcher system was carried out by PRB, with whom Bull had re-established a close relationship after moving to Brussels. In 1988, PRB signed a contract with Jordan to develop and produce very large quantities of a solid propellant based on a specification provided by ATI. This was ostensibly for use by the Jordanian army's artillery, but the unusual type and large quantities required gave rise to suspicions that this was not the case. In March 1989, however, the Belgian air force reportedly flew a consignment of propellant to Baghdad.

As work progressed on the project, Iraqi technicians visited both Forgemasters Engineering and Walter Somers. By early 1989 the latter had manufactured and delivered a number of tubes; deliveries were completed in March 1990. ATI technicians, working with their Iraqi counterparts, used these tubes to build the twenty-metre-long barrel of a smaller prototype launcher, nicknamed 'Baby Babylon', which was horizontally mounted on converted railway bogies. According to accounts reportedly given later by former SRC personnel, a test firing took place in

April at which a scaled-down projectile was successfully fired into a mountainside at a range of about one mile. Other reports contradict this account, stating that the barrel exploded when 'Baby Babylon' was fired.

Based on the known details of Bull's technology, the type of projectile likely to have been developed by SRC for use with this type of launcher would possibly have been an advanced version of the 'Martlet' type developed by Bull during the 1960s for the HARP project. This consisted of a fin-stabilised rocket which would have been launched initially by the charge fired by the launcher. The rocket, fitted with a sabot which encased it during its passage up the barrel of the launcher, would probably have been powered by binary fuel, which would mix and ignite after launching, thus preventing any risk of it exploding during the initial stage of propulsion. On leaving the muzzle of the launcher, the sabot would fall away from the rocket, which would carry on to its target height. At that point the motor would burn out and the rocket body fall away, leaving the satellite in position in geo-stationary orbit. The maximum weight limit of the payload would probably have been about 200kg and thus the proposed Franco-Brazilian satellite's weight of 150kg would have been well within this limitation.

During the period from late 1988 until the beginning of 1990, Forge-masters Engineering Ltd carried out the manufacture of the larger tubes. The company later maintained that it was unaware that these were apparently destined to be the barrels of two huge test guns codenamed 'Big Babylon'. Each barrel comprised twenty-six sections totalling 156 metres in length with a bore diameter of one metre. By early 1990, a total of forty-four tubes had been shipped to Iraq.

Gerald Bull's death was a major setback for 'Project Babylon'. Approximately three weeks later, on the morning of 10th April, British Customs officers raided a Bermuda-registered cargo vessel, the *Gur Mariner*, which was docked at Teesport, near Middlesbrough. Chartered to the Iraqi Maritime Organisation, she was shortly due to sail for the Iraqi port of Umm Qasr with the final consignment of eight tubes manufactured by Forgemasters Engineering. At the same time, Customs officers also raided the offices of Walter Somers Ltd and Sheffield Forgemasters and confiscated documents relating to the supply of the tubes to Iraq.

The Customs raids were apparently the result of information passed on by intelligence sources. According to one report, which has been supported by a Middle East intelligence source close to Tehran, a Muslim employee of Walter Somers Ltd passed information to the Iranian intelligence service, SAVAM. The Iranians distrusted the British, maintaining that Britain would rather encourage Saddam Hussein in his campaign against Iran than deter his attempts to enlarge his arsenal. They therefore decided to pass the information on to others whom they felt sure would take the implications of Saddam Hussein acquiring such a launcher system seriously – the Israelis. This was effected via a Palestinian based in Lebanon who has worked for some time as a double agent for Mossad and for the Lebanese Deuxième Bureau. In due course, Mossad passed the information about the tubes to the British.

This was not the first occasion on which Iran and Israel had cooperated against their common foe. In 1987, the Iranians used the same conduit for passing the photographs and information concerning the missile 'kits', including the prototype Condor-2, shipped by Egypt to Iraq for testing against Iranian targets – a member of an Iraqi Shia clandestine opposition group had obtained them and passed them to the Iranians, who in turn handed them over to the Israelis via the Palestinian double agent.

Meanwhile, authorities in other European countries had also seized consignments of tubes and components en route by road for Baghdad. In Greece a British lorry heading for Iraq was impounded. Its cargo was a single large tube, one end of which was fashioned in such a way as to give rise to belief that it might have formed part of a large breech.

A total of sixteen directors and executives from Sheffield Forgemasters and Walter Somers Ltd were questioned by the British authorities. Subsequently, the managing director of Walter Somers, Peter Mitchell, and Dr Christopher Cowley, the metallurgist and SRC director, were arrested and charged with knowingly being concerned in the export of prohibited equipment under the Export of Goods Control Orders of 1987 and 1989 and under Section 68 of the Customs and Excise Management Act 1979. Subsequently, the Department of Customs and Excise prepared charges to be brought against a total of eleven individuals, including three men working in Brussels.

Elsewhere, other consignments of components had been seized. Fifteen tons of steel were confiscated from the Societa delle Fucine steelworks at Terni by the Italian authorities who also impounded four containers holding seventy-five tons of steel parts at Naples. These were about to be loaded on to a vessel, the *Jolly Turchese*, which was due to sail for the Jordanian port of Aqaba. In northern Italy, one and a half tons of components were seized from warehouses belonging to two companies in Brescia, one of the centres of the Italian arms industry.

In West Germany, thirty-seven tons of forged steel parts, reported to be components for a hydraulic system, were seized at Frankfurt airport. These had been manufactured by a Belgian company, Rexroth, which was a subsidiary of the German firm of Mannesmann, one of the largest

manufacturers of steel pipes worldwide. Mannesmann had also participated in defence contracts and is the parent company of Krauss-Maffei,
the manufacturers of the Leopard II tank.

It was rumoured that the Spanish company Trebelan had been linked
to the supply of roller-mounted steel cradles for 'Project Babylon'. These
reports were subsequently strengthened by confirmation from the Spanish government that in April 1989 the company had supplied Iraq with two
transporters designed to carry missiles or large artillery weapons. However, such items were not on any list of goods prohibited for export and
thus the company had not committed any offence.

Inevitably, the Iraqis strongly denied that the tubes formed part of any
launcher or weapon system, maintaining that they were required for
petro-chemical applications. However, the evidence overwhelmingly
contradicted them. In November 1990, the Iraqis lost an appeal in the
High Court in London against the impounding of the tubes.

During the aftermath of the seizure of the tubes and components, there
was inevitably much speculation in the media as to the nature of the
'Super Gun'. There were conflicting accounts and opinions as to the
purpose of the project, but once the initial excitement had died down
some rather more probable theories prevailed. One of these maintained
that the tubes were intended for use in testing missile boosters, but this
application would have required tubes of a uniform thickness. Moreover,
the tubes had been of pre-stressed, layered and compressed steel produced by a process known as 'autofrettage' – the method used in the
manufacture of artillery gun barrels.

Other theories stated that 'Project Babylon' was designed to be some
form of long-range weapon system capable of launching chemical and
nuclear warheads. However, the size and weight of the barrel alone
precluded any form of mobility and thus would have made it highly
vulnerable to attack. Moreover, after the Israeli bombing of Tammuz I in
1981, the Iraqis were only too well aware that the construction of such a
huge weapon would have invited some form of pre-emptive strike by
Israel. These factors alone made it hardly feasible as a weapon, even if a
large part of it had been buried underground. Furthermore, it is known
that the Iraqis, having lost the surveillance cover provided by the
American-manned Saudi AWACS during the Gulf War, were anxious to
replace it as soon as possible with a satellite surveillance system of their
own to cover Israel, Syria, Iran and their own northern borders.

On considering the information available, the only logical explanation
of 'Project Babylon' is that it was a development and construction
programme for a launcher designed to propel payload-carrying projectiles

into space. Such projectiles could well have carried a satellite of the type under discussion between the Iraqis and the Brazilians or, alternatively, a nuclear weapon to be recalled into the earth's atmosphere and programmed to deliver itself into a given area. Canadian intelligence sources have been quoted as saying that, at the time of his death, Bull was working on a form of binary hydrogen fuel for use with long-range projectiles and that he was also apparently involved in the development of projectiles designed to re-enter the earth's atmosphere – a former Canadian colleague of his was quoted as stating that Bull was interested in thermal protection for missile warheads. Moreover, PRB apparently possessed the technology to produce the 'Martlet'-type projectile designed to launch payloads from a gun-type launcher and to transport them into space.

Needless to say, there has also been much speculation as to how long the British government had been aware of 'Project Babylon' before the Customs seizures in April 1990. The directors of Sheffield Forgemasters stated that they contacted the Department of Trade and Industry when first approached by the Iraqis in 1988 with an enquiry concerning artillery gun barrels. The company was advised that an export licence would not be granted for such items and it accordingly informed the Iraqis that they would be unable to fulfil any such orders. When the company was approached a second time by the Iraqis through SRC, it contacted the DTI again after the meeting in Brussels in June 1988 and obtained a verbal clearance that there would be no problems with a petro-chemical project for Iraq. Sheffield Forgemasters then apparently wrote to the DTI, supplying full details of the specifications of the tubes, and received a reply confirming that if the tubes were for petro-chemical applications an export licence would not be required.

It transpired that Sheffield Forgemasters were not alone in their doubts about the Iraqi contract. In June 1988, SRC had changed the specifications of the tubes ordered from Walter Somers Ltd and this had aroused the suspicions of the company's management. The managing director, Peter Mitchell, contacted the Conservative member of parliament for Bromsgrove, Sir Hal Miller, who also contacted the DTI and was told that there was no objection to the contract being fulfilled. In 1989, Mitchell contacted Miller again when Walter Somers Ltd received a second contract from the Iraqis for another quantity of steel tubes. Once again, the response from government departments was that there was no objection to the contract being fulfilled.

In early April 1990, a few days before the Customs seizure of the tubes at Teeside docks, Peter Mitchell contacted Sir Hal Miller yet again when Walter Somers Ltd was approached about a further contract to supply a structure which the company suspected might be some form of traversing and aiming mechanism for a large barrel. Miller telephoned the office of Alan Clark, the Minister of State for Defence Procurement, and discussed the matter with Clark's Parliamentary Private Secretary, who apparently promised to pass on the information. Miller later confirmed that this had been done because he was aware that a government department had contacted Walter Somers Ltd. By now, however, the company's management was sufficiently concerned to decline the contract.

The government had previously also received a warning from another source. Astra Holdings had purchased PRB from its previous owners, Gechem, a subsidiary of Société Générale de Belgique, for £22 million in September 1989. On inspecting the company's books, the Astra management discovered details of the Jordanian contract which stipulated extremely large quantities of the unusual solid propellant specified by the SRC subsidiary, ATI. Senior Astra executives were apparently concerned because they knew that a propellant of this type and quantity would not have been for use with weapons of the type with which the Jordanian army's artillery units were equipped. They were also worried about the involvement of SRC. Accordingly, the chief executive of Astra Holdings, Christopher Gumbley, and a director of PRB, John Pike, contacted the Defence Export Services Organisation of the Ministry of Defence. At subsequent meetings with members of the security services, Gumbley and Pike are reported to have handed over documents which clearly showed the role played by Gerald Bull.

There is evidence that the government was already concerned over SRC's activities at that time. In September 1989 Richard Needham, the junior Northern Ireland minister, wrote to Kevin McNamara, the Shadow Northern Ireland spokesman. In his letter, Needham explained that an application for a development grant submitted by SRC Composites, a company jointly owned by SRC Engineering of Geneva and the Iraqi-owned British firm Technology Development Group had been turned down on the grounds that it was believed that the company intended to manufacture and export missile components. Needham's letter indicated that government suspicions had initially been aroused at the time of the purchase of the factory, which was previously owned by the Lear Fan company, for the very high price of £3 million when the site had previously been valued for only £650,000.

The reference to the production of missile components related to the fact that the factory had previously been used for the production of a turbo-prop executive aircraft manufactured from carbon fibre and advanced composite materials. Amongst its equipment were a number of filament-winding machines which could have been used to manufacture missile components. It was these machines which made the factory such an attractive proposition to SRC Composites Ltd, whose board of directors included two Iraqis, Nassir al-Nainsi and Fadel Jawad Khadum, both of whom were prominent figures in Baghdad's covert procurement network in Europe, as mentioned in the previous chapter.

Needham's letter also made the following revealing statement: 'The Foreign and Commonwealth Office said that Iraq was known to be involved in an advanced ballistic development programme in co-operation with other countries, including Argentina. Composite materials, which the former Lear Fan factory produced, could be used in ballistic missiles and other weapon systems.'

In the light of these facts and this statement, and in view of the warnings passed on by three companies and a member of parliament, not to mention the known efficiency of the Secret Intelligence Service and the other British security services, it is hard to believe that the government was unaware of SRC's activities and its involvement with 'Project Babylon'. It is more likely that Whitehall was fully aware of what was going on and was biding its time for its own reasons before making a move.

This view is strengthened by statements subsequently made by Sir Hal Miller, whose exchanges in the House of Commons indicated that the Department of Trade and Industry had not told the complete truth when Nicholas Ridley, Secretary of State for Trade and Industry, informed the House on 18th April 1990, 'On the information available at the time [1988], the department did not think an export licence was needed.' Sir Hal ridiculed the idea of the Israelis having been the initial source of information about 'Project Babylon', informing the House that in 1988 he had personally approached the Department of Trade and Industry, the Ministry of Defence and 'a third agency' on behalf of Water Somers Ltd, passing on the company's offer to withdraw from the contract or, alternatively, to proceed and enable investigations to be carried out at the same time. This offer was repeated when a second contract was offered by the Iraqis twelve months later.

The revelations concerning 'Project Babylon' caused a furore in the House of Commons and heated exchanges between government departments. Accusations and recriminations were exchanged between the Department of Trade and Industry, the Ministry of Defence and the Customs and Excise as to whether the tubes were intended for military use as part of a giant gun capable of launching projectiles over hundreds of miles or whether they were simply for use in a petro-chemical plant and thus did not require a licence for export. The Department of Trade and Industry cast aspersions on the Customs and Excise's insistence that the tubes were part of a giant weapon and a programme of leaks took place to support the DTI standpoint. This resulted in criticism of the Customs and Excise action by the Labour opposition in the House of Commons, to the extent that the Prime Minister was forced to make a statement defending the Customs and their actions.

In fact, the Customs and Excise had good reason for sticking to their theory. Prior to the inspection of the seized consignment of tubes by a Ministry of Defence armaments expert on 12th April, investigators of 'Target Team A', the London-based squad which works full-time on the illegal export of arms, had used a computer to match the specification of the tubes to those shown in a book – *Project HARP*, written by Dr Gerald Bull and Charles H. Murphy. The book contains the detailed specification of a HARP gun – the Paragon – located in Barbados. Pages 230, 231 and 232 show a diagram of the weapon in its assembled form. On comparing details from the book and from documents confiscated from Sheffield Forgemasters, the computer had found that they matched perfectly.

In November 1990, further facts were suddenly and unexpectedly revealed about another project which had been conducted by an SRC subsidiary. The Customs and Excise investigators attempting to unearth the facts behind 'Project Babylon' discovered that another long-range artillery weapon system had also been under development for Baghdad. The existence of this other project, codenamed 'Project 839', was revealed after the construction of a computer model based on some of the drawings and specifications seized during the raids on Sheffield Forge-masters and Walter Somers Ltd earlier in the year.

From the model, it rapidly became apparent that the weapon being developed under 'Project 839' was a railway-mounted long-range weapon similar in configuration to the huge rail-mounted guns used by the Germans in both world wars. In the case of the 'Project 839' weapon, however, its range was to be a staggering 466 miles when firing a 52kg shell – sufficient to reach targets in Saudi Arabia. The investigators learned that the Iraqis had planned to construct seventy-five of these weapons, which would have been sited in positions near the border with Iran, each consisting of a stretch of railway line heavily fortified against air attack.

The discovery of 'Project 839' possibly explains the existence of certain of the components known to have been delivered previously to Iraq or impounded by Customs authorities in different parts of Europe – items which had puzzled investigators as clearly not being for use in a large static launcher: the roller-mounted cradles and two special 'transporters' previously manufactured in Spain; the Belgian-made parts for hydraulics systems; and the suspected breech section discovered on the lorry impounded by the Greek authorities. The documents accompanying this consignment revealed it to be part of 'Project 839'. Moreover, 'Project 839' is almost certainly the ultra-long-range artillery weapon system which was reported to have been discussed by Bull during his meetings in Baghdad in January 1988.

At the same time as the facts concerning 'Project 839' were revealed, it was announced that a decision had been taken 'at the highest level' to drop all charges against those involved in 'Project Babylon', including Dr Christopher Cowley of SRC, one of the principal characters in the affair. This sudden change of heart by the British authorities is rather strange, bearing in mind that their previous strength of conviction was apparently sufficient for them to arrest and charge two of the individuals concerned and to prepare charges against nine more. In the light of the evidence revealed in December 1990 of Department of Trade and Industry knowledge of exports of arms-related equipment to Iraq, the question arises as to whether the dropping of charges was designed to prevent further embarrassment to politicians and high-ranking civil servants.

DICTATORSHIP
AND INVASION

7 · The Making of a Dictator

A few years ago an Egyptian journalist was granted an interview with Saddam Hussein. Two hours before the meeting, the president's press secretary showed him a video of *Aliyam Altawilah* (*The Long Days*), a film which was about to be released. It was a dramatisation, using top box-office stars, of the life and super-heroic deeds of Saddam Hussein, his struggle to build the Ba'ath party and to create a modern Iraq.

'What did you think of the film?' the president asked the reporter.

'Wonderful, Mr President! Perhaps the most important chapter in the history of Iraq is now a film,' replied the journalist. The president asked him if it was sufficiently realistic. In order that the Iraqi people could learn about their country he had instructed the director to make it 'didactic, truthful and historically accurate, as well as accessible to the majority of viewers'.

'Yes, Mr President, it certainly meets that criterion,' the journalist enthused, 'except for one scene – when your comrade cuts into your leg using a razor blade to get a bullet out. The actor who was playing your part only grimaces. I think he should scream in pain. It would be more realistic and show people that you, as a human being, have physically suffered.'

The president replied, 'I didn't think it was realistic either. I wanted the director to reshoot the scene because I remember the day when it happened. I did not grimace or move an inch until the bullet was out.'

This was genuinely Saddam Hussein's image of himself – a great leader and a man of superhuman qualities and impervious to suffering. It was all part of the myth he had created. As he manipulated and murdered his way to power, he never sought the affection of his people by attempting to be one of them. Nor did he feel the need to share his life with the Iraqi people. He resorted to a brutal and, in his eyes, more efficient and persuasive method of imposing his personality upon Iraq – terror.

Saddam Hussein was born in 1937 in Al-Auja, a village composed of a few mud huts and rarely shown on any maps. It is situated near the remote small town of Takrit on the northern bank of the River Tigris one hundred miles north of Baghdad. The area at that time could be described as backward; the Mosul–Baghdad railway line only passed through Takrit because decades earlier it was the centre of the raft industry as well as the manufacture of leather products. There was no electricity or running water and cow dung was burned for fuel.

Three 'works of art' have been devoted to the Iraqi leader, a film of his own 'struggle' and two biographies: Dr Amir Iskandar's *Saddam Hussein: The Fighter, the Thinker and the Man* and Fuad Mattar's *Saddam Hussein: A Biography*. The three works boast his genius in handling firearms from the age of ten, one of them describing how his wife Sajeda proudly helped him dress and loaded his submachine gun on the night of the 1968 coup, while his infant son Udai played with a hand grenade. Indeed, Saddam's talent in violence was more highly praised in his biographies than his skills as a statesman.

He grew up surrounded by violence. His father, Hussein al-Majid al-Takriti, was killed by bandits either just before or just after Saddam's birth. The details are sketchy and at times contradictory. Saddam himself has done little to correct them since the mystery lends him a further mythological dimension. One story, told by an official who turned against the dictator, claims that Saddam's father simply left his family. Whatever the truth, Hussein al-Majid was not present when his wife gave birth at her brother's house in the Alharah quarter of Takrit. Her brother in law, Hassan al-Majid, gave the baby the name Saddam – meaning 'Clasher'.

His mother's decision to remarry an already married man, Ibrahim Hassan, gave the young Saddam a severe shock that marked the first unhappy episode of his life. The stepfather was a brutal and illiterate man who denied Saddam any education, forcing him instead to work as a farmhand and shepherd. He often told the boy's mother, 'He is a son of a cur, give him away,' complaining of Saddam's fighting with the neighbours' children while his older step brother Adham, who was much quieter, was well behaved. Although one Muslim opposition figure claims Saddam's stepfather sexually abused him, it seems unlikely since, once in power, Saddam would almost certainly have killed his stepfather in order to ensure his silence. Saddam proved to be a man who would not tolerate 'gossip' about himself or his family. A Takriti officer, General Omar al-Hazzah, once told a woman friend that he had slept with Saddam's mother. As the woman's house was bugged by the Mukhabarat, Saddam was soon informed of the conversation. General al-Hazzah, his son and the woman friend were executed while their houses were flattened by bulldozers. A similar incident involved the assassination of a top official and the imprisonment of his wife because the Mukhabarat recorded a conversation in which the pair discussed the origins of one of Saddam's mistresses.

At the age of ten Saddam turned up at his uncle's house in Takrit with a pistol. No one knows whether his stepfather had finally thrown the boy out or whether he had simply run away. His uncle, Khairallah Tulfah (who was dismissed from the army in 1941 for joining a pro-Nazi organisation), enrolled Saddam in the local primary school with his own son Adnan, who later became defence minister but was killed in a mysterious helicopter crash after he grew too popular in 1989.

Saddam, inspired by photographs of his uncle in army uniform, wished to become a soldier but his poor academic record made entry to the military academy impossible. He inherited from his uncle an admiration for Nazi principles and thus, when he enrolled in the Karch secondary school in Baghdad, he was attracted to the ideas of the Ba'ath nationalist movement. The movement had been established in Damascus in 1943 by two Syrians, Greek Orthodox Christian Michel A'flaq and Sunni Muslim Salah al-Bitar. Their philosophy was based on the ideology of German national socialism and on Italian fascism. Such ideas were fashionable at the time among Arab nationalists in the Levant who aspired to a new national identity and an end to the domain of colonial powers: France in Syria and Britain in Iraq. The Ba'ath did not recognise national borders and referred to the former Ottoman empire provinces as Al'Umma al-Arabiyah ('The Arab Nation'). The central executive body, the National Command, was based in Damascus and had overall responsibility over regional commands in Iraq, Trans-Jordan and Palestine. The Ba'ath party had only a very small number of followers and secured very few votes in elections. As a result, it designed a two-tier strategy in the early 1950s. The first aim was to recruit army officers with nationalist sympathies in the hope that military coups could be staged all over the Arab world. The second aim was to establish a civilian movement by attracting militant students and other civilian elements. They would not be required to fight an election but to fight opponents on the streets and university campuses. In the mid-sixties, when Ba'athists were in power in both Syria and Iraq, the movement split, causing the bitter rivalry which has existed between the two countries ever since.

The school which Saddam joined in the 1950s was, like many Iraqi schools, full of nationalist teachers and students, the majority of whom were fervid supporters of Nasser.

Saddam's fellow pupils knew of his skill with firearms. He was barely sixteen when he joined his uncle Khairallah Tulfah in killing another Takriti, Abdallah al-Rashid. Twenty-eight years later the murdered man's nephew, General Maher Abd al-Rashid, took his revenge in a typically Takriti manner. During a visit to Iraqi frontline positions during the Gulf war, Saddam Hussein and his entourage were suddenly at risk from an Iranian counter-attack. In the process of saving him from falling into the hands of the advancing Iranian troops, al-Rashid made Saddam ask for help by swearing 'Bihyiat Abdallah al-Rashid', in the name, that is, of the uncle to whose murder Saddam had been a party nearly three decades before.

Saddam was just twenty when he joined his uncle in another killing, this time of Sa'doun al-Alousi, a civil servant. Saddam was caught but freed due to lack of evidence. Having been expelled from school he found himself unemployed but shortly afterwards a great opportunity appeared. He was called at short notice to join the Ba'ath six-man assassination squad endowed with the task of killing Prime Minister Abd al-Karim Qasim.

The fiasco which resulted has already been described. After having their wounds treated, Saddam Hussein and one of his men fled to Takrit from where, with the aid of the chief of the Syrian intelligence service, they crossed the border into Syria and made their way to Cairo.

One of Saddam's biographies says he fainted for a few minutes when the blade cut into his flesh and the bullet was pulled out with a pair of scissors. The other book gives more details, saying he fainted for a few moments when his comrade poured iodine into the bleeding wound. The film shows him only grimacing, and Saddam himself says he felt nothing. The doctor who dressed his wound tells a different story. Now living in Britain, he says he saw no bullet at all!

Once in Cairo, Saddam lived comfortably. He was given an allowance of E£84 (£97) a month by the Egyptian Mukhabarat's Arab Interest Bureau and installed in a flat in the Nile-bank quarter of Dukkie. The Cairo authorities, irritated by Qasim's close relations with the communists, ignored Iraqi requests to hand him over. The police in Dukkie threatened Saddam Hussein with deportation on a number of occasions for provoking street fights with other Iraqi and Arab students. Eventually, the Egyptian Mukhabarat co-operated in bringing his cousin Sajida, whom he subsequently married, to Cairo. They thought that the presence of a wife might act as a curb on his activities.

At that time Saddam was still only an associate member of the Ba'ath party, according to some old members. It was Midhat Juma'h, the head of the Ba'athist cell in Cairo, who eventually granted him full membership.

Saddam enrolled at Cairo's Qasr al-Nile private sixth form college at the age of twenty-three but he failed to achieve passes in any of his exams. His biographies maintain that he studied law at Cairo University but there is no proof of this in the university's records. When he later returned to

Iraq as the Ba'ath party's leading assassin, he let it be known that he had been studying law in Cairo and intended to take his degree. A day was appointed for him to go to Baghdad University to take the exam: he turned up in full military-style uniform, wearing a pistol which he drew from its holster and placed on his desk to make him 'feel more comfortable'. The degree was granted.

After the Ba'ath party came to power in February 1963 with the overthrow of General Qasim, the party leadership refused to recognise Saddam's membership and he had to wait until the Takritis amongst them nominated him for full membership. The Takriti officers group, which included Ahmad Hassan al-Bakr, Herdan al-Takriti, Mahdai Amash, and Saddam's brother-in-law Adnan Khairallah, had visions of the Takritis eventually controlling the Ba'ath party and ultimately Iraq.

Saddam was promoted into the Regional Command Council and it was soon found that this was his metier. He was put in charge of a special force responsible for terror and assassination and was an interrogator and torturer in the Qasr al-Nihayyat ('The Palace of the End'). This was also the headquarters of the National Guard, the para-military organisation which formed the powerbase of the Ba'ath party.

Eyewitnesses say Saddam excelled in creating new methods and revealed a sadistically inventive mind. He designed new instruments of torture and then experimented with them on his victims. One Iraqi, who was fortunate enough to survive falling into Saddam Hussein's hands in 1963, recalled his experiences at a human rights conference in London some years later. 'My hands and feet were tied together and I was hung by my feet from the ceiling. Saddam had converted a fan to take the weight of a man's body. As I was spun round, he beat me with a length of rubber hose filled with rubble.' Saddam also had a macabre and sadistic habit of presenting victims with a list from which they had to select the method by which they would 'prefer' to be tortured.

The secrets of the palace of Al-Nihayyat first became known after the November 1963 coup which overthrew the Ba'athists. 'When army officers reached the cellars of the Qasr al-Nihayyat in 1963', writes Iraqi historian Hanna Batatu, 'they found all sorts of loathsome instruments of torture, including electric wires with pincers, pointed iron stakes on which prisoners were made to sit, and a machine which still bore traces of chopped-off fingers. Small heaps of bloody clothing were scattered about and there were pools of congealed blood on the floor and bloodstains all over the walls.'

By the summer of 1963, Saddam was urging the party to put him in charge of creating a special security apparatus modelled on the Nazi SS.

This was the Jihaz Haneen mentioned in a previous chapter. Saddam wanted this apparatus to be a party-based alternative to the power wielded by Ba'ath members in the Army's officer corps. Only a few months later, before the Jihaz Haneen had become fully established, Saddam's foresight was proved: the first Ba'athist regime was overthrown by party members in the Army siding with non-Ba'athist fellow officers.

When the Ba'ath party lost power in November 1963, Saddam went underground but concentrated on building up the strength of the Jihaz Haneen. It operated in strict secrecy and the select few picked to join it were, without exception, members of Saddam's own family and tribe. They eventually became specialists in intelligence and security. During this period Saddam carried out a campaign of assassinating communists, students and workers in unions. By this means the members of the Jihaz Haneen gained the experience which made them a disciplined, brutal and ruthless fighting force. When the party eventually seized power again in 1968, their loyalty to their leader was beyond doubt and, above all, none of them was sufficiently well educated to exercise initiative outside the framework set by Saddam. During their underground years, Saddam and the Jihaz Haneen turned their guns on anyone whose ideas or activities posed a threat to the Ba'ath or undermined Arab nationalism. In some instances, they even disposed of a few Ba'athists as well.

Saddam Hussein's analysis of the lessons learned in November 1963 were simple. He believed that a 'rightist military aristocracy' was to blame for the downfall of the regime, facilitated by the talk of a well-disciplined secret security organisation. He refused to consider that a policy of terror, lack of a clear political programme and the party's deeply rooted hatred of democracy might have been to blame.

Non-Ba'athist Iraqis who knew Saddam in those days say that he regarded killing as a normal profession. They recall how he would excuse himself in the middle of a game of dominoes and disappear for a while, to carry out a liquidation, subsequently reappearing to continue the game. Saddam's name sent tremors through student organisations all over colleges and academic establishments in Baghdad. An Iraqi academic, now living in London, was a first-year student in 1966. He recalls how a group of left-wing students were holding a poetry- and play-reading evening when they heard screams, the smashing of glass and shots being fired. 'Someone put their head round the door and said one word: "Saddam!" They all ran like hell for it.' Similar stories are repeated by many who were students during this period.

After the November 1963 coup, Western capitals saw in the ousted Ba'ath party a political force with whom they could deal – a non-communist force which would keep Iraq out of Nasser's domain. It is noteworthy that critics of the Ba'ath link events such as Ba'athist-organised assassination attempts against Iraqi heads of state with moves by the latter to take economic or political measures which threatened Western interests. For example, following nationalisation of banks and certain foreign companies in 1964, the Ba'ath party instructed Saddam to assassinate the president Abd al-Salam Arif. The proposed assassination was designed to trigger off another Ba'ath coup. Critics say it was a plan on behalf of the CIA but according to some Ba'athist defectors the CIA did not have direct contact with the Ba'ath itself but with army officers who were co-ordinating a joint coup with the party. The main contact with the Americans was Iraq's own ambassador in Washington, Dr Nasser al-Hanni. He reported to Abd al-Razaq al-Nayyef, the deputy head of the Iraqi intelligence service in Baghdad.

Although this attempt on Arif's life failed, the Ba'athists executed a successful coup on 17th July 1968. Once again there were rumours of CIA involvement. Former Ba'ath party members have claimed that the agency had been supplying the Jihaz Haneen with the names of left-wing activists whom Saddam then had systematically executed. In addition, Saddam had made several contacts with the Americans and the British in Beirut (where Dr Nasser al-Hanni had become Iraqi ambassador in 1967, following the severing of relations between Iraq and the US over the Six Day War). But the evidence suggesting Saddam sought their co-operation is circumstantial; all Ba'ath party members who spoke to journalists about these contacts, or who themselves took part and could thus testify about them, were brutally assassinated. Some former party members, one of whom served as an official in the Ministry of Oil, point at strong links between the Ba'ath secret apparatus and British intelligence officers, saying that Britain wanted to see an Iraqi regime in power which would grant oil companies favourable concessions. Whatever the truth, no satisfactory explanation has ever been given as to how the Ba'ath party, with a membership of only nine hundred, managed to seize power again in 1968.

Saddam's biographies minimise the role of the chief co-ordinators of the coup and give the credit for its success to Saddam Hussein. What actually transpired was that Ba'athist senior army officers, led by General Ahmad Hassan al-Bakr, Secretary-General of the party in Iraq, had already been plotting a coup.

Then, according to Ba'athist defectors, al-Bakr's conspirators made contact with the Americans in Beirut with a view to obtaining support for the coup. They did not receive a firm answer. The CIA knew of another, non-Ba'athist, coup in the making – organised by al-Nayyef and some of his men together with the commander of the Presidential Guard, Ibrahim al-Daoud, and a number of nationalist officers.

According to Iraqi sources King Hussein of Jordan was also aware of 'officers plotting to overthrow the Iraqi government', having been alerted by the British. King Hussein sent a warning to President Abd al-Rahman Arif, who had already received another from his prime minister, Taher Yehyia. Arif had foolishly asked the Mukhabarat, of which al-Nayyef was the deputy head, to investigate the report after the latter had sworn an oath on the Koran that he was loyal to the president.

Having been informed by the Americans in Beirut about al-Bakr's proposed coup, the Iraqi ambassador, al-Hanni, warned al-Nayyef against including the Ba'athist officers in his plans. But already General Herdan al-Takriti, a leading member of the Ba'ath party, was in contact with two of al-Nayyef's men: Sa'doun Ghidan, the commander of the 1st Tank Battalion of the Presidential Guard, and a Mukhabarat officer, Major Ahmad Mukhlis, from al-Nayyef's office. Agreement had been reached for the two conspiring groups to co-operate and to contact officers from tribes and families that had long-standing disputes with President Arif's family or with the family of Prime Minister Taher Yehyia. One officer whose tribe was feuding with Prime Minister Taher Yehyia and his family commanded a troop of four tanks at the gates of the presidential palace. In the early hours on the morning of 17th July, he observed Saddam Hussein and some of the Jihaz Haneen approaching. He and his men were about to open fire on them but his commanding officer, Sa'doun Ghidan, managed to prevent him doing so. He claimed that Saddam and his men had arrived to assist President Arif because Taher Yehyia was planning a coup.

It transpired years later that, on the day before the coup, Saddam had suggested to his group of conspirators that once they were inside the presidential palace they should kill al-Nayyef and the members of the other group. Al-Bakr and Herdan al-Takriti, together with other officers, voiced objections on the grounds that it would be too dangerous; the Presidential Guard were much stronger in numbers. Saddam Hussein therefore took it upon himself to carry out the task, together with members of the Jihaz Haneen dressed as army officers. Saddam planned to hijack the coup since his name had not been put forward for a leading post in the new regime.

When, on the morning of 17th July 1968, Saddam Hussein and a dozen members of the Jihaz Haneen, including his half-brother Barzan (who was barely eighteen years old), his half-brothers Sabawai Ibrahim and Wathban Ibrahim, his cousin Ali Hassan al-Majid and many of his Takriti relatives, arrived at the presidential palace, al-Daoud had already arrested the president. Arif had come out with his hands held high, holding a signed blank sheet of paper for his 'resignation' as soon as al-Daoud fired three shots outside his room.

Saddam was now pursuing his own plans. After al-Bakr had been appointed president, the Revolutionary Command Council was formed. Saddam, who was made a member responsible for security, plotted against al-Nayyef. His first move was to win over one of al-Nayyef's most trusted men, Hammad Shihab, a Takriti officer who commanded the 10th Armoured Brigade which had ensured the success of the coup. He persuaded Shihab to demand a place on the Revolutionary Command Council and supported him in doing so. He then planned with al-Bakr to remove al-Nayyef, who was now prime minister and who had called a press conference saying that he would review all concesssions granted to foreign oil companies. Al-Nayyef's men, the commander of the 1st Tank Battalion of the Presidential Guard and his brother, were both promoted and transferred to posts elsewhere. Meanwhile, Ibrahim al-Daoud, the commander of the Presidential Guard, was sent to Jordan to inspect Iraqi troops based there.

The president invited al-Nayyef for lunch on 30th July, thirteen days after the coup. Saddam Hussein arranged with Shihab for units of the 10th Armoured Brigade to move to the vicinity of the palace. After lunch al-Bakr and al-Nayyef went to the president's office at which point the president excused himself. Saddam, who had never met al-Nayyef before, entered the room holding a pistol and saying, 'So you want to implement your new oil policy, son of a whore!' He then slapped the prime minister's face. Al-Nayyef, who knew of Saddam's reputation, broke down and begged for his life. Saddam later said that al-Nayyef had been lucky. He would have enjoyed killing him but could not risk a battle with the Presidential Guard, who outnumbered his own men. Al-Nayyef was immediately despatched from Iraq on an aircraft to West Germany where he was to be the ambassador. Ten years later he was assassinated in London on Saddam's orders.

For several years after 1968, Saddam concentrated on building up his security apparatus, the Jihaz Haneen. Although al-Bakr was the country's president, it was generally known who was the real power in the land: Saddam himself – Al-Sayyed al-Na'eb (Mr Deputy) as he preferred to be called. He invented the title and the post of the Deputy Secretary-General of the Revolutionary Command Council and retained his vision of a future when the party would become the state and would have supremacy over the armed forces and all else.

Saddam Hussein was the only person who could authorise the issue of firearms to party members; the Jihaz Haneen was in full control. Within three months the age of terror had officially begun. In October 1968, three months after the coup, the regime claimed that it had discovered a major pro-Israeli spy network. In fact, it was a plot, and one which illustrates Saddam's facility for long-term planning. Two years earlier an Israeli agent had been killed in the Hotel Shattura in Baghdad, minutes before an Iraqi intelligence team was due to arrest him. He was discovered to be in possession of a notebook listing names and telephone numbers, including those of Sa'doun Ghidan, the former commanding officer of the Presidential Guard's 1st Tank Battalion, and Shafiq al-Dragi who was head of the Mukhabarat. The notebook mysteriously disappeared but emerged again in 1968 containing a few more names, names of men Saddam wanted purged. It was simple to convince the Iraqi people that they were collaborators controlled by the former deputy head of the Mukhabarat, the exiled al-Nayyef.

The second part of the plot was carried out by the Jihaz Haneen. One of its members, Sadiq Ja'fer, delivered letters to the homes of those who were to be purged. They were written in such a way as to incriminate the recipients as Israeli agents. The Mukhabarat arrived to arrest the men just a few minutes after delivery of the letters. Members of the Iraqi Jewish community, which traditionally sympathises with the Communist party, were also arrested. Eleven of them were among the first fourteen 'spies' to be publicly hanged on 27th January 1969.

Another member of the Jihaz Haneen, Salah Omar Ali al-Takriti, was put in charge of the investigations. His methods made those of the dreaded Mehdawi courts of 1959 pale into insignificance. The public hangings turned into a national holiday with live television and radio coverage, and the Ba'ath party organised the transport of some hundred thousand 'workers and peasants' from outside Baghdad to join in implementing justice. The Iraqi public was encouraged to come out and watch the executions in Baghdad's 'Liberation Square'. President al-Bakr and Saddam Hussein were amongst the first to arrive. Members of Shabybabt Alba'ath (the Ba'ath student organisation) lined the road while the two leaders drove round the square in an open car. Families picnicked under trees while watching the hangings. This public orgy of death went on for twenty-four hours while al-Bakr made nationalist, anti-Zionist and anti-imperialist speeches against a background of hanging bodies. It was the Iraqi people 'punishing the spies'. Saddam was later to confide to one of his aids that modern satellite methods at espionage had made spies in the traditional sense redundant. 'We hanged them to teach the people a lesson,' he said, adding that anyone thinking of organising a coup or undermining the authority of the state should think twice.

Saddam was determined that the 1968 coup would be the last. While the leaders of the Ba'ath government had unanimously handed him the responsibility for security, Saddam was planning for the long term: he intended to be the leader of Iraq.

Whenever anybody was identified by the public as 'a hero', Saddam would move quickly to liquidate him. In 1969, he planned the assassination of PLO leader Yasser Arafat. He had discovered that some Iraqis believed Ba'athist propaganda about the Palestinian cause and had joined Fateh, the main organisation of the PLO. One Iraqi, Iyad Abd al-Qadir, joined the Palestinian resistance and was killed by Israeli forces during a Fateh-organised operation on the occupied West Bank. During his funeral in Baghdad, there were no pro-Ba'ath slogans shouted by the people; instead they hailed 'the martyr', Palestine, Fateh and Arafat. When Arafat delivered a speech he failed to acknowledge the Ba'ath's leadership. A few days later, as his American-made white Pontiac passed in front of Abu Gharib barracks an army lorry rammed into it. Arafat was not seriously injured, suffering only a broken arm, and during the evening he laughed off the incident, telling the press, 'I was attacked by Zionist agents during one of my missions'. Arafat had learned his lesson – in 1990 he insisted that Saddam was the leader who would liberate Palestine.

Following the 1968 and 1969 purges against politicians, Jews and left-wing activists, the regime turned to suppressing the Shia, who form the majority of Iraq's population, by destroying their Islamic leadership. When Seyyed Muhsin al-Hakim, the world spiritual leader of the Shia faith, travelled from the holy city of Najjaf to Baghdad, thousands blocked the streets just to receive his blessing. This display of popular support for a non-Ba'athist figure alarmed the party leadership. Saddam Hussein arranged for a solution. A week later a 'spy' was 'persuaded' by the Jihaz Haneen to confess on television that Seyyed Muhsin al-Hakim's eldest son was 'a spy and a conspirator' in the service of Iran. Muhsin al-Hakim returned to Najf, a humiliated and lonely figure. His son went underground and was condemned to death *in absentia* by a 'revolutionary court'. In January 1988, whilst in exile in London, he was invited to participate in an Islamic conference in Sudan. On the day after his arrival, members of the Jihaz Haneen murdered him in the lobby of the Hilton hotel in Khartoum, after which they walked calmly to a waiting car with diplomatic number plates and were driven to the sanctuary of the Iraqi embassy.

As the propaganda war against Iran intensified in the early seventies, the government announced the uncovering of two 'pro-Iranian coups'. More of Saddam's opponents from the military or from the old guard of the Ba'ath party were purged. The norm was to shoot the condemned men in the front yard of the court. (On one occasion a young officer was shot by mistake.) As a means of spreading fear, families of 'traitors' who were shot by the firing squad were presented with an official invoice to pay for the bullets that had executed their relatives. Thus by 1973 the majority of the military wing of the party had been effectively eliminated, leaving President al-Bakr totally isolated. His duties were ceremonial and his only function was to sign any orders presented to him by Saddam Hussein.

After the oil price boom in 1974, Saddam had at his disposal huge sums of money with which to widen his base of support inside the army. He transferred his relatives from the Jihaz Haneen to command army units and exploited every chance to consolidate his grip, allowing his opponents to defeat each other. He convinced the Ba'ath party to invite the communists to form with them a national unity government. This move allowed Iraq to assume militant anti-Western policies and guaranteed a friendship treaty with Moscow which supplied Baghdad with arms. However, on the same day that President al-Bakr was signing the national unity charter with the communists, Saddam distributed amongst the members of the Jihaz Haneen a leaflet entitled 'How to Destroy the Iraqi Communist Party'. Saddam was later to slaughter communists by the hundreds, even while they were still in theory his coalition partners.

In addition to the Shias, Saddam wanted to control the Kurds. Although they had observed a truce signed with the former regime, hostilities in Kurdistan were resumed again in 1969 when they pressed for the implementation of autonomy plans agreed in 1966.

Saddam told the party that he would solve the problem. He personally directed by radio a two-man assassination team of the Jihaz Haneen as they machine-gunned the car of Idriss al-Barzani, the son of the Kurdish leader Mula Mustafa al-Barzani.

Saddam then tried to assassinate the father a year later. Two of his representatives went to hold talks with him. They were given a 'tape recorder' and were told by Saddam to press the button as soon as Mustafa al-Barzani started to talk, in order to 'record his exact demands'. However, the tape recorder contained a small bomb which was triggered when the button was pressed and both men were killed. Barzani escaped with light injuries because his servant, who was serving his coffee, took the full blast.

A few years later, Saddam invited a number of pro-Ba'athist, non-Iraqi journalists to tell Arab readers outside Iraq how he was personally conducting a war against 'a CIA- and Iranian-inspired plot to undermine the eastern wall of the Arab nation'. Years later, it was revealed by a Ba'athist defector that Saddam had been planning during the mid-1970s to take over the leadership of Iraq. But because of the inability of his forces to score a decisive victory over the Kurds, despite total control of the skies and massive firepower, he had to wait a few more years.

The conflict over the Shatt al-Arab waterway had started with Iran a few years earlier. In 1937, under pressure from Britain, a treaty was concluded which obliged Iranian ships and vessels sailing through the waterway en route to Iranian ports to fly an Iraqi courtesy flag and to pay dues to the Iraqi authorities. In 1969 the Shah refused to allow that situation to continue; he sent his ships through the waterway and refused to pay the dues. It was the first sign of the Shah's new role as the strong man and policeman of the Gulf – a role that Saddam was to aspire to play a decade later.

Iraq launched a propaganda war against the Shah, and deported the Shia in their thousands. The Shah replied by giving his full support to Mulla Mustafa al-Barzani, the Kurdish leader who was fighting for the independence of his region in the north of Iraq.

For Saddam Hussein, personal ambition and the iron will to defeat any enemy standing in his way were essential factors in his bid to exercise total control over Iraq; his ambition was such that it took priority even over national interests. So instead of accommodating the demands of the Kurds, who represent one fifth of the Iraqi population, he opted instead to surrender some of his nation's rights.

In a conference held in Algiers in 1975, Saddam Hussein and the Shah reached an agreement which had brutal effects on the Kurds: the Shah immediately, without any warning, cut off all Iranian support for the Kurds whilst Iraq accepted the 'thalweg', the central line of the navigable channel, as the border in the Shatt al-Arab. The result was that the Kurdish revolt collapsed, al-Barzani was forced into exile and the Baghdad government was able to impose its own ideas of autonomy on Iraqi Kurdistan. For the Iranians, there was a new acknowledgement of their dominant position in the Gulf, an end to a dispute which had occasionally spilled over into frontier incidents, and a new boost for the Shah as he reached the apogee of his international standing.

For Saddam Hussein personally, it was a humiliating admission of the impotence of his country; it rankled with him and became one of the prime excuses for his decision to go to war in 1980.

*

In 1978 Egypt's policy of peace with Israel gave Saddam another opportunity to bid for the leadership of the Arab radical camp. The few members of the Ba'ath who knew that Saddam's ambition went beyond his commitment to the nation, warned President al-Bakr and suggested a pact with Syria to undermine Saddam's powerbase. However, thanks to his powerful secret organisation that had wired every office and every bedroom of Ba'ath party members, Saddam Hussein was able to make his move first.

It was on National Day, 17th July 1979, that Saddam finally declared himself president. President al-Bakr had resigned the day before 'owing to poor health'. In fact, he was already under house arrest.

Five days later, in a scene reminiscent of Stalin's reign of terror, Saddam prepared to deliver the final blow to his opponents and assume absolute power. He carried out a spectacular purge in a closed session attended by nearly one thousand party cadres. A videotape of the meeting was later distributed among party members as a warning of things to come. It began with prominent members of the party – mainly the old guard – reading confessions of their participation in Syrian-backed plots against the nation, the party and its leadership. The confessions went on, individuals stepping forward to confess as Saddam Hussein read their names from a list.

According to eye-witnesses, Saddam played a psychological game of cat and mouse. He would mention a name, then pause; then skip this name for another one; meanwhile half the named men had fainted with terror.

The meeting broke out into hysterical acclaim for Saddam as he broke down in tears while condemning his comrades to death. The purges went on for days. Some say that the number of those involved was approximately five hundred whilst others quote double that, but no one really knows. What *is* known is that Saddam and a dozen top officials (half the members of the Revolutionary Command Council – the other half having already confessed to high treason), formed the firing squad to execute the rest of the leadership. This was Saddam's 'Night of the Long Knives' and blood was on all their hands. Saddam emerged invincible; the party was now the state and the nation was subordinate to the party. He himself was the party.

Saddam and his relatives from the tribes of Takrit controlled all aspects of life in Iraq. One of his first presidential decrees was to abolish family names. New ID cards were issued and all new birth certificates were to record only the child's first name and the father's name. Saddam aimed to hide the fact that all those in top posts shared the family name al-Takriti.

All children of the nation were equal before the one, the leader, the father. The personality cult had started.

His picture was on postage stamps, on wrist-watches, and on T-shirts. The airport at Baghdad is called Saddam International Airport and his birthday became a national day. Even the war with Iran was called the War of Saddam. A new offence was created called 'Insulting Alqa'ed – The Commander'. One day, Saddam was visiting a school and he asked a boy of six, 'Do you know who I am?'. 'Yes, you are the man who makes my father spit on the television every time you appear.' The boy's entire family disappeared and their house was demolished.

After the Night of the Long Knives in 1979, Saddam's propaganda machine published his personal telephone number. Ordinary people would telephone the 'Father' of the nation with any problem. Every night on television, someone would recount how Alqa'ed had solved his problem on the telephone. However, for every one that phoned about street lights or to increase his pension, ten others would telephone to inform on their relatives or colleagues. 'He has implicated ordinary people in the violence of the party,' said a former Ba'athist.

After he had consolidated his grip on power, Saddam Hussein's speeches concentrated on one question: Was it Iraqi patriotism or Arab nationalism that was needed? In a speech delivered in 1979 Saddam said: 'The glory of Arabs stems from the glory of Iraq. Throughout history, whenever Iraq became mighty and flourished, so did the Arab Nation. This is why we are striving to make Iraq mighty, formidable, able and developed, and why we shall spare nothing to improve welfare and to brighten the glory of Iraqis.'

Saddam, whose vision of his holy mission went beyond the Ba'ath party and its principles, presented a new ideology based on the superiority of a home-grown Abbassiyed heritage. In the eighth-century AD, the Muslim Abbassiyed state stretched from Morocco, which also ruled large parts of Spain, to what is now Pakistan. Twice the size of the Roman Empire, it was the largest imperial system that the world has ever seen and it lasted until 1258.

Following the invasion of Kuwait on 2nd August 1990, Iraq directed broadcasts at Muslim countries throughout the Middle East, trumpeting the glories of the Muslim Empire during the period that Baghdad was its capital. Saddam Hussein wanted to create a popular dream of the rebirth (the meaning of the word 'Ba'ath') of a united Muslim Arab empire ruled by a strong man from Baghdad. The name 'Abbassiyed' hit the airwaves, reminding Muslims of the fact that President Saddam is often referred to by the name of one of the Abbassiyed Caliphs: Al-Mansour Be-allah, 'The One Whom God Made Victorious'.

The name 'Abbassiyed' comes from Alabbas, the uncle of the prophet Muhammed, another great historic character whom Saddam Hussein claims as a distant relative. A carefully drawn family tree has been created, leaving the final link between the founder of the Takriti clan and the prophet to the imagination of the people.

One of the great Caliphs of Abbassiyed was Haroun al-Rashid (AD 786–809); he, too, has been taken as a model by the Iraqi dictator. Unlike Saddam, the Caliph Haroun al-Rashid was an enlightened leader who liked to appear unannounced in different parts of Baghdad, or in the countryside, to see how the common man lived. Saddam does not generally go so far as to disguise himself and go out alone in this way but it is still the image which he cultivates and exploits. During carefully arranged visits to specially vetted lower-middle-class family homes or to peasants huts, Iraqi television shows the president 'dropping in' and sharing the family's modest dinner, later joining in the afternoon or evening prayers with the father and his sons.

Only once did Saddam go out alone in his own car. At one time during the Gulf War there was a shortage of flour, and therefore of bread. The people of the new Baghdad suburb of Thawra, went on a rampage, burning and looting and demanding action from the authorities. The leader roared in rage, shouted for his driver to bring a car and drove himself at high speed to Thawra, while the trembling driver screamed for the bodyguards to go after the president.

Parked outside the mosque, Saddam threw off his shoes and climbed the steps of Al-Manbar (the pulpit) and began shouting down to the people who crowded below: 'Good for nothings! Ungrateful, and wretched mob! People of discord and dissembling and evil! I built you this whole suburb! I gave you the shops you have just burnt down! And, if you had asked, I would have given you bread! Now I will see all your sons go in the army and I will send taxmen to collect money for the damage you have done!'

The crowd stood impassively, but by the time the guards arrived they were shaking the president's hand, and shouting blessings on 'their father', Saddam.

Saddam was inspired in this incident by a Al-Hadjadj bin Yusuf al-Thaqafi, who was appointed governor of Kufa and Basra in AD 694 by Abd al-Malik bin Marawan, the Ummiyed caliph. Al-Hadjadj had been sent to quell disturbances in the region and he took the most drastic measures recorded by Muslim historians. On the day he arrived in Kufa he promptly beheaded a dozen dissidents, putting the heads on public display in the courtyard of the mosque as the public were called for an assembly. He climbed the steps to the Manbar and addressed the assembled populace. 'I see heads before my eyes that are ripe and ready for my sword to pluck them. And I see blood glistening between the turbans and the beards. O people of Iraq, people of discord and dissembling and evil character! I cannot be squeezed like a fig or scared like a camel with old water skin. Amerrul Mo'meneen ['The Commander of the Faithful', a title for the Caliph] emptied his quiver and bit his arrows to find me the bitterest and the hardest of them all. He aimed me at you. For too long now you have been swift to sedition; you have lain in the lairs of error and have made a rule of transgression. By God, I shall skin you like bark, I shall truss you like a bundle of twigs, I shall beat you like stray camels. By God, what I promise, I fulfil; what I purpose, I accomplish; what I measure, I cut off. Enough of these gatherings and this gossip. I swear by God that you keep strictly to the true path, or I shall punish every man of you in his body.'

The speech, which is learnt by heart by every Iraqi pupil, is a well-known piece of classical Arabic literature, used by writers to describe a state built on absolute tyranny. However, Saddam was the only Arab ruler who dared to deliver a modern form of the speech to his unfortunate people and to go on implementing Al-Hadjadj's measures.

On his way to becoming a dictator Saddam clearly grasped the importance of the media. All great tyrants, ancient and modern, have used the power of persuasion to extend and consolidate their grip on the nation. While he was establishing the Jihaz Haneen, before he became president, Saddam planned with selected journalists to take control of the media. He put thousands of journalists all over the Arab world on his payroll so that they would slowly build up his image. When he became president in June 1979, the Iraqis had already become accustomed to the media referring to him with such honorifics as Alza'Im (the Leader), to be followed by such adjectives as: Al-Muheeb (the Awesome); Al-Rukn (the Corner Stone); Al-Mulham (the Inspired); Al-Faris Al-Mighuar (The Aggressive Knight); Al-Awhad (the Only One); Al-Mul'Lem (the Tutor).

The terror machine that ruled the party evolved into a gigantic structure once Saddam took total control of it. He created the perfect Orwellian state, complete with a Big Brother, who ruled through terror and oppression. It has carved out its own existence in an almost mythological realm that has its own history and geography inside the collective mind of the Iraqis. A state whose efficiency makes its faithful citizens happily accept that they have four fingers instead of five on each hand, it goes beyond any perfection that O'Brian's innovations could achieve.

Saddam Hussein is a complex personality. He is both the thug who rules by fear, and the stern paternalistic guardian of the nation. He is portrayed as the far-seeing statesman he imagines himself to be, the general who leads his armies to victory, the architect, the economist and designer of modern Iraq and the leader of the pan-Arabism. He is not to be underestimated. He is a consummate politician, a skilful negotiator and publicist and a successful administrator. He is also a killer who started his 'profession of death', as some Arab intellectuals call his political career, at a young age and has never lost his taste for blood.

Saddam is always armed with a pistol, especially in his meetings. 'Beware of meetings around long tables,' he once told an astonished President Mubarak and King Hussein during an Arab Cooperation Council meeting. Shortly afterwards there was a 30-second power cut. Saddam dived under the table. When the lights came on again he had his pistol in his hand.

During a cabinet meeting in Baghdad when Iraq had suffered reverses in the war with Iran, Saddam said he had heard that some people were considering the possibility of claiming that Iran was fighting not Iraq but Saddam Hussein himself. He could then step down temporarily, allowing a ceasefire to be negotiated. While others in the cabinet kept their thoughts to themselves and showed no reaction, the Minister of Health smiled, although he didn't say a word. It was an indication that he was thinking about the idea. Saddam Hussein shook his head and laughed, saying in a reassuring voice, 'We can trick them, eh?' The Minister of Health nodded. 'Very wise. Let us go into the next room to discuss the plan further,' said the president. They did so, and a few seconds later a single shot was heard. The president returned, holstering his smoking pistol, and the cabinet meeting continued. An announcement of the minister's death was made the following day, implicating him in a corruption scandal involving the taking of bribes for allowing the importation of medicine which was past its expiry date.

A similar incident occurred at a cabinet meeting held to discuss the loss of the Majnoon islands, the occasion on which the Iraqis are first known to have used chemical weapons. One minister suggested that Saddam Hussein should give the armed forces more freedom to take decisions on the ground instead of 'the government directing them'. Saddam took this as a personal insult and looked at his bodyguards who escorted the minister away. After three days without a sign of her husband, the minister's wife spoke to Sajeda Hussein on the telephone. She handed the telephone to her husband who said: 'Your husband is a traitor. He had sold his soul, and now he is just a body. But, because Sajeda promised you that he will return, you will receive him in the morning.' The woman's doorbell rang at 5 a.m. the next day. When she opened the door, she found two sacks containing the torn and mutilated body of her husband.

Each year, when Saddam Hussein celebrates his birthday, he chooses a different theme and a different historical figure to emulate. In 1990, he chose Sargon the Great, ruler of the Empire of Agade which flourished about 2300 BC in what is roughly now Iraq. The birthday celebration included a tableau depicting the legend of the newborn Sargon being found in a basket floating among the reeds at the side of a river. History records that Sargon went on to win thirty-four battles, and clay tablets recounting his exploits describe him as having been 'triumphant from the Lower Sea [the Gulf] to the Upper Sea [the Mediterranean]'.

Selecting Sargon, the great warrior who won all his battles, as the symbol for 1990 meant that Saddam – who claimed he was already under siege from the forces of imperialism, Zionism and Arab reactionaries – was preparing for war.

Saddam's propaganda machine had plundered the rich history of the Middle East to portray the dictator in many different guises; he appears as an ancient warrior, a pre-biblical hero, a modern nationalist, a pan-Arab hero or an Islamic conqueror, depending on the political mood of the day. But the people close enough to know him, and the very few of them who have survived after defecting from his camp (the ratio is one in fifty-five), say that the calm, stone-faced dictator is in real life insecure, cowardly and always in search of an identity. That is why he changes his personal theme from year to year.

When Saddam Hussein declared war on Iran on 22nd September 1980, the oil-rich Arab states, led by the Sabah ruling family of Kuwait and by the Saudis, were all behind him. They were anxious to stem the Islamic tide generated by the revolution in Iran.

Huge posters covered the walls of every Iraqi city. An image of an Arab Muslim hero was now needed and Sa'd bin Abi Waqqass was chosen. He was a warrior who led the Mohammedan Arab troops to defeat the Persian army in the Al-Qadissiyah battle in AD 633, in which the armies of Islam defeated the forces of Zoroastrian Persia and opened the way for Islam eastwards. As the backing of wealthy Arabs was needed during the eight-year conflict, the war was hailed by the Iraqi press as 'Qadissiyaht Saddam'. The Army started a daily newspaper called 'Al-Qadissiyah'.

However, when the war ended, a new image was required, one which could promote Saddam's ambitions for the future: the rebuilding of Iraq, the leadership of the Arab world and above all the presentation of Iraq as a fortress guarding the eastern gate of the empire he wished to lead.

More posters emerged, this time showing Saddam with Nebuchadnezzar II, King of Babylonia from 604 to 562 BC. Shortly before his accession, he led the Babylonian army at the battle of Carchemish in central Palestine. The Egyptian army was defeated and Nebuchadnezzar brought Palestine and Syria into his empire. When the Egyptians assisted the Hebrew inhabitants of Judah to rebel in 596 BC and again in 587–586 BC, Nebuchadnezzar marched to capture Jerusalem and took large numbers of Israelites into captivity. They were among the slaves who built the Hanging Gardens. They were kept prisoners for half a century 'by the waters of Babylon', an ambitious irrigation scheme in the marshlands of the Shatt al-Arab. Similar schemes are on President Saddam Hussein's agenda for the upper Gulf and they were behind his short-lived capture of the area around Abadan in Iran in 1980. They are also part of the reason for his insistence on holding one of the Kuwaiti islands. He needs land to the east and the west of the Shatt al-Arab river system in order to build a new complex of canals on the model of the Babylonian water scheme. These would have enormous economic and strategic value.

In the poster, Nebuchadnezzar is helping Saddam Hussein rebuild Babylon – a task on which the Iraqi president has actually embarked. Hundreds of thousands of special bricks are being placed in the new city wall which bear an Arabic inscription which reads, 'Rebuilt during the era of the awesome cornerstone leader, President Saddam Hussein'.

Saddam's Orwellian 'state of fear' constantly changes allegiances, national aims and principles. This naturally involves a process of writing and rewriting history, a trick once employed by Stalin. Every Iraqi civil servant under Saddam Hussein is a Winston Smith, constantly feeding the present into the 'memory hole' to rewrite the past. As soon as the future becomes the present it is thrown into the 'memory hole' and today's lie becomes the correction of yesterday's error – and there is always someone who has to pay with his life for that mistake. Today's lie could as easily turn into tomorrow's truth, for the only truth is what Saddam wants, or thinks he wants, and not even what he says because that too could change.

The leader's biographies – or more accurately autobiographies since he dictates them to the authors – are constantly written and rewritten. The details change according to the enemy of the day irrespective of historical accuracy. One indelible fact remains throughout all his histories: it was Saddam Hussein who singlehandedly created the Ba'ath party (Stalin at least had the modesty to reserve this role for Lenin), and it was the 'inspired leader' who led the tanks during the 1968 'revolution', despite the fact that Saddam has never served in the army.

8 · Saddam's Long Arm

For six years Ayatollah Sayyed Mahdi al-Hakim lived in Britain with his wife and four children. The fifty-three-year-old highly respected Shia clergyman used to hold Friday prayers in a mosque in West London, attracting huge crowds. Despite the high esteem and affection in which he was held, however, he was a sad man. In 1969, accused by the Ba'athist regime in Baghdad of being a spy, he had been forced to flee his home in Iraq. Seventeen members of his family, men and women, young and old, had been executed by Saddam Hussein's government. Their only crime was that they had been popular with the Shia who form the majority of the Iraqi population.

The ayatollah's father, the late Ayatollah Mohsen al-Hakim, was one of the 'grand' ayatollahs, or 'Marges', of the Shia branch of Islam. His younger brother, Hojatoleslam Mohammad-Baquer al-Hakim, is the leader of the Tehran-based Supreme Assembly of the Islamic Revolution of Iraq. For the last few months of 1987, Hakim had tried to group all the Iraqi opposition groups together to form an alliance, in an attempt to rid the Iraqi people, Shia and Sunni, Kurds and Arabs, Assyrians and Jews, of the rule of Saddam Hussein.

Al-Hakim had just returned from his twentieth trip abroad during 1987. This time he had visited Iran, the United Arab Emirates and Saudi Arabia, to sound out officials on his proposals to end the Gulf War. Soon after his return to Britain, he was invited to address a Muslim conference in Sudan. Accepting the invitation, he arrived there on 17th January 1988. As he was waiting in the lobby of the Hilton hotel in Khartoum, three members of Saddam Hussein's Jihaz Haneen walked over to where the learned man was sitting. One shot him at point-blank range whilst the others each fired two shots into the air. Sudanese security men watched impassively without making any attempt to intervene. The three Iraqis then walked calmly out of the hotel and headed for a waiting car bearing diplomatic number plates, which subsequently drove them to the Iraqi embassy in Khartoum.

Al-Hakim's murder was seen by opponents of the Baghdad regime as part of the stepping-up of a campaign by Saddam Hussein to eliminate leading political opponents. They proceeded to lobby the British government to press Iraq to cease its terrorist activities against its opponents in Britain, but the Foreign Office and Whitehall appear to have taken no action.

Three days before Saddam's men gunned down Al-Hakim, an Iraqi businessman, Abdullah Ali, was murdered in London by Iraqi Mukhabarat agents who lured him into a restaurant in West London and poisoned his drink with thallium, well known as a favourite poison of the Iraqi intelligence service. A few weeks later the same method of liquidation was used against Kurdish leaders during a meeting in Iraq.

On 25th January, the wife of a prominent left-wing Iraqi dissident was stabbed to death in Oslo. A week later, in Turkey, police told journalists that an Iraqi activist, Qassem Emin, had died after being severely tortured. He had been found with his throat slit.

Soon after the invasion of Kuwait, Hussein Samidah, an officer in the Mukhabarat, defected to Canada, where he was extensively debriefed by the Canadian intelligence service. He confirmed that the Western European branch of the Mukhabarat, headed by Saddam Hussein's half-brother Barzan al-Takriti, had recruited a number of citizens of European countries who were of Iraqi origin. Samidah gave further detailed information, which we have put together here with information obtained from other defectors.

In 1990, the Mukhabarat was headed by Saddam's half-brother Sabaawi Ibrahim. With a massive budget equivalent to hundreds of millions of American dollars, Sabaawi Ibrahim heads an organisation which numbers over 125,000 in strength. It has a section responsible for dealing with military intelligence, the 'Alistikhbarat al-A'askariyah', and another tasked with carrying out espionage operations outside Iraq, the 'Jihaz al-Amn al-Kharji'. The latter controls Iraqi terrorists or forms contracts with either 'freelance' terrorists based in Lebanon or with Palestinian and Lebanese groups such as Abu Nidal and Abu al-Abbas, both of which were based in Baghdad at the time of the invasion of Kuwait, or with other smaller groups in Lebanon who are opposed to Syria and its Shia allies. Terrorists from all those groups, as well as the Amn-Kharji's own agents, carry out acts of terror abroad on behalf of the Baghdad regime.

Unlike other Arab dictators, Saddam Hussein does not tolerate opposition abroad. In the secret charter of the Jihaz Haneen, Section B of Article 1 identifies the 'Duty and Objectives of the Special Apparatus Members' as being to convince Ba'ath party members and the public in general that opposition to the party and its leadership do not exist. Jihaz Haneen achieves this through a two-tier policy: media and terrorism. The first is carried out by placing Arab journalists on the organisation's payroll or pressurising them into co-operation, whilst the second is effected by terrorising any opposition into silence.

For example, prior to the invasion of Kuwait, governments in the Middle East either censored press coverage hostile to Saddam or restricted the activities of the Iraqi opposition groups. Since such tactics did not succeed in the West, the Amn-Kharji used terror to silence opposition or to 'liquidate those who will not be silenced'.

One of the popular stories exchanged by Saddam's opponents maintains that the president once confided to a number of his close inner circle that the code of honour and loyalty to the family, as seen in his favourite film, Francis Ford Coppola's *The Godfather*, was the ideal code of ethics to which every human being should aspire. He declared that once loyalty to the family (i.e. the party and its leader) was in doubt, then the life of the individual concerned had no meaning and was worthless.

Thus, former Ba'ath party members or officials who desert Saddam Hussein are regarded as traitors. Some of them are simply punished if they are unfortunate enough to fall into the hands of the Jihaz Haneen, whilst those who publicly divulge information about the regime and its activities are hunted down and liquidated.

When Saddam Hussein succeeded in fusing the identities of state and party into one, he gave sweeping powers to the secret organisations within the party. Thus in Iraq all members of opposition groups are regarded as 'criminals' and so could be 'legitimately' terrorised under specially made laws. The logic behind the action is simple: all Iraqis are one family, the godfather is Saddam Hussein, therefore any form of dissent is an act of treason; traitors must be punished.

The hanging of *Observer* journalist Farzad Bazoft in March 1990 is an example. He had been considered a component in the Ba'athist propaganda machine and a friend of Iraq. He was an Iranian and, in Iraqi eyes, had no right to follow the traditions of Western journalism but to be an 'Arab journalist' and follow the Ba'ath party's line. Thus, when he was discovered carrying out an investigation into the explosion at the Al-Hillah military industrial complex, the Ba'athists were angered and decided to treat him as a criminal. If Bazoft had managed to leave Iraq and publish his report, he would most probably have been assassinated by one of the Ba'ath party's secret organisations abroad.

Saddam Hussein's secret organisations, although part of the state, are given the role of 'revolutionary opposition' when active abroad, and thus resort to the same methods of terror and assassination which Saddam himself used when he was a 'revolutionary' in opposition in Iraq between 1963 and 1968. The intellectual justification for this is that the Ba'ath party abroad is in opposition to 'an oppressive world controlled by Zionist and imperialist forces hostile to Arabs', and that members of Iraqi opposition groups are agents of such forces who thus must be liquidated.

When, in 1969, General Herdan al-Takriti, who in 1968 was defence minister, deputy prime minister and a member of the Revolutionary Command Council, had a disagreement with the leadership, he heard the news of his replacement from Baghdad Radio when he was in Algeria, where he wisely decided to stay. He subsequently sent for his wife and children, but meanwhile foolishly granted interviews to the press in which he expressed his grave concern over the Iraqi government's excesses in dealing with opposition. The Ba'athists used his wife to teach him a brutal lesson.

Prior to leaving Baghdad airport with her three children to join her husband in Algeria, Mrs al-Takriti was told she had to be vaccinated before departure and was accordingly given an injection. By the time the Iraqi Airways jet landed at Algiers airport, she was dead and her three children were screaming in shock. General al-Takriti retaliated by calling a press conference and giving the press a detailed account of how the 1968 coup had been carried out, highlighting the connection between Saddam Hussein's Jihaz Haneen and America's Central Intelligence Agency. Three months later he was invited for lunch with the Iraqi ambassador in Kuwait. As he sat next to the diplomat in his car, a Mukhabarat agent walked calmly up to the vehicle and shot General al-Takriti dead before crossing the road to a waiting car and being driven away. The Kuwaiti police did not even attempt to stop the vehicle, which had Iraqi number plates.

Saddam's long arm has not confined its activities to the Arab world. Soon after the Ba'athist coup of 1968, Iraqi agents tried to assassinate Ayad Allawi, a Shia opposition clergyman in London.

In 1978 there was a series of Iraqi-sponsored acts of terrorism on British soil as Saddam Hussein was preparing for the final stages of his take-over of the party and was purging his opponents.

Said Hammami, the Palestine Liberation Organisation representative in London who was advocating direct negotiation between the Palestinians and the Israelis, was assassinated by a member of the Abu Nidal terrorist group who was also an officer in the Mukhabarat. It was during a period when relations between Iraq and the West had cooled as a result of Baghdad having adopted an 'anti-imperialist' line. When the investigations into the murder, as well as those concerned with the liquidations of a number of Iraqi dissidents living in Britain, uncovered the extent of the Mukhabarat network of terror in Britain, eleven Iraqi 'diplomats' were ordered out of London. As usual, the initial Foreign Office reaction was to adopt a low-key response for fear of provoking Iraqi retaliation. However, one particular official, who was on the Iraq desk at the time, took a different view and summoned the Iraqi ambassador, threatening him with the severing of diplomatic relations if Iraq retaliated by expelling British diplomats. Needless to say, Baghdad backed down.

Since 1979, Iraqi students in Britain have been subjected to a campaign of terror. Their independent union, the Iraqi Students' Society (ISS) was declared illegal in Iraq by Saddam Hussein and so it officially ceased to exist. In accordance with Article 1 of the Jihaz Haneen's charter, the members of the illegal student union became 'non-persons'. They were to be terrorised into deserting the union or be liquidated.

One of the 'fronts' used by the Iraqi Mukhabarat in Britain is the National Union of Iraqi Students (NUIS). The average age of its members is thirty-five, although some are in their late forties. One of the rewards given to 'successful' Mukhabarat agents is an overseas post for four years, during which they are enrolled in universities as post-graduate students. As such, they try to recruit other Arab students to join a front organisation of the pan-Arab Ba'ath party called the Arab Society, which has branches in many universities worldwide. With huge budgets at their disposal, they spend lavishly on parties and other social activities.

However, the main role of the Mukhabarat 'students' is to harass and attack dissident students and other targets dictated by Baghdad. On 1st May 1979, members of the Ba'athist NUIS attacked a festival organised in Manchester by foreign students. Their sole reason for doing so was the fact that the Iraqi Students' Society was participating in it. The NUIS students used iron bars and clubs in the attack, but no charges were subsequently brought against them by the police. Also in 1979, details of a death list, drawn up by Mukhabarat agents at the Iraqi embassy in London, were revealed. The Committee Against Repression and for Democratic Rights in Iraq (CARDRI) and a number of human rights organisations joined students in demanding an investigation by the government but to no avail.

In February 1981, the Liverpool University Student Union wrote to the Iraqi embassy in London, protesting at the Iraqi 'spy activities on the campus'. A document had been found, written in Arabic and dated that month, giving detailed instructions to NUIS students on how to observe and report on the activities of other Iraqi students suspected of 'holding opposing views'. Each student was required to give a report on other students in their colleges. Those who refused to do so would have had their grants cut, or would have been threatened with retaliation against their families in Iraq. Iraqi students who continually refuse to co-operate initially receive threats and then are subjected to attacks. On 6th February 1981, two badly injured Iraqi students were rushed to hospital in Cardiff after being stabbed and beaten by Ba'athist students on the university campus. Three days earlier, female Iraqi students at Cardiff had also been attacked.

On 19th February 1981, as a number of Iraqi students held a protest outside the Iraqi embassy in Kensington, they were photographed by Mukhabarat agents. During the following months, the majority of them were attacked and beaten up.

It was not until the deportation in August 1990 of a number of Iraqi 'students' from Britain who were members of Mukhabarat that people began to accept what had been reported on different occasions in the press: that for several years there was an informal, tacit agreement on terrorism between the Iraqis and the British government that the Baghdad regime would not mount terrorist attacks on British soil. Whilst a carefully orchestrated campaign of leaked information ensured that the image of certain regimes in the Middle East, such as Libya and Syria, was such that they engendered hostility amongst the British public, little mention was made of Iraq.

Iraq was spared certain measures taken by London against countries like Iran, Syria and Libya, which 'sponsored terrorism'. Iraq's activities were generally tolerated, despite endless protests to the Foreign Office from Iraqi opposition groups and human rights activists, who also supplied the Home Office with names of Iraqi students who were Mukhabarat agents. No action was taken.

On 30th April 1980, four gunmen took over the Iranian embassy in Princes Gate, West London. At the time, they claimed to be from Iranian Arabistan, demanding independence from 'Persian Iran'. In fact, the operation was masterminded by the Iraqi Mukhabarat to highlight public awareness worldwide that the Arabs of the Arabistan area, which is situated on the borders with Iraq, were Arabs rather than Iranians. It was one of the objectives of Saddam Hussein's war against Iran which would begin four months later. The siege lasted several days, during which the gunmen shot one of the hostages whilst lengthy negotiations were still being conducted. It was abruptly ended when troops of 22nd Special Air Service Regiment (SAS) stormed the embassy, rescuing the surviving hostages. During the assault, all but one of the gunmen, a nineteen-year-old identified later as 'Ali', were killed. According to a source close to the

SAS, Ali 'sang like a bird' during subsequent interrogation. He apparently revealed that all six men had undergone training beforehand at an Iraqi army special forces base and that their weapons had been supplied by the Iraqi embassy on their arrival in London. He also identified a Mukhabarat officer, codenamed 'The Fox' but whose real name was Sami Muhammad Ali, as being the mastermind behind the operation. Despite a search by the police and the security services, however, 'The Fox' succeeded in escaping from Britain and returning to Iraq.

Ali was subsequently prosecuted and sentenced to a long term of imprisonment, which he is still serving. Despite the evidence obtained from him as to the Baghdad regime's involvement in the affair, there were no recriminations against Iraq and no diplomats were expelled.

A month later, former Iraqi Prime Minister Abd al-Razzaq al-Nayyef, who had organised the 1968 coup, was gunned down near his home in Kensington. A few weeks later two Mukhabarat agents visited a small village in Surrey to call at the home of Dr Tahseen Me'alla who had treated Saddam Hussein's leg wound after the unsuccessful assassination attempt on President Abd al-Karim Qasim in 1959. The doctor himself was away at the time, and as his wife opened the door the two men charged in carrying axes. Mrs Me'alla screamed and, in the ensuing uproar, with neighbours rushing out of their houses nearby, the two Iraqis fled. Although Dr Me'alla subsequently explained the situation to the police, there is no evidence to suggest that the Iraqi embassy in London was later rebuked by the Foreign Office and warned about Mukhabarat operations in Britain.

In 1982, the Mukhabarat sent one of its officers to London to activate a cell of 'sleepers' led by the nephew of Sabri al-Banna, better known as Abu Nidal, who is the head of the terrorist group which bears his name. The cell was tasked with the assassination of the Israeli ambassador in London, Shlomo Argov. In due course, they ambushed him on the steps of the Dorchester Hotel in Park Lane, shooting him in the head. The assassin himself was shot and wounded by the Metropolitan Police Special Branch officer who was escorting the ambassador; the two other members of the cell were later arrested. It was widely believed that the Palestine Liberation Organisation had been responsible; the Iraqis' aim was to goad the Israelis into taking large-scale retaliatory action against the PLO in Lebanon.

However, the fate of opposition figures is less horrific than that of those who betray the family, the defectors who break their oath of fidelity to the organisation. Majid Hussein knew that he was under sentence of death as long as Saddam Hussein ruled in Baghdad. In September 1980, only four days after war erupted between Iran and Iraq, he had defected from his post as a captain in the Mukhabarat. At that point, he had nine years' service behind him as an agent, during which time he had also served as Saddam Hussein's bodyguard. His defection took place whilst he was in Kuwait on a mission to blow up an oil installation. From there he fled to Syria, subsequently travelling to Yugoslavia, Bulgaria, Switzerland, Austria and West Germany. Other intelligence services kept an eye on him as he moved from place to place, keeping one step ahead of the vengeful Mukhabarat. On one occasion, at Munich airport, he was approached by a CIA agent who offered him a collaboration agreement but Hussein declined.

In early 1983, Hussein moved to Sweden, where he sought political asylum on the grounds that he was a defected agent. He declared that he had been subjected to assassination attempts and that his death sentence had been published in an Iraqi newspaper. The Swedish authorities, however, did not appear to believe him, and for two years his application for asylum was passed between the immigration authorities, the police and the labour department with none of them prepared to take a decision. In the autumn of 1984, he took the desperate step of offering the Swedish security police top-secret information in exchange for the right to remain in Sweden. When his offer was refused, he turned to the media and revealed his network of contacts. Moreover, he disclosed what he knew about Iraqi agents working in Scandinavia.

Hussein also declared that he was in possession of information about the Swedish security police commissioner who, in 1979, had been convicted of spying for Iraq, and about the suspected Norwegian spy, Arnet Trayholt, and his contacts with Baghdad. The security police still did not believe him because the possibility that Hussein still worked for the Mukhabarat could not be discounted. In their opinion, his flight and the information which he had revealed could all have been part of a plan to infiltrate him into Iraqi exile circles.

This suspicion against Hussein was shared by many Iraqis in Sweden and he therefore had some difficulty in establishing contact with them. However, amongst a handful of close friends was Salman Mourad with whom he shared a flat in Mashda. 'It was madness that the Swedish security police for two years did not manage to sort out whether Majid was an Iraqi spy or not,' said Mourad.

Hussein did not only appear in the Swedish press. In the Iraqi exile paper *Attiyar*, published by the Iraqi Uma party from exile in London, he revealed information about secret negotiations at presidential level in Iraq and described methods of torture used by the Iraqi security services. The articles caused a big stir in the Arab world and were quoted in several papers throughout the Middle East.

After his revelations, Majid Hussein realised that he was in grave danger. He asked the police several times for protection, but they ignored him. They told him that he was in Sweden, not in Iraq. Since he had been refused protection, Majid knew he had to be very careful. He never went out alone.

On 9th January, however, Hussein made an exception. During the day, he had visited a compatriot at his office in Kunstarten in Stockholm. Suddenly an Arab woman, who gave her name as Nina, appeared in the office, asking for help. She said that she was looking for a dentist but had seen an Arabic nameplate on the door to the office and wondered if the two men could help her. They were unable to do so, but the meeting ended with Majid Hussein inviting his Iraqi friend and Nina back to his home.

During the evening, Majid Hussein gave his guests dinner. At about eight o'clock his Iraqi friend left and Hussein was alone with Nina. At ten o'clock she wanted to leave but Hussein offered her a bed for the night. She insisted, however, on going back to Stockholm. Hussein escorted Nina to the railway station. He was never seen again. Six weeks later the Swedish police told his friends he had left voluntarily. They thought that Hussein had probably completed his mission for the Mukhabarat and returned to Iraq.

However, on 20th March 1985, it became clear what had befallen Majid Hussein. Police in Hadinhar announced that the body of a man, who had been murdered and dismembered, had been found in the River Ede at Gredi, twenty-five miles south-west of Stockholm. It was subsequently confirmed that it was the body of Majid Hussein and that it had apparently been lying there since the beginning or middle of January, soon after his disappearance.

Despite evidence of acts of terrorism by the Mukhabarat, relations between Britain and Iraq improved as part of the West's efforts to use Saddam Hussein as a bulwark against the tide of Islamic fundamentalism emanating from Iran. However, Britain's diplomatic relations with other Arab states, who are important in the sense of keeping contacts and diplomatic channels open with radical Arab elements, had collapsed owing to Prime Minister Margaret Thatcher's policy of shadowing American foreign policy – which itself was a disaster – and thus there were no diplomatic relations with Syria or Iran. Moreover, permitting President Reagan to use Britain as a launching base for his bombing raid against Libya in 1986 had served to isolate Britain still further from the radical Arab camp. The Foreign Office appeared to be prepared to turn a blind eye to Iraq's terrorist activities on British soil in order to maintain the status quo as far as relations with Baghdad were concerned.

Iraqi opposition groups in February 1990 wanted to hold a press conference and publish a document – signed by prominent Iraqi figures and former Iraqi ministers – warning the British public against Iraqi acts of terror. The Foreign Office urged them not to go ahead for fear of harming Anglo-Iraqi relations. Two months later, despite mounting evidence of the brutal excesses of the Ba'athist regime both in Iraq and in Britain, Foreign Secretary Douglas Hurd stated in the House of Commons that severing relations with Baghdad would leave Britain without an embassy between the Khyber Pass and the Mediterranean. British and other Western policy-makers and strategists saw Iraq purely as a key regional power who possessed the largest oil reserves after Saudi Arabia, as a profitable export market and as a force to help keep the Iranians in check.

9 · The Gathering Storm

Historians will debate for a long time when exactly Saddam Hussein made the decision to invade Kuwait and how far he planned to go. Since it seemed irrational to invite the whole world to fight against him, a number of Saddam's critics, both Arab and Westerners, believe that anger overcame his careful calculations and the sabre-rattling turned into a real invasion that went beyond what Iraqi army generals had planned. What strengthens this belief is the number of purges and arrests that followed the invasion as top army officers voiced their objections.

Other observers disagree, saying it was a long-term plan and part of Saddam's bid to lead the Arab world on his own terms and in his own Ba'ath style. But for most the question remains: When did he start planning to invade Kuwait?

In Washington, US State Department officials came round to accepting the explanation of the long-term plan, but also argued among themselves and with Arab diplomats as to when the signals from Baghdad became clear enough for the alarm to be sounded. By September 1990, they agreed that the Iraqi leader had begun to implement the plan to take over Kuwait seven months earlier, in February 1990. They take this date as the start of Saddam's policy of heightening tensions with the West and the time when the anti-Western Arab nationalist vocabulary re-emerged to colour his rhetoric, having disappeared during the war with Iran.

American analysts, who were then wondering about Saddam's real motives, said after the invasion that they were twofold. Firstly, to disguise his real intentions, which were to bully the Kuwaitis until they gave up a large slice of their wealth to cover Iraq's massive debts, and conceded territory demanded by Saddam by placing part of their land under Iraq's control, thus giving him direct access to the Gulf. Secondly, to gather popular Arab support by attacking the triumvirate of 'Zionism', 'Western imperialism' and 'Arab reactionary forces', the last meaning the wealthy oil sheikhs towards whom the majority of Arabs shared the Iraqis' resentment.

Many American analysts agreed with their Arab colleagues that Saddam's resentment and anger towards Kuwait and other Gulf states had first surfaced immediately after the ceasefire in the Gulf War.

The authors believe that the plan to subject the Gulf states to his will and to impose his strategy on the region, including total control of Kuwait – and certainly placing Iraqi forces on one or two of the Kuwaiti islands as well as on a large part of the coast by force or by concession – had been carefully worked out during the war with Iran. The desire, however, to impose his hegemony on the region started even before the war with Iran: it started with the fall of the Shah.

In 1983, when Iraq was under massive Iranian pressure, Kuwait – which had virtually turned into an Iraqi port for shipping Iraq's oil and importing the heavy gear needed for industry – began, along with other Gulf states, to inject massive funds into the Iraqi war machine. However, their generosity was not enough for Saddam Hussein. He wanted a political commitment to his leadership, one that would remain intact when the Iranian threat was over.

Once the war was finished, the Gulf states, who had formerly been united by fear of Iran's fanatical soldiers, failed to agree on what new dangers faced the region. For the Saudis, Iran and the revolutionary Islamic groups that operated under its banner were the main danger, as they challenged the Saudi royal family's self-proclaimed right to rule over the holiest of Muslim shrines. It is for that reason that Saudi Arabian intelligence operations were directed against subversive Shia elements worldwide, whilst their agents in Europe continued the policy of buying influence and building Islamic centres all over the world to sabotage Khomeini's power over Muslims. For other Gulf states, internal dangers like Shia and left-wing groups were a more pressing concern, but they tackled it differently. To the disapproval of the Saudis, they sought to improve relations with Iran.

The Kuwaitis had their own internal problems. Chief amongst these was action by disillusioned Shia who, at the height of the Gulf War, attacked French and American interests because the emirate backed Iraq. In 1983 they tried to assassinate the emir, but the Kuwaiti rulers, unlike the Saudis, have always been pragmatic and know how to manipulate their three big neighbours, Iran, Iraq and Saudi Arabia. They saw no real danger from Iran during its war with Iraq, apart from the odd missile attack on their installations, which was regarded as a 'pretty low-key response to the massive support we gave to the Iraqis', as one top Kuwaiti official put it in September 1990. They even knew that, had their Shia population, roughly 35 per cent, been treated better, they would have created few problems.

Kuwait had no illusions as to the real threat. 'I was urged by my ministers to press Iraq with settling the borders dispute,' said the deposed emir, Sheikh Jaber al-Ahmad al-Jaber, to Arab leaders in Cairo one week after he fled his Dasman palace, 'but I said no, not while my Iraqi brothers were at war.' He then burst into tears and added from the depth of his grief, 'It was at a time when we were supporting the brothers against the cousins, and put all our facilities at their disposal; it wouldn't have been very gallant to press our claim during their plight.'

However, the deposed emir knew that 'Arab brotherhood' or 'gallantry' had nothing to do with postponing the border question at the time. He, like the rest of Arab leaders from the Gulf States, had received two messages from Saddam. The first hinted that terrorists of organisations like the Abu Nidal group could reach them 'in their bed chambers'. The second came from Saddam himself at the height of Iranian pressure on Iraq's second city, Basra, which was close to falling to an attack mounted by human waves of Iranian fanatics, for whom victory came second to martyrdom. Saddam hinted that if the Iranians were to break through his defence lines he would pull his forces north to a second defence line, leaving the Basra–Kuwait highway wide open for Iranian troops to move south. The sheikhs, who had problems with their own Shia population, had no choice but to pay 'protection money' to Saddam to stop what was for them the greater evil. 'Didn't the great America, with all its fleets and nuclear weapons, back him too?' replied one exiled Kuwaiti official, after the invasion, to the suggestion that they shared responsibility for creating the monster.

Ironically, Saddam Hussein combined the two threats in a message to President Bush during his meeting with April Glaspie, the American ambassador, on 25th July. He firstly reminded her of who protected American interests against Iran. 'You know you are not the ones who protected your friends during the war with Iran,' he said. 'I assure you, had the Iranians overrun the region, the American troops would not have stopped them.' In other words, he was in a better position to guard the security of the Gulf than the Americans who could not, in practice, safeguard their interests without him. He also touched a raw nerve exposed by the Vietnam War: 'Yours is a society which cannot accept ten thousand dead in one battle in one week, then another ten thousand the second week.' Finally came the threat of terrorism: 'We cannot come all the way to you in the United States, but individual Arabs may reach you.'

Had American diplomats cared to listen carefully, or at least bothered to read reports by many analysts, they would not have been taken so totally by surprise. There was nothing new in Saddam's messages or tactics, as he had said or carried them out before. The threats had been constantly repeated in the Arab press in one form or another, including those publications printed in Europe which hailed Iraqi-backed acts of terror as the 'heroic fight against Imperialism and Zionism'.

In 1983, the editor of a London-based Arab newspaper had just returned from Baghdad where he had spent three weeks seeking financial help for his publication. Previously, five weeks in Saudi Arabia had produced nothing. He recounted the details of a meeting he had in Baghdad with one of President Saddam's aides. The editor had started by praising the 'brave stand of the Iraqi Arab army in defending the heart of Arab land and the Muslim shrines' against the Persian forces. He then told the Iraqis how his paper, which was with Iraq in the same trench as 'the Arab nationalist forces', was suffering from lack of funds whilst oil sheikhs spent lavishly in European casinos. On the same day, an editorial appeared in his paper in London, conveying the same message to the readership but identifying Kuwait and the Sabah family as the 'mean sheikhs' who, instead of providing for the forces 'that stop Iran overrunning their land', spent 'the wealth of the Arab nation' in America and Europe which financed Zionist aggression.

The editor, whose paper prints only a few thousand copies and is not widely read, returned to London with three cheques totalling just under $2 million. He told other Arab journalists how the Iraqi official quoted Saddam Hussein as saying, 'Their help is not enough and not coming from the heart; they don't give a damn about the Arab nation. They just want us to stop Khomeini getting to them. But wait until we finish this war, then Arab soldiers will get their rightful share of Arab wealth.'

The whole episode indicated two important trends. First, Saddam's Ministry of Information paid $2 million just to give certain messages to Arab diplomats, analysts, rivals, friends or neutrals, indicating the direction in which Saddam Hussein wanted events to go. It was important to publish this message in London, for the city has historically been the most important listening-post for Arab diplomats, where they conduct their secret or open diplomacy. Secondly, the Arab editor's story indicated the aspirations of Ba'athist policy and hinted at how events would unfold. It was a sign of the way the Ba'ath leadership was prepared to finance the media in order to shape the collective mind of the Arabs and prepare them for the day on which Saddam Hussein would assume the role of leader of Arabia. The pro-Saddam Arab press, as well as hundreds of Arab journalists on Baghdad's payroll, continued to write in this vein from 1983 until the invasion of Kuwait.

After the August 1988 ceasefire in the Gulf, Kuwaiti papers, the pro-Saddam Arab press, as well as some Saudi publications which were infiltrated by Ba'athist journalists, stepped up their criticism of those who had not helped Iraq. A few articles were also printed in the guise of analysis by military experts using maps and diagrams, indicating that, had Iraq had access to the Kuwaiti islands and the waters of the Gulf, it would have defeated Iran in the early days of the war.

Iraq's foreign debts were over $70 billion in 1988, and the Iraqi treasury proposed some measures to curb public spending. Baghdad's Ministry of Information budget in 1988 for bribing Arab journalists and sponsoring Arab papers outside Iraq was over $57 million. For the 1989 budget the ministry proposed a 75 per cent cut but Saddam refused and instead increased it by 25 per cent. He argued, 'We made large sacrifices. Let us pretend that we lost another couple of battle tanks or fired another half a dozen missiles. That would pay for this budget.'

Twenty months later, in August 1990, the same London-based Arab editor left Baghdad just as the United Nations Security Council was about to implement sanctions. He had received another $4 million in cheques and lines of credit. His brief was to carry on with the same theme of 'Arab nationalism versus the Zionists and the imperialist-backed oil sheikhs'. This theme was vigorously pushed by the pro-Saddam press, which took a markedly more anti-Western tone during the period dating from the Farzad Bazoft affair up to the August 1990 crisis.

At the end of the war with Iran, few would doubt that the regional balance of power had already shifted in Iraq's favour. Richard Nixon's 'twin pillars' policy was ancient history and Iran would clearly take many years to recover as a regional power, while Saudi Arabia, despite all of its expensive military hardware, had no illusions about its real weight. Thus the way was open for Saddam to exploit his position of power and to try to realise his ambitions. However, his economy was crippled by debts and his programme of semi-liberalisation did not convince foreign private investors that the regime was serious about changing its repressive methods. Several countries, led by Britain and France, did extend generous lines of credit for weapons and other purchases but Baghdad failed to attract any foreign entrepreneurs to invest in its state-owned businesses. Saddam was unable to win the confidence of Western businesses which he so badly needed. One American official, former Assistant Secretary of State Richard Murphy, recalled how in 1988 the Iraqis were 'clearly nettled and aggravated that the Arabs – and indeed the world – were not sufficiently grateful for Iraq's sacrifice in the war, that none of us appreciated what Iraq had done for all of us.'

By the end of 1988, as the Palestine Liberation Organisation was being courted by Egypt to denounce terrorism and to adopt the two-state solution in line with the United Nations 1947 partition of Palestine, Saddam Hussein was forging a two-tier foreign policy which seemed somewhat contradictory.

First, as part of the settling of old scores, the Iraqi leader wanted to keep up pressure on his Arab enemies, particularly his arch-rival, the other Ba'athist regime in Syria. (The Arab Socialist Ba'ath party had split in the mid-1960s, the Syrian branch claiming they were the true Ba'athists led by the Syrian president Hafez al-Assad.) Assad, an A'lwiyet from a Shia minority who rules ruthlessly over a Sunni majority, saw the priority of the Arab nations as confronting Israel, not their Muslim brothers in Iran, so he sided with Khomeini against his sworn enemy Saddam Hussein – a Sunni who rules ruthlessly over a Shia majority. Assad's action was a 'mortal sin', not to be forgiven by a man like Saddam, who adheres to a code of practice similar to that of the Sicilian Mafia when it comes to matters like avenging the honour of the Ba'athist family. So the first part of Saddam's post-war foreign policy was to keep secret contacts with the opposition and terror groups whom he was financing to undermine his Syrian rivals in Lebanon, as well as building a number of secret Ba'ath organisations in many Arab and Muslim African countries, such as Mauritania and Somalia.

The second part of his foreign policy was to join a secular, moderate Middle East camp led by Cairo – not because he was advocating peace or moderation, but because it offered a back door to the United States and the West. Meanwhile his 'sponsored' media would keep the pressure on the oil sheikhs, all of whom had many skeletons in their cupboards.

One morning in November 1988, the Egyptian Minister of Arts, Farouk Hosni, the youngest member of President Hosni Mubarak's cabinet, was waiting at Cairo airport to welcome a low-key Iraqi minis-terial delegation. To the atonishment and embarrassment of the waiting officials, Saddam Hussein himself stepped out of the special jet, leading a bewildered Mubarak two hours later to say to him in front of a large gathering of reporters, 'I thought that they were joking when they said you were here. I had to leave my guest to lunch by himself.'

The surprise visit was initiated by Saddam himself. He was pressing ahead with the idea of creating the Arab Co-operation Council (ACC), a grouping of Egypt, Iraq, North Yemen and Jordan, whose accord was signed in 1989. The West interpreted Saddam's presence in a Common Market type of grouping with pragmatic leaders such as President Mubarak and King Hussein of Jordan as a further assurance that Iraq was not planning to follow an extremist course.

However, other countries in the region suspected that Saddam might have had other reasons for wanting to form the ACC. When Kuwait, Saudi Arabia, Bahrain, Qatar, the United Arab Emirates and Oman formed the Gulf Co-operation Council in 1980, Iraq was excluded because the Ba'ath government's foreign policy was not in accordance with that of these Gulf states.

Now, the Kuwaitis welcomed the accord as a way of diverting Saddam Hussein's attention away from the Gulf to the 'Fertile Crescent', where successive Iraqi regimes, long before the birth of the Ba'ath party, had attempted to create a stronger unified Arab body with Syria and Jordan.

Two of the prospective members of the ACC were already attuned to some of the Iraqi dictator's ideas. King Hussein had quietly been nodding assent to Saddam's suggestions that rich Arab countries should pay more to poorer countries. His own country's economic boom, created by the Gulf War, when Jordan became the only supply route to Iraq for eight years, was coming to an end. In September 1988, Hussein had surrendered Jordan's administrative role in the Israeli-occupied West Bank. Up to this point they had been paying the salaries, for instance, of teachers and civil servants there. The money had been donated by the PLO and other Arab organisations and had been lodged in Jordanian banks. The surrender of the administrative role therefore meant the loss of millions of dollars.

For Yemen (then North Yemen), which was amongst the poorest of Arab nations because oil was not discovered there until late 1989, an alliance with Saddam seemed an attractive proposition. Since Ibn Sa'ud annexed their only two oil-rich provinces, O'ssiran and Najran, in 1934, the Yemenis have constantly been made to feel pressure from Saudi Arabia. Only Egypt, suspicious of Saddam's real motives, had misgivings about the ACC, but the pact was duly signed on 19th February 1989.

The thought of a troublemaker like Saddam being present in their own backyard was one of the Saudis' worst nightmares. Iraq was now in a grouping politically and demographically much stronger than the Gulf Co-operation Council, and with formidable economic potential in the longer term. Above all the ACC geographically encircled the GCC's main core, Saudi Arabia, from the north, north-west, north-east and south.

The signing of the ACC accord served as a constant reminder to the Saudi oil princes that they were no longer the sole dominant power which could dictate policies in the southern tip of the Arabian Peninsula. The nightmare came true in 1990. Shortly before Saddam invaded Kuwait in August, he positioned two squadrons of MiG fighters in Yemen, now part of a powerful Arab organisation which proceeded to throw sand in the gears of the Egypt–Saudi–Western vehicle by escalating the popular protest of rejecting the presence of American troops on Arab sand.

At the time of signing the accords of the ACC, Iraq owed Egypt some $3.5 billion for arms and missiles which Cairo had supplied during the war with Iran. Another $850 million was owed to Egyptian workers in Iraq. Saddam had no intention of paying these debts, and instead wanted to persuade Cairo that Egypt was more likely to get its money by backing him in demanding a share of the Gulf states' oil wealth. Egyptian sources associated with ACC meetings recalled how Iraqis, including the president himself, had tirelessly spent the first year of the Council's short life reminding them of Egypt's sacrifices in four wars to defend Arab Palestine, whilst the oil sheikhs were as ungrateful as ever. The Iraqis had stressed that it was the Yom Kippur War that had created the massive jump in oil prices, but the Egyptians themselves had not benefited. After he invaded Kuwait in 1990, Saddam Hussein offered the Egyptians their 'fair share of oil wealth' if they would drop the idea of supporting the Emir of Kuwait and of allying themselves with the Americans against Iraq.

In one closed meeting of the Arab Co-operation Council in 1989, Saddam reminded both King Hussein and President Mubarak of the Gulf states' obligations, according to the 1967 Khartoum summit, to pay the front-line states money to enable them to confront Israeli aggression. He repeated details of the Rabat summit in 1969 when the late President Nasser had walked out in anger, refusing to get into the limousine provided by 'Arabs' and returning to his hotel in a taxi hailed in the street. He had been disgusted by the way the late Sheikh Sabah Salim al-Sabah, then Emir of Kuwait, challenged as to why the support due under the 1967 Khartoum agreement had not been forthcoming, had tried to question details of expenditure.

At the time of signing the ACC pact, the Arab States League, whose Cairo headquarters had long been deserted thanks to the Iraqi-led chorus denouncing Egypt's peace with Israel, seemed another legacy of Nasser's days which had no practical use in the post-oil-boom era. A third grouping of nations was formed in early 1989 when Libya, Tunisia, Algeria, Morocco and Mauritania signed the Union of Arab Maghrib accord. This left Marxist South Yemen, impoverished Sudan and fragmented Lebanon out in the wilderness. Most important, however, was the degree of isolation of Ba'athist Syria, the only Arab state which posed a real threat to Israel but which had supported Iran in its war with Iraq. It remained bogged down in Lebanon, where Saddam Hussein continued to fight his war with Iran by arming the Christian general Michel Aoun with sophisticated weapons to fight Syria and its Muslim allies. Mutual distrust after the breakdown of the Arab consensus during the war with Iran was all too apparent.

The Egyptians began a series of diplomatic manoeuvres to reassure Arabs in many quarters that the ACC was not against their interests. The Syrians were alarmed because of Saddam's activities in Lebanon, which Assad had always regarded as his own territory. Cairo sent them reassuring messages as well as confiscating a number of arms shipments sent by the Iraqis to Lebanon through the Suez Canal.

President Mubarak, locked in a bitter fight with the International Monetary Fund over rescheduling the country's massive debts, also invited King Fahd of Saudi Arabia for a state visit. He wanted to persuade the Saudis to pay money they owed Egypt for the Arab Industrial Board and to use the Saudi monarch's influence with the IMF. The visit was scheduled for 27th March 1989, just over one month after the signing of the ACC agreement.

Just two days before he landed at Cairo airport, King Fahd had visited Baghdad where he signed a 'non-aggression pact' with Saddam Hussein which raised a number of eyebrows. 'If Margaret Thatcher were to show up tomorrow in Paris and sign a non-aggression pact with President François Mitterrand,' wrote Andrew Gowers in the *Financial Times*, 'people would think it more than a little odd, even alarming. That, in the context of the Gulf, was roughly the effect of King Fahd's visit to Baghdad.'

Meanwhile, other Gulf Co-operation Council members such as Kuwait, the United Arab Emirates and Oman were improving relations with Iran as swiftly as possible.

While the Egyptians, along with King Hussein of Jordan, were emphasising the economic nature of the Arab Co-operation Council and playing down its political significance, Saddam Hussein had already made it clear that security issues would be high on its agenda and that he wanted all members to sign bilateral or collective non-aggression pacts similar to that reached between Iraq and Saudi Arabia.

The Saudis did not publicise details of the accords of the non-aggression pact and their wish was briefly respected by Iraqi officials. However, as soon as Fahd was embracing President Mubarak in Cairo, Saddam Hussein, who seldom talks to reporters, said the accords set out 'the concept of non-interference in the internal affairs of the two sisterly countries and non-use of force and armies between the two states'. The mention of force took observers by surprise, because Saudi Arabia had been Iraq's leading ally during the latter's war with Iran. However, the president's revelation of the details of the pact captured the attention of observers familiar with Arab politics. More than one Western ambassador in Baghdad subsequently filed reports to his foreign ministry warning that he had no doubt that 'Saddam Hussein's vision of Iraq's position in the world is as the leading Arab country', adding that the Arab Co-operation Council was a 'vehicle for his re-entry into Middle Eastern politics'. 'What is not clear,' the report continued, 'is whether Iraq regards these non-aggression pacts as a way of soothing the concerns of other Arab countries, or is an implied threat to force concessions from them.'

The idea, then, of Iraq using force against Saudi Arabia under any scenario was ruled out; even after the invasion of Kuwait, the United States eventually accepted that Iraq never intended to attack Saudi Arabia. However, as far as oil politics was concerned, Saudi Arabia was almost bound to be irritated by the emergence of such a powerful rival. Riyadh knew full well that Iraq, with huge oil reserves second only to its own, could threaten its pre-eminence in OPEC. Observers and analysts at the time of the signing of the non-aggression pact paid particular attention to the clause covering non-interference in each other's internal affairs, the most significant clause in the accord. Arab Gulf states still harbour vivid memories of the then-radical Iraq's subversive activities throughout the Arabian Peninsula during the 1970s: the underground Ba'ath party organisations it maintained in other countries, and the assassination of opponents, as well as its support for a secessionist rebellion in Dhofar in southern Oman.

Four days after he invaded Kuwait, the Iraqi president summoned Joseph Wilson, the US chargé d'affaires in Baghdad, to assure him that Iraq had no intention of taking any action against Saudi Arabia because of the non-aggression pact. 'You know, some Western circles were annoyed and some were joking about the idea of the agreement, comparing it to agreements between Britain and France, for example. Thank God Kuwait did not sign that agreement with us. I was very happy when we decided to support the revolutionary group in Kuwait because there was no agreement between us and Kuwait. If there had been, we couldn't have done that.'

According to our research, there was no evidence to suggest that the US State Department had actually noted the indications of how the new alignments between states who crossed each other's path of interests were reshaping the geopolitical map of the Middle East in early 1989. Even in Europe, especially in London where some reports were received, placing a question mark against Iraq's intentions, no danger signals were detected and business with Iraq was conducted as usual. The view held in London,

Washington and by many Arab diplomats was that Saddam Hussein had emerged seasoned from the war and was now merely attempting to regain for Iraq the dominant position in the region which it deserved by virtue of its size.

Six weeks before they signed the non-aggression pact with the Saudis, the Iraqis had offered the Kuwaitis the opportunity to sign a similar agreement. As the Kuwaitis knew that there was a price to pay, their prime minister, Sheikh Sa'ad al-Abdallah al-Salem al-Sabah, declared that he was going on a visit to Baghdad as he thought he could negotiate with Saddam. Sheikh Sabah al-Ahmad al-Jaber, the longest-serving foreign minister in the Arab world, an able diplomat, wise statesman and a wily negotiator, advised the prime minister against the visit, saying the Iraqis would set a diplomatic trap for him.

The visit was unusually long and the Kuwaiti guest had a pretty rough time at the hands of his host, according to well-placed Kuwaiti and Iraqi sources. As the prime minister knew what the Iraqis were seeking, he thought to outwit them by first reminding Saddam Hussein of the huge debts – estimated at $20 billion – owed by Baghdad to Kuwait; this also was against his foreign minister's advice.

Saddam is said to have ignored the debt issue and all the while pressed Sheikh Sa'ad al-Abdallah to discuss the border, three miles of which remained in dispute, and in particular the Iraqi demand for access to the two islands just off the coast, Bubiyan and Warbah. He told his guest that his concern was the security of maritime access to Iraq's Gulf port of Umm Qasr, which the Iraqis always maintained would be greatly enhanced if they were allowed their own facilities on Bubiyan Island. He proposed some form of leasing arrangement for the island, which, he told Sheikh Sa'ad al-Abdallah, would not compromise Kuwaiti sovereignty. The Kuwaiti prime minister went home without having reached any agreement, but he had already exposed his hand to Saddam Hussein.

The rough treatment of its highly embarrassed prime minister sent shockwaves through Kuwait. Mindful of Qasim's claim in 1961 which had spoilt their first taste of independence, many Kuwaitis realised that Saddam, now seen by fellow Arabs as 'the great warrior who had fended off the Persian enemy at the eastern gate of the Arab fortress', was turning on them to settle old scores by exercising historical Iraqi claims to parts of Kuwaiti territory. In addition, the Kuwaitis feared that openly permitting Iraq to install facilities on Bubiyan would compromise their newly rebuilt relations with Iran and their ostensible position of 'neutrality' in the Gulf.

There were more surprises to come. In March 1989, the two countries suddenly announced an agreement for Iraq to supply Kuwait with some

350 million gallons of drinking water per day and five hundred million gallons of irrigation water per day via pipeline from its rivers. It was the idea that Iraqi Prime Minister Nuri al-Sa'id had thought of some thirty-five years earlier and which had been turned down by Sheikh Abdallah al-Salim.

This development had the effect that Baghdad wanted. It demonstrated that the new generation of the Sabah family were more trusting than their forebears had been in the 1950s, and it gave certain signals to the outside world. Some observers saw the water agreement as an indication of progress on other issues.

Just a few months after the ceasefire with Iran, when Kuwait had restored diplomatic relations with Iran, Iraqi troops made at least one illegal incursion over the border, in case Kuwait had forgotten who was the dominant force in the area. Another incursion took place in October 1989, a few days after the new Iranian ambassador had taken up his post in Kuwait on 29th September.

By the end of 1989, Iraq was in severe financial difficulties and was renegotiating its debts with most of its creditors. The French, as well as the British, were keen to shore up Saddam's ailing economy. France was arranging for licensed assembly of Mirage F1 fighters in Iraq, while Britain signed a facility for £450 million of new credit.

Nearly half of Iraq's $80 billion or so of debts was owed to Arab states, mainly in the Gulf. Most of these creditors reconciled themselves to the idea that Saddam Hussein would never pay his debts. Unlike the Kuwaitis who foolishly kept reminding the Iraqis of their debts and trying to use them as a bargaining chip, the Saudis were no longer even bothering to keep a record of the loans to Iraq on their books.

The significance of foreign debts and Iraq's ailing economy in shaping Saddam Hussein's future policies was again misread by policy-makers in the West. Analysts in Britain discounted the possibility of a major Iraqi drive for pan-Arab unity under its leadership since 'the regime's overriding priority in the aftermath of the war with Iran will be with domestic reconstruction'. Those same analysts also predicted that Iraq's continuous suspicion of Iran would prompt Saddam to be more friendly: 'If the Iraqis continue to fear Iranian resurgence, then they have a stake in not alienating the Gulf States.'

However, the Ba'athist drive for a wider role in Arab politics was evident, and the Arab press continued peddling this theme. During the Gulf War, the bulk of the politically or economically heavyweight Arab nations, with the exception of Iraq's bitter rival Syria, had been led by Egypt and Saudi Arabia into a unified bloc supporting Saddam's campaign and seeming to dance to his tune. Not one single word was published in Arab newspapers about the Iraqi mass slaughter of the Kurds or the use of chemical weapons against Iran. Only the Syrian government-controlled press exposed 'the crimes of the Iraqi regime' and its grounds for doing so was hatred of Iraq rather than moral outrage. Just a few weeks before Iraq invaded Kuwait, the press there was applauding the murder by hanging of *Observer* reporter Farzad Bazoft and parroting Iraqi news agency claims that he had been in the employ of the British and Israeli intelligence services.

In fact, the vast majority of the Arab media welcomed Iraq's use of chemical weapons and the development of weapons of mass destruction. One editorial after another in so-called independent Arab papers, including those based in London and Paris, praised Saddam Hussein's efforts in producing such weapons, as this arsenal 'will lend strength to all Arabs since chemical weapons would balance Israel's possession of nuclear weapons'.

Helped by state-controlled Arab media, the Iraqi leader deluded himself into believing that it was Iraq alone who had brought about what he saw as a victory over Iran. 'You know that Iran agreed to the ceasefire not because the United States had bombed one of the oil platforms but because of the liberation of the Fao. Is this Iraq's reward for its role in securing the stability of the region and for protecting it from an unknown flood?' said Saddam Hussein to April Glaspie at that famous meeting one week before the invasion of Kuwait.

The Arab media continued to hail Saddam as a hero, thus feeding his delusions of grandeur and his ambition to become the leader of the Arab world, the new Nasser. As for almost any post-1948 Arab leader whose domestic policy goes bankrupt and whose economy deteriorates in tatters, Palestine became a trump card for Saddam. Yet he was not as mad as large sections of the Western media depicted him – on the contrary, he was calculating and cunning. Despite his aggressive talk, he had no wish to take on Israel in a battle he was more than likely to lose. Even if he had been able to inflict heavy losses on Israel – and his media doubtless would have presented that as a victory – it would have led nowhere. Iraq has no common border with Israel and neither Syria nor Jordan would have permitted the use of their territory as a battleground to satisfy the megalomaniac ideas of the Iraqi dictator. King Hussein had lost half of his kingdom – the West Bank – when he went to war against Israel in 1967 and he would not make the same mistake twice.

Since the late President Anwar Sadat of Egypt left him waiting for talks in Geneva in 1977 and went ahead with a bilateral peace treaty with Israel,

18 Saddam's mother and step-father.
19 (below left) The young Saddam.
20 (below right) Saddam Hussein in disguise during his flight from Iraq after
    the assassination attempt on General Qasim in 1959.

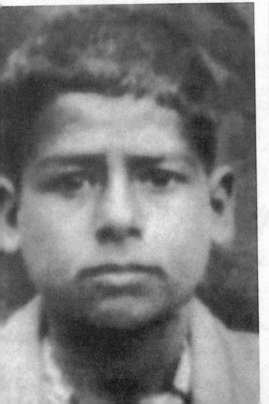

21 (above) Former Iraqi Defence Minister Adnan Khairallah was killed in a mysterious helicopter crash after he had become popular with the Iraqi people.

22 (left) Saddam the devout Muslim, worshipping in Mecca in 1990.

23 (opposite top) Saddam courts King Hussein of Jordan (centre) and President Mubarak of Egypt (left).

24 (opposite below) Saddam Hussein and King Fahd. The two signed a non-aggression pact in 1989.

25 In May 1990, Saddam used the Arab summit in Baghdad to demand money from his oil-rich neighbours.

26 (below left) The arrest and execution of *Observer* journalist Farzad Bazoft in March 1990 turned world press opinion fiercely against Saddam Hussein.

27 (below right) Sheikh Saad of Kuwait embraces Izzat Ibrahim, head of the Iraqi delegation at the Jeddah meeting which, on 1st August 1990, failed to resolve their countries' differences.

28 2nd August 1990: Kuwait was captured in a few hours.

29,30 Demonstrations against George Bush and Margaret Thatcher take place in Baghdad after they responded quickly to the invasion and took a tough stand.

31 US Ambassador April Glaspie. She told Saddam just before the invasion,
'We have no opinion on the border dispute with Kuwait.'

32 The US 82nd Airborne Division arrives in Saudi Arabia on 9th August
1990.

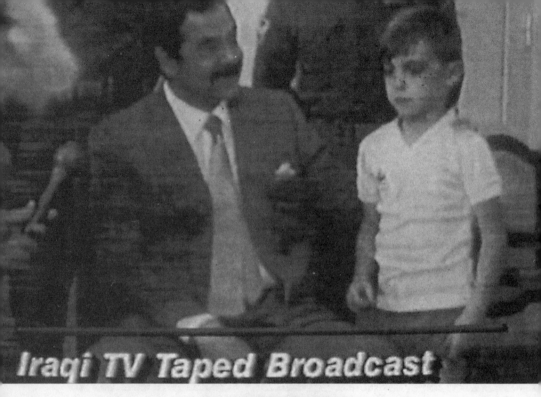

Iraqi TV Taped Broadcast

33 23rd August: Saddam
    appears on TV with
    British hostages.

34 King Hussein visits
    George Bush in
    Washington in an
    effort to defuse the
    crisis.

President Hafez Assad of Syria had known that his country would be the main battleground for any decisive war to come against Israel. He had sought to give his country 'strategic parity' with Israel, but he was abandoned by his Soviet patrons in 1988. Given Syria's battered economy, Assad had no chance of getting the arms he needed.

Saddam Hussein, however, although he had directed them against the wrong enemy at the wrong time, already possessed arms in plenty – thanks to a combination of Western dismay at the emergence of the Islamic revolution and the greed of arms suppliers from East and West. Even after the Gulf War was over, companies around the world competed for Iraqi arms orders. Meanwhile, Saddam Hussein continued his quest for a nuclear capability. Above all, he already possessed chemical weapons and had shown, during the Gulf War and immediately afterwards in Kurdistan, that he was prepared to use them. Chemical weapons were easy to make, relatively easy to use and devastating in their effect; the psychological effect alone of such weapons was sufficient for Saddam's requirements. So much so that, although Saddam had no intention of fighting Israel, chemical weapons were a factor the Israelis took seriously: they conducted gas drills and, in early October 1990, issued gas respirators to the whole of the Jewish population – but not to the impoverished Palestinians of the West Bank and Gaza, who were required to purchase them.

While Nasser had engaged Israel in wars which cost Egypt and its people dear, Saddam Hussein thought of a way to gain from Israel some concessions on Palestinian rights by the *threat* of war as opposed to war itself. However, such a threat had to be a completely credible one which would run the risk of high numbers of casualties, something to which Israel is extremely sensitive. For Israel, one thousand dead would be the equivalent of British deaths totalling 18,660, given the ratio of population. A war would also have put an end to Jews emigrating to Israel at a time when it wanted to absorb Soviet Jews to double its population.

Saddam Hussein wanted to capitalise on the West's negative attitude to the way he had conducted the war against Iran. The latter stages of the Gulf War were an indication of the shape of wars to come. The key factor was the ballistic missile which could reach targets in territories with which the attacker had no common borders. What Saddam Hussein planned to do was to seek 'Aslihatul Dammar el Shamel' – the weapons of mass destruction, including a nuclear capability in addition to the chemical weapons which he already possessed. At the same time, he would make himself the acknowledged champion of the Palestinians who were frustrated by their betrayal by the Gulf sheikhs and by the lack of any progress as a result of Yasser Arafat's moderation. As far as Saddam Hussein was concerned, whether or not they saw him as a credible liberator was irrelevant as long as the Arab media presented him as the leader who would win the rights of the Palestinian people.

There was another flag for Saddam Hussein to wave besides that of Palestine – the banner of Arab unity from the Atlantic Ocean to the Gulf: the old Ba'athist ideology of pan-Arabism as the ideal shape of a nation to confront Israel. Saddam was more explicit than former Arab leaders who used the same rhetoric. Not only should the burdens be spread over the whole Arab nation, but also the benefits. In other words, the rich oil states should share their wealth with their poorer brothers – an idea which had already occupied many columns in Arabic newspapers, including those in Kuwait, argued by well-known names from Nasser's camp such as his autobiographer Mohammed Heikel. Whether they penned such arguments on Saddam's behalf or of their own initiative mattered little; the important thing was that they had already generated the desired debate.

Saddam knew that Nasser had made a mistake in raising the flag of Arab unity at a time when Egypt was paying the salaries of teachers and providing textbooks for schools all over the Arab world, as well as financing and arming the Algerian and Yemeni revolutions. However, Nasser had lacked the modern wealth generated by oil. Oil could give Saddam all the wealth he needed, but the debts of the war with Iran were draining the Iraqi economy. These debts had to be written off if he was to embark upon the crusade of leading the Arabs, starting with the Palestinians.

At the end of 1989, Iraq's ambitious missile programme had two major setbacks. One was the huge explosion which devastated the missile solid-fuel manufacturing facilities in Al-Hillah on 18th August 1989 and destroyed a great deal of the equipment and research results. The second came in early December 1989, when a Tammuz-1 rocket, which was supposed to have launched a satellite, flew for less than half a minute before exploding in mid-air. It was discovered that a wind tunnel at the multi-million-dollar missile research and development centre at Saad-16 near Mosul was of faulty design and needed to be rebuilt.

On 15th September 1989, the Iraqis had arrested the *Observer* journalist Farzad Bazoft, whom they knew well and had cultivated for a long time, at Baghdad airport. His 'crime' was to have visited the site of the Al-Hillah explosion with a British nurse, Daphne Parish. As part of their building-up of tension with the West, the Mukhabarat broadcast a television film of Bazoft 'confessing' that he was a spy. To keep their options open the Iraqis, who had at that time not identified an enemy, forced Bazoft to say he was spying for Israel via the British embassy. This was an indication of where events would lead.

Building up a wave of public enmity to Israel was an easy task. Israel is identified as the number one enemy by the Arab populace even in Egypt, which has a peace treaty with the Jewish state. However, implicating the British embassy was an interesting turn, especially when an all-party group of British members of parliament were on a 'freebie' to Baghdad on the day that Bazoft was arrested. After the televised 'confession', the British embassy made a strong protest and nothing was thought of it. But was it not Britain, the former colonial power in the region, who saved Kuwait from the Iraqi claws in 1961? Again, no one in London or Washington seemed to take note.

With the plight of Bazoft in their mind, a number of British journalists began 1990 by pressing human rights issues in Iraq. Meanwhile, British and other Western companies – who had queued up six months earlier to attend Baghdad's armaments exhibition – were contributing to the construction of Saddam Hussein's machine of terror. Saddam skilfully used press coverage to heighten tension with the West.

As the East European tyrannies crumbled during the closing days of 1989 and, on the remains of the Berlin Wall, people from once-divided countries held the biggest New Year's Eve party in the world, the new decade had already dawned in an Arab region still ruled by Western-backed Arab monarchs and dictators.

One such dictator was planning, not to change his ways, but to devise new plans. Saddam Hussein's closest associates and top security men later told of being shown videos of the execution of Nicolai Ceauşescu and his wife in Romania and being warned that, if anything similar happened in Iraq, past events had made it certain that the leader would not be alone in suffering the anger of the people – they would all suffer a similar fate. However, Ceausescu's experience also proved the truth of the old adage 'Those who live by the sword die by the sword'. Saddam Hussein knew that in order to forestall such events in Iraq he had to provide a diversion for his people – one that would bring considerable material benefit in order to improve his own political standing.

As Saddam observed Iraq's neighbours carefully, it was plain that they were all too preoccupied with their own problems to prevent him embarking upon a new adventure for which Kuwait was the obvious target. It provided the opportunity to resolve once and for all the long-standing border dispute; 'correcting the British colonialists' drawing of the border and the return of Kuwait to Iraq' had been a popular Iraqi demand since the 1930s. In addition, the Kuwaitis were reluctant to sign a non-aggression pact with Iraq. Most importantly, however, a majority of the poorer Arabs as well as the educated middle classes had long shared the Iraqis' resentment towards the Kuwaitis and other wealthy Arabs from the Gulf. Saddam Hussein was convinced that Kuwait was the answer to his problems. He merely had to secure some form of legitimacy by gathering popular support for the move against Kuwait, and to decide on the timing.

At the time Saddam Hussein began to lay the plans which would culminate in the events of 2nd August, Iran was still concentrating on rebuilding its ravaged economy and undertaking a major reconstruction programme. Syria was heavily involved in Lebanon thanks to Israel's efforts at destabilisation and Iraq's support, with Israeli assistance, of General Michel Aoun. Meanwhile, Egypt was in deep economic trouble and fighting a continuous battle with the International Monetary Fund. All the while, the United States was ignoring the basic historical fact that it has always been during periods when Egypt's influence was weak that dictators such as Saddam Hussein have emerged to plunge the Middle East into turmoil. Israel was suffering from an internal crisis as the Intifada was entering its third year whilst Prime Minister Yitzak Shamir was too locked into his own biblical ideology to listen to voices advising a dialogue with the Palestinians. This led to tension in relations with Washington, which was at the same time trying to gain favour with Baghdad. Thus the scene was set for Saddam Hussein to make his move.

Early in 1990, Saddam coupled his policy of acting the 'anti-Western imperialism' Arab hero with his quest for money. On 19th February, a meeting of Arab Co-operation Council foreign ministers was held in Baghdad. Saddam surprised the gathering by demanding that American warships be withdrawn from the Gulf. At the time, American officials overlooked the significance of this demand.

It is worth reflecting at this point on the reasons for the presence at that time of American and other Allied warships in the Gulf. Kuwait's support for Iraq had inevitably incurred the wrath of Iran. After a series of attacks on oil tankers, Kuwait had sought support from the Americans and had requested that its vessels be reregistered under the American flag. When the Americans did not respond enthusiastically to this suggestion, the Kuwaitis approached the Soviet Union, which immediately agreed to charter to Kuwait three Russian tankers. This automatically necessitated the deployment of Soviet naval forces as protection, providing Moscow with a valid excuse to increase its presence in the Gulf.

Washington immediately changed its mind and agreed to allow the reflagging of Kuwaiti tankers under the Stars and Stripes. Thus, playing the Soviet card resulted in Kuwait achieving what it wanted: the involvement of the United States.

There were no incidents involving Soviet ships before the end of the war. But in July 1987 the first of eleven Kuwaiti tankers hoisted the Stars and Stripes and sailed into the Gulf with an American captain, only to hit a mine on this highly publicised first trip. As a result, the escorting American warships had to huddle behind the massive tanker for protection as they headed up Al-Ahmadi port in Kuwait.

The Kuwaitis' intention had been twofold: to seek immediate protection for their vessels but also, in the long term, to obtain an American guarantee for the security of their country, as Britain was no longer in a position to provide protection in the same way as in 1961. More clearly than most, the Kuwaitis had foreseen that, after the Gulf War, Saddam Hussein would constitute a problem. High-ranking Kuwaiti officials, including Sheikh Ali Khalifa, then Kuwaiti oil minister, made no secret of their hope that America would remain in the Gulf once hostilities were over.

When the Iraqi dictator demanded the withdrawal of American warships from the Gulf, State Department officials in Washington were puzzled. Only a week earlier, Assistant Secretary of State John Kelly had told Saddam Hussein that President Bush wanted good relations with Iraq, 'relations built on confidence and trust'. They decided, however, that Saddam's demand was not a hint of a change of policy to come but, rather, an over-reaction by an angry Arab leader to a recent broadcast by the Voice of America which had apparently caused anger in Baghdad. The programme, called 'No More Secret Police', had started with the statement: 'The success of dictatorial rule and tyranny requires the existence of a large secret police, while the success of democracy requires the abolishment of such a force.' The editorial went on to list a number of countries – including Iraq – where secret police forces were still playing an important political role, and had prophesied that the 1989 wave of freedom should make 1990 belong not to dictators and their secret police but to their peoples.

Failing to interpret the signals from Baghdad, Secretary of State James Baker believed he had defused the issue by directing his ambassador in Baghdad to apologise to the Iraqis and to reassure Saddam Hussein of America's wish for good relations. In effect, this was appeasement of a dictator. Saddam was later to use the media again to heighten tension with the West and to divert attention away from his plans.

On 24th February 1990, during the Arab Co-operation Council summit in Amman, he repeated his call for the withdrawal of American warships from the Gulf. He then proceeded to expand on his theme with even more passionate conviction, declaring that American interests in the region were not compatible with those of the Arabs. Saddam called upon Arabs to withdraw part of their wealth from the United States and invest in Arab countries, the Soviet Union and Eastern Europe. He warned that increasing economic pressure and Western plots had weakened the Soviet Union to the extent that America would be the only remaining super-power in the Middle East. He added that the inevitable conclusion would be that Washington would take care to advance the interests of Israel in the region and warned that the Israelis were likely to attack the Arabs within five years. However, with his plans and with Arab strength, if plans were made beforehand, Israel could be defeated. 'We can see the bright lights of Baytulmaqdes [Holy Jerusalem] before our eyes,' said the Iraqi president to the perplexed leaders of the ACC, 'clear signs on the path of liberating Baytulmaqdes.'

Next day, during a closed session, he heightened tension still further, and almost caused Egypt's President Hosni Mubarak to lose his temper – an apparently rare occurrence. Saddam declared that Iraq badly needed money to repair its economy, which was damaged when he defended the interests of the oil sheikhs. 'I need $30 billion in fresh cash,' said Saddam to an amazed President Mubarak. 'Go and tell them in Saudi Arabia and the Gulf that if they don't give Iraq this money we will know how to get it.' At this point President Mubarak interrupted him sharply. 'I will not allow myself, as President of Egypt, to be a party to extortion.' The figure quoted by Saddam was the exact amount that had been in the Iraqi treasury at the beginning of the Gulf War ten years earlier. Saddam departed and the meeting ended in disarray as King Hussein and President Mubarak exchanged looks, whilst the official who had been re-cording the minutes was instructed to delete certain remarks from them.

Saudi Arabia had already given Iraq more money than it considered to be reasonable. However, King Fahd saw that with the Iraqi army still mobilised and no peace treaty between the Gulf War antagonists, there remained a threat from the possible resumption of hostilities. Saudi Arabia was still targeted by Iran for an annual attack every Haj season and was facing growing trouble with its Shia population, as well as a worldwide campaign by the majority of Muslims, whom oil money never reaches and who question the Saudi royal family's competence to rule over the Muslim holy shrines. The Saudis were infuriated by Kuwait mending fences with Iran and responded by placing pressure on Kuwait, arresting some seventy Kuwaiti Shia pilgrims and beheading seventeen of them on an unproved charge of planting bombs.

The Saudis agreed to Iraqi demands that the huge loans made between 1980 and 1988 should be turned into outright grants. They were rewarded with the treaty of non-aggression from Iraq, which made the ever-fearful Saudi princes smile at each other as their less trembling fingers played with their worry beads. 'Alhamdullah we have bought a few more years of peace.'

10 · The Screw Tightens

In September 1989, *Observer* journalist Farzad Bazoft and British nurse Daphne Parish were detained by the Iraqi Mukhabarat. Demands for their trial or their release were ignored. Then suddenly, six months later, they were put on trial in Baghdad. The Iraqi authorities had no intention, however, of making it a proper trial, even by the shabby standards of the Iraqi Ba'athist judiciary; it was from the start to be a show trial designed to provoke strong public reaction in the West. The British lawyer hired by the *Observer* to defend Bazoft was denied a visa to go to Iraq and the so-called 'revolutionary court' refused to include as defence evidence sworn affidavits signed by many British and non-British journalists. This evidence included statements by members of an Independent Television News camera crew who had actually entered the military industrial complex at Al-Hillah, but did not face charges. Bazoft and Parish, by contrast, had only driven around the outside of the perimeter fence.

The only evidence against Bazoft was his own confession, which he withdrew in court, saying he had made it under duress. Neither the prosecution nor the defence lawyer attempted to cross-examine those who had interrogated him during his six months of detention. The sole piece of material evidence presented in court was a soil sample in a test-tube which had been found in his luggage. Bazoft admitted that this was to be examined for traces of chemical agents as part of his investigation as a journalist into the possibility of chemical weapons being produced at Al-Hillah. The prosecution presented no documents or correspondence between Bazoft and any agents or diplomats, nor any between Bazoft and his alleged partner Parish. There were no exhibits of any tapes of recorded conversations or telephone calls, and no witnesses were called for either side. Above all, there were no formal charges made against the defendants. When the 'judge' harshly asked Parish, 'Do you plead guilty or not guilty?' he was somewhat taken back and angered by her unexpected reply of 'Guilty of what? I have not been charged yet. What is the charge, your honour?'

People who are sentenced to death for spying in Iraq, or those who are purged for high treason from the party or the armed forces and condemned to death, are usually hanged – often in public – within the next twenty-four hours, if not within minutes of the sentence. Bazoft, condemned to death on 10th March 1990, was not executed until 15th March. The Iraqis gave the Western media five days to create what the Iraqi press repeatedly called a 'vicious campaign by the West'.

Sixteen hours before Bazoft's execution in the notorious Abu Gharib prison in Baghdad – he received no warning of it until twenty minutes beforehand, when British consul Robert Keely had the distressing task of breaking the news to him – Saddam Hussein addressed a meeting of farmers' leaders. Well into their fifties, they all had bitter memories of British rule and some of them were called to give accounts of the suffering of their fathers at the hands of the British. Saddam himself then launched a bitter attack on Britain, seeking the endorsement of the farmers for the execution of a 'British spy who works for Israel'.

Saddam's timing was perfect: there was a massive outcry against foreigners and the victimisation of Iraq in the Western press. Bazoft's body was not released to the British embassy until a week later and did not arrive in Britain until 27th March, giving Western newspapers another two weeks to fill their columns with more anti-Saddam articles. Even during his funeral on Saturday, 31st March, the London bureau of the Mukhabarat, based at the Iraqi embassy, and the Ba'ath party Jihaz al-Khas, based in the Iraqi Cultural Centre in Tottenham Court Road, organised a small but noisy and forceful group to disrupt the service in London's Regent's Park mosque, thus producing further anti-Saddam publicity.

Since Bazoft was allegedly spying on a missile site, it was natural that more columns in the press would be given to investigating Iraq's missile programme. As British journalists, angered by the murder of their colleague, wrote profiles of the 'Butcher of Baghdad', they quoted numerous examples of his unparallelled brutality, such as the gassing of Kurdish civilians and the murders of his exiled opponents. It occurred to very few of them or to other observers that this was precisely the sort of publicity that Saddam Hussein wanted in order to raise his profile amongst the people as the hero of the Middle East. Even statesmen like President Mubarak, King Hussein and King Fahd misread the signals. They hinted in private that the episode was a mistake since there was no need to put Bazoft on trial and thus focus the world's attention on Iraq's missiles and chemical weapons.

Arab journalists on the Ba'ath party's payroll began to launch a propaganda campaign, starting with more allegations that Bazoft had spied for Israel and Britain. They then broadened their focus, citing the

Western media's 'anti-Saddam campaign' as a prelude to a possible Israeli strike against Iraq's arsenal, on the lines of the Osirak raid of 1981. On this occasion the CIA was not accused, for once, as an intelligence service which could have employed Bazoft. But then it was not America which had carved Kuwait out of the Basra velayet in 1922, double-crossed the Arabs who followed the Sharif of Mecca by not giving them an independent state from the Mediterranean to the Gulf, and betrayed League of Nations trust when Palestine was put under its mandate only to be handed to the Jews on a platter. It was Britain.

Arab editorials tirelessly listed Britain's crimes against the Arab nation, and in particular against Iraq and Palestine. One article in the London-based *Al-Arab* newspaper attacked journalists who questioned the legality of the court that had condemned Bazoft. On the following day, the same writer penned another column attacking Prime Minister Margaret Thatcher for her undemocratic way of dealing with trade unionists and for her pro-Zionist bias. On the third day, the same writer doubled the size of his column to write a historic defence of the so-called Arab hero Saddam Hussein, who had been subjected to a conspiracy directed by Zionists, Imperialists and Arab reactionary forces – the name given in radical Arab nationalist media to the oil sheikhs.

On 28th March 1990, the day of Bazoft's memorial service at St Bride's church in Fleet Street, British Customs and Excise officers, with the help of the US Customs Service arrested the group of Iraqis and Britons attempting to smuggle the consignment of krytrons out of Britain to Iraq.

The ease with which the operation was carried out, and the degree of Iraqi carelessness in letting themselves be caught red-handed, leaves it open to doubt whether the Iraqis were genuinely trying to smuggle the krytrons out, or whether the operation was a bluff. According to intelligence officers from more than one service, this was a 'sting within a sting'. Two days after the Heathrow seizure, a defence correspondent who is a former employee of Marconi asked British Secretary of State for Defence Tom King at a press conference, 'But these capacitors have many other uses, don't they?' This statement caused ears to prick up in certain quarters of the Western media.

Some British journalists questioned the authenticity of the story, suggesting that the Iraqis had deliberately allowed themselves to be caught in order to give the impression that they were well on the way to producing nuclear weapons.

The thesis adopted by every Arab newspaper was that the 'sting' operation by the British and US Customs was part of a plan by Mossad and the CIA to draw attention to events in Iraq, or even to prepare the way for pre-emptive action against it. Another piece of the jigsaw puzzle fell into place on 2nd April 1990 when Saddam Hussein went out of his way to admit in a warning to Israel, during a radio broadcast, that Iraq possessed chemical weapons.

Two weeks earlier the Israeli media had been covering the Bazoft affair in depth. While censorship by the Israeli authorities against the Palestinian press – in Arabic, English, French or Hebrew – is even more strict than that which Saudi Arabia imposes on its own newspapers (Palestinian papers on the West Bank and in Jerusalem and Gaza are not allowed to reprint or repeat material published in Israeli papers except as the military administration sees fit), nevertheless the Israeli media are encouraged to appear as liberal as their Western counterparts. This is part of Israel's public relations exercise with the West. In the coverage of the Bazoft affair, Israeli journalists expressed their concern over the plight of their Iranian-born colleague, but more emphasis was placed on Saddam's arsenal of chemical weapons and missiles. This triggered a debate on Israeli television and in the newspapers. One option which was openly discussed was that of destroying Iraq's chemical capability, just as in June 1981 Israeli aircraft had bombed the Iraqi nuclear reactor at Al-Tuwaitha.

It was this talk of attacking Iraqi targets which prompted Saddam Hussein's speech on 2nd April – 'Whoever threatens us with the atomic bomb, we will annihilate him' – to members of the armed forces, during which he also openly mourned the murder of his friend Gerald Bull, the Canadian inventor of 'Project Babylon'. He cited the uproar in the West over the krytron capacitors as both part of a Western Zionist plot to bar Iraq from achieving the technology it needed to defend itself, whilst Israel already had atomic weapons, and 'a screen provided by the West for Israel to attack us'. He denied that he was building a bomb: 'Why should we need an atomic bomb?' he asked. 'Don't they know that we have "Al-kimawi al Muzdawaj" [the binary chemical weapon] to cause fire to devour half of Israel if Israel, which has atomic bombs, dared attack Iraq?' In reports of the Iraqi leader's speech, that crucial conditional clause was usually omitted by the Israelis, and by the Americans, who issued stiff warnings to Saddam Hussein. At the time, Saddam was in fact far more frightened by Israel than Israel was by him. He knew that the Israelis possessed nuclear warheads and delivery systems and understood that they would not hesitate to use them; what he was trying to do was use the threat of Israel to unite the Arabs under his leadership.

The millions of dollars that the Iraqi Ministry of Information had invested in Arab journalists and in the Arab press began to pay dividends. A huge campaign in large sections of the Arab media – 'Minal Muhett illa Alkhaleej' ('from the Atlantic to the Gulf') – was now in full swing. It supported Saddam Hussein and warned against imperialist-sponsored Zionist aggression against Iraq which would deprive the Arab people of the chance that at last loomed, of reaching military parity with Israel, an opportunity resulting solely from the efforts of the leader Saddam Hussein. The Iraqi, Libyan and Saudi Arabian press in Europe combined their pro-Saddam Arab leadership campaign with an attack on British hypocrisy. Many editorials quoted Margaret Thatcher's statement, 'Nuclear weapons kept the peace for forty years in Europe', and asked why the same was not applicable to the Middle East.

Politicians from many Arab countries went out of their way to condemn what they called 'the Western propaganda campaign' against Baghdad. Amongst the loudest voices of the politicians and media defending Saddam and condemning the Western media campaign were those of the Kuwaitis. It was one of the more craven examples of Arabs toeing Saddam Hussein's line, reinforcing his belief in his own importance.

However, the most encouraging signals for Saddam came from Washington, which reinforced his misconception that the American government's objective was to improve relations with Iraq at any price. Not only were the excesses of his regime ignored, but the administration also argued strongly against efforts by Congress to limit American help for Iraq because of its treatment of the Kurds and other minorities. That led him to believe that the Americans would make the US media kowtow to their authority in the manner of Arab regimes.

When Saddam was angered by a Voice of America broadcast comparing him to deposed Romanian leader Nicolai Ceauşescu, he raised the matter with American officials, saying it would spoil relations with Iraq. As a result he received a written apology. Under-Secretary John Kelly complained to Secretary of State James Baker that those 'democracy pushers' in Voice of America were undermining his efforts to court Saddam Hussein into the Western camp, and demanded they be muzzled. Baker agreed and instructed the United States Information Service, which had produced the editorial, to obtain clearance on its editorials in future from the State Department. Six weeks later, in Iraq, Saddam held talks with five senators, which were widely celebrated by the Arab press. Once again the Iraqi leader complained about the offending broadcast and an article in the *Washington Post*. Senator Bob Dole of Kansas replied that the American media fed on themselves and repeated what they considered to be a fashionable story at the time. Senator Dole ingratiatingly, if inaccurately, assured Saddam Hussein that the person responsible for the offending article had been fired.

This episode gave Saddam the impression that Washington was supporting him as the guardian of their interests in the Gulf. He interpreted it as a green light to continue forcing his policies on his neighbours so long as American interests seemed better served under his guardianship.

On the countdown to the strike against Kuwait, tension had also been building up in Egypt after the arrival at Cairo airport of the bodies of hundreds of Egyptians who had been working in Iraq. They bore the marks of bullet wounds and other evidence of death by violence. President Mubarak was coming under pressure to take action. Again, this was a deliberate Iraqi policy to destabilise the Egyptian government which, from the point of view of the radical camp which Saddam aspired to lead, was identified with the West and had relations with Israel. It was also to blame, according to the Palestinians, for the failure of PLO chairman Yasser Arafat's moderation which ultimately had achieved nothing with Israel.

Saddam was still not sure about reactions from Iran to his next initiative, and needed to allow himself room for a sudden but decisive U-turn if he was to grant concessions and make peace with Iran. Two weeks after his Army Day speech against Israel, which made him the target of an attack by the 'Zionist media', he sent a private letter to Iran's president Ali Akbar Hashimi Rafsanjani, offering to return to Iran some unspecified territories and to exchange prisoners-of-war as a first step along the road of settling the 'unfortunate conflict between the two sisterly Muslim nations'. The Egyptian, Omani and Saudi intelligence services knew of the letter immediately, whilst those in the West were informed of it a few weeks later. They all differed in their interpretations of it but agreed that Saddam Hussein was obviously anxious to settle differences with Iran before he opened another front somewhere else. Egypt accordingly quickened the pace of its rapprochement with Saddam's bitter rivals in Damascus.

Another report presented to the US State Department indicated that Baghdad had placed orders for American wheat and essential commodities in quantities that exceeded the usual requirements for its population.

The Israelis sent urgent messages to the Americans, warning that they would be next on Saddam's list – especially when he called for an Arab summit in Baghdad after requests from Yasser Arafat to discuss the immigration of thousands of Soviet Jews arriving on land in the occupied territories.

When the Arab summit finally got under way in late May 1990, not all the Arab leaders were happy about Saddam Hussein raising tension with the West. King Fahd, King Hassan of Morocco and Oman's Sultan Qaboos stayed away, sending deputies instead, whilst President Hafez al-Assad of Syria boycotted the summit. President Mubarak tried in vain to persuade Assad to go with him to Baghdad in order to present a united front on the issue of Jewish immigration to Israel from the Soviet Union. According to sources close to Damascus, President Assad replied, 'If I wasn't one hundred per cent sure that Saddam's summit has nothing to do with the Palestinian issue, I would come with you even if I had to go on foot. But Saddam has other plans, none of them in the interests of the Arabs.'

During the summit, Saddam delivered a fiery speech as he repeated earlier calls for the Arabs to liberate Jerusalem. He called for the liberation of the Palestinian people from the slavery which American military and economic backing for Israel was imposing on them. In the closed sessions, however, Saddam pressed ahead with his cash demands and this time accused the Kuwaitis and the United Arab Emirates of undermining the Iraqi economy by overproduction of oil. 'We cannot tolerate this type of economic warfare that is waged against Iraq,' he thundered. He wanted some $27 billion from the Kuwaitis for oil which he claimed had been pumped from the Iraqi section of the disputed Rumailah oil field, accusing the Kuwaitis of having drilled diagonally. He declared that the money would also compensate for the loss of revenue Iraq had suffered as a result of Kuwait's overproduction.

The Kuwaitis seemed unprepared to confront Saddam's outburst. They replied that they did not have such funds available at that time, thinking that they could outwit Saddam Hussein in negotiation. However, they had misinterpreted the Iraqi dictator's real intentions. While both Western and Arab miscalculations led to the crisis, the Kuwaitis' mistakes cost them their country. Despite their wiliness and their reputation as the most sophisticated of the Gulf States in foreign policy, the Kuwaitis, like other Arabs, could not bring themselves to believe that there would be actual military aggression which would turn them into the Palestinians of the 1990s. The result was that they misread all the signals given by Saddam Hussein in the month before the invasion.

11 · The Sword of Damocles

'Stop thief!' shouted the wolf at the little lamb. 'Eating the food of my cubs! I will tear you to pieces!'

'That's impossible. I only eat grass, sir,' replied the lamb as he moved quickly to the stream.

'You're polluting the water I drink!' protested the wolf loudly.

'That's impossible. I'm downstream from you, sir,' replied the lamb, trembling.

'I am talking about last year,' said the wolf as he came closer to the lamb.

'That's impossible. I wasn't even born last year, sir.'

'It must be your father, the spitting image of you,' said the wolf as he pounced on the lamb, 'but there is no time to look for him right now.'

from the classical Arabic beast-fables book
Kallila wa Dimnah

Since early 1990, the Iraqis had been pushing for the price of oil to go up. Their anger was boiling over, but it was not until July that the affair spilled out into the open. Kuwait had given Saddam Hussein the excuse to make his move by going its own way in mending fences with Iran in 1989, an aim which had always been on Kuwait's agenda. During a meeting in November 1987 in Kuwait, two weeks after the Iranians fired a Silkworm missile from the Fao Peninsula and destroyed a platform in the Al-Ahmadi oil terminal, Kuwait's foreign minister, Sheikh Sabah al-Ahmad, dismissed the incident as irrelevant in the long history between neighbours who would have to live together and improve relations once the crisis was over. There were further signs in the months leading up to the 1990 invasion that Kuwait was continuing its old policy of playing one of its giant neighbours off against the other.

Iraq had been calling for a summit meeting of oil-producing countries to force an increase in the price. However, it was agreed to hold a Gulf oil ministerial meeting in Jeddah before the Geneva OPEC meeting at the end of July 1990. However, the events during the Baghdad Arab summit in May had proved revelatory, the deep divisions in the Arab family being plain for all to see.

A month later the Iraqis sent their deputy prime minister, Sa'doun Hammadi, one of Saddam's most trusted envoys and a member of the Ba'ath party regional command, to Kuwait and other small Gulf states to prepare for a joint Arab policy after the price of oil dropped from $18 to $14 a barrel. Iraq's idea was that all members should reduce production in order to push the prices up. However, Hammadi had another message to present to the sheikhs: Iraqi children were hungry while others lived in luxury, protected by Iraq's giving 'streams of blood' (or, as Saddam was to tell the American ambassador later, 'in a war to stop the Khomeini flood while the Americans themselves couldn't stop them'). Hammadi also presented each Gulf state with a demand for $10 billion to help Iraq to rebuild its economy after the war with Iran, which Hammadi said was 'in defence of the eastern wing of the Arab nation'.

The fact that Saddam had started the war himself was ignored, the large sums of money previously donated by the Gulf rulers conveniently forgotten. Saddam Hussein had already decided to force Iraq's creditors to drop their claims. Some, like the Saudis, did so. In Kuwait, Sa'doun Hammadi presented a long list of Kuwaiti assets and many bank accounts all over the world, indicating that Saddam Hussein possessed full details of them and that the emirate had sufficient funds to be able to afford this 'small contribution' to Baghdad's coffers. However, the Kuwaitis infuriated Saddam by offering Hammadi the insulting sum of $500 million, to be paid over three years.

It was a major blunder by the Kuwaitis. As the oil-producing Arab Gulf states made many excuses not to hold a summit, a meeting on a lower level was convened. On 10th July, oil ministers met in Jeddah to discuss the Iraqi demands. Oil is one of those commodities which encourage strange alliances and Iran had already joined Iraq in protesting that the UAE and Kuwait had violated oil quotas by producing too much and lowering the price. With mighty Saudi Arabia joining the chorus of disapproval, the two violators of OPEC policy agreed to cut their production levels.

This was a major economic loss to Kuwait. Its oil policy, devised by the emirate's oil minister Sheikh Ali Khalifah, was coherent and well thought out. The logic behind their policy was simple, but economically far more advanced than the policies of its neighbours. Kuwait is no longer a traditional Third World oil producer and it has invested its vast oil wealth in the down-stream oil economy worldwide: refineries, petro-chemical industries and a large chain of filling stations. To maximise the profits in overseas activities, which at the time of the invasion were earning Kuwait more than oil did at home, it needed to maximise production of crude oil. It earned higher revenues for itself by expanding its market share than by raising prices; there was no point in Kuwait having to pay dearly for crude for its ancillary industries. So Kuwait was producing four hundred thousand barrels per day more than its quota of one and a half million.

For the United Arab Emirates, the story was different. Behind a façade of modern buildings and an imitation of Western lifestyle, they remain a classic Third World oil producer, substituting the loss in revenue from the drop in oil price by increasing production, and motivated by tribal rivalry as much as anything else. The two main producers, Abu Dhabi and Dubai, each wanted to maximise cash flow in order to outdo the other in road and building construction, together with some development projects, as they competed for leadership of the loose federation of seven emirates. Thus the UAE was producing a staggering 1.1 million barrels per day more than its OPEC quota permitted.

Iraq would not accept the logic behind the Kuwaiti oil policy. Investing money in the West, from the Ba'athist point of view, was betraying the Arab nation. For Saddam, who is ultra-xenophobic and often sees himself as the target of foreign conspiracies, the activities of Kuwait and the UAE were proof of his suspicions.

When oil ministers met in Jeddah on 10th July and the Saudis joined Iraq in pressurising Kuwait and the UAE to cut production, the Iraqis listened carefully to what Saudi oil minister Hisham al-Nazzer was saying. On the previous night, the Iraqi Mukhabarat had managed to tap King Fahd's telephone conversation with the Emir of Qatar, Sheikh Khalifah al-Thani, and concluded from the transcript that Saudi Arabia, traditionally the most influential OPEC member, was conspiring to arrange a common bloc of Gulf oil producers against Iraq. The Iraqis saw this as Fahd and al-Thani drawing the Gulf producers together, preparing to deflect Iraqi anger the following day whilst in the long term preparing a pro-American policy.

The fact that the transcript also proved that Saudi fears about another war in the region were genuine was overlooked when Saddam Hussein's propaganda later presented the Iraqi people with the proof of the Saudis' treason.

King Fahd began the conversation with the usual Arabic greetings, wishing Allah's blessing upon al-Thani's health and upon his household. Then came the Arabic phrase widely used when someone is fed up: '*Kefayiah, bellah kefayiah* . . . We have had enough. Israel threatens Iraq and now Iraq threatens Israel. Now we're back to the story of Abd al-Nasser before 1967. We want to think the matter over. May Allah's blessing be upon you, may Allah preserve you.'

AL-THANI: '*Allah yehfazhak* [protect you]. I shall always be with you.'

KING FAHD: '*Allah yebarik feek* [bless you]. I wanted to tell you that I instructed Hisham [Nazzer, Saudi Arabia's oil minister] to inform his brothers [the other ministers] not to pay attention to what the Iraqi minister said. Iraq is in trouble. There's a sensitive situation between Iraq and Israel. Every day we are worried by something. The Iraqi minister said some meaningless words. The important thing is we put everything in order during these two months, especially when things become quiet, and we follow a defensive stand. Two months are left to us. As Gulf states, we shall meet and organise matters. The same applies to Iraq. The Iraqis have lost their temper. Now they are saying all kinds of things. And you know that when someone loses his temper his words become unreasonable.'

AL-THANI: 'True, by Allah what they say is unreasonable.'

KING FAHD: 'We don't want that.'

AL-THANI: 'I am sure it is unreasonable.'

KING FAHD: 'We don't want problems with Israel. We don't want problems with Iran.'

AL-THANI: 'True, by Allah.'

KING FAHD: 'But we are envied as Gulf states. Yet where were those who now envy us when we were poor? They did not say, "Our brothers have nothing."'

AL-THANI: 'No, they did not.'

KING FAHD: 'And when we became rich we did not stop helping them.'

AL-THANI: 'They know us only when we have something. Otherwise, they did not know us.'

KING FAHD: 'When we were poor, riding donkeys and finding difficulties in coming across a date, by Allah, a date we couldn't find, no one asked about us. And since we became rich we have not stopped helping them.'

AL-THANI: 'Allah bless you.'

KING FAHD: 'All I want to do is stop the bad temper. When things become quiet it will be easy to talk to Iraq. Saddam thinks highly of you. All we must do is to stop this bad temper. I told my minister to meet their minister in Iraq tomorrow. Before you meet with Iraqis, all of you must agree as Gulf ministers. Keep quiet even if the Iraqi minister says something bad.

These people [the Iraqis] have got themselves into a problem with Israel, but they have nothing to do with Israel. Seven hundred kilometres separate them from Israel. The matters must be dealt with wisely.'

AL-THANI: 'By Allah what you say is true.'

KING FAHD: 'And our brothers in Iraq have put themselves into a maze.'

AL-THANI: 'True, by Allah.'

KING FAHD: 'They have given themselves the same problems as Abd al-Nasser, and he could not solve them. How can we fight the whole world? By Allah, between us, I think the Palestinians have pushed matters too far. They are losing nothing.'

AL-THANI: 'True.'

KING FAHD: 'I hope Abu Ammar [PLO Chairman Yasser Arafat] will be reasonable. I told our Palestinian brothers, we will do our best so that we might not lose the West Bank and Gaza. I don't want to see the West Bank and Gaza lost by sheer words.'

AL-THANI: 'That's disastrous.'

KING FAHD: 'One must be reasonable and think carefully. Look at the Soviet Union. Who ever thought the Soviet Union would reach such an agreement with America?'

King Fahd then suggested the Iraqis were calling the conference for a time when the ruler of Qatar would be away. 'As a principle, if they had that idea, I said it can't be. Let oil ministers first meet and discuss with each other. It will be better if ministers of oil, foreign affairs and finance meet in every country to discuss all the political, financial, social and petroleum aspects.'

AL-THANI: 'True.'

KING FAHD: 'At that time you might think of a summit meeting. But don't think of holding a summit if there's a chance of failure.'

AL-THANI: 'And Kuwait?'

KING FAHD: 'Probably our Iraqi brothers will agree to dismiss the idea of a summit meeting.'

AL-THANI: '*Alhamdulellah* [Allah be praised].'

KING FAHD: 'It's easy to start a conflict but it is very difficult to stop it. Israel is our number one nightmare. It has two hundred nuclear warheads and forty-seven atom bombs. Its people are mad. All our Palestinian brothers have to do is to do their best and we will help them. They have got to put their hand on the West Bank and Gaza. They don't have to go to the extreme. In that case Israel would make them real colonies.'

AL-THANI: 'We have to gain one position after another.'

The two leaders then exchanged further courtesies until the end of the tape.

It was not exactly a conspiracy to deliver OPEC to the hands of America and Palestine to the Zionists, as the Radio Baghdad commentator maintained in the programme which made the tape public: 'An Arab king in a conversation with his conspirator brother, another Arab ruler; they were both conspiring against the Arab people of Iraq.'

Despite the paranoia of the *nouveaux riches* that they are only liked for their money, Fahd was, naïve as he sounded, genuinely concerned about what he might do to help the Palestinians hold on to something of the little that was left of their homeland. There was a tinge of panic in his voice which occasionally hit a very high pitch as he seemed to hint at buying time rather than becoming caught up in financing another war initiated by Saddam Hussein.

The Iraqis were right about one thing. There was a conspiracy initiated by King Fahd: persuading al-Thani to use his absence as an excuse not to go ahead with a summit meeting for Gulf oil producers. In Iraqi eyes that meeting could turn into a trial for the accused – Sheikh Jaber of Kuwait and Sheikh Zaid bin Sultan of the UAE. They believed the Saudi strategy was, by using the Emir of Qatar's absence from the region to postpone the meeting, to let Kuwait and the UAE get away with a policy that, according to their figures, would cost the Iraqi treasury about $6 billion a year. This figure was increased to $14 billion in a speech by Saddam Hussein a week later. Reducing the meeting from summit level to ministerial level was also preventing Saddam from bullying the Kuwaitis and the UAE into making a firm commitment to paying what he wanted.

From Saddam Hussein's point of view, it was an insult to suggest his bad temper and uncontrolled speech would lead to Israeli gains. In addition, he feared the spread of the idea that he was seven hundred kilometres (450 miles) away from Israel and thus could only fight the Israelis with words rather than deeds. Such talk had made Fahd a 'traitor' indeed. For Saddam it was also the proof that the smaller Gulf States were not as independent as they claimed to be, that they were given instructions by the Saudi king. In fact Saddam Hussein in his search for a solution after his invasion of Kuwait, ignored the Gulf States and sought direct talks with King Fahd. This he made clear during a meeting with Yasser Arafat and King Hussein in Baghdad on 4th December 1990, after the United Nations Security Council specified 15th January as the deadline to withdraw from Kuwait.

Fahd and al-Tahni's conversation made Saddam fear a united front by the Gulf States against his interests. If they were suddenly to increase oil production and reduce the price by $10 a barrel, it would cost him $10 billion in lost revenue.

Still the Iraqis said nothing, but when the UAE and Kuwait agreed under Saudi pressure to cut production without going into lengthy discussion to sort out a long-term plan as expected it became obvious to the Iraqis that a Fahd–Khalifah plot was being implemented to keep them quiet, after which matters would carry on as before. Saddam Hussein told the American ambassador two weeks later that he possessed intelligence reports that 'America's friends' had deliberately avoided a summit meeting and were just paying lip-service to the agreement to restrict production, whilst in reality planning for their oil policy to return to its previous status after two months.

A day later, the Iranian foreign minister, Ali Akbar Velayati, called in at Kuwait on his way home from acrimonious talks with his Iraqi counterpart in Geneva. It was a bad portent for Iraq, which feared that Kuwait might be seeking Iranian protection as it became increasingly worried by Iraqi criticism and the spate of demands from Baghdad.

As Iraq's national day, 17th July, approached, clouds were gathering over the Gulf. Saddam wanted to make his speech the start of a new crusade. A signal was to go to Britain that the period of heightened tension was over. The British nurse Daphne Parish was released, thanks to mediation by Saddam Hussein's friend, President Kenneth Kaunda of Zambia. During his press conference, President Kaunda accused British journalists of causing the death of their colleague Farzad Bazoft by 'angering Saddam Hussein and launching an unfair campaign against him'.

While the British media were focusing on the Parish–Kaunda press conference at Lusaka and the subsequent jamboree at Gatwick Airport on Daphne Parish's arrival in Britain, another unusual event took place in Tunis. On 15th and 16th July, there was a meeting of foreign ministers of the Arab League, at the request of the PLO, to discuss the increasing number of Soviet Jews arriving in Israel and the failure of American attempts to stop Israel housing them in the occupied West Bank and East Jerusalem. Up until then, all quarrels inside the Arab family had been fought behind closed doors. However, as one Arab nationalist wrote in a

Muslim paper, all the old rules had been broken over the past decade or so, when 'infidels and old colonialists were called in to solve our problems'.

Egypt had made peace with Israel whilst Iraq fought its Muslim neighbour Iran. As a result, Iranians closed down the Israeli embassy in Tehran and hoisted the Palestinian flag over it instead. Arab Syria sided with Persian Iran against Arab Iraq whilst the custodians of Mecca called upon infidels to help in evicting the occupiers of Alka'bah, the holiest of all Muslim shrines where an argument in a loud voice, let alone a shooting, is considered to be a mortal sin.

As the old order collapsed, Saddam had made the decision to become the Patriarch of the Arab family, by force if necessary. However, it was also characteristic of him, the head of the Takriti Mafia, to want retribution for the blood of the members of the family who had protected the rich. Those who were starving the people by forcing down oil prices must be punished.

While Arab foreign ministers gathered in Tunis, Saddam's arch-rival, Syria's president Hafez al-Assad, was in Alexandria with President Mubarak, the snub being yet another insult to Baghdad. The Iraqi foreign minister Tariq Aziz, a tough and committed Ba'athist, did not beat about the bush or use mediators in accordance with the normal customs of Arab politics. In his speech to the foreign ministers in Tunis he said, 'We are sure some Arab states are involved in a conspiracy against us. We want you to know that our country will not kneel, our women will not turn to prostitution and our children will not be deprived of food.'

Half an hour earlier, Tariq Aziz had sent a letter to Arab League Secretary-General Chadli Kleibi, in which he openly accused the Kuwaitis of 'stealing' $2.4 billion worth of oil by drilling into the three-mile area of the Rumailah oil field claimed by Iraq. The Kuwaitis, stunned by the unexpected attack and the unusually direct tone of the accusation, then received another warning that Iraq was no longer regarding ownership of the three-mile-long oil field as a commercial dispute and that it would be applying political pressure. Mighty Iraq, with its population of more than ten times that of Kuwait and its one-million-strong army, accused its tiny neighbour of aggression against it. The explanation given – and repeated a week later to the Americans – was that Kuwait had surprised Baghdad by moving the border posts, Customs and Immigration offices from their previous positions; the Kuwaitis noted that both were still in Kuwaiti territory, and replied that if they had been moved, then it was for administrative and practical reasons imposed by the flow of traffic.

At the risk of even further aggression, the Kuwaitis did not back down but responded with a show of defiance. They countered by accusing the Iraqis of 'stealing' oil from Kuwaiti wells, adding that they would not be fooled by Iraq's over-reaction – it was merely an attempt to intimidate creditors to write off Iraqi debts. The Kuwaitis' reply intimated that they had no intention of following in the Saudis' footsteps and writing off the debts owed to them by Baghdad.

Infuriated by such a tiny neighbour daring to defy the 'leader of the Arab nation which broke the might of Iran', Saddam Hussein declared a day later that the campaign against Kuwait was a national policy. He chose 17th July, the twenty-second anniversary of the Ba'ath party's accession to power, on which to make a fierce attack against the Gulf States in a televised speech that was seen in many Gulf countries. 'They are trying to undermine Iraq after its military triumph,' he accused the Gulf leaders. 'Instead of rewarding Iraq, which sacrificed the blossoms of its youth in the war to protect their houses of wealth, they are severely harming it.' Overproduction of oil was 'an evil act against Iraq'. Then he directed his anger against Kuwait and the UAE because it was their practice of overproduction which had pushed the price down to $14 a barrel. He described this as 'an American plot to deplete Iraq's oil revenues', and said Iraq's lost revenues were 'usurped rights'. Then he threatened stronger action to come: 'Raising our voices against the evil is not the final resort if the evil continues . . . there should be some effective act to restore things to their correct position.' Saddam used an old Iraqi saying, that 'cutting necks is better than cutting the means of living'.

The angry speech coming from a brutal dictator who knew all about 'cutting necks' sent tremors through the Gulf leaders, and confusing signals that alarmed Western capitals. Iraqi foreign minister Tariq Aziz maintained the pressure by giving more interviews and using words like 'Kuwaiti violation' of Iraqi territories. It was a reminder that the border dispute would soon be put next to the oil quota on the political agenda again.

The ones who trembled most were the Kuwaitis. The next day, the Kuwaiti prime minister, Sheikh Sa'ad al-Abdallah, called the newly elected fifty-member Kuwaiti National Council into a closed session. As Kuwait's foreign minister Sheikh Sabah al-Ahmad rushed to Riyadh on 18th July to persuade King Fahd to intervene in the dispute, Iraq, although not spelling it out, hinted that the crisis could be defused if Kuwait were to reach an agreement on oil quotas and pay the money demanded by Baghdad. Tariq Aziz spoke to reporters of his country's 'sincere efforts to continue brotherly dialogue', but he also hinted that things could become dangerous for the Kuwaitis if they did not accede to

Iraq's demands. Aziz condemned Kuwait's refusal to stick to the OPEC quota as 'short-sighted, selfish and dangerous'.

A cabinet meeting was convened in Kuwait to respond to Arab League Secretary-General Chadli Kleibi's memorandum containing Tariq Aziz's letter of 16th July, in which the latter accused Kuwait of stealing $2.4 billion worth of oil from the Rumailah oilfield. The ministers were unprepared and confused about Saddam's real objectives, having turned down his demand to write off the war debts and to give an extra $10 billion in aid. Each tried to guess from his own narrow experience what Saddam's motives really were. There were suggestions from Kuwait's friends in London and Washington that Iraq was making noises to force the price of oil up before an OPEC meeting in Geneva just over a week later.

This analysis was not accepted. However, Sheikh Ali Khalifah, who was by now finance minister, declared that Iraq was trying to salvage its economy and was blaming the Gulf States for its own economic failures. 'Iraq's tone will not change, even after Geneva. Iraq is going to continue escalating the level of confrontation,' he predicted. He proposed involving the other six Gulf States by stating that a solution should be sought through the Gulf Co-operation Council. Sheikh Salem al-Sabah, the interior minister, then asked whether other Arab states had supported Iraqi claims against Kuwait. He was the minister in charge of the police force which throughout 1989 and 1990 suppressed demonstrations by pro-democracy activists seeking restoration of the parliament suspended by the emir, Sheikh Jaber, and was the first to suggest that Iraq may have profited from the political turmoil which preceded the elections to the interim national assembly on 10th June, although this was not what the pro-democracy activists had in mind.

Sheikh Nawaf al-Sabah made no suggestions as to how to solve the crisis, but accused Iraq of pushing its military installations and agricultural areas across the frontier. At this point Mr Abd al-Rahman al-Awadi, the Minister of State for Cabinet Affairs, returned to the view that Iraq was attempting to extort money. 'We must keep cool. The Iraqis are going too far and we need to move very quickly to find a political solution to the crisis.' Foreign Minister Sheikh Sabah al-Ahmad, the most senior member, was the first to draw attention to the explosive nature of the border issue which made 'Iraqi aggression a real possibility'. He suggested starting 'intensive diplomatic contacts with GCC [Gulf Co-operation Council] countries' and asking GCC Secretary-General Sheikh Abdallah Bishara to contact 'our brothers in the GCC'. He also proposed sounding out Egypt and Jordan, whilst correctly predicting that Libya and Algeria might take Iraq's side.

Another accurate prediction was made by Justice Minister Dhari al-Othman who concluded that the oil price issue raised by Iraq was a pretext for something else. He feared that Iraq would not pay attention to Arab mediation but would proceed with its plans, illustrating his point by using the famous tale from *Kallila wa Dimnah* the tenth-century Arab book of fables of beasts' wisdom quoted at the beginning of this chapter. 'Iraq and Kuwait are just like the wolf and the lamb.' Two more ministers, Abd al-Wahab al-Fawzan, the Health Minister, and Fahd al-Hisawy, Minister of State for Municipal Affairs, agreed with him. They urged a quick response to the crisis, saying that Iraq might act before it talked and that Kuwait must be prepared for 'a military threat'.

Mr Salman al-Mutawa, Minister of Planning, was among those who misjudged the gravity of the situation. He declared that the Iraqi memorandum was weak and easily answered. Prime Minister Sheikh Sa'ad al-Abdallah agreed with the possibility of the Iraqis taking military measures. However, he predicted a limited operation to seize land in the border areas of Ritqa and Qasr, and urged the Ministries of Defence and the Interior to be on the alert. After the meeting the Kuwaitis cancelled military leave and raised the state of alertness of its minute armed forces.

The prime minister discussed the history of the border dispute and did not rule out the idea of leasing Bubiyan and Warbah Islands to Iraq after getting an agreement from the GCC. The cabinet began to calculate Iraq's total debts and a figure of $35 billion was mentioned as being owed to both Kuwait and Saudi Arabia; there was no accurate figure on how much Iraq owed Kuwait alone, but $13.5 billion was mentioned. Then followed a discussion of the possibility of writing off the debts: a number of ministers said they should be kept on the books and no decision was made.

Sheikh al-Sabah's visit to Riyadh was the signal for the start of frantic Arab diplomacy to avert a crisis. Meanwhile, Saddam Hussein kept turning the screw. By 21st July, intelligence sources had reported the movement of 30,000 Iraqi troops to the borders with Kuwait. However, William Webster, America's Director of Central Intelligence, did not see invasion as an imminent danger; it was 'just sabre-rattling to push the price of oil up and achieve other demands put forward by the Iraqis'.

The US State Department clearly restated its policy for the region: 'We remain determined to defend the principle of freedom of navigation and to ensure the free flow of oil through the Strait of Hormuz,' said spokeswoman Margaret Tutwiler on record. However, that was the beginning of a series of unclear signals. By omission, it could be interpreted that America, now importing more than half of its oil and receiving from the Gulf three times as much as it had a decade earlier, was more committed to the flow of oil than to upholding the principles of international law. Also, there was no specific message or signal given to Baghdad of a possible response to an assault on Kuwait, since the statement was a formulation used repeatedly during the Iran–Iraq War to warn Iran against attacking Arab tankers when American warships were sent to escort Kuwaiti tankers in 1987.

Meanwhile, the Egyptian intelligence service reported that more Iraqi troops were preparing to move south: 'Between six and eight armoured divisions as well as the same number of mechanised divisions began routine preparation for action,' a report said. In Cairo, President Mubarak had to cut short talks he was holding with a number of Arab foreign ministers, in preparation for an Arab summit that he was due to host in November 1990, and fly to Baghdad.

President Mubarak subsequently informed the Kuwaitis that Saddam Hussein had assured him that he was not going to invade Kuwait. Mubarak relayed the same message to both King Fahd and President Bush. The Iraqis were to deny later that they gave such assurances.

Two hours after the Egyptian leader had left Baghdad to visit Kuwait and Saudi Arabia, Iraqi Foreign Minister Tariq Aziz repeated his earlier criticism of Kuwait and the United Arab Emirates. The US State Department, realising the ambiguity of their earlier statement, repeated it with a clearer commitment: 'We also remain strongly committed to supporting the individual and collective self-defence of our friends in the Gulf, with whom we have deep and long-standing ties.' However, in her replies to reporters, Margaret Tutwiler clearly ruled out any American commitment to defending Kuwait if Saddam decided to take military action: 'We do not have any defence treaties with Kuwait and there are no defence or special security commitments to Kuwait.'

So what kind of response were the Iraqis led to expect as their troops continued to mass on the border with Kuwait? To underline this 'vague commitment', Washington quickly arranged a show of strength on 24th July by deploying six combat vessels on a joint military exercise with the United Arab Emirates, the first ever, and sending warships to patrol the northern Gulf. Still there was no specific warning given to Iraq and no American naval vessels were deployed to Kuwaiti waters.

There were reports from the CIA of more troop movements, whilst spy satellites presented the National Security Council with evidence of armoured columns moving on the Basra–Zubair road towards the borders with Kuwait. Cairo and Riyadh received intelligence reports of armoured brigades from the élite Republican Guards moving from the central sector south towards Basra as the number of Iraqi troops on the border trebled. President Bush gave another unclear warning: 'There is no place for coercion and intimidation in a civilised world.' 'Not even a hint of a new arms deal with Kuwait came from Washington,' said one Arab diplomat later, adding that the least President Bush could have done was to contact Mikhail Gorbachev in Moscow and ask him to restrain Saddam Hussein.

However, the view held by politicians in many capitals of the world, including Washington – although it was not a view shared by intelligence chiefs – was that Saddam was getting more aggressive than usual in bullying Kuwait on the eve of the Geneva OPEC meeting: after all, oil prices kept on creeping up with the news of more deployment of troops.

The State Department, it seems, had deluded itself into believing that it had defused the crisis by sending warships to the UAE coast, whilst considering that the world could live with another temporary increase in the price of oil. Unlike the 1961 border crisis, when the British Foreign Office instructed Ambassador Sir Humphrey Trevelyan to seek clarification from the Iraqis and to give them an unequivocal warning, the State Department did not give any clear instructions to April Glaspie. As Saddam was weighing the costs and estimating the political expediency of his next move, he wanted to know the American position. He summoned April Glaspie for a meeting at 1 p.m. on 25th July 1990, just one day before the OPEC meeting was due to take place in Geneva.

The Iraqi president told Mrs Glaspie that he wanted to hold a comprehensive political discussion with her which would form a message that was to be taken to President Bush. He raised several points at the meeting. First, he explained his urgent need for money, but the figure he mentioned excluded some $35 billion owed to Saudi Arabia and Kuwait as well as over $3 billion owed to Egypt. 'Iraq came out of the war burdened with $40 million debts, excluding the aid given by Arab states, some of whom consider that too to be a debt. Although they knew – and you knew, too – that without Iraq they would not have had these sums and the future of the region would have been entirely different.' He then explained that he considered the Kuwaiti and UAE oil policies to be acts of economic aggression: 'When planned and deliberate policy forces the price of oil down without good commercial reasons, then that means another war against Iraq, because military war kills people by bleeding them, while economic war kills their humanity by depriving them of their chance to have a good standard of living.' He went on to differentiate between his people and the oil-rich Arabs of the Gulf: 'People who live in luxury and economic security can reach an understanding with the United States on what are legitimate joint interests. But the starved and the economically deprived cannot reach the same understanding.'

Saddam Hussein told Mrs Glaspie that American manoeuvres and State Department statements had encouraged the Kuwaitis and the UAE to 'disregard Iraqi rights'. 'I say to you clearly that Iraq's rights, which are mentioned in the memorandum [sent to Kuwait via the Arab League on 16th July], we will take one by one.' He clearly wanted an answer from the ambassador or a hint from Washington. 'The United States must have a better understanding of the situation and declare who it wants to have relations with and who its enemies are.'

As the president said he wanted to find a solution within an Arab framework, he hinted that the United States should advise the Kuwaitis to take care in their dealings with Iraq: 'We do not ask you to solve our problems. I said that our Arab problems will be solved amongst ourselves. But do not encourage anyone to take action which is greater than their status permits.' Thus, when April Glaspie told him towards the end of the meeting that 'We have no position on Arab–Arab disputes', Saddam Hussein interpreted this not as polite fence-sitting diplomacy but as American permission to do as he liked.

He then chose to warn the Americans by use of an analogy. After reminding the ambassador of the role that Iraq played to stop the 'Iranian Islamic flood', he gave her an account of the background of Iraqi relations with Iran, hinting at the possibility of enlisting their support against the United States if Washington became involved in moves against Iraq. 'In 1974, I met with Idriss, the son of Mullah Mustafa Barzani [the late Kurdish leader]. He sat in the same seat as you are sitting in now. He came asking me to postpone implementation of autonomy in Iraqi Kurdistan, which was agreed on 11th March 1970. My reply was: We are determined to fulfil our obligation. You also have to stick to your agreement. When I sensed that Barzani had evil intentions, I said to him: Give my regards to your father and tell him that Saddam Hussein says the following. I explained to him the balance of power with figures. I finished this conversation with the result summarised in one sentence: If we fight, we shall win. Do you know why? I explained all the reasons to him, plus one political reason – you [the Kurds in 1974] depended on our disagreement with the Shah of Iran [the Kurds were financed by Iran]. The price for the support of the Iranians in a conflict is their claim on half of the Shatt al-Arab waterway. If we could keep the whole of Iraq with the Shatt al-Arab, we will make no concessions. But if forced to choose between half of the Shatt al-Arab or the whole of Iraq, then we will give the Shatt al-Arab away, to keep the whole of Iraq in the shape we wish it to be.'

Although this might seem a clear enough hint about the similarity of the situations, Saddam gave more details on how far he was prepared to go in the process of repeating history. 'We hope that you are not going to push events to make us bear this wisdom in mind in our relations with Iran. After that [meeting with Barzani's son], we gave half of the Shatt al-Arab away [1975 Algeria agreement] and Barzani died and was buried outside Iraq and he lost his war.' He then paused, and began to speak slowly as he looked at the American ambassador, directing his speech at her: 'We hope we are not pushed into this. All that lies between relations with Iran is the Shatt al-Arab. When we are faced with a choice between Iraq living proudly and the Shatt al-Arab, then we will negotiate using the wisdom we spoke of in 1975. In the way Barzani lost his historic chance, others will lose their chance, too.'

As Mrs Glaspie sought clarification of the situation on the border, she assured Saddam Hussein that the priority of President Bush's administration was to improve relations with Iraq. 'As you know, he [President Bush] directed the United States administration to reject the suggestion of implementing trade sanctions,' she said to Saddam. When he joked that there was nothing left for Iraq to buy from the United States except wheat which, he was afraid, 'You will say we are going to make into gunpowder', the ambassador firmly replied, 'I have a direct instruction from the President to seek better relations with Iraq.' At this very moment, Iraqi armoured columns were pouring southwards in the direction of the Kuwaiti border.

Saddam Hussein cunningly manoeuvred her into repeating this assurance by asking: 'But how? We too have this desire. But matters are running contrary to this desire.' The ambassador indicated that the State Department was making sure that Saddam would not come under criticism from the American media: 'This is less likely to happen, the more we talk. For example, you mentioned the issue of the article published by the US Information Service and that was sad. And a formal apology was presented.' After apologising for another programme on ABC news, she gave Saddam further assurance: 'Mr President – not only do I want to say that President Bush wanted better and deeper relations with Iraq, but he also wants an Iraqi contribution to peace and prosperity in the Middle East. President Bush is an intelligent man. He is not going to declare an economic war against Iraq . . . It is true what you say that we do not want higher prices for oil. But I would ask you to examine the possibility of not charging too high a price for oil.'

She was given the opportunity to suggest what price the US might like to see as a result of the next day's OPEC meeting. At this point, Foreign Minister Tariq Aziz intervened in the conversation to say, 'Our policy opposes sudden jumps in oil prices.' Saddam Hussein added, 'Twenty-five dollars a barrel is not a high price.' Again the ambassador missed the chance to say what price the US would see as reasonable and instead she merely said, 'We have many Americans who would like to see the price go above twenty-five dollars because they come from oil-producing states.'

At another point during the interview, Saddam Hussein went into a detailed explanation of what he believed was a conspiracy to lower the oil price (at this time the Americans did not know that the Mukhabarat had listened to King Fahd's telephone conversation with the Emir of Qatar). Saddam simply said that he possessed some intelligence reports which stated that the Gulf States were only going to stick to the new oil policy for two months and no more.

The ambassador twice asked for clarification on the situation on the border. Saddam Hussein responded initially by giving a long speech containing details on the oil prices quarrel and the Jeddah oil ministers' meeting. The ambassador did not press hard for an assurance but asked for 'an assessment of the efforts made by your Arab brothers and whether they have achieved anything'. Saddam informed her that a meeting would be held in Jeddah between Iraqi and Kuwaiti delegations, after which Sheikh Sa'ad al-Abdallah, the Kuwaiti prime minister, would come to Baghdad for direct talks on 28th or 30th July. He repeated what he had told President Mubarak a day earlier: 'Assure the Kuwaitis and give them our word that we are not going to do anything until we meet with them.' But he added a conditional clause: 'When we meet and when we see that there is hope, then nothing will happen. But if we are unable to find a solution, then it will be natural that Iraq will not accept death, even though wisdom is above everything else. There you have good news.'

According to a report in the *Washington Post* on 20th October, President Bush sent a message to Saddam Hussein on 28th July, stressing once again United States commitment to its friends in the region. In his message Bush declared that the use of force to resolve Iraq's grievances against Kuwait was unacceptable and that the United States would 'support other friends in the region', a reference to Kuwait, Saudi Arabia and other moderate Arab states. However, like the earlier message given by April Glaspie, it also stressed the desire to improve relations with Iraq. President Bush's message failed to give Baghdad a specific warning about the consequences of military action against Kuwait, even though by then there were some nine divisions of troops massed on the Iraqi borders.

When the OPEC delegates led by the thirteen oil ministers gathered in the Sheraton Hotel in Geneva on 26th July, all their attention was on the Gulf. The unofficial gossip outside the conference concentrated on whether Saddam was bluffing or daring to challenge America and occupy part of Kuwait. As Saddam cast his shadow over the meeting, the Saudis, who usually made the running, kept an unprecedentedly low profile. When the previously unknown Iraqi minister, Issam al-shalabi, arrived at the conference, he set a target of $25 a barrel, $7 above the current price. This took many delegates by surprise – after all, there was a world glut of oil in the middle of a hot summer. Everyone looked to the Saudis, who traditionally argue for a 'reasonable' price. They have always maintained that oil producers have to import large quantities of products manufactured in oil-importing countries, therefore a reasonable price should reduce the imports bills paid for in hard currency.

At this historic OPEC meeting, yesterday's enemies saw eye to eye on oil prices. The Iranians and the Iraqis went out of their way to agree with one another over arguments affecting the price as they found allies from the four corners of the globe amongst people with whom they usually hardly exchanged a word. Venezuela became the leading producer to argue in favour of the status quo, while countries like Nigeria, in desperate need of maximum revenues, found themselves on the side of the Iraqis.

The next morning, when Iran suggested a compromise price of $23, Iraq reluctantly agreed. Nigeria and others abandoned any attempt to play a role and the Saudis stepped in to play their usual trump card: unless the ceiling price was set at $21, they would 'play with the tap' to achieve what they wanted. After the Kuwaiti, Iranian, Iraqi and Saudi ministers had held further talks, the whole of the OPEC delegation agreed to the price set by the Saudi minister, Hisham al-Nazzer, at $21. The Iraqis said they were happy with the outcome and had no intention of 'policing' the quotas. All the same, a second part of the agreement called for production to be limited to 22½ million barrels per day and no one doubted that if the usual quota-busters tried their tricks again they would be in trouble. There was also some small print compelling signatories to link any future increase in production to a rise in prices. Thus all was well that ended well: OPEC meetings seemed to be returning to the tradition of being gentlemanly affairs. Some of the oil producers jokingly suggested that such a crisis from time to time would be very beneficial for oil prices.

Meanwhile, in the heat of the desert thousands of miles away from the air-conditioned halls and muzak of the Geneva Sheraton, Iraqi troops were still massing. More contacts took place between Cairo, Kuwait City, Washington and Riyadh. President Mubarak, King Hussein, Prince Sa'ud (the Saudi foreign minister) and even PLO Chairman Yasser Arafat began another round of talks, visits, telephone calls and more meetings to contain the crisis.

On Saturday, 28th July, the Egyptian intelligence service placed a report on President Mubarak's desk which warned that an invasion of Kuwait was likely within a week. Mubarak had, or so he thought, received a personal assurance from Saddam four days earlier that there would be no invasion. He asked for another report. On the following day, 29th July, his intelligence service, with very good sources on the ground, prepared another, much longer and more detailed report which proved highly alarming to the Egyptian leader. 'Drivers who regularly cross the borders on the Basra–Kuwait highway reported long hold-ups because slow-moving columns of tanks, armoured personnel carriers and artillery were moving south – repeat – south . . . Army camps, tents and other field facilities began to appear near the crossing point . . . The same drivers report that the size of camps and number of troops have doubled as they spent two days in Kuwait and returned to Basra,' a crucial extract from this three-page report said. It was obvious that, far from moving away from the borders, Iraqi forces were moving towards them.

President Mubarak then went over, with a fine-tooth comb, the minutes of the talks he had held with Saddam in Baghdad in an effort to read between the lines.

Meanwhile in Washington satellite photographs showed more troops heading south towards the Kuwaiti border. On the night of 29th July, the CIA was preparing another report that the Iraqi forces drawn up on the border numbered some 100,000 troops, supported by three hundred battle tanks. The report concluded that invasion was 'probable'. On the afternoon of Saturday, 28th July, the State Department had received further information from an American oil expert who claimed that he had held a discussion with an Iraqi friend who told him: 'You will see by next week [that Iraq will be] protecting the people of Kuwait,' adding that American was 'a paper tiger that won't do anything'. State Department officials advised him not to be concerned; they were aware of all Iraqi actions.

Also on 28th July (Saturday is the start of the working week in the Arab world), whilst good news was coming from Geneva, there was another alarming signal from Baghdad. Iraq announced the postponement of talks with Kuwait which were to have taken place in Jeddah as a prelude to

Sheikh Sa'ad's visit and final talks in Baghdad. April Glaspie received a message from President Bush to be delivered to Saddam Hussein, but it was essentially a repetition of the statements which she had made previously. During that meeting on 25th July, Saddam had mentioned Saturday 28th or Monday 30th as the date Sheikh Sa'ad would come to Baghdad, after a meeting in Jeddah – but that meeting had been put off indefinitely, and did not in fact take place until the Tuesday. Had Glaspie looked into her notes of 25th July meeting, she would have realised that Saddam Hussein had said, 'Nothing will happen while there are talks' – but the talks had been postponed. The US State Department has refused to comment on what communications took place between them and the Iraqis on that Saturday. However, the Iraqis report that the embassy sent President Bush's message and that there were no further contacts with April Glaspie. She went on her annual period of leave on Monday, 30th July, as did the Soviet ambassador in Baghdad.

On the same day, the CIA presented another report. While most newspapers were beginning to question Saddam Hussein's real motives after the build-up of his troops, the *Washington Post* published a long article estimating the numbers of troops at over 100,000 and expressed grave concern. However, the report also quoted State Department officials who had stated that the Iraqis were bluffing. Meanwhile, politicians throughout the West had dismissed the warnings of their own intelligence chiefs. The view held by top officials in capitals like Washington and Cairo, as well as by a large contingent in the Foreign Office in London, was that Saddam was still sabre-rattling. They based their views on some of the following reasoning: Iraq had already used the threat of force to get a rise in oil price, but the increase had been only $3 a barrel (giving the Iraqi treasury an extra $3 billion); Iraq wanted more and was repeating the same tactic; it was logical for Saddam to extend the same threat on the eve of the Jeddah talks between Iraqi and Kuwaiti delegations. In fact, the State Department analysis suggested that Iraq's postponement of the talks for another three days lent support to this view, as it only served to make the Kuwaitis more anxious to give in to Iraqi demands.

As the Iraqis and Kuwaitis were arriving in Saudi Arabia, there were more warning signals from intelligence. The Egyptian Mukhabarat stated in a report dated 1st August that invasion was 'imminent', but did not give specific details of how far the Iraqi troops were prepared to go. The CIA continued to give what their chief William Webster was to describe later as 'very useful and timely information'. In addition, there would have been information coming from the National Security Agency (NSA) which obtains intelligence from satellite reconnaissance data and electronic monitoring (ELINT), and would have received information from American-manned Saudi AWACS aircraft as well as from the American warships which had been sent to the northern waters of the Gulf on 24th July. The NSA should have been able to pick up radio communications between Baghdad and Iraqi forward formations and units on the border prior to the invasion. By 1st August, the NSA had not reported anything unusual and apparently continued to cast doubts on CIA reports and further data gathered by intelligence services on the ground.

There is no evidence – at the time of writing this book – to suggest that the Kuwaiti intelligence service was carrying out any surveillance of the Iraqi formations on the border or that it had transmitted any warnings, despite the state of alertness agreed by the Kuwaiti cabinet at its 18th July meeting. Nor is there evidence to suggest that the Israelis had taken steps to instruct Mossad to maintain tight surveillance on events. A few days earlier, Mossad had submitted a report stating, somewhat vaguely, that the Iraqis might advance into Kuwait territory. (In fact, the Israeli prime minister Yitzhak Shamir first heard what had happened from his ambassador in Washington, Moshe Arad, who had been briefed by the State Department a few hours after the invasion.)

On 31st July, Under-Secretary of State John Kelly told a congressional hearing that the United States was doing all in its power to help its friends in the region and to preserve stability, but in reply to a question he repeated the statement made by the State Department spokeswoman Margaret Tutwiler a week earlier, 'We have no defence treaties with any Gulf countries.'

Saddam managed to camouflage his intentions well. Western military attachés, who are not normally allowed to drive more than twenty-five miles outside the Iraqi capital, were invited to see for themselves what was going on in the border area. They were free to drive around. It was their reports, stating that they had not seen evidence of large ammunition convoys leaving depots and that Iraqi tanks were not equipped for action, which gave the impression that Saddam had not deployed his armoured divisions for an invasion.

Western embassies on the ground had no clear idea, and were not given specific instructions, as to what evidence they should have been seeking. To them, everything looked calm and businesslike as usual. Some West European expatriates working in Iraq asked their embassies if it was safe to drive to Kuwait or down the motorway to UAE, where they could enjoy the beaches and drink alcohol. Most of the embassies advised them to continue as normal, but warned them to expect delays because of heavy traffic on the Basra–Kuwait highway.

NSA satellite pictures showed that the armoured brigades of the Republican Guards' 3rd Division had not moved to the front. Mindful of the successful coups using armoured formations in the 1950s and 1960s, Saddam Hussein had, since 1972, permitted only his élite units to be equipped with radios. Thus NSA reports concluded that the three hundred or so Iraqi tanks on the borders were not a real attack force. As for Iraqi Mirage fighters at the air bases near the front, they did not have missiles or bombs mounted and there was no movement registered of such weapons being taken from bunkers and ammunition stores. In fact, the weapons had been removed from the aircraft on 16th July, one day before the parade on Revolution Day, a normal precaution observed in Iraq to avoid a military coup or an assassination attempt when aircraft flew in formation over Baghdad.

Satellites, AWACS aircraft and warships in the Gulf did not pick up any signals between Baghdad and the troops massed by the border for one perfectly simple reason – there were none. The Iraqis sent orders by the slower but effective means of dispatch riders and field telephones linked by short cables which were difficult for the NSA's advanced technology to detect. Only the Egyptian and Jordanian intelligence services could sense clearly what was transpiring, because they had worked with Iraqi army personnel and knew how they operated. That is why, when the West was not paying much attention during the two weeks that preceded the invasion, President Mubarak of Egypt and King Hussein of Jordan took things seriously and started Arab diplomatic initiatives. They were given continual assurances by Saddam Hussein himself that there would be no invasion, and so Mubarak's last political decision just a few hours before the invasion was to overrule his intelligence service's suggestion to contact Saddam with a view to dissuading him from the action which he was to take in less than twelve hours. On 1st August a crisis meeting was held at the White House; the CIA's conclusion was 'They are ready; they will go.' Yet the Americans still issued no last-minute warning to Saddam Hussein.

It transpired later that on Wednesday, 1st August, less than fifteen hours before the Iraqi tanks rolled off across the border, an emergency meeting was called at the Department of Defense and headed by the chairman of the Joint Chiefs of Staff, General Colin Powell. The general assembled his top brass in the 'tank' – a sealed, secure meeting-room in the heart of the Pentagon where war plans are discussed with no possibility of being bugged.

During the ten months of Powell's tenure of his post, United States forces had been deployed on no less than five separate occasions, including a rescue operation to extract Americans trapped in Liberia by the civil war; military assistance to the government of President Cory Aquino of the Philippines against a coup attempt; not to mention Panama, where the rapid deployment of US forces, backed up by 'heavy metal music', toppled President Manuel Noriega.

During the 'tank' meeting, an assessment of the situation in the Gulf was given by General Norman Schwarzkopf, commander of the US army's Central Command (CENTCOM), which is a formation with responsibility for covering 10 million square miles of territory from the eastern coast of Africa to Pakistan, where 70 per cent of the world's proven oil reserves are contained. The command was created in 1983, growing out of former President Jimmy Carter's Rapid Deployment Force which was created to protect the oil fields of the Middle East after the fall of the Shah in 1979. However, the 'Bear', as General Schwarzkopf was nicknamed when he commanded the force that invaded Grenada in 1983, said he could not 'kick some butt down there' because CENTCOM had been caught unaware of Saddam's imminent invasion. He said he could activate a main battle plan – known as Operations Plan 90-1002. However, this plan, first drawn up in 1980 and relying on deploying heavily armoured forces on the ground as well as offensive fighters and bombers for counter-attack, was designed to cope with a Soviet attack from Afghanistan on the Gulf or an Iranian attack on the oil fields. There was no plan prepared for the eventuality of an Iraqi attack on Kuwait. Plan 90-1002, or a version of it, was to be deployed later. So the 'tank' meeting ended some thirteen hours before the invasion, with the Pentagon impotent. It had no plans at its disposal, not even a simple preventive measure to provide a trip-wire against Saddam Hussein if he were to cross the border into Kuwait.

In the heat of the desert, the Iraqi–Kuwaiti meeting in Jeddah went ahead on the night of 31st July and on 1st August with hope, and with rather more wishful thinking than certainty, in Washington and Arab capitals that the crisis would be defused. The Kuwaiti team was headed by the prime minister, Sheikh Sa'ad al-Abdallah, whilst the Iraqis were led by Saddam's deputy, Izzat Ibrahim, another dedicated Ba'athist.

The account of what transpired during the Jeddah talks is the subject of controversy. Baghdad entrusted telling its version of events to Dr Mohammed al-Mashat, a particularly unpleasant character – he divorced his American wife and sent her home in order to win Saddam's confidence – who was notable, during his time spent as a diplomat in London, for his ability to make enemies (his reward was appointment as Iraqi ambassador to Washington). Al-Mashat subsequently declared that the

Kuwaitis had no intention of negotiating a settlement to the dispute and that they had come to the meeting in bad faith. He continued by saying that they were 'arrogant and conducting themselves like small-time grocery-store keepers. The gap was irreconcilable, so the meeting collapsed.'

As expected, the Kuwaitis gave a different version of events as their Sheikh Sabah al-Ahmad detailed in a subsequent interview with the Cairo weekly *Al-Mosawar*. He maintained that Kuwait had finally agreed at the Jeddah talks to write off the Iraqi debts and to lease Warbah Island to Iraq as an 'oil outlet for the Rumailah field', in order not to give the Iranians the wrong idea. 'Iraq asked us to drop the $14 billion debt and we did not object,' he said. 'Iraq asked for Bubiyan Island. We agreed to give them Warbah Island instead.'

The official Kuwaiti version, which was given to the Americans and repeated in the Cairo summit on 9th August, was as follows: the head of the Iraqi delegation, Izzat Ibrahim, opened the meeting with a list of demands, including disputed territories, oil-pumping rights and a further $10 billion from the Kuwaitis. The Kuwaitis objected, saying these were confrontational demands and not the basis for negotiations between two sisterly nations. Mr Ibrahim asked them to consider the demands further and to meet the next day.

When the meeting reconvened on the following morning, Kuwaiti prime minister Sheikh Sa'ad al-Abdallah met alone with Izzat Ibrahim. The Kuwaitis did not give a full account of what happened at that meeting, beyond what Sheikh Sabah said in Cairo. However, according to the Kuwaiti official version, they did not discuss anything of substance. Mr Ibrahim developed a headache during the meeting and retired to his room. Sheikh Sa'ad pleaded with him not to leave, but to no avail. The Saudi foreign minister, Prince Sa'ud al-Faisal, who in theory chaired the meeting, did not succeed either in persuading him to stay. The Kuwaitis maintain that they were prepared to write off Iraq's debts and to lease one of the islands under discussion, but both sides needed further instructions from their capitals. Both delegations agreed to meet a few days later in Baghdad after more consultations in their respective capitals.

Using our Iraqi, Kuwaiti and Saudi sources, and bearing in mind the Kuwaitis' and Iraqis' past experience in negotiations, we have strong reasons to think that the scenario of the meeting between Izzat Ibrahim and Sheikh Sa'ad could well have taken place along the following lines: Ibrahim made it plain that all Kuwait had to do was to agree to the demands, which comprised an undertaking not to exceed oil quotas in the future – which had already been given in Geneva; ceding the southern portion of the Rumailah oilfield to Iraq; writing off the $14 billion of Iraq's debt to Kuwait and paying some $2.4 billion for oil illegally extracted. Sheikh Sa'ad, representing a nation described by fellow Arabs as having survived by 'bribing its way out of trouble', was ready to agree to write off the debts but baulked at the territorial concessions – perhaps trying to outwit the Iraqis in the same way as he had tried unsuccessfully a year earlier. He had studied a suggestion made a few weeks earlier by the Iraqis, who had stated that they would agree to a non-aggression pact in return for a concession on the borders, giving Iraq the whole of the Rumailah oil field, the Warbah and Bubiyan Islands, and territory south of Umm Qasr, to enable them to build a canal as part of Saddam Hussein's water project.

Sheikh Sa'ad, who unlike his Iraqi counterpart had the authority to make concessions, saw this meeting as an opportunity to settle once and for all the outstanding issues with Iraq. He thought that it was only reasonable, having agreed the principle of territorial adjustments and money, to expect Iraq to enter into negotiations. As the history of diplomacy had showed, Kuwait could end up with the favourable terms which they had achieved so many times in the past. However, Izzat Ibrahim spoke for a dictatorship in which only one man could make decisions: Saddam Hussein. It is very probable that he developed a convenient headache to avoid a situation that would have obliged him to set a date for continuing the discussion. It is, however, equally likely that the thought of returning to Baghdad to inform his master that the price for achieving settlement of his demands on Kuwait was a commitment not to make any future claims or extort money gave him a real headache.

Whatever Ibrahim thought, a few hours later Saddam Hussein's tanks put an end to his headache and to Sheikh Sa'ad's diplomatic designs.

12 · Into Kuwait

As Iraqi troops massed on the Kuwaiti border towards the end of July, the assumption of analysts around the world was that, should Saddam Hussein take offensive action, the worst that would occur was the seizure of the Rumailah oilfield territory and the islands. Yet when his tanks rolled over the border in the early hours of 2nd August they did not halt at the edge of that area sliced away from the province of Basra by Percy Cox almost seventy years before. They thrust all the way through to the heart of Kuwait City.

It was a swift takeover that gave no chance for any intervention by Kuwait's allies and there was little or no attempt by the Kuwaiti armed forces to engage the Iraqis. An Egyptian defence expert, who had recently been involved in installing Ammoon missile defence systems in Kuwait, confirmed that the multi-role missile could easily have been used against advancing armoured vehicles, with devastating effect. 'The Kuwaitis had enough of those missiles to pin down Iraqi tanks for at least half a day, if not longer,' he said. 'And they were shown how to do it.' The Kuwaitis were also equipped with a selection of anti-tank weapons mounted on jeeps or armoured personnel carriers.

A Kuwaiti hospital doctor later told us that, for days after the occupation, he had been very worried about his son who was a soldier. He had been called – on his portable telephone – to return to his unit but a week later had turned up at the hospital. It transpired that his unit had been assembled not to fight but to flee across the borders to Saudi Arabia. The Saudis told them to dig trenches. They were left in the heat, without adequate supplies and apparently received minimal assistance from the Saudis.

There is little evidence that the 16,000 strong Kuwaiti army, with its six armoured and mechanised brigades and its 420 tanks, received any orders to fight at the borders. Only when the Iraqis were on the streets of Kuwait City did a few gallant defenders attempt some form of resistance. They were mercilessly gunned down and it later emerged that they were Shia who opposed the rule of the Sabah family. Regarded as second class citizens by the ruling elite in the emirate, they died defending a state which had previously refused even to grant them its citizenship.

Kuwaiti pilots did fly their thirty odd Mirage, Skyhawk and Hawk fighters, but not to fight the advancing Iraqis. They headed south to Saudi Arabia. Kuwait's tiny navy did not become involved in any action at all, nor were its eight missile craft and fifteen fast patrol boats engaged. Their role was to protect Kuwait from smugglers, and particularly from the Iraqi dhows which occasionally attempted to land valuable cargoes of alcohol, a commodity much sought after in the officially 'dry' emirate.

For months after the invasion, Arab and western strategy makers have argued about whether Saddam Hussein actually intended to occupy the whole of Kuwait or, as was the view held by the US State Department, based on intelligence sources, had only intended to secure the disputed territories. Meeting no resistance, the argument goes, he seized the opportunity to occupy the whole country. Given the subsequent massive build up of international forces and the claim that Saddam's occupation of Kuwait was only a prelude to the invasion of Saudi Arabia, it is a crucial question. It is unlikely that anyone will ever find out exactly what were the orders issued to the Iraqi Chief of Staff, Major General Abd al-Karim al-Khazragi; he was executed two months after the invasion, together with senior officers of his staff, on Saddam Hussein's orders. But it is known that only twenty-four tanks in the whole Iraqi invasion force were carrying ammunition for their main armament of 125mm guns. Furthermore, the Mirage fighters had no missiles mounted.

In mid-August, a rumour emerged, later traced back to Kuwaiti officials, that Baghdad's plan was to send troops directly to the Dasman Palace on entering Kuwait. The Emir was to be offered a choice: if he agreed to 'co-operate' and order an end to all resistance, and if he agreed to stay on as head of a quisling government that would ally itself with Baghdad, then his life would be spared. If, as expected, he refused such a proposal, he would be killed.

However, such a scenario seems unlikely. Iraqi troops did not initially head directly for the Palace. The leading elements of lightly equipped Iraqi armour paused for two hours on arrival at the outskirts of Kuwait City whilst waiting for the twenty-four fully armed tanks and other units of the Republican Guards. It subsequently took a further two hours to occupy the city centre and seafront area where eighteen of the fully armoured tanks took positions directing their guns to the sea. By 4 p.m. they had been joined by another 120 tanks.

Meanwhile, there had been plenty of time for the Emir to escape. His bodyguard implemented a well rehearsed plan of evacuation: they bundled him into his armoured Mercedes saloon which, followed by a convoy of similar cars carrying ministers and the Emir's personal guards, his wives and children, sped off along the motorway towards Saudi Arabia.

Altogether, from the moment they received the first warning of tanks crossing the borders to the moment of the Emir's departure and their own flight, Kuwaiti officials had six hours to organise themselves.

There is no evidence that one single official spent time organising resistance or even trying to contact Iraqi commanders in a last ditch attempt to avert disaster. It seems, from the reports of journalists who later interviewed them, that they spent the few hours contacting their banks in order to withdraw their money or ensuring that all information concerning Kuwait's gold reserves had been removed.

By the time the Iraqis reached the Dasman Palace, the Emir was gone. During the morning of the 2nd August he arrived at the new seat of the Kuwaiti government in the Saudi Arabian summer capital of Taif, ensconcing himself in the al Hada Sheraton Hotel. Soon afterwards, he started broadcasting to his people inside Kuwait.

Seven hours after the first Iraqi tank crossed the borders, it was all over. There was no one in authority from the Sabah family left in Kuwait.

During the first few hours of the invasion the Iraqi Mukhabarat moved into action. Whether or not he had intended full-scale occupation, Saddam Hussein ensured that the long arm of his intelligence services could reach all 'traitors'. Equipped with the names and addresses of hundreds of Iraqi opposition members from the Communist Party or from the Shia Islamic Dawa Party, its agents began rounding them up. Three hours later, as they were being driven blindfolded to Iraq, thousands of Iraqi troops were pouring into Kuwait from the direction of Basra in airconditioned buses.

Subsequent resistance was sporadic and disorganised. Individuals, mostly Shia, sniped at Iraqi troops but this was soon countered by tanks shelling tower blocks still inhabited by Kuwaiti and European civilians. The snipers gave up.

In Baghdad, the Iraqi government news agency claimed that the Kuwaiti government had been overthrown by a group of Kuwaiti revolutionaries who had asked for assistance from Iraq, and that a group of nine 'unknowns' had been named as the provisional government. It later emerged that the so-called acting prime minister was an Iraqi, and a relative of Saddam Hussein. In fact, he was a Mukhabarat officer, Colonel Ala'a, who had previously served in Iraqi embassies in various parts of the Arab world. After 8th August there was no further mention of the new government.

There had for some time been a growing movement for democracy in Kuwait, mainly amongst former members of the National Assembly. The Emir, under pressure from the Saudis to give up his experiment in democracy, had dissolved the assembly in 1986 when it became increasingly critical of his conduct of affairs. After the invasion, the Iraqis quickly contacted those members of the Kuwaiti opposition in the city, and sent messages to the larger number outside. But on 2nd August, not a single member of the opposition could be found to co-operate with them.

It was the height of the hot weather, when most rich Kuwaitis (and there are few who are not) traditionally escape to Europe. Those who were left in the emirate were mainly minor officials, or the poorer elements of the Kuwaiti community, including the Shia, and about a million foreigners. Palestinians and foreign nationals from the Indian sub-continent, the Philippines and Egypt were numbered in tens of thousands; Americans, Europeans and Japanese in hundreds. Many of them would become part of the massive human tragedy which would take place in refugee camps on the Jordanian border in the weeks following 2nd August.

On the day of the invasion, the Kuwaiti Ambassador in Baghdad denounced it as flagrant aggression; a few days later he was again produced on television to recant. Looking sick and frightened, and mumbling his words, resembling Farzad Bazoft in his famous televised confession in October 1989, the ambassador declared that he had been misguided and had not learned history well. He added that he now understood that the Iraqi action had been necessary and he endorsed it; nothing has been heard of him since.

President George Bush, together with other world powers and Arab leaders, reacted swiftly to events. Resolution 660 (see page 308) was passed unanimously by the UN Security Council on the evening of 2nd August and all Iraqi and Kuwaiti assets were frozen at the request of Kuwaiti ambassadors abroad. In less than a week, the European Commission and the United Nations had passed resolutions imposing sanctions against Iraq. (A detailed diary of events can be found on pages 299–307.)

There is no doubt that the almost universal condemnation of his invasion took the Iraqi leader by surprise. It is likely that he expected the crisis to be solved within the 'Arab family' and did not anticipate interference from outside nations. On previous experience, he could have expected a meeting of Arab heads of state, urging Iraq to withdraw. After further explaining its grievances against Kuwait, Baghdad would oblige, taking the emirate's wealth with it and retaining the disputed oilfield and the islands. Events would be concluded with embraces and kisses of apology between the two brothers Saddam and Sheikh Jaber and the world would learn to live with yet another annexation along the lines of Israel's in South Lebanon, the Golan Heights and the West Bank; Saudi Arabia's in part of Yemen; Morocco's in the Spanish Sahara; and China's in Tibet.

Under the old world order, the Soviet Union would have supported this Arab solution and vetoed any Security Council resolution condemning Iraq. However, by August 1990 national interests had changed. On the day of the invasion, US Secretary of State James Baker was in Irkutsk, Siberia, on an ambitious and carefully designed diplomatic mission to further improve increasingly warm relations with the Soviet Union. Within a few hours he had agreed with his Soviet counterpart, Eduard Shevardnadze, the draft wording of the UN Security Council Resolution No. 660, ordering unconditional Iraqi withdrawal from Kuwait.

Later on during the crisis, when Saddam Hussein detained thousands of foreign nationals as hostages for over four months, the Soviet Union sent Baghdad the sternest of all the warnings it had given so far. They made it clear that if Soviet hostages were not released quickly, Moscow would send troops to join the allied forces in the Gulf. Clearly, the Iraqi dictator could no longer rely on Soviet support. Unknown to him, the Soviets had already passed to Britain's ITN television, satellite photographs of what was suspected to be a uranium enrichment plant in Iraqi Kurdistan.

Most interesting of all, however, was the hostile reaction to the invasion from other Arab nations whose support enabled President Bush to persuade the United Nations Security Council to move swiftly in deploying American forces on Arab soil.

Of all the Middle Eastern leaders, President Mubarak was the most determined to reverse Saddam Hussein's fortunes. From the time of its 1979 peace treaty with Israel, Egypt had lost its leadership of the Arab world and Mubarak saw in the new crisis a chance of regaining the role and obtaining increased economic aid. (After Egypt's immediate condemnation of the invasion, Washington proceeded to write off $7.6 billion of military debts, whilst over $1.1 billion in aid was promised from the West and Japan.) Personally angered because he had been deceived by Saddam's promise not to invade Kuwait, he had rapid consultations with Egyptian opposition leaders and found that the inclinations of his people matched exactly the policy which he believed would bring the greatest rewards for Egypt. So Cairo quickly turned down an Iraqi offer to pay billions of dollars, and return over $30 billion of Egyptian assets in Kuwait, if Egypt would adopt a neutral line.

During the months leading up to the invasion, anger against the Iraqis had been escalating in Egypt. Thousands of Egyptians were resident in Iraq. Many had moved to the southern part of the country during the 1970s to advise on the best way of cultivating the wetlands of the Shatt al-Arab area north of Basra. Later, during the Gulf war, Egyptians in their hundreds of thousands went to Iraq to run its industries and to replace over a million Iraqis serving in the army. They injected the rapidly developing society with valuable management skills, using them to good effect in the expanding arms industry.

By late summer 1989, however, thousands of Egyptians were returning to their homeland with sad tales of the way they had been treated. Some recounted how they had been cheated out of money, forced to enlist in the army, sent to Basra to work on water projects while the city was under artillery bombardment or, ultimately, attacked by Iraqis returning from the war to find their jobs no longer open. Several hundred Egyptians were killed in such attacks, but the Iraqi authorities made no effort to charge those responsible. After the invasion, Egyptians working in Kuwait or Iraq were expelled, losing all their savings and most of their belongings. President Mubarak therefore had no difficulty in persuading his parliament to endorse his decision to dispatch troops.

While securing Egypt's support against Iraq was vital, one of President Bush's chief tasks was to convince King Fahd of Saudi Arabia to invite foreign troops on to Arab soil to 'protect' his kingdom.

Prior to the invasion, the Saudi Royal Family had been under attack from many directions. Shia and radical Muslims worldwide were calling for the internationalisation of the Islamic holy shrines, accusing the Saudis of being unfit to be their custodians. The notion of 'infidel' troops, with their 'unclean' food and their 'godless social habits', setting foot on the holy land of Arabia would only heighten such criticism.

King Fahd had emerged as an important Arab leader during the Gulf War, when he had helped to finance the Iraqi war effort. He had also shown himself to be a wise and powerful statesman open to change. Since becoming king in 1982, Fahd has ruled by consensus, striking a careful balance between the emirs. (They are descended from one father – King Abd al-Azziz ibn Sa'ud, the founder of the Kingdom – but from different mothers from different tribes.) He also has to strike a balance between the modernists, of whom he is one, and the traditionalists; and between the western educated technocrats and the strong traditional religious establishment (the ulamas) led by the Mufti, Sheikh bin Baz. In 1986 he issued a fatwa that the earth is flat and that to think of it as a globe is blasphemy.

For six days after 2nd August there was no mention of the invasion in the Saudi media. Saudis were tuning to Egyptian television and radio or to the BBC World Service to learn what was happening in Kuwait. During frantic diplomatic efforts, visits and contacts with nearly all Arab capitals, King Fahd had hoped that, persuaded by Arab opinion, Saddam Hussein would come to his senses and that the Iraqi invasion would turn out to be just a modern, heavy handed and brutal version of the traditional raids carried out by Arab tribes across unrecognised borders.

However, he underestimated the importance of one factor: oil. The necessity of securing its supply meant that western policy makers would never be prepared to treat Saddam Hussein's invasion as a matter to be solved within the Arab family.

On 3rd August US Secretary of Defense Richard Cheney met with King Fahd and his brothers for three hours. The Saudis have for years relied on the US to obtain and interpret all military intelligence data in the region. When, according to an eyewitness at the meeting, King Fahd and his brothers were shown satellite photographs purporting to show Iraqi tanks massed to attack the kingdom, they looked at each other, then back at the photographs, then at each other again. Who could tell from the dotted lines whether they were looking at a mass of armoured vehicles or a herd of camels? Nevertheless, they were convinced formally to request assistance from the United States – assistance which, it was made perfectly clear, was going to be sent no matter what the response from the Saudis. The Pentagon in Washington had already placed on stand-by elements of the 82nd Airborne Division, the North Carolina-based spearhead of the United States' rapid deployment forces.

A few days later, when an emergency Arab summit had endorsed the decision to call in multi-national troop support, King Fahd appeared on television, a medium which he loathes, to make his emotional announcement *Bismellah al-Rahman al-Raheem* (in the name of God the Merciful, the Compassionate). In a soft monotone and barely looking at the camera he told his people that 'regrettable events' and the kingdom's wish to 'contain' the dispute, as well as its demand that the ruling family of Kuwait should be restored, had forced him to invite 'troops from friendly nations to help defend the kingdom'.

The swift dispatch of American troops was announced as a means of forestalling any Iraqi takeover of the airfields in the eastern province of Saudi Arabia, or a quick drive on to Dhahran. Yet it seems extremely unlikely that Saddam Hussein ever intended to invade Saudi Arabia. He had only recently signed a non-aggression treaty with King Fahd, but had he seriously intended to seize the Eastern provinces and prevent American aircraft or troops from landing, or to capture the oilfields, he could have done so swiftly and easily. The Iraqi army's airborne forces, numbering in excess of twenty brigades of special forces and paratroops, would have been capable of seizing landing fields and holding them for a few hours until support arrived from the armoured divisions advancing rapidly over the border.

In fact, once Kuwait had been secured, Iraqi deployments were entirely defensive and the much-cited move towards the Saudi border was merely the extending of front lines and the fortifying of defensive positions. This is an exercise at which the Iraqis are particularly expert after eight years of trench warfare with Iran. They were measures that any commander would have taken in the circumstances.

In fact, American officials have since admitted in interviews that there was no evidence to suggest that Saddam Hussein was going to invade Saudi Arabia. In fact, the American move was designed to prevent him, with his missiles pointing at Saudi oilfields, from dictating Arab oil policy and world oil prices.

When the dust of 2nd August had begun to settle, some observers also began to suspect that the American military deployment was intended for the total overthrow of Saddam Hussein and the destruction of Iraq's military potential. It was an aim that many international diplomats believed was shared and encouraged by Margaret Thatcher who quickly agreed to contribute additional warships and aircraft, together with nearly 15,000 troops.

In his evidence to Congress during October, Rear Admiral Eugene Carroll revealed America's true aims when he described the buildup of forces in Saudi Arabia as 'the creation of an offensive war-fighting force directed at Iraq.' A truly defensive and truly international effort would not have required such a massive sea-lift, he added. Certainly the effort was a huge one: some 800,000 tonnes of matériel had to be moved in the initial phase, followed by 1.7 million tonnes for a sustained presence.

Not only did the Iraqis have no intention of attacking Saudi Arabia, they also avoided the sort of provocative actions that might have precipitated a war. When, during October, an Iraqi border patrol captured five soldiers of the *13e Regiment des Dragoons Parachutistes* (a French Army special forces unit specialising in long range deep penetration reconnaissance) inside Iraqi territory, they maintained that the Frenchmen had lost their way and handed them to the French embassy in Baghdad. Baghdad confined its aggression towards the allies to the media, directing it mainly against leaders of Arab states and singling out Margaret Thatcher, representative of the old colonial power, from amongst Western leaders, referring to her as 'an old hag in whose head the devil has found a comfortable dwelling'.

The emergency Arab summit held in Cairo on 8th/9th August marked the collapse of the Arab States League when it voted to invite in foreign troops. (Iraq and Libya voted against the resolution while Algeria, Sudan, Yemen, Jordan, Mauritania and the PLO abstained.)

During the summit an anti-Iraqi bloc, led by Egypt and including the Gulf states, took a tough line with Baghdad and demanded an unconditional withdrawal. Syria, Iraq's bitter rival, joined the Cairo camp and was later rewarded when it was given tacit approval by the Americans and the French to take control of Lebanon and destroy the forces of the Iraqi-backed Christians led by General Michel Aoun. And furthermore, diplomatic relations with Britain were resumed, having been severed in 1986 when Syrian diplomats were allegedly involved in aiding a Jordanian in his attempt to blow up an Israeli airliner at Heathrow. The fact that the Damascus regime has a deplorable record on human rights, and it tops the US State Department's list of countries sponsoring terrorism, mattered very little when President Bush met with President Hafeze al-Assad in Geneva on 23rd November to secure Syrian military participation against Iraq.

Saddam Hussein did not attend the summit but sent his foreign minister, Tariq Aziz, who proceeded to threaten officials from smaller member states with the consequences of voting against Iraq. He walked hand in hand with PLO leader Yasser Arafat, whose organisation sided with Iraq. Palestinians in the occupied territories and in refugee camps saw in Saddam a great hero willing to confront America and Israel.

The Iraqis' best hope during the Cairo summit was to persuade Arab radicals such as the Libyans, the Algerians and the Palestinians, to undermine pro-western support. They attempted to do so but with little effect. According to an eye-witness, the Libyan leader, Colonel Muammar Gaddafi, sat with Libyan and Palestinian officials in the lounge of the conference building after the morning session, claiming that the conference was part of an 'imperialist conspiracy against the Arab nation'. Told of the remark by an aide, President Mubarak appeared in the lounge. 'Muammar,' he said, 'if you think I would be party to such a conspiracy, as you say, then I would long ago have sent a couple of armoured divisions to occupy Libya; I had a hundred and one pretexts for doing so, as you know.' As Gaddafi sat speechless, the Egyptian leader walked over to him, placed a hand on his shoulder and said, 'Come, I will buy you lunch.'

Despite the vote against him, Saddam Hussein still hoped to keep the matter an Arab affair with the help of King Hussein of Jordan. The king was alone amongst Arab leaders in being able to speak on equal terms with President Bush, Prime Minister Margaret Thatcher, President Francois Mitterrand or Saddam Hussein. Moreover, there were a number of powerful factors influencing the sympathies of the normally pro-Western monarch.

Seventy per cent of Hussein's 2.6 million subjects are Palestinians who support Iraq against the West and have seen little in the way of help from wealthy Arab states or the West. In 1951 King Hussein's grandfather, King Abdallah, was assassinated on the steps of the mosque in Jerusalem, because he had made peace with Israel. Hussein was only fifteen at the time and one of the four bullets touched the top of his ear.

When the Cairo summit convened, the Jordanian monarch surprised the West by supporting Iraq against any action by the United States. The king, for all his refusal to endorse the Western viewpoint, insisted that he was misunderstood. He maintained that he was not backing Saddam but was acting as an honest broker, seeking a way out of the imbroglio. He was also well aware that any war in the region would be a major disaster to his kingdom, placed as it is between Saudi Arabia, Iraq and Israel. During his rule as the longest surviving Arab monarch, Hussein has learned some bitter lessons. During the Six Day War in 1967, he lost half his kingdom to Israel because of his brief association with Nasser, a man for whom he had little liking. (He has, however, shown a personal liking for Saddam Hussein, seeing in him the ultimate hope of recovering the lost half of his kingdom, the West Bank.)

There were also economic reasons for King Hussein's position. During the Gulf War Jordan prospered as Aqaba became a main port for the import of all the goods Iraq needed and in return Iraq supplied cheap oil to the kingdom. At the time when sanctions were imposed, Saudi Arabia was supplying twenty per cent of Jordan's oil requirements. The Saudis agreed to increase this to fifty per cent but a month later closed down the pipeline altogether, angered at King Hussein's ambivalent attitude. The result was to make Jordan even more dependent on Iraqi oil.

Jordan was recognised by the United Nations sanction committee in New York as the country of most strategic importance if sanctions were to work. It was fully appreciated that if Jordan were to cut off its oil imports from Iraq, the country would come to a standstill, and so trade between the two countries was allowed to continue. However, other sanctions-breaking moves were taken more seriously. Every day at least two, and often four, civil airliners flew in from Baghdad; on the outward flight to Amman, they took refugees, journalists, diplomats and a few other privileged passengers from Iraq. Flying back to Baghdad, it was clear that the holds were full. The total tonnage was not very significant but the psychological impact was a great bonus for the Ba'athist regime which thrived on propaganda. Equally, 'food donated by the children of Jordan and Palestine to the children of Iraq' was dispatched to Baghdad with much publicity given to Iraq's struggle for the central Arab cause: Palestine.

If King Hussein had tried to go against general opinion in Jordan, there would have been riots in the streets and eventually a confrontation which might have involved either Iraq or Israel, or both. King Hussein, who has survived many crises in his thirty-seven-year rule, was walking a tight-rope. His main hope was to be the centre of secret diplomacy concentrating on finding an Arab solution.

By the second week of December 1990, King Hussein and Yasser Arafat were working together with the Algerian President, Chadhli bin Jadid, to persuade King Fahd and Saddam Hussein to meet face to face in search of an Arab solution. King Hussein had tried to negotiate a solution a few days after the invasion but had been pre-empted by US Secretary of State James Baker's announcing to journalists on 6th August that he had agreed with President Mubarak to send troops; this despite the Egyptian leader's advice to his American guest not to reveal the fact before the Cairo Summit meeting on 9th August. Clearly the US, having misread the situation before 2nd August, did not wish to be outmanoeuvred again.

The CIA, meanwhile, was searching for every shred of evidence from non-American sources that would emphasise to President Bush that its reports of a planned invasion had been accurate and it was the administration's political assessment that had been wrong. They seized upon a report leaked to the press in Europe and the Middle East a few days after the invasion, which claimed to explain why Yemen and King Hussein of Jordan appeared to have sided with Saddam Hussein and had objected to the deployment of American troops. Saddam Hussein's plan, according to the report, was to invade the coastal eastern part of Saudi Arabia and to take the rich oilfields in the north east. Meanwhile, King Hussein, whose great grandfather had been driven out of Mecca by ibn Sa'ud, would order Jordanian forces to advance along the Red Sea coast and capture Mecca, Jeddah and the coastal area of Hijaz. At the same time, Yemeni troops would move northwards and capture the oil-rich Saudi provinces of O'sir and Najran. Thus the kingdom of Saudi

Arabia would be dismembered whilst the Saudi Royal Family would be forced to withdraw to their original homeland in the central highlands of Najd. The Saudis, angered by the report, immediately deported tens of thousands of the 1.5 million Yemenis in the kingdom. The report was widely quoted in the pro-Saudi Arab press. More careful and experienced journalists among those to whom the report was leaked made the effort to double check its sources; they traced it back to the Israelis.

Israel remained generally quiet as the crisis unfolded: the Americans realised very well that Israeli involvement would jeopardise the Arab consensus they were relying upon, and would make it impossible for Arab countries to send troops to Saudi Arabia.

However, the Israelis did all that they could to encourage a military confrontation with Saddam Hussein. Of all the countries in the region, Israel least wished Iraq to accept Resolution 660 and withdraw, as this would leave the Iraqi war machine intact. Throughout 1989 and 1990, when Iraq was no longer distracted by a war with Iran, a good deal of misinformation and straightforward disinformation had been put out by Israel: intelligence estimates passed on to the West constantly inflated Iraqi strengths and capabilities whilst seeking to show that Baghdad was bent on further expansion. In the first week of the invasion they announced that any Iraqi move into Jordan would be a *casus belli*. This notion gave Saddam Hussein the opportunity to confuse the situation further. He realised very well that opposition to Israel was the one thing which could unite the Arabs; Iraqi propaganda constantly harped on the links between America and Zionism, and talked of the conspiracy between Israel and America to carve up the Arab nation.

The Iraqi dictator hinted strongly that should the allied forces assembled in Saudi Arabia attack Iraq, he would in turn take action to involve Israel. An Israeli strike against Iraq would make it extremely unlikely that Arab troops would remain in the American-led multinational forces fighting their Iraqi brothers.

So two days after Saddam Hussein annexed Kuwait as the 19th province of Iraq, he made a link between possible withdrawl and the Palestinian issue, offering to accept Resolution 660 if Israel would abide by Resolution 242, now twenty-three years old, and withdraw from occupied Arab land. His offer found massive popular support in the Arab world, even inside the camps of his enemies.

In fact the indications are that Saddam Hussein had no intention of remaining in Kuwait in the long term. Iraqi troops systematically stripped Kuwait of everything which could be removed and transported it to

Baghdad: research laboratories, scientific equipment, gold bullion, cars, spare parts, hospital equipment, weapons and other military equipment, and even traffic lights. By the 10th December, it was estimated that the total value of items removed from Kuwait was in the region of $45 billion. This well organised 'official' looting was organised and carried out by the Mukhabarat with special forces units under their command; any ordinary soldiers caught looting were hanged from cranes. When Mukhabarat agents went to the Emir's stables, they asked for each horse by name.

Between the time of April Glaspie's meeting with Saddam Hussein on 25th July and 6th August no attempt was made at direct consultation between Washington and Baghdad. But on the sixth the Iraqi leader, apparently perplexed by America's swift reaction against him, tried to reassure Washington that Iraq could still be the guardian of US interests in the region. Twelve hours before Secretary of State James Baker announced that the United States would be sending troops to Saudi Arabia, the Iraqi president summoned the American chargé d'affaires in Baghdad, Joseph Wilson.

He opened the meeting by again hinting at the possibility of making peace with Iran. It would put the United States in 'a tight position', he said, hinting at angry Muslim reaction around the world if American troops were to land in Saudi Arabia. He then alluded to the border dispute between Iraq and Kuwait, so reminding Wilson of the previously stated American official position of having no opinion on such disputes. 'Kuwait was a state without any real frontier. Even before 1961 it was not a state. So, up until now Kuwait has been a state without borders.' He then gave an assurance that Iraq had a non-aggression pact with Saudi Arabia and hinted at a possible pact with Kuwait if a deal was to be reached. 'You know that we were the first to propose a security agreement with Saudi Arabia which includes non-intervention in each other's internal affairs and non-recourse to force and we signed that agreement. We proposed the same agreement to Kuwait but they refused to sign the agreement with us, probably under the advice of a foreign power, possibly Britain.'

The Iraqi leader continued by stating that he was willing to give the Saudi Arabians any guarantees that they wanted but he denied having given any assurances to Arab leaders about Kuwait, claiming that they misread his words. 'I did not give that promise to any Arabs. I promised that I would not take any military action before the meeting that we agreed upon in Jeddah. This is what happened.'

He even offered the United States a 'sweetener' in the event of a peaceful solution. 'You know that you have been buying oil from Iraq since I came into power, although our relationship was severed during that time. You bought more oil after resuming our relationship in 1984. Up until the time you decided to boycott Iraqi oil, you were buying about one third of our oil output. We know that your interest lies in trade and the continuing supply of oil. So what makes you discuss military options, which you will no doubt lose? Why do you want to be our enemies . . . ? We see that your interests could be looked after by a strong nationalistic and realistic regime in the area.'

Saddam Hussein then suggested that de-escalating tension would reduce oil prices, as the following exchange with Wilson indicates:

Wilson: 'Thank you Mr President. I will address your words to my government and I will convey your message by telephone immediately and will also put it on paper. As you have said correctly, this is a dangerous time, not only for American/Iraqi relations but for stability in the area and in the world.'

Saddam Hussein: 'Why dangerous for the world?'

Wilson: 'As I understand it, there is a sense of insecurity and unrest in the world markets.'

Saddam Hussein: 'This is your fault. We accepted $25 per barrel and if it was not for your boycott position, the price of the barrel would be around $21. When you boycott five million barrels in one go, then instability occurs. We feel that dealers will feel the benefit of it, but not the American people.'

The US did not accept Saddam's blandishments. James Baker, who had gathered support from all over the world, announced that evening that America would be sending troops.

The Iraqi media escalated the attack on Saudi Arabia which, it trumpeted, had invited 'infidels' into the heartland of Islam. Saddam Hussein himself took the opportunity to become more obviously Muslim than the ayatollahs whom he had spent eight years fighting.

Despite the number of countries ranged against him, the Iraqi leader retained an amazing ability to improvise on the diplomatic front. He proceeded to make peace with the Iranians, offering to return to them all that the Iraqis had fought for during eight years of bloody conflict. The agreement also allowed him to redeploy a large proportion of his army which had until then been tied down in the north of Iraq.

He played the hostage card very carefully and brutally. Learning from the Iranian experience of taking American hostages in 1979, he made sure that the situation was brought to every front room in the West. In order to thwart any attempt at their rescue and at the same time avert any pre-emptive strikes by allied forces, hostages were dispersed amongst military establishments of strategic value to form a 'human shield'. Journalists from the Western media were allowed into Baghdad where they talked to the hostages as well as to Iraqis. Amongst the latter, Saddam Hussein's popularity seemed intact.

Every time the hostages disappeared from the front page, he made a number of carefully staged appearances with American and British families – in the same way that besieged terrorists have brought hostages to a window to warn against any action that might be taken against them. Using such methods, he was able to keep the issue on television screens worldwide for several weeks. He also took the opportunity to improve his personal image. During a television interview with British families, one British wife commented that it was not very gallant to hide behind women and children. Saddam Hussein responded by ordering the immediate release of the women and children but continued to detain the men.

Meanwhile, peace groups from those nations contributing to the multinational force, and an American congress mindful of the lessons of Vietnam, were pressing an increasingly belligerent President Bush (who had failed to give a clear explanation to the American people of the real objectives of deploying troops in the Arabian desert) to find a peaceful solution. In addition, prominent figures in the West started carrying out a series of visits to Baghdad on humanitarian grounds, most of which resulted in the release of hostages. Inevitably, media organisations such as BBC, ITN, ABC, CNN, CBS devoted a considerable amount of air time to interviewing politicians who had visited Baghdad. They included former West German chancellor Willy Brandt, and former British prime minister Edward Heath and Labour MP Tony Benn.

The French, who had earlier proposed a peace conference on the Middle East to solve all problems, including the Kuwait and Palestine issues, were rewarded by the release of all their hostages. It was subsequently revealed that Iraqi foreign minister Tariq Aziz had attended a meeting in Tunisia with Claude Cheysson, the former French foreign minister, to discuss a peace plan.

Iraqi tactics were working and more debate on the human aspect of the problem was generated in the West. By early December a number of leading retired military figures as well as top strategists presented an intellectual argument against the war based on the possibility of very high casualties amongst allied troops as well as the devastating effect on the world economy of blazing oil wells.

President Bush, who on 29th November had succeeded in persuading the United Nations Security Council to pass Resolution 678 giving Iraq a deadline of 15th January 1991 to evacuate Kuwait, appeared uncertain in December 1990. Cracks had started to appear in the alliance. Egypt and Syria had told the Americans that military operations should be confined to Kuwait and that there should be no air raids on Iraqi cities. Slowly, public opinion in America turned against the use of force against Iraq. It was only the Israeli lobby that continued to push for war, along with the military, led by Chairman of the Joint Chiefs of Staff General Colin Powell. They wanted to retain America's dominant role in the crisis and at the same time cure the United States of the 'Vietnam Syndrome'. However, Congress, the media and the American public were clearly asking, 'What are the objectives of American policy in the Gulf?'

Studies warned that the destruction of the Iraqi armed forces could result in a reversal of the situation in early 1990 as there would be no regional counterbalance to powers such as Iran or Syria. There was also criticism of America's alliance with Arab regimes whose records on human rights were not much better than Iraq's. There were further reports that Turkey would make it a condition of maintaining sanctions against Iraq that there would be no discussions on autonomy for the Kurds.

In early December, President Bush surprised his own administration by suggesting his Secretary of State visit Baghdad for direct talks with Saddam Hussein, and that Iraqi foreign minister Tariq Aziz visit Washington.

Four days later Saddam Hussein announced that all foreign 'guests' were free to go. Realising that the Iraqi president was only playing for time, refusing to receive Baker before 12th January, Bush cancelled Aziz's visit to Washington.

By Christmas, when there had been no contact between Iraq and the US for two weeks, war looked more likely than it had at any point since 2nd August. At the same time, the Bush administration was beginning to lose its grip on events. As the Iraqis, with their considerable intelligence networks around the ports and bases in Saudi Arabia, were well aware, US forces could not be ready to take the offensive by 16th January. Furthermore, the commitment of some of the European allies, led by France and Germany, seemed to be waning. On New Year's Eve they made it plain to Bush that the final decision to go to war must not be his alone. German Foreign Minister Hans-Dietrich Genscher called for an EC foreign ministers' meeting to be held in Luxembourg on 4th January.

In America, Congress was determined not to give the president a 'blank check for war' and questions about political, economic and environmental expediency, as well as the human cost, became more persistent.

The first hundred hours of 1991 saw frantic efforts by European politicians to provide Saddam with a means of withdrawing from Kuwait without a total loss of face. (See Diary of the Gulf Crisis.) Ministers at the 4th January meeting (with the exception of those from Britain and Holland) unofficially accepted the principle of an international conference on all the problems of the Middle East (including the Palestinian question) as a *quid pro quo* for Iraqi withdrawal. The Kuwaitis, Israelis and Saudis, meanwhile, resigned themselves to letting the war take its bloody course since the alternative was to leave Saddam armed and ready to attack another time.

President Bush had little choice but to return to diplomacy if he were not to lose the initiative to Europe. On 3rd January, having learned that a close confidant of President Mitterrand, Michel Vauzelle, had travelled to Baghdad for talks with Saddam, Bush suggested a meeting in Geneva between James Baker and Tariq Aziz.

Britain, meanwhile, aimed to distance itself from the European peace moves and declared that war was imminent. It ordered eight Iraqi diplomats out on 3rd January, hoping that Iraq would retaliate by expelling the last six British diplomats and thus save Britain from having to close its Baghdad embassy in preparation for war. The Iraqis called Britain's bluff, however, and did nothing. Furthermore, and contrary to American expectations, they agreed the next day to send Aziz to Geneva. (The EC meeting then invited Tariq Aziz to talks in Luxembourg on 10th January and it was later revealed that France and Germany had planned to invite him whether or not he accepted America's invitation to Geneva.)

During the 4th January EC meeting French Foreign Minister Roland Dumas, after consultation with his German counterpart, presented a seven-point plan for a peaceful solution. To Britain's dismay, the plan included an offer to extend the 15th January deadline should Iraq announce its intention to withdraw from Kuwait. Three hours later, President Mitterrand dropped another diplomatic bombshell by suggesting that, should Iraq fail to meet the deadline, there should be a further meeting of the UN Security Council before military action was taken. (Yasser Arafat and Saddam Hussein seized on this suggestion, repeating it a few days later.)

On 5th January, Michel Vauzelle met Saddam Hussein for talks that lasted four and a half hours. According to sources associated with the event, the Iraqi leader said he would consider making a 'great sacrifice' if the Allies would show a more positive attitude, by which he meant open a bargaining dialogue.

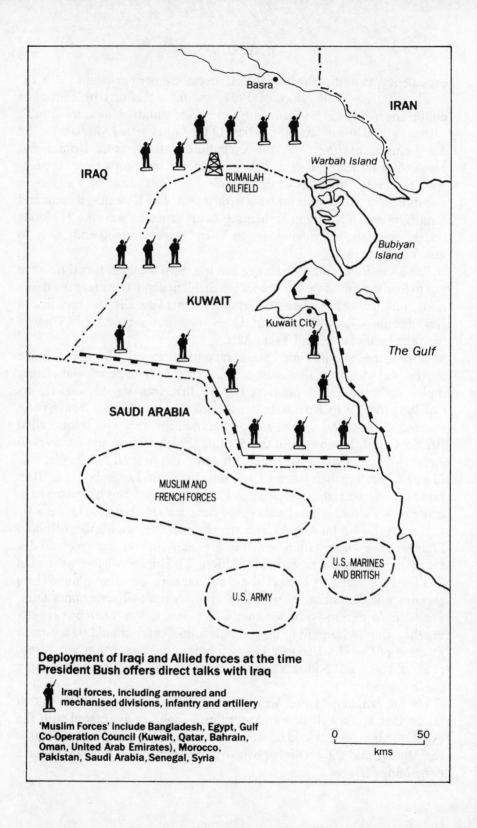

**Deployment of Iraqi and Allied forces at the time
President Bush offers direct talks with Iraq**

Iraqi forces, including armoured and
mechanised divisions, infantry and artillery

'Muslim Forces' include Bangladesh, Egypt, Gulf
Co-Operation Council (Kuwait, Qatar, Bahrain,
Oman, United Arab Emirates), Morocco,
Pakistan, Saudi Arabia, Senegal, Syria

The French, who showed by their clandestine bargaining with Saddam a better understanding of his mentality than either America or Britain had displayed, seemed, with German, Italian and other European backing, to be moving events towards the American and Israeli nightmare: a partial withdrawal by Iraq which would leave Saddam Hussein in control of his war machine and present the prospect of many years of tangled diplomacy. Suspicion that France might have been engaged in secret discussions with Iraq was increased when Aziz turned down the invitation to Luxembourg. He claimed that, since the foreign ministers had refused to endorse the proposal for an international conference on the Middle East, their policy was clearly dictated by Washington. The assumption was that he was providing France with ammunition to encourage Europe to make a more concrete offer.

As the world's press poured into Geneva for the 9th January talks (seen as possibly the last chance for peace), each side prepared to cover itself whatever the outcome. President Bush wanted to be able to tell his voters that he had done all he could to avert war, while the Iraqis wanted to drag the proceedings past the 15th January deadline.

As the clock ticked towards midnight in early 1991, it became clear that the rush by an over-committed America to protect its interests and friends had placed the US and its allies in an almost impossible position. The deployment of Western troops on Muslim soil, protecting a regime seen by radical Muslims as unfit to rule over Mecca and the holy shrines, can only inflame the passions of Arab nationalists and Muslim fundamentalists. As America's commitment to the Shah of Iran illustrated over a decade ago, the presence of American troops is likely to undermine the stability of the very regimes they are intended to sustain.

President Bush was caught in a cleft stick. Allowing time for sanctions to work would mean large numbers of troops remaining in Arabia. And if, at the end of the crisis, Saddam Hussein were to remain in power, then the oil sheikhs who invited in the infidels would have little chance of survival without a permanent US presence in the region.

Should, on the other hand, Saddam be removed by a destructive war, then a new generation of Arab nationalists would emerge whose anger would eclipse all past experience of Middle Eastern terrorism. More dangerous still would be the committed Islamic fundamentalists on either side of the Gulf: in Lebanon, Syria, Israel and even in secular Egypt. (A war would be likely, for instance, to destroy Shia holy shrines at Najjaf and Karblaa in southern Iraq, both close to chemical weapons sites.)

Policy makers in the West should remind themselves that it was fear of these very Islamic forces and the desire to keep them east of Shatt al-Arab that led Western powers into a course of action, the value of which was no more than a mirage in the Arabian desert.

Diary of the Gulf Crisis

17th July Saddam Hussein launches a bitter attack on Kuwait and the United Arab Emirates, saying they have exceeded their oil quotas. Iran agrees.

25th July Saddam receives American ambassador April Glaspie. He warns that he may make a deal with Iran and hints at invading Kuwait. Glaspie misreads the signals.

26th July OPEC conference in Geneva eventually agrees on $21 a barrel oil price for member nations.

31st July and 1st August Kuwaiti and Iraqi delegations meet for talks in Jeddah. Talks break down as the Kuwaitis take an intransigent stance.

2nd August Iraq invades Kuwait at about 3 a.m. GMT.

4th August The European Community takes a collective decision to impose immediate economic sanctions against Iraq.

6th August United Nations Security Council passes Resolution 661, imposing sanctions against Iraq. Saddam summons American chargé d'affaires Joseph Wilson in an attempt to strike a deal with the United States at the expense of Kuwait.

8th August Saddam Hussein annexes Kuwait. Iraqi oil exports come to a standstill. Leading elements of US 82nd Airborne Division arrive in Saudi Arabia. Allied warships gather in Gulf. Hostages captured in Kuwait arrive in Baghdad.

9th August Emergency summit meeting of Arab States League in Cairo. Meeting splits into factions and no results achieved. Iraq orders all Western embassies in Kuwait to close and their staff to Baghdad within two weeks. Border between Jordan and Iraq closed to Westerners trying to leave Iraq. King Fahd attacks Iraq's invasion of Kuwait.

10th August Saddam Hussein calls upon Muslims to take up arms in Jihad Muqadas (holy mission) to liberate the Muslim shrines in Saudi Arabia. Arab summit in Cairo votes to send Arab forces to Saudi Arabia and the other Gulf states.

12th August RAF aircraft arrive in Sultanate of Oman. Egyptian 3rd Mechanised Division arrives in Saudi Arabia. Briton shot on Kuwait–Saudi border whilst trying to escape.

13th August Pakistan announces it will send troops to support Saudi Arabia. Saudi Arabian warships turn back Iraqi tanker approaching pipeline terminal at Mu'ajjiz.

14th August Syrian troops begin arriving in Saudi Arabia. United States holds discussions with Britain, France, Soviet Union and China over establishment of joint military command structure under United Nations.

16th August United States announces despatch of 45,000 marines to the Gulf. European Community offers aid to Jordan if it complies with United Nations sanctions. Saddam Hussein attacks President Bush in television broadcast. Iraq orders all Britons and Americans in Kuwait to assemble in hotels prior to being transported to Baghdad.

17th August Special committee of United Nations Security Council convenes to discuss compliance with sanctions against Iraq. Iraqi troops commence withdrawing from Iran whilst Iranian prisoners, captured during Gulf War, are released by Iraq. King Hussein returns from United States after failing to achieve anything during talks with President Bush.

19th August Iraq announces it will release hostages from those countries not sending forces to Gulf. United Nations Security Council demands that Iraq release all hostages.

20th August Iraq gives foreign embassies in Kuwait five days to move to Baghdad, warning that they will otherwise lose their diplomatic status. Hostages are despatched to military and strategic installations in Iraq in attempts to avert possible strikes by allied forces. Britain, Italy, Sweden and Denmark refuse to close their embassies. Saudi Arabia fails to win sufficient support for convening of special meeting of OPEC. Iraqi Deputy Prime Minister arrives in Moscow.

21st August Iraq moves Scud missiles and launchers to Kuwait. Iraqi Foreign Minister Tariq Aziz is prepared to discuss Gulf crisis with the United States. President Hosni Mubarak urges Saddam Hussein to withdraw from Kuwait. Prime Minister Margaret Thatcher rules out negotiations with Baghdad over hostages. Iraq announces completion of withdrawal of its troops from Iran. Meeting of Western European Union in Paris agrees to support dispatch of military forces by Britain, France and the Netherlands to the Gulf.

22nd August President Bush authorises call-up of US military reserves for active duty in the Gulf.

23rd August The five permanent members of the United Nations Security Council reach agreement on a formula to put forces in the Gulf under a UN umbrella. Saddam Hussein televised with British hostages and their children. Thousands of refugees flee from Iraq to Jordan despite closing of border on the previous day. King Hussein arrives in the Yemen.

24th August Foreign embassies still in Kuwait come under siege from Iraqi troops.

25th August Iraqi Foreign Minister Tariq Aziz agrees to meet UN Secretary-General Perez de Cuellar in Amman. Iran agrees to open its border for refugees. First French troops arrive in the United Arab Emirates.

26th August Qatar announces agreement for Western forces to be deployed on its territory. Israel seeks fighter aircraft and surface-to-air missiles from the United States. British Secretary of Defence Tom King departs for Saudi Arabia for talks. Britain and France reject the idea of negotiations with Iraq, despite declaration by Perez de Cuellar that the time is right for a diplomatic solution. A quorum of Arab States League members agree to meet in Cairo to discuss the crisis.

28th August Saddam Hussein proposes talks with the United States and Britain and announces that all women and children hostages are free to leave. President Mubarak announces he will request withdrawal of foreign forces from Gulf if Iraq withdraws from Kuwait. The PLO sends an envoy to Iran to seek help in defeating the UN embargo on Iraq. The US Senate questions contributions from other nations and to what extent America will have to make sacrifices for the Gulf. Ten of thirteen OPEC ministers support increase in oil production by Saudi Arabia and other Arab states. An American held in Basra dies.

29th August Bahrain's Foreign Minister warns military action might be required to liberate Kuwait if sanctions fail. Iraq asks Turkey for food and medical supplies. Britain sends another warship to the Gulf. Japan offers aid to multinational force in the Gulf.

30th August Iraq threatens to attack Saudi Arabia and Israel in the event of war. Perez de Cuellar arrives in Jordan for talks with Iraqi foreign minister. President Bush announces plan to persuade allied nations to share cost of enforcing United Nations sanctions.

1st September Two thousand women and children begin to leave Iraq and Kuwait. American politician Jesse Jackson brings forty-seven of the estimated 1050 American hostages home.

4th September Moscow calls for an international peace conference to settle all Middle East problems.

9th September Almost total agreement is reached between Presidents Gorbachev and Bush during the summit in Helsinki.

14th September Iraqi soldiers violate diplomatic rules by entering the homes of four French diplomats in Kuwait. Three Frenchmen are abducted.

15th September President Mitterrand despatches units of the Foreign Legion to Saudi Arabia and France expels fifty Iraqis. Baghdad declares the violation of French diplomatic immunity by Iraqi soldiers was a mistake.

20th September Iraq threatens to destroy all oilfields in the Gulf if attacked.

21st September Iraq expels seventeen diplomats from six countries, including Egypt.

23rd September President Mitterrand proposes a plan to settle all Middle East disputes.

25th September United Nations Security Council votes for an air embargo on Iraq.

3rd October President Mitterrand visits French troops in the Gulf as well as Saudi Arabia and Abu Dhabi.

8th October Israeli police kill more than twenty Palestinians at the Temple Mount in Jerusalem after they lose control of a crowd throwing stones at Jewish worshippers.

9th October Saddam Hussein calls upon the Arabs to liberate Jerusalem. The Soviet Union and Iraq agree to release fifteen Soviet nationals from Iraq. Iraqi Foreign Minister Tariq Aziz calls for negotiation between all parties concerned in the Gulf crisis.

12th October The Speaker of Egypt's People's Assembly, Dr Rifaat al-Mahgoub, is assassinated by unidentified gunmen.

14th October Iraq denies role in death of Mahgoub. Iran and Iraq formally resume diplomatic relations. The UN Security Council unanimously condemns Israel for the death of the Palestinians in Jerusalem. Syrian troops complete occupation of Beirut, after crushing Christian leader General Aoun.

16th October Britain increases its commitment by deploying the 7th Armoured Brigade and supporting troops. The US asks Pakistan to deploy an armoured division to Saudi Arabia.

20th October Former British Prime Minister Edward Heath arrives in Baghdad on a humanitarian mission to secure the release of British hostages, contrary to Foreign Office policy.

21st October A teenage Palestinian stabs three Jews dead and wounds another in Jerusalem in revenge for the killings of 8th October. Mr Heath meets with President Saddam Hussein and secures the release of over forty elderly and sick hostages.

23rd October President Bush declares that there will be no settlement with Saddam Hussein until Iraq withdraws from Kuwait.

28th October Soviet envoy Yvgeny Primakov meets Saddam Hussein in Baghdad to discuss the possibility of a peaceful settlement. Saddam Hussein removes his oil minister from office for instituting petrol rationing.

29th October All 298 French hostages arrive in France. The French government denies that a deal was made with the Iraqis in exchange for the hostages' freedom. In France, President Gorbachev declares that war is not acceptable as a means of settling the crisis and calls for an Arab summit to settle it.

31st October President Mubarak rejects the idea of an Arab summit before Iraq withdraws from Kuwait. The Iraqi ambassador in Washington calls for further negotiations to resolve the crisis. Egyptian, Syrian and Saudi Arabian foreign ministers meet in Riyadh after Syria has expressed doubts over American plans for the region.

1st November The Iraqi government rubber-stamps a parliamentary vote to free all Bulgarian hostages on the grounds that their country is not part of the 'imperialist plot'.

2nd November US Secretary of State James Baker begins a Middle East and European tour of allied nations. Libya expels the Abu al-Abbas terrorist group who move to Iraq.

3rd November EC foreign ministers recommend that individual politicians should not go to Baghdad. Iraq threatens an all-out war, which would reach Israel, if the United States attacks.

4th November Baghdad orders British hostages to telephone home.

5th November US Secretary of State James Baker agrees with King Fahd and Saudi leaders the chain of command for allied forces in the Gulf. (The United States to command any offensive outside Saudi Arabia but joint command to be exercised on Saudi soil.) Baker addresses troops of 82nd Airborne

Division. Wives of British hostages held in Iraq announce they will go to Baghdad as guests of the Iraqi government to plead for their husbands' release.

6th November Former West German Chancellor Willy Brandt arrives in Baghdad to try to negotiate freedom for the hostages. Saddam Hussein announces that he will release 106 hostages, mainly Japanese and twenty-nine of other nationalities, as a gesture towards former Prime Minister Nakasoni, who had arrived in Baghdad the day before.

7th November Arab diplomats reveal that France's former Foreign Minister Claud Cheysson met a week earlier with Tariq Aziz in Tunisia to negotiate a deal for the release of the French hostages.

8th November British Labour Member of Parliament Tony Benn announces he will go to Baghdad to explore a peaceful settlement and to negotiate the freedom of more hostages. Ten British women, whose husbands are trapped in Iraq, ignore Foreign Office advice and leave for Baghdad.

9th November Willy Brandt departs from Baghdad with 200 hostages.

10th November US Secretary of State James Baker arrives in London for talks with the Prime Minister and the Foreign Secretary. Margaret Thatcher is reported as stating that she sees no need to obtain a United Nations Security Council resolution for approval of military action if sanctions against Iraq fail. Egyptian and Saudi Arabian foreign ministers arrive in Damascus to meet with their Syrian counterpart after doubts are expressed over Syria's commitment.

13th–15th November President Bush tours European capitals. More hostages are released. President Mubarak carries out a surprise trip to Libya then travels on to Syria.

16th November President Mubarak returns to Cairo, calling for a halt in military action for another three months.

20th November President Bush suffers a setback after failing to secure Soviet support for a United Nations resolution giving sanction for military action. US fails to persuade Saudi Arabia to end its policy of forcing 1.5 million Yemenis to return home.

21st November Iraq announces it will release more hostages, including German and Irish workers who have completed contracts. President Bush arrives in Jeddah for a meeting with King Fahd.

22nd November Prime Minister Margaret Thatcher resigns. Britain announces that it will send 14,000 additional troops to the Gulf.

23rd November After meeting President Mubarak in Cairo, President Bush meets with President Assad of Syria in Geneva.

24th November British women meet Saddam Hussein to plead for their husbands' release. Poll of American public opinion shows growing support for diplomatic solution by ratio of 7:3. Reports from Iraq of incidents and internal trouble. A Kuwaiti organisation is blamed for attacks on Iraqi schoolgirls.

25th November Labour Member of Parliament Tony Benn and former World Heavyweight Boxing Champion Muhammad Ali travel to Baghdad.

26th November Saddam Hussein talks for three hours with Tony Benn and promises to release more British hostages.

27th November Saddam Hussein agrees to release the husbands of the women he had met three days previously.

28th November United Nations Security Council members are shown evidence of Iraqi atrocities in Kuwait. UN Security Council asks the Secretary-General to safeguard a copy of Kuwait's population register to foil attempts by Iraq to repopulate the emirate with Iraqis.

29th November The UN Security Council lays down a deadline of 15th January 1991 by which Iraq must comply with Resolution 660 to withdraw from Kuwait or face military action by allied forces.

30th November President Bush offers direct talks with Iraq and announces that he will send US Secretary of State James Baker to Baghdad and that he will receive Iraqi Foreign Minister Tariq Aziz in Washington.

3rd December US Defense Secretary Dick Cheney testifies before Senate Foreign Relations Committee, stating that sanctions are not proving effective. Baghdad starts releasing 1000 Russians after Moscow threatens to send troops to the Gulf if its citizens are not released.

4th December Iraqi Minister of Health reports death of 1000 children because of lack of medicine, and calls for the lifting of sanctions.

5th December Iraq formally accepts talks with the United States. Iraq announces that all Soviet experts are allowed to leave, but demands that Moscow pay compensation for cutting short their contracts.

6th December Saddam Hussein announces that all Western hostages will be released by Christmas. The Bush administration vehemently rejects claims that it is seeking a Middle East peace conference, and denies it has weakened its outright opposition to 'linkage' between the Gulf crisis and the Palestinian question.

9th December 500 Western hostages are allowed to leave Iraq as the exodus begins. King Hussein of Jordan reveals that behind-the-scenes diplomacy was under way to arrange for direct talks between King Fahd and President Saddam Hussein.

12th December Algerian President Chadli bin Jadid arrives in Baghdad as part of a diplomatic effort to end the crisis.

14th December President Bush cancels Tariq Aziz's proposed visit to Washington on 17th December after Baghdad's failure to fix a date, earlier than their suggested 12th January, for James Baker to meet with Saddam Hussein in Baghdad. Moscow expresses regret but puts the blame on Iraq.

16th December In Cairo, Algerian President Chadhli bin Jadid suggests a new peace plan: Iraq is to withdraw while Arab forces guarantee security. It meets with little Arab response.

17th December Secretary of State James Baker warns NATO foreign ministers that Saddam Hussein might withdraw from most, but not all, of Kuwait before the deadline of 15th January in an attempt to split the allies. President Bush sends Iraq a tough warning and escalates his attack on Saddam Hussein. Britain advises nationals to leave the Gulf region.

18th December EEC foreign ministers refuse to meet with Aziz unless Iraq agrees on holding talks with the United States. US Secretary of Defense Dick Cheney and General Colin Powell visit Saudi Arabia.

20th December Former British Prime Minister Edward Heath testifies before the Congressional Armed Services Committee and calls for negotiation rather than war.

21st December UN Security Council passes a resolution to protect Palestinians under Israeli occupation but does not call for an international conference. Israel rejects the proposal and the PLO claims it does not go far enough. Iraq attacks it. Arab press hail the deployment of the Egyptian 4th Armoured Division to the front line on the borders with Kuwait as a signal that the allies mean business.

22nd December Gulf Co-Operation Council starts 11th Summit meeting in Doha, Qatar; Iran is invited as observer. President Bush and Prime Minister John Major meet in Washington. Mr Major says Britain is still committed to US policy in the Gulf.

23rd December The Gulf heads of state call, with Iran's agreement, for a new security system in the region. US Defense Secretary Dick Cheney and Chief of Staff General Colin Powell give a stern warning to Saddam Hussein during a press conference in Cairo after meeting with President Mubarak. Iraqis say the land will burn under the feet of the Americans if they attack. Reports circulate that British troops have ammunition for less than two weeks' fighting.

24th December Cheney says Saddam will be totally defeated if he does not withdraw. Saddam Hussein summons all his ambassadors from abroad. He says on television that Tel Aviv will be his first target if hostilities break out whether or not Israel is involved.

26th December Two Iraqi ships are intercepted by US ships and boarded by both American and British marines. Baghdad calls it an act of piracy. John Major repeats demands that Iraq must withdraw from Kuwait before 15th January 1991. Defense Secretary Dick Cheney tells President Bush American troops will not be ready for operation until two weeks after the 15th January deadline. State Department orders all non-essential staff in embassies in Sudan, Mauritania and Jordan to move out before January 15th.

27th December In a meeting with the Iraqi ambassadors who were recalled to Baghdad, President Saddam Hussein offers high level direct talks with the United States but says they must include the Palestinian issue. Joseph Wilson, the American *chargé d'affaires* in Baghdad, reveals he had been discussing with the Iraqis renewed efforts for direct talks. The Kuwaiti Foreign Minister in exile, Sheikh Sabah al-Salim, says the time for peace offers has passed.

28th December It is revealed that Franco–Algerian diplomatic efforts have been trying to find an Arab solution. US sends two carrier groups led by *USS Roosevelt* and *USS America*. Reports emerge that Britain is to deploy *HMS Invincible*. Iraqi opposition members declare an alliance of 17 groups (including Muslims, Liberals, Communists, Kurds and Nationalists) in Damascus and call for the removal of Saddam Hussein and elections.

29th December Claims appear in the British press that US and British forces have between them some 1000 tactical nuclear weapons ready to use in the conflict. Front-line observation posts report that Iraqi troops are still pouring into Kuwait.

30th December President Bush says he feels that Saddam Hussein will withdraw. Following German and French expressions of concern at Bush's handling of the crisis, EC foreign ministers announce they will hold an emergency meeting on the Gulf on 4th January to break the diplomatic deadlock.

31st December US Vice President Dan Quayle visits troops in Saudi Arabia and asks Gulf states for more money to finance allied forces. Luxembourg Foreign Minister Jacques Poos, who chairs the EC council of ministers from 4th January, says he expects the council to send him on a mission to Baghdad to talk with Mr Aziz. Saddam Hussein spends New Year's Eve with troops on the front.

1st January 1991 President Mubarak urges Iraq to withdraw from Kuwait to avoid an inferno that would claim thousands of lives. Iraq calls him a liar and a clown. President Bush meets with defence and top security advisers and announces he will send Secretary of State James Baker on a mission to meet with Saddam. EEC ministers say they will meet Iraqi Foreign Minister Tariq Aziz in Europe. A suggestion emerges of fixing a meeting between Aziz and Baker in a European city. Iraq calls for those over seventeen to report for military duty. London cuts the Baghdad embassy staff from sixteen to six. (There were thirty before 2nd August 1990.)

2nd January Crown Prince Hassan of Jordan opens a joint conference with the Green Party in London, addressed by Tony Benn and Edward Heath on the effect of a war in the Gulf on the environment. The French say sanctions should be given more time to work and criticise the Americans for deploying so many troops that they can no longer afford the time necessary. King Hussein of Jordan arrives in London on a peace finding tour of Europe. Michel Vauzelle, President of the French National Assembly, arrives in Baghdad on a private mission to explore ways of peace. In London 2500 naval reservists called up. British troops move nearer to the Kuwaiti borders.

3rd January King Hussein holds talks with Prime Minister Major. President Bush invites Tariq Aziz to hold talks with James Baker in Geneva on 6th and 7th January. Saddam Hussein refuses to meet Baker before 15th. Britain expels eight Iraqi diplomats and 67 students after the Iraqi press attaché warns reporters that war would be likely to lead enraged Arabs to carry out violent attacks in Europe. President Bush gives Iraq a last chance for peace by inviting Tariq Aziz to hold talks in Geneva with James Baker between the 7th and 9th. The Egyptian, Syrian, and Sudanese presidents meet with Colonel Gaddafi in Libya to close ranks. In Islamabad, Iran, Pakistan and Turkey call for an urgent meeting of Islamic countries to seek a peaceful solution. Listeners to the BBC's Africa service vote Saddam Hussein Man of the Year 1990.

4th January In Iraq Tariq Aziz holds talks with M. Vauzelle. Iraq says Aziz will talk to Baker in Geneva on 9th January. The pope sends a message to the EEC foreign ministers' meeting in Luxembourg, calling for a peaceful solution.

solution. The French, supported by the Germans, propose an extension to the 15th January deadline in return for an Iraqi promise to withdraw from Kuwait. The foreign ministers say they will invite Aziz to Luxembourg for talks on 10 January. President Mitterrand states the UN Security Council should meet again if Iraq fails to meet the deadline. The Congressional Foreign Relations Committee tells president Bush he has 'no blank check' for war.

5th January Michel Vauzelle holds four-and-a-half-hour talks with Saddam Hussein while Tariq Aziz says he will not meet with EC foreign ministers since European policy is dictated by Washington. UN Secretary General Perez de Cuellar meets with President Bush at Camp David, and declares there is no need for another Security Council meeting. American officials say Baker is prepared to discuss all Middle East issues with Aziz but will reject any linkage to withdrawal. Documents leaked to the *Observer* show that the Ministry of Defence asked the National Health service to prepare 7500 beds in British civilian hospitals to cater for casualties, should war break out.

6th January President Saddam Hussein delivers a fiery speech on Army Day saying his people are ready for 'the mother of battles', adding that all Middle East issues are part of one battle. John Major leaves for the Gulf and Egypt as James Baker arrives in London to start a European tour. King Hussein arrives in Bonn for talks with the Germans and the Americans say James Baker will show Tariq Aziz evidence that US satellites can pinpoint details of Saddam's moves and could target him and possibly kill him in the event of war. Five major airlines including Pan Am and SAS cancel their flights to Israel on the basis that it could be an early target in a war, while Germany and Sweden advise their nationals to leave the country.

9th January Six-hour meeting in Geneva between Baker and Tariq Aziz (who is accompanied by Saddam's half-brother Barzan al-Takriti) ends in failure. Baker refuses to turn the 'discussion' into talks. Aziz attacks the West's double standard of allowing Israel to ignore UN Resolutions and threatens to attack Israel if war starts. President Mubarak warns that Egypt will change position if Israel gets involved. France presses for EC peace talks with Iraq in Algeria. UN Secretary General announces he will go to Baghdad to see Saddam on 12th January. Saddam Hussein warns that US troops will 'swim in their own blood' if war starts. At midnight, the Foreign Office orders British diplomats out of Iraq.

Summary of the United Nations Resolutions Covering the Gulf Crisis

1 Resolution 660, 2 August
The Security Council condemns the Iraqi invasion of Kuwait; demands that Iraq withdraw immediately and unconditionally all its forces to the positions in which they were located on 1 August 1990; calls upon Iraq and Kuwait to begin immediately intensive negotiations for the resolution of their differences and supports all efforts in this regard.

2 Resolution 661, 6 August
The Council determines that Iraq has failed to comply with Resolution 660; decides to take the following measures:
• All states shall prevent the import of all products originating in Iraq or Kuwait; any activities that would promote the export of any products from Iraq or Kuwait; the supply of any products, including weapons, but not including supplies intended strictly for medical purposes, and, in humanitarian circumstances, foodstuffs, to Iraq or Kuwait.
• All states shall not make available to any undertaking in Iraq or Kuwait any funds and shall prevent their nationals from making available any funds.
• A committee of the Security Council to be established to examine reports on the implementation of the present resolution, and to seek from all states further information regarding the action taken by them.

3 Resolution 662, 9 August
The Security Council decides that annexation of Kuwait by Iraq has no legal validity; calls upon all states, international organisations and agencies not to recognise that annexation; further demands that Iraq rescind its actions purporting to annex Kuwait.

4 Resolution 664, 18 August
The Security Council demands that Iraq facilitate the immediate departure from Kuwait and Iraq of the nationals of third countries; further demands that Iraq take no action to jeopardise the safety, security or health of such nationals; demands that the government of Iraq rescind its orders for the closure of diplomatic missions in Kuwait and the withdrawal of immunity.

5   Resolution 665, 25 August
The Security Council calls upon those member states deploying maritime forces to the area to use such measures as may be necessary to halt all inward and outward maritime shipping in order to inspect their cargoes and verify their destinations.

6   Resolution 666, 13 September
The Security Council decides that, in order to determine whether or not humanitarian circumstances have arisen, the committee shall keep the situation regarding foodstuffs in Iraq and Kuwait under constant review; requests that the Secretary-General seek information on the availability of food in Iraq and Kuwait; requests further that particular attention be paid to persons who might suffer specially.

7   Resolution 667, 16 September
The Security Council strongly condemns aggressive acts perpetrated by Iraq against diplomatic premises and personnel in Kuwait, including the abduction of foreign nationals; demands the immediate release of those foreign nationals as well as all nationals mentioned in Resolution 664; further demands that Iraq immediately protect the safety and well-being of diplomatic and consular personnel and premises in Kuwait and in Iraq and take no action to hinder the missions in the performance of their functions.

8   Resolution 669, 24 September
The Security Council entrusts the committee established under Resolution 661 with the task of examining requests for assistance under the provisions of Article 50 of the Charter of the UN and making recommendations for action.

9   Resolution 670, 25 September
The Security Council decides that all states should deny permission to any aircraft to take off from their territory if the aircraft is carrying any cargo to or from Iraq or Kuwait other than food in humanitarian circumstances, or supplies intended strictly for medical purposes.

It decides further that all states shall deny permission to any aircraft destined to land in Iraq or Kuwait to overfly its territory unless the aircraft lands in order to permit inspection; or the flight has been approved by the committee established by Resolution 661, or the flight is certified by the UN.

The Security Council decides to consider, in the event of evasion of the provisions of Resolution 661 or of this Resolution, measures directed at the state in question to prevent such evasion.

10   Resolution 674, 29 October
The Security Council demands that Iraq cease and desist from taking third-state nationals hostage, mistreating and oppressing Kuwaiti and third-state nationals and any other actions that violate the decisions of this Council, the UN Charter, the Fourth Geneva Convention, the Vienna Conventions on Diplomatic and

Consular Relations and international law; it invites states to collate information on the grave breaches by Iraq as per above; demands that Iraq ensure access to food, water and basic services to Kuwaiti nationals and nationals of third states in Kuwait and Iraq.

The Security Council reminds Iraq that it is liable for any loss, damage or injury arising in regard to Kuwait and third states, as a result of the invasion and occupation of Kuwait; invites states to collect relevant information regarding their claims for compensation by Iraq. The Council reposes its trust in the Secretary-General to make available his good offices and to undertake diplomatic efforts in order to reach a peaceful solution to the crisis and calls upon all states to pursue their efforts to this end; requests the Secretary-General to report on the results of his good offices.

11   Resolution 677, 28 November
The Security Council asks the Secretary-General to safeguard a smuggled copy of Kuwait's population register to foil attempts by Iraq to repopulate the emirate with Iraqis.

12   Resolution 678, 29 November
The Security Council, noting that Iraq refuses to comply with its obligation to implement Resolution 660 and subsequent resolutions, demands that Iraq comply fully with all relevant resolutions and decides, while maintaining all its decisions, to allow Iraq a final opportunity, as a pause of goodwill, to do so.

It authorises member states co-operating with the government of Kuwait, unless Iraq on or before 15 January 1991 fully implements the foregoing resolutions, to use all necessary means to uphold and implement Security Council Resolution 660 and to restore international peace and security in the area; requests all states to provide appropriate support for the actions undertaken in pursuance of this resolution.

Chronology of Events

1534 The Ottoman Turks, under Suleiman the Magnificent, conquer Baghdad.

1917 The Ottomans relinquish control of Baghdad to Britain.

3rd October 1918 Ottoman rule over the Arabs symbolically ends as the bedouin army of Faisal, the son of Sharif Hussein of Hijaz, and leader of the Arab revolt against the Turks, enters Damascus.

2nd June 1920 Widespread tribal uprisings in Iraq against British military rule.

24th July 1920 French forces oust Faisal and occupy Damascus. The French mandate over Syria begins.

27th August 1921 Britain installs Faisal as monarch in Iraq under mandate from the League of Nations. Faisal is accompanied by an entourage of Iraqi supporters from the days of the Arab revolt. Satia'al-Husri, a Syrian pan-Arabist thinker, arrives with Faisal and gradually takes over the educational system.

10th October 1922 The Anglo-Iraqi Treaty, which sets out the scope of Britain's involvement in Iraqi affairs, is signed.

16th November 1930 The Iraqi parliament ratifies a new Anglo-Iraqi Treaty, which sets a date for the termination of the British mandate over Iraq on conditions favourable to Britain.

3rd October 1932 The independent state of Iraq is formally admitted to the League of Nations.

13th December 1932 The first communist proclamation appears in Iraq, written in long hand by 'Fahd', the future leader of the Iraqi communist party (ICP).

August 1933 The Assyrian Affair. The army under General Bakr Sidqi initiates a pogrom of the Assyrian community with the support of the government and against the express wishes of Faisal. Sidqi becomes a national hero.

8th September 1933 King Faisal dies and is succeeded by his son Ghazi, a keen supporter of the army's actions against the Assyrians.

29th October 1936 Bakr Sidqi overthrows the government in the Arab world's first military coup.

28th April 1937 Saddam Hussein is born in the desert town of Takrit.

11th August 1937 Sidqi is assassinated by army officers. Six more coups follow in quick succession, ending in 1941.

1st April 1941 Four pan-Arabist generals proclaim a state of emergency. A government of national defence headed by Rashid'Ali al-Guilani is formed and immediately supported by the Axis powers. Pro-British Iraqi politicians flee.

May 1941 British forces, landed in Basra, defeat the Iraqi army on 19th May. Rashid'Ali and the generals escape to Tehran on 29th May.

24th July 1943 Arab Ba'ath movement, a group of ten people, publishes its first programme in Damascus.

April 1947 The first congress of the Ba'ath party is held, representing a membership of a few hundred. In Iraq, Ba'athist ideas are introduced by Syrian teachers in 1949.

1956 President Nasser of Egypt nationalises the Suez Canal, and the Canal Zone is occupied by Anglo-French troops who are eventually withdrawn after pressure on Britain and France from the United States.

14th July 1958 A secret organisation of two hundred 'free officers' overthrows the monarchy in a coup acclaimed throughout Iraq. Brigadier Abd al-Karim Qasim, who led the coup, emerges as prime minister and commander-in-chief of the armed forces.

24th July 1958 Michel'Aflaq, founder of the Ba'ath party, arrives in Baghdad calling for instant unity with the newly formed United Arab Republic. In opposition, the ICP projects Qasim as the sole leader.

30th September 1958 Abd Al-Salam Arif, a free officer of pan-Arabist persuasion and organiser with Qasim of the 1958 coup, is removed from his posts as deputy prime minister and minister of interior. The split between Qasim and Arif draws attention to the irreconcilability of the pan-Arab and Iraqist trends among the coup makers of 1958.

1st May 1959 Demonstration of about half a million people calling for communist representation in government.

September 1959 The writings of Michel'Aflaq are collected and published for the first time under the title *Fi Sabil al-Ba'ath* (*On the Way to Rebirth*).

7th October 1959 A Ba'athist assassination squad fails to kill Qasim. A member of the team, twenty-two-year-old Saddam Hussein, escapes to Syria and then to Egypt. Seventy-eight Ba'athists implicated in the incident are brought before Mehdawi's people's court. Their defiant militancy leaves a deep impression.

1st January 1960 Qasim announces that all political parties will be legalised but the Iraqi communist party is rebuffed. Anti-communist measures continue until the end of the regime.

10th September 1960 Iran, Iraq, Saudi Arabia and Venezuela meet in Baghdad to agree on a common oil policy.

15th January 1961 Oil producers, meeting in Venezuela, adopt a constitution for the Organisation of Petroleum Exporting Countries (OPEC).

March 1961 Ba'athist agitators lead a demonstration against the Qasim regime.

September 1961 The Iraqi army launches its first major offensive against the Kurds in mountainous terrain. By the spring of 1962, a costly full-scale guerrilla war develops, which Qasim cannot win.

24th December 1962 The Ba'athists successfully organise a nationwide strike of all secondary-school and university students, which continues until the fall of the regime.

8th February 1963 A Ba'athist coup overthrows Qasim amidst several days of terrible street fighting. The first Ba'athist regime is installed. Its nine-month rule is marked by a relentless settling of accounts with communists and their fellow travellers. Abd al-Salam Arif becomes president.

18th November 1963 Following bitter infighting between moderate and radical factions of the Ba'ath, Arif overthrows the Ba'athist regime. He is supported by moderate Ba'athist officers. The Ba'athist National Guard militia controlled by the civilian wing of the party takes to the streets and is crushed by the army. Arif appoints Ahmad Hasan al-Bakr, a former free officer and long-standing Ba'athist, vice-president. However, gradually all Ba'athists are eased out of the new military regime, which leans towards Nasserism.

February 1964 Michel'Afalq recommends the elevation of Saddam Hussein to the regional command of the Iraqi branch of the Arab Ba'ath Socialist party.

18th April–6th August 1966 Prime Minister Abd al-Rahman al-Bazzaz negotiates a temporary end to the Kurdish war, tries to curb army privileges and bring about an atmosphere reminiscent of the old regime.

June 1967 The Six Day War brings military catastrophe to the Arab world. All officer-led regimes are discredited.

6th September 1967 The Ba'ath party leads a large demonstration against the new Arif regime. It calls for action against the 'fifth column' responsible for the June defeat.

17th July 1968 In alliance with non-Ba'athist army officers, the Arab Ba'ath Socialist party organises a successful coup that overthrows the Arif regime.

30th July 1968 The Ba'ath cast out their former allies in a second carefully planned coup. Supreme authority passes to the Revolutionary Command Council (RCC) chaired by Ahmad Hasan al-Bakr, secretary-general of the Arab Ba'ath Socialist party, who also becomes president and commander-in-chief of the army. Saddam Hussein, already assistant secretary-general of the party, becomes deputy chairman of the RCC in charge of internal security.

February 1969 Aziz al-Haj, leader of the Iraqi communist party central command, is arrested and makes a public confession, which leads to the capture of the whole politbureau.

8th August 1969 The Kurdish village of Dakan in Mosul is the scene of a major army atrocity. The war against the Kurds is stepped up.

October 1969 Former prime minister Abd al-Rahman al-Bazzaz is tortured and imprisoned for fifteen years on charges of being a Zionist agent.

14th December 1968 Iraqi television presents graphic details of an alleged Zionist spy ring of Iraqi Jews broken up in Basra.

5th January 1969 The new regime's first batch of 'spies' are put on public trial. Seventeen defendants, including thirteen Iraqi Jews, are hanged in Liberation Square amid speeches and much fanfare. Hundreds of thousands of people attend the spectacle.

21st January 1970 The regime reports that a new conspiracy is foiled. Within a week forty-four people have been executed.

11th March 1970 A manifesto on Kurdish autonomy is published amidst much fanfare. On paper the Kurds are granted more rights as a nationality than ever before. The fighting stops and the Ba'ath government gains time to consolidate.

10th July 1970 The Arab Ba'ath Socialist party announces conditions for the communist party to join it in a Progressive National Front. The Iraqi communist party central committee prevaricates.

15th October 1970 Herdan al-Takriti, a prominent Ba'athist officer, former member of the Revolutionary Command Council, and former deputy prime minister and defence minister, is gunned down in Kuwait.

August 1971 Abd al-Karim Nasrat, early Ba'athist and organiser of the militia that was used in the overthrow of the Qasim regime in 1963, is stabbed to death in his house.

September 1971 Iraqi state security fails in an attempt to assassinate the Kurdish leader, Barzani.

November 1971 Fuad al-Rikkabi, the leader of the Ba'ath party from the inception of an Iraqi organisation until 1959, is murdered in prison.

April 1972 Iraqi–Soviet Friendship Treaty is announced.

May 1972 The Iraqi Petroleum Company is nationalised.

8th July 1973 Nadhim Kzar, chief of internal security, is executed, along with at least thirty-five others in the wake of an attempted coup.

July 1973 A National Action Charter, first announced in 1971, is signed by the Arab Ba'ath Socialist party and the Iraqi communist party, in which the latter accepts all the July 1970 conditions.

March 1974 Following the collapse of the 1970 Kurdish autonomy accords, all-out war begins. The Kurdish towns of Zakho and Qala'at Diza are razed to the ground. Hundreds of thousands of Kurds flee the cities. Brutalities break all previous records.

December 1974 Five Shi'ite clergy are executed for unknown reasons.

6th March 1975 The Algiers agreement between the Iraqi Ba'athist government and the Shah's regime in Iran is promulgated. Iraq formally concedes to Iranian territorial demands in return for the Shah's support against the Kurds. The Kurds' lines of supply are cut off and resistance crumbles. The government launches its policy of mass Kurdish deportations and re-settlement.

February 1977 Shi'ite clergy head a demonstration on the religious occasion of 'Ashura' in the city of Karbala. Some two thousand people are arrested and eight clergy executed. Mass deportations into Iran of Iraqi Shi'ite 'fifth columnists' begin about this time. By the late 1970s some 200,000 Iraqi Shi'ites have been dumped inside Iran, stripped of their nationality and property.

October 1978 Ayatollah Ruhollah Khomeini is expelled from Iraq and flees to France.

16th January 1979 Shah Mohamed Reza Pahlavi is overthrown and leaves Iran for good.

1st February 1979 Ayatollah Khomeini returns to Iran from exile in France to a rapturous welcome in Tehran.

June 1979 Saddam Hussein becomes president of Iraq. Ahmad Hasan Al-Bakr is stripped of all positions and placed under house arrest.

July 1979 Massive purge amongst top echelons of Ba'ath party in Iraq. One third of the members of the revolutionary command council are executed. By 1st August some five hundred top-ranking Ba'athists are said to have been executed.

1st November 1979 Iranian students storm the US embassy compound in Tehran, taking the staff hostage for 444 days, and demand the extradition of the Shah. All Iranian assets in the United States are frozen.

26th December 1979 Soviet troops enter Afghanistan.

9th April 1980 Mohammed Baqir al-Sadr and his sister Bint al-Huda, symbols of the Shi'ite opposition in Iraq, are executed.

24th April 1980 American attempt to rescue hostages held in Iran fails disastrously.

4th September 1980 Iranian shelling of Khanequin and Mandali; the day on which Iraq claims the Gulf War began.

17th September 1980 Iraq abrogates Algiers treaty with Iran.

22nd September 1980 Saddam Hussein launches full-scale war against Iran. The bloodiest war in Middle Eastern history, it lasts eight years. Casualties are estimated at two million. Dissent spreads to the army, the rank-and-file of the Ba'ath party and the 'people's army'. Repression extends to all sections of the population.

24th October 1980 Iraq captures Khorramshahr.

November 1980 Setting-up of the Democratic Patriotic Front, which includes the Iraqi communist party, the Kurdistan democratic party and the Kurdistan socialist party. They adopt the armed struggle.

19th January 1981 The United States and Iran sign an agreement to free American hostages and unfreeze Iranian assets. Hostages fly to Germany as Ronald Reagan takes presidential oath of office.

7th June 1981 Israel destroys the French-built Osirak nuclear reactor near Baghdad in an air raid.

September 1981 Iraqi armed forces pull back east of the Karun river in Iran.

10th April 1982 Syria stops pumping of Iraqi oil through pipeline to Mediterranean.

April 1982 Popular uprising in Iraqi Kurdistan. Thirteen women among those killed.

24th May 1982 Iran recaptures Khorramshahr.

6th June 1982 Israel invades Lebanon.

July 1982 Iranian troops cross into Iraqi territory.

12th August 1982 Iraq declares maritime exclusion zone around Iran's Kharg Island oil terminal.

17th November 1982 Setting-up in Tehran of the Iraqi Muslim opposition umbrella organisation SAIRI (Supreme Assembly for the Islamic Revolution in Iraq).

May 1983 Turkey invades Iraqi Kurdistan with the full co-operation of the Iraqi regime.

23rd October 1983 Suicide bomber causes death of 241 American marines in Beirut.

1st March 1984 First confirmed use of chemical weapons by Iraq. Iraqi troops driven out of the Majnoon marshes and oil field. Start of the Tanker War with Iraqi missile attack on British oil tanker.

4th March 1985 Beginning of the first 'War of the Cities', with Iraq bombing Ahwaz and Iran firing missiles at Baghdad.

14th July 1985 Iran warns that ships sailing into the Gulf may be stopped and searched.

10th February 1986 Iranian troops capture the Fao Peninsula.

March 1986 UN report confirms that Iraq has used chemical weapons.

3rd November 1986 The Lebanese magazine *Al Shira'a* publishes details of what became known as the 'Irangate' scandal, in which US National Security Adviser Robert MacFarlane and Lt-Col. Oliver North were alleged to have clandestinely sold arms to Iran and used the proceeds to fund the Nicaraguan 'Contras'.

17th May 1987 In Gulf waters, an Iraqi fighter fires an Exocet missile at the American frigate USS *Stark*, killing thirty-seven of its crew. Washington accepts the Iraqi explanation that it was a mistake.

19th May 1987 The United States announces it will reflag eleven Kuwaiti oil tankers to afford them protection.

22nd July 1987 The first convoy of reflagged tankers escorted by American warships sails. Two days later, the tanker *Bridgetown* hits a floating mine.

31st July 1987 Clashes between Iranian pilgrims and Saudi Arabian security forces in Mecca leave more than four hundred dead.

28th March 1988 Iraqi forces use chemical weapons against the town of Halabja, in the first-ever use of chemical weapons by a state against its own citizens. Further targets include civilians in the Bassay Valley in October.

18th April 1988 Iranian forces are driven out of the Fao Peninsula.

25th May 1988 Iraq recaptures territory opposite Basra.

25th June 1988 Iraq drives Iranian forces out of the islands on the Majnoon marshes.

3rd July 1988 All 290 passengers travelling in an Iranian airbus are killed when it is shot down by USS *Vincennes*.

18th July 1988 UN Secretary-General Perez de Cuellar receives Iran's acceptance of Resolution 598 calling for a ceasefire and withdrawal of troops to the internationally recognised border, as well as the establishment of a commission to decide responsibility for the war.

February 1989 Iraq, Egypt, Jordan and North Yemen establish the Arab Co-operation Council.

May 1989 Iraq and Saudi Arabia sign a non-aggression pact.

August 1989 Huge explosion destroys missile site in Iraq killing 700.

15 September 1989 *Observer* journalist Farzad Bazoft is arrested at Baghdad airport.

10th March 1990 Farzad Bazoft is condemned to death by an Iraqi court after being found guilty of spying. He is executed on 15th March.

21st March 1990 Jonathon Moyle, editor of *Defence Helicopter World*, is found murdered in hotel room in Santiago, Chile.

22nd March 1990 Dr Gerald Bull, inventor of 'Project Babylon', is murdered outside his Brussels flat.

28th March 1990 British Customs and Excise officers at Heathrow Airport seize a consignment of American-manufactured 'krytron' capacitators bound for Iraq.

10th April 1990 Customs officers at a British port seize a consignment of tubes destined for 'Project Babylon'.

27th May 1990 Arab summit in Baghdad. Saddam Hussein's first criticism of Gulf oil producers.

9th July 1990 Gulf oil ministers meet in Jeddah.

14th–15th July 1990 Arab foreign ministers meet in Tunis. Iraqi Foreign Minister Tariq Aziz accuses Kuwait of stealing oil from Iraqi part of Rumailah oil field.

17th July 1990 President Saddam Hussein attacks Kuwait and the UAE policy of overproducing oil and pushing prices down in his national day speech. He threatens to cut throats.

Select Bibliography

BOOKS

A. Abbas, *Saddam's Iraq – Revolution or Reaction?* (Zed Books, London 1986)

Abo Eslam A. Abdalla, *Saddam Hussein – The Roots & the Crimes* (Bait Al Hekma, Cairo 1990)

Muhammad Morsy Abdullah, *The United Arab Emirates – A Modern History* (Croom Helm, London 1978)

Ervand Abrahamian, *Radical Islam – The Iranian Mojahedin* (I. B. Tauris, London 1989)

Said K. Aburish, *Beirut Spy* (Bloomsbury, London 1989)

James Adams, *Trading in Death* (Hutchinson, London 1990)

Walid Al-Heli, *Human Rights in Iraq 1968–1988* (Media Research, London 1988)

Hassan Al-Alawi, *Abd al-karim Qasim: A Vision beyond Twenty Years* (Dar al-Zawra, London 1983)
  The Iraqi Shi'ite and the State 1914–1990 (Dar al-Zawra, London 1990)

E. Ashtor, *A Social & Economic History of the Near East in the Middle Ages* (Collins, London 1976)

Frederick W. Axelgard, *A New Iraq? The Gulf War & Implications for US Policy* (Prager, Washington, DC, 1988)

Gamal Badawi, *Black Days in Baghdad*
  Al-Zahra Lillam Al-Arabi (Ciro 1990)

Frank Barnaby, *The Invisible Bomb* (I. B. Tauris, London 1989)

Christopher Bellamy, *The Evolution of Modern Land Warfare* (Routledge, London 1990)

John Bulloch and Harvey Morris, *The Gulf War* (Methuen, London 1989)

Stuart A. Cohen, *British Policy in Mesopotamia 1903–1914* (Ithaca Press, London 1976)

Anthony H. Cordesmann, *The Iran–Iraq War and Western Security 1984–1987* (Jane's Publishing Company, London 1987)

John F. Devlin, *The Ba'ath Party – A History from its Origins to 1966* (Hoover Institution Press, Stanford 1976)

Christopher Dobson and Ronald Payne, *The Dictionary of Espionage* (Harrap, London 1984)

Mahmoud al-Durrah, *The Mosul Nationalist Revolution in 1959* (Al-Yaqadha Al-Arabiyah, Baghdad 1987)

Paul Eidelberg, *Sadat's Strategy* (Dawn Books, Quebec 1979)

Marion and Peter Farouk-Sluglett, *Iraq Since 1958* (I. B. Tauris, London 1990)

General Mohammed Fawzi, *The Three Years War 1967–1970* (Dar Al-Mustaqbal Alarbi, Cairo 1984)
October 1973 War (Dar Al-Mustaqbal Alarbi, Cairo 1986)
Strategy for Reconciliation (Dar Al-Mustaqbal Alarbi, Cairo 1988)

K. G. Fenelon, *The United Arab Emirates* (Longman, London 1973)

R. Garaudy, *The Case of Israel* (Shorouk International, London 1983)

Akram Hadi, *The Crimes of Saddam's Regime* (Council of Islamic Revolution Publications Centre, Tehran 1988)

Mohammed Hassanin Heikal, *The Thirty Years War: The Suez Files* (Al-Ahram Publications, Cairo 1986)
The Thirty Years War: 1967 – The Explosion (Al-Ahram Publications, Cairo 1990)

Brigadier Khalil Ibrahim Hussein, *Al-Shawaf Revolution in Mosul: The Struggle Between Abd al-Karim Qasim and Abd al-Salam Arif* (Maktabit Bashar, Baghdad 1987)

Dilip Hiro, *The Longest War* (Grafton, London 1989)
Islamic Fundamentalism (Paladin, London 1988)

International Institute for Strategic Studies, *The Military Balance 1990–1991* (Brassey's, London 1990)

Dr Amir Iskandar, *Saddam Hussein: The Fighter, the Thinker and the Man* (Hachette, Paris 1980)

Saad Saleh Jabr, *Frankly Speaking* (Al Taiyar Al-Jadid Publications, London 1985)

Eliyahu Kanovsky, *The Economic Impact of the Six Day War* (Praeger, New York 1970)

Abbas Kelidar, *The Integration of Modern Iraq* (Croom Helm, London 1979)

Samir al-Khalil, *Republic of Fear* (Hutchinson Radius, London 1989)

Dr Suad Khairi, *The 14th July Revolution in Iraq* (Dar Ibn Kahldoun, Beirut 1980)

David A. Korn, *Human Rights in Iraq* (Human Rights Watch, New York 1990)

Peter Mansfield, *Kuwait – Vanguard of the Gulf* (Hutchinson, London 1990)

Fouad Matar, *Saddam Hussein – A Biography* (Highlight Productions, London 1990)

Helmut Mejcher, *Imperial Quest for Oil: Iraq 1910–1928* (Ithaca Press, London 1976)

Judith Miller and Laurie Mylroie, *Saddam Hussein & The Crisis in the Gulf* (Times Books, New York 1990)

Victor Ostrovsky and Claire Hoy, *By Way of Deception* (St Martin's Press, New York 1990)

James A. Paul, *Human Rights in Syria* (Human Rights Watch, New York, 1990)

Ronald Payne, *Mossad – Israel's Most Secret Service* (Bantam Press, London 1990)

Amos Perlmutter, Michael Hanel and Uri Bar-Joseph, *Two Minutes Over Baghdad* (Corgi, London 1982)

Tallal Ahmed Abd al-Quader, *Saddam: The Funny Side of the Iraqi Dictator* (Dar Al-Waie Al-Arabi, London 1990)

Fahd Quahtani, *Juhyiman's Earthquake in Mecca* (Al-Jazira Publications, London 1987)
>   *Communists in Saudi Arabia* (Al-Safa Publications, London 1988)
>   *Conflict Within Al-Saud: A Study in the Political System and the Foundation of the State* (Al-Safa Publications, London 1988)
Dr Hassan Quaid, *History of Kuwait* (Dar Asharq, Doha-Qatar, 1990)
Philip Robins, *The Future of the Gulf* (Royal Institute of International Affairs, London 1989)
Hassan Shabbr, *Political Parties in Iraq from 1908 to 1958* (Dar Al-Turath Al-Arabi, Beirut 1989)
Ahmad al-Shaieb, *The Improvising Dictator* (Al-Ouruba Publishers, Cairo 1990)
Behrouz Souresrafil, *Khomeini and Israel* (C.C. (Press) Ltd, London 1989)
Leonard Spector, *The New Nuclear Nations* (Carnegie Endowment, Washington, DC, 1985)
Leonard Spector with Jacqueline R. Smith, *Nuclear Ambitions – The Spread of Nuclear Weapons 1989–1990* (Carnegie Endowment, Washington, DC, 1990)
Stockholm International Peace Research Institute, *SIPRI Yearbook 1987* (Stockholm 1988)
John M. Stopford, John H. Dunning and Klaus O. Haberich, *The World Directory of Multinational Enterprises* (Macmillan Reference Books, London 1980)
Adel Thabit, *Farouk: A King Betrayed* (Akhbar al-Yom, Cairo 1988)
Humphrey Trevelyan, *The Middle East in Revolution* (Macmillan, London 1970)
Steve Weissman and Herbert Krosney, *The Islamic Bomb* (Times Books, New York 1981)
Marion Woolfson, *Prophets in Babylon* (Faber & Faber, London 1980)
Robin Wright, *In the Name of God* (Bloomsbury, London 1990)
Royal United Services Institute Defence Yearbook (Brassey's, London 1989)

PERIODICALS

Armed Forces Journal International
Aviation International
De Volkskrant
Defence
Defence Journal
Defense & Foreign Affairs Weekly
Der Spiegel
Flight International
Focus
GHT International
International Defense Review
Jane's Defence Weekly
Jane's Soviet Intelligence Review
Jeune Afrique
Le Canard Enchainé
L'Express
Le Point

Middle East Defence News
Middle East Economic Digest
Middle East International
Military Powers
Military Technology
New Statesman & Society
PAIS
Profil
'RAIDS' Magazine
Sozialdemokratischer Pressedienst
Stern Magazine
The Listener
The Middle East
Third World Defence
Time
US News & World Report

PARLIAMENTARY PAPERS

Hansard

Federal German Parliamentary Report (18th January 1989) On Participation by German Nationals in the Construction of a Chemical Weapon Factory in Libya.

DOCUMENTS

'Nuclear Exports: The Challenge of Control', Leonard Spector (Carnegie Endowment for International Peace, Washington, DC, 1990)

Fact Sheet on Military Expenditure and Iraqi Arms Imports (Stockholm International Peace Research Institute, Stockholm 1990)

'Export of Terror – A Documented Diary', compiled by the Iraqi Students Society

International Conference on Combating the Use of Chemical and Biological Weapons, 24–7 May 1989, documents and texts compiled by the International Commission of Health Professionals

'Biological and Chemical Warfare Second World Congress' (Department of Organic Chemistry, University of Amsterdam)

Country Report on Iraq (*Economist* Intelligence Unit, London 1988)

Cabinet and Foreign Office Papers 1957–9

President Gamal Abd al-Nasser's Speeches and Interviews, 1967–70 (Al-Ahram Centre for Strategic Studies, Al-Ahram Publications, Cairo 1973)

Documents on Saddam's Crimes (Islamic Centre for Political Studies, Tehran 1983)

'Iraqi Assassinations Abroad' (Centre for Human Rights in Iraq, London 1988)

Documents and Leaders' Speeches from 2nd August to 2nd October 1990 (Falcon Press, London 1990)

Index